# GAA GRASSROOTS

*In memory of two great GAA men:
Eugene McGee and Jo Jo Barrett*

# GRASSROOTS

## STORIES FROM THE HEART OF THE GAA
### VOLUME 1

#### COMPILED BY PJ CUNNINGHAM

*Ballpoint Press*

Published in 2021 by Ballpoint Press
4 Wyndham Park, Bray,
Co Wicklow, Republic of Ireland.

Telephone: 00353 86 821 7631
Email: pj@gaastories.ie
Web: www.ballpointpress.ie

ISBN 978-1-9160863-7-1

© Text copyright PJ Cunningham and Ballpoint Press, 2021

All rights reserved. No part of this publication may be reproduced, stored in a retrieval system, or in any form or by any means, without the prior permission in writing of the publisher, nor be otherwise circulated in any form of binding or cover other than that in which it is published and without a similar condition including this condition being imposed on the subsequent publisher.

While every effort has been made to ensure the accuracy of all information contained in this book, neither the author nor the publisher accept liability for any errors or omissions made.

Book design and production by Joe Coyle Media&Design,
joecoyledesign@gmail.com

Front cover map by Ryan McGuinness at gaapitchfinder.com

Printed and bound by GraphyCems

# Contents

| | |
|---|---|
| Acknowledgements | 11 |
| Réamhrá Uachtarán Chumann Lúthchleas Gael | 13 |
| Message From The GAA's Director of Communications | 15 |
| The Phantom Croke Park Sub, by Tommy Moyna | 17 |
| Fallout From War In Bronx Landed Down Under, by Mike Burke | 23 |
| Priest's Mass Appeal To End GAA, by Anon | 28 |
| From World Cup To Eadestown Junior Bs, by Niall Quinn | 29 |
| 'Yarra' Survived Bloody Sunday Bullet To Star For Dubs, by David Carroll | 33 |
| Getting A Kick Out Of Football In The Rare Ould Times, by Keith Barr | 37 |
| Reducing Goalpost Height For Crucial Final, by Aonghus Ó Maicín | 41 |
| Fine Gael GAA Team's Ambush On Fianna Fáil Hurling Rivals, by Mike Monaghan | 43 |
| Tears That Became Part Of Nicky Rackard's Finest Hour, by Mick Byrne | 45 |
| Scores To Last A Millennium At 'The Hyde', by Paddy Joe Burke | 49 |
| The Exploits Of Churchill, by Robert Bunyan | 52 |
| Victory Achieved After A Very, Very Short Second-half, by Collette Bonnar | 53 |
| Inspirational Manager For Connemara Gaels New York, by Pat Uniacke | 56 |
| When A Thump Of A Ball Echoes Across The Globe, by Declan Coyle | 57 |
| Player Sought Free Junket... With Wife | 60 |
| Memories Of My Dad, Michael O'Hehir, by Tony O'Hehir | 61 |
| Legendary Voice Turned Into Medic, by Barney McDonald | 63 |
| Putting The Boot Into Wellingtons, by Martin Fitzpatrick | 64 |

# GRASSROOTS

| | |
|---|---|
| A Major Challenge... And That Was Just Getting To The Game, by Rose Kelly | 65 |
| Cherished Days Together As Father And Daughter, by Rose Maloney Quinn | 69 |
| Lollie, The Subway Kid And Me, by Frank Lynch | 75 |
| The Long And Short Of My Camogie Dress Dances, by Eileen Ludlow | 81 |
| Pigeons Coming Home To Roost, by Mick Hackett | 84 |
| Stitched Up By A Neighbour's Red Hand, by Fionnuala McNicholl | 85 |
| Derry Game Records New Score, by Seamus McRory | 88 |
| A Different View Of The 1996 Meath-Mayo Fracas, by Seán Boylan | 89 |
| Fans Protest As Payne Stewart And I Shoot The Breeze In Croker, by Brian Jaffray | 91 |
| Gate Opening That Cost Carlow Thousands, by Tommy Murphy | 95 |
| I Was A Sixties 'Wag' – And Proud Of It, by Joan Cleere | 99 |
| My Father The Ref Saved By Honest Kicker, by George Murphy | 102 |
| Deireadh Seachtaine Na Síob – Cluiche Ceannais Peile, by Brian Mac Lochlainn | 103 |
| Michael Hogan's Girlfriend On Bloody Sunday Was...?, by Oliver McMahon | 107 |
| Still Playing... After All Those Years, by John Arnold | 110 |
| Sons Starred For Kildare But Mother Only Had Eyes For Páidí, by John Kelly | 111 |
| The Referee Sorted The Problem, by Seán Nugent | 114 |
| Scaling New Heights In Gaelic Park, by Liam Fardy | 115 |
| The Clash Of The Ash, by Joe Kearney | 119 |
| The Magnificent Seven Who Went To Jail For Playing GAA, by Michael Commins | 121 |
| When Football's Loss Was Tug-of-war's Gain, by Tom Lynch | 125 |
| Black '47 In Ireland Became A 'Golden Year' In Cavan, by Pat Lynch | 133 |

## CONTENTS

| | |
|---|---|
| A Royal Tale Of Two Patrick Rattys, by Michael O'Brien | 137 |
| What Happened Next After Ref Sent Me Off, by John Lynch | 139 |
| Refereeing To Sound Of A Train, by John Arnold | 142 |
| Germans Invading... Stop... Can't Fulfil Fixture... Stop..., by Pádraig MacMathúna | 143 |
| Arnotts And Dublin Break New Ground In GAA Sponsorship, by Bill Kelly | 147 |
| Pushing Myself To Beat Christy Ring, by James Power | 155 |
| About A Boy Who Played Camogie, by Dermot Gilleece | 157 |
| The Only Radio In The Parish, by Robin O'Connell | 162 |
| Ecstasy And Agony Following The Banner In The Mid-Fifties, by John Ryan | 163 |
| One Free In Entire Game, by Anon | 168 |
| A Place Apart – And Yet Just Like Any Other, by Declan Bogue | 169 |
| How We Played Hurling In Canada – Without Hurleys, by Bernie Comaskey | 175 |
| Young Ring Fan Vs Major Star, by Barrie Henriques | 178 |
| Milk Truck Expedition To Thurles That Turned Sour In Victory, by Donal Herlihy | 179 |
| Brexy The One-Handed Wonder, by Gerry Tolan | 186 |
| Player Sent Off Twice In Different Countries In The One Day, by Gerry McLaughlin | 187 |
| Ag Bualadh Báire Leis Na Síoga | 189 |
| A Scór Night Of Error When Robert Emmet Captained Kerry, by Joe Hunt | 191 |
| Paddy Writes His Own Long John Story, by Jamesie Murphy | 194 |
| 'Breaking In' To Local Hospital After Our Daughter's Birth, by Bernard Flynn | 195 |
| Putting Unholy Order Into My Banger Days, by Ricey Scully | 199 |
| Minor's March Of Time On Sideline, by Sean Nugent | 204 |
| The Great St Mel's College Breakout Of 1963, by Denis Glennon | 205 |
| All-Ireland Final Fever Hits The Equator, by Norman Freeman | 209 |

## GRASSROOTS

| | |
|---|---|
| Tullogher Rose From Dead To Meet Challenge, by Jamesie Murphy | 212 |
| Award For The Man Who Hated Players, by Larry McGann | 213 |
| Writing The History Of Phantom Pregnancy Final, by Billy Keane | 217 |
| Wexford And I Ripped To Pieces, by Tim Horgan | 222 |
| Bobby Charlton In Genuine Awe Of Hurlers, by Gerry McGrath | 223 |
| Last Charge Of The Bike Brigade, by Michael McDonnell | 227 |
| Family Warning For Phil 'The Gunner', by Paul Fitzpatrick | 230 |
| GAA's Own Case Of 'Sudden Death', by Jackie Napier | 231 |
| Memories Of Unbelievable Coincidence And An Action-Packed Day, by Michael Duignan | 233 |
| 'Cabbage' Failed To Bring Home The Bacon, by Jim Brophy | 238 |
| Croats, Serbs And The Fighting Irish, by Ciarán Macken | 239 |
| Ghost Train Into The Past, by Seán O'Grady | 243 |
| The Game That Never Finished, by Peter Gordon | 245 |
| Why Silence Is Golden After Picking A Team, by Jackie Napier | 248 |
| Days Of Great Escapes And Mysterious Disappearances, by Sean O'Dwyer | 249 |
| A Case Of No Sliotar, No Game, by John Arnold | 252 |
| Four Years In The Young Life Of A GAA 'Sham', by Barrie Henriques | 253 |
| Playing With Two Legends Of Different Eras, by Seán O'Sullivan | 259 |
| The Soccer Man Who Led Rebels To Hurling Paradise, by Frank F Murphy | 261 |
| Stuck Up Player With The Flour Power Togs, by Jamesie Murphy | 264 |
| The Pitch With The Humped Back Middle, by Pat Healy | 265 |
| The Day The Bomb Dropped On Kerry In 1982, by John B. Keane | 267 |
| The Man Who Scored Twice With The One Shot, by Donal O'Shea | 270 |
| Forgetting My 'Name' While Playing Féile Illegally In Roscommon, by Joe Connolly | 271 |

## CONTENTS

Three Amigos Who Caused Havoc At Every Turn, by John Caplice — 274

Three All-Irelands – The Good, The Bad And The Bubbly,
  by Dan Kerr — 275

Injured For Bloody Sunday Game, by Alice Glover — 278

There Is An Isle Of Hurling, Though I Didn't Know It Then,
  by Mae Leonard — 279

High Spirits See Galbally Home, by John Cummins — 286

Is Maith An tAnlann An tOcras, le Eilís Uí Bhriain — 287

Fun And Games On And Off The Field, by Nudie Hughes — 289

Dubs Win On Back Of Our Dollymount Tidal Wave,
  by Maeve Edwards — 295

First Hurling Game Ever Played, by John Arnold — 298

The GAA, The Guards... And All Things In Between,
  by Pat McGilloway — 299

Cameo Mocked By Hands Of Time, by Paul Mulcaire — 306

A (W)hole New Ball Game In This Minefield, by Peter Makem — 307

Moving The Goalposts 1927-style, by John Arnold — 310

How Quick Thinking Flattened A Bigger Opponent,
  by Dermot O'Brien — 311

The Summer Of Sweeney And Ballygar, by Noel Hughes — 315

Winning While On The Run, by Stan McCormack — 318

Micheál's Voice Transported Us To The Land Of Tír Na nÓg,
  by Art Ó Súilleabháin — 319

Whatever Happened To The Fahey Cup? by Tommie Kenoy — 321

By The Way, You Wouldn't Be Anything To...?, by Peter Nolan — 323

Player's Name Taken For Unholy Moment, by Seamus McRory — 326

Inch By Inch, Row By Row, by Joe Kernan — 327

Priest Left Holding Glass Of Water, by Nioclás Ó'Griobhtháin — 332

Uplifting Twist In Marathon Final Series, by John Lennon — 333

Officiating An Unusual Pitch Battle, by Tom Farrell — 336

Antrim On The Cusp Of New Era When Troubles Took Hold,
  by Declan Bogue — 337

Playing GAA In 'The Blacks' Before GAA Was Founded,
  by Paddy Phelan — 345

# GRASSROOTS

| | |
|---|---|
| Policeman Flew Under The Ban, by Anon | 348 |
| A Giant Of The Alley Called 'Tatters', by Éamon Ginnane | 349 |
| Getting Rid Of All Things English, by Anon | 352 |
| Rock And Roll Like Never Before, by Enda McEvoy | 353 |
| Winners Forged From Feuding Cornafean-Slashers' Rivalry, by George Cartwright | 357 |
| The Match That Changed Football, by Anon | 360 |
| Cusack Stand Intro And UDR Outtro, by Micheál Rodgers | 361 |
| 'God Save Ireland' Played The 'Tans, by Stan McCormack | 364 |
| Kerry Win 'Sam' In Cork Dearg Agus Bán Colours, by David Devane | 365 |
| A Sevens' Squad That Tamed The Wilds Of Boho, by Seán Treacy | 367 |
| Hega's Verbal Assault On Tipp, by Kieran Burke | 370 |
| Earning The Right To Have A Jersey On The Coffin, by John Bermingham | 371 |
| Opening Up A Brave New World, by Jim Berry | 375 |
| Escaping A Lynching In Our Pub, by Sean O'Dwyer | 378 |
| For And Against – The Leech Brothers In Louth County Final, by Mickey Leech | 379 |
| A Case Of Writing To Myself, by Larry Ryan | 382 |
| Tight Timetable For Railway Station And Football, by Dick Stokes | 383 |
| A Lucky Escape On Bloody Sunday, by Larry Ryan | 386 |
| Wartime Champions Deprived Of Medals Due To Gold Scarcity, by Fintan Mussen | 387 |
| A Whiter Shade Of Pale Green, by Louis Brennan | 390 |
| Chairman Sends Off County Secretary And Future GAA President, by Seamus McRory | 391 |
| GAA's Global Story Eloquently Told By Ladies From The Land Of The Rising Sun, by Páraic McGrath and Joe Trolan | 395 |
| Getting Ready For Grassroots, Volume Two | 398 |
| About PJ Cunningham | 400 |

# Acknowledgements
## PJ Cunningham

Beginning work on this book coincided with the advent of Covid 19 restrictions in 2020. Despite the omnipresence of the cussed virus, this project was very fulfilling and rewarding. I was finally doing something that I had long-fingered for years.

It meant meeting, when restrictions were lifted, or talking by phone to hundreds of people with stories to tell. Many took the time to initiate contact by post or email to discuss potential stories for the book. Some were sons, daughters or relatives who asked me to contact their elderly relatives who they felt had GAA nuggets waiting to be unlocked from their memories. It is a matter of great satisfaction that scores of these stories are now captured in written form for posterity in this volume.

Indeed such was the quantity and quality of the response from GAA folk all over Ireland and across the globe that it became obvious from an early stage to Alan Milton, Communications Director of the GAA and myself that it would be necessary to do a second volume of Grassroots. I would likes to sincerely thank all those who make this book and indeed the next one possible for their wonderfully unique contributions.

The key to getting such a response was the fact that the GAA saw the value of what I proposed to collect and opened its social and normal media outlets to reach out to as many people as possible.

When embarking on such an undertaking, the value of family and friends' support is invaluable and I would like to thank many people for keeping me going over the time of researching, writing and editing.

Three people especially helpful in directing the thrust of the book were former Meath star Bernard Flynn, former Offaly dual player Ricey Scully and Jackie Napier, a great Wicklow Gael who possesses a treasure trove of stories of his own.

My thanks to my brother Ed for reading all the stories and offering suggestions and to Dr Joe Kearney, whose pen never ceases to produce words in a magical array and who also doubles as an éminence grise for good advice.

Design guru Joe Coyle, as ever, worked the oracle in getting the production over the line and I'd like to thank Ryan McGuinness at gaapitchfinder.com for the map artwork on the front cover. Each 'light' on the map represents a GAA club.

And to Ray McManus at Sportsfile for making his vast library of top-class photos available to the project.

I am eternally grateful to the GAA for its support through presidents John Horan and Larry McCarthy, with my former journalistic colleague Alan Milton a constant positive influence in pushing the project along.

Lastly to my wife Rosemary and our family for their suggestions; without them I'd have been lost.

*P. J. Cunningham*

**PJ Cunningham**
Editor

# Réamhrá Uachtarán Chumann Lúthchleas Gael

Is cúis mhór áthais dom an deis seo a bheith agam fáilte a chur roimh an foilseacháin seo atá lán le scéalta saibhir an Chumainn.

The folklore and stories that have built up around our games and the GAA in general, are part of the reason that the organisation occupies the special place that it does in society.

It's worth trying to visualise the Ireland of 1884 into which the GAA was born and the way in which the fledgling association captured the imagination of the public.

Not only did it meet its stated intention at the outset of preserving our pastimes and cultural traditions, but in so doing, it created rivalries where none had previously existed by pitting one townland, village, parish or town against another.

The stories of success and failure, of gallant efforts and triumphant legends are the sort many of us were raised on and as these tall tales are passed on from one generation to the next, they are quite often accompanied by a layer of embellishment.

The GAA is essentially about people and about place and these two powerful ingredients feature in many of the stories submitted for this publication.

Leaving aside the GAA momentarily, the importance of 'béaloideas' or folklore to life in Ireland and to those who left here to make their home elsewhere around the globe, is well documented.

An organisation and movement like the GAA with its wide network of clubs and more than 700,000 members, was always going to seep into the DNA of the nation and feed into that revered oral tradition.

The exercise undertaken by PJ Cunningham, with the blessing of the GAA, sought to safeguard the future of some of the more colourful memories as well as bringing local stories beyond their traditional confines.

The GAA museum is already home to the GAA Oral History Project and this is another piece of work that will serve us well, not least for future generations.

The spread of stories, from both a chronological and geographic perspective, is a strength of the book and it should be a great source of pride to all of those whose submissions made the cut given the level of interest that the project generated.

The GAA has always been about more than just games. The reach and influence of the Association and the focal point it provides in so many communities, means it has attained a special status in the lives of so many.

This book captures that essence and I believe it will provide many hours of happy reading for those who engage with it. Here's to Volume II!

Rath Dé ar an obair,

**Labhrás Mac Carthaigh**
Uachtarán Chumann Lúthchleas Gael

# Foreword
## Message from the GAA's Director of Communications

Cuirim fáilte ar leith roimh an leabhar nua seo agus roinnt de na scéalta is suimiúla in ár gCumann iontach bailithe le chéile in aon áit amháin den chéad uair.

PJ Cunningham is a persuasive man. I should know. A proud son of Offaly, he was one of my first bosses in the very different world of journalism around the turn of the millennium.

As the Sports Editor of Ireland's then best-selling newspaper *The Irish Independent*, he had a knack of managing a team of sub-editors and reporters to ensure the Irish sporting landscape was comprehensively covered and given his grá for our native games, the activities of the GAA were not neglected.

In addition to overseeing a convivial atmosphere of co-operation, respect and productivity between a team laden down with strong characters – sometimes an achievement in itself – PJ was also a man for the odd brain wave.

Ahead of his time, he once tasked this green horn journalist to watch the 2000 All-Ireland football final multiple times with stopwatch in hand to determine how many players touched the ball over the course of that meeting of Galway and Kerry and for how long. It's called Opta today.

Back then the findings were quite startling and my VHS recorder caved in soon after from the incessant stop-start nature of the exercise. Crucially though, it did earn the eager rookie reporter a Davin Stand ticket for the game.

Little did I think then in another guise that PJ would be approaching me with an idea that the GAA should make an attempt to capture some of the stories that make the organisation the technicolour miracle that it is.

While the idea was a good one from the onset, a period of gestation ensued before the project was granted lift off. And so followed a clarion call for tales, yarns and fables from every corner of the organisation across Ireland and around the globe that generated considerable interest from the get go. On reflection why would anyone have been surprised?

All of our clubs have local legendary stories that we roll out, dust down and share with locals and visitors alike in victory and defeat.

They impart character, humour and underpin the history of our clubs, and by extension the areas that host them. They provide insight to those who steps we follow and whose colours we inherit and wear with pride.

The thought dawned on me at an early stage that many of these same stories were quite simply too good to be the preserve of any one club or any one generation. If they weren't committed to paper (or screen!) might they be lost to those who will follow us? The answer to that question lies somewhere between possibly and probably.

To that end, this exercise, which has seen the Clara man traipse across the nation and back, has been a huge success. A rich repository of stories has been recorded and will doubtless be a source of pride to families and clubs who have helped secure it.

I laud PJ's perseverance and tenacity and know he has amassed enough submissions to contemplate a second offering – something I look forward to assisting with and reading in due course.

Beirigí Bua.

**Alan Mac Maoldúin (Milton)**
Stiúrthóir Cumarsáide (Director of Communications)
Cumann Lúthchleas Gael

# The Phantom Croke Park Sub

## Tommy Moyna

The year 1945 is one indelibly chiselled in the memory board of my young life. Myself and my identical twin Michael, known universally as Mackie, were 15 going on 16 and all we wanted to do was play football.

The world was still in a state of chassis then for sure. We had 'The Emergency' in Ireland and World War Two elsewhere. We grew up knowing no better than the rationing and shortages that people the length and breadth of the land felt at the time.

Our parents had come back from America in the 1930s. Actually my father stayed on for a while longer but my mother and her young family of five, including three born in New York, headed back to Ireland to set up home.

She scouted around for a while and eventually bought a business in Scotstown which has the Moyna name over the shop door to this day. We grew up working in the business from the time we could contribute though not many people know Mackie was very ill during his younger years.

Indeed, those who would later see his unrivalled strength as he burst out from the fullback position with the ball while playing for college, club, county and province found it hard to believe that the same Mackie was the subject of daily prayer in national school that God would spare him. This frail boy became a man mountain and I remember the sheer power of his body knocking an opponent aside one day – the poor fella ended up with three broken ribs just from the force of the fall.

To a certain extent, his frailty as a child was partly the reason why he and I didn't go to the same secondary school. I went to the nearby St Macartan's as a border for £40 a year but my mother, Catherine, decided the 'grub' was better with the Marists in St Mary's, Dundalk and she enrolled the 'delicate' Mackie there.

That was another reason why the two of us didn't play for Monaghan in the 1945 Ulster minor championship. During the 'Emergency', petrol was scarce and the government had to ration it for commercial and essential travel purposes.

It was deemed that Mackie could declare for Louth but not travel to and from Monaghan out of school unless he did so by train. That was ruled out by my parents so the upshot was I went to play for Monaghan while Mackie helped Louth to a Leinster minor final appearance where they lost out to Dublin, who would later go on to win the All Ireland that year.

During holidays and whenever we were allowed out we were always in search of a game of football. It was a signal year for us as our club, Scotstown, began playing under its own name rather than Knockatallen (the mountainy side of the parish) and myself and Mackie – as 15-year-olds – played in the first match against Killeevan.

Back then, it is important for younger readers to remember that every club usually only had one team – there were few with minor or juvenile set-ups. So our aspiration was to play with the senior team even at 15-16 – and we did so proudly in the club colours.

To pick a Monaghan minor team, the county board decided to have a trial match between a team from north and south of the county. However, there was great disappointment in our house when the local newspaper carried the names of the teams and subs without a Moyna name to be seen.

That was where my mother came in. The man over the team, Pat McGrane, was a pig buyer and was at the fair day in Scotstown soon after where both cattle and pigs were sold on the streets. Pat was a great GAA man in the county and was responsible for driving the project which ended up in the county board buying the Clones pitch.

He was also good with a quick answer so when my mother tackled him over her boys not getting a look in with the minors, he left her speechless with his reply.

"Your lads. Sure didn't I see them playing in the senior championship. And both of them played very well. They're already on the team. It's to find lads around them that we're looking for now with this trial game."

Without boasting, Pat was right that both Mackie and myself played well in that senior match. Why wouldn't we? We were young bucks full of running and we both had a good pair of hands, which was very important then. We lined out on that historic championship occasion with Jack McCaffrey's grandfather left-full back on the team. Mickey Fitzpatrick was an older man playing alongside Mackie in defence and I can remember him saying: "I'll do the backing, Mackie, and you do the fetching."

We played that match about a month before our 16th birthdays. It was a special game because, as I said, Scotstown was affiliated in its own name as a senior club for the first time. We cycled to all the games and that first one was uphill virtually all the way to Latton. We togged out behind a big rush bush and stopped half way home after the game in Ballybay where Mrs McGrane gave us a cup of tea and a sandwich. That revived us and gave us the energy to arrive home before dark. I don't ever remember cycling to a match without myself or one of the lads getting a puncture. The great thing then was we would all dismount and we'd have the repairs done in no time. Then we'd all get up on the bikes again and head for wherever we were playing.

The county minor scene became complicated for us Moynas that same year due to the school situation. Mackie and I were playing in different provinces. Monaghan played Cavan in the first round and had no trouble beating them. We were also too strong for Tyrone in the semi-final which meant we would face Down in the final in Clones.

I remember everything surrounding that day as well as yesterday and at the time of writing this story I'm now 92 years of age. At the start of a game back then, there were eight-a-side lined up at the halfway line for the thrown in.

I had a look at the referee and calculated that his best throw would land somewhere in the middle of the eight places. I had the reputation of having a good pair of hands, so I backed myself to catch the throw in.

Which I did – and I went hand to toe the whole way into the Down defence selling dummies wholesale before burying the ball in the back of the net.

Now I'd like to tell you I had a great game after that but the truth is I hardly felt the weight of the leather from there to the final whistle.

The reason was ice cream. Our goalkeeper Jim Lonergan and myself had arrived early in Clones for the match and to kill time, we walked down the town. As we passed the Venice Café, our eyes were attracted to a new sign which read – 'Ice Cream On Sale Now.'

Due to 'the Emergency,' such luxuries had been absent in shops, so that day Jim and I got our first taste of proper ice cream. And it was the nicest thing I ever tasted. So good in fact that I had another, and another… and another.

I ate so much that I found it hard to walk up the hill by the chapel in Clones and into the GAA grounds.

I came out before the match with a full stomach as we warmed up. Due to the feed of ice cream I wasn't feeling well so after I caught the ball, ran the pitch and scored the goal, I knew I was in trouble. I trotted back out to midfield and began throwing up… gallons of white stuff spewing out of me.

The boys who were playing with me wondered what was happening and asked: "Tommy what ails ya?"

And I said: "I ate four ice creams up at the Venice Café before the game."

They should have taken me off because I never kicked a ball and Tommy and the ice cream story became a great joke with my teammates for years after that. Of course, I always had a good response as we won on a scoreline of 1-8 to 0-8, I'd point out that my goal was the winning margin.

Having held on to win that game, we were put in by the county board to what was called 'collective training' for two weeks in preparation for the All Ireland semi-final. An official letter arrived at our house inviting both myself and Mackie to report to the AOH (Ancient Order of Hibernian) Hall in Clones and we ate our meals at the nearby Hibernian Hotel.

Don't ask me why Mackie was included – maybe Pat McGrane didn't want to face my mother's wrath again. The other lads never said a word either, probably thinking that he had come in to keep me company and make up the numbers in the practice. Mackie did all the drills under Pat, got the rubs after training, then ate the same food and slept like the rest of us on the army beds six inches off the floor.

There were absolutely no tactics, only building us up. We'd play a bit of football. Kick the ball out to 10 players in midfield and they'd kick it back in to 10 people around the goal. Anyone who could catch a ball in those circumstances would be noted.

Looking back on it, you'd think that Pat knew Mackie might be needed as backup but I can tell you truthfully that nothing like what eventually happened ever entered our minds.

He travelled down to the All-Ireland semi-final game against Leitrim in Croke Park with us. We went by train to Dundalk and changed to catch the Belfast train to Dublin. Seeing Croke Park for a young lad who had just turned 16 was something else. I remember running out onto the pitch with a great feeling that I could jump over the Hogan Stand.

From the word go, we found it hard against Leitrim, who we would learn later was one of the 'oldest' minor teams ever to play in Croke Park. I couldn't honestly tell you if I was playing well because I was in a bubble and slightly in awe of being in Croke Park. The first half was a low scoring affair; I think all the players – and not just me – were more enamoured with the surroundings than playing good football.

I didn't win the throw-in that day – the ball went way over my head – and I remember trying to close people down and get on as much ball as I could during the first half. Then near half-time I was going for a ball with one of their players. I put my hand under the bouncing ball to collect it and the Leitrim man quite legitimately drew on the ball in the same moment but caught my right wrist with his boot. It snapped. The pain instantly shot up my arm and I knew I was in deep trouble.

By the time the St John's Ambulance fellas arrived out onto the pitch I was in agony. They put me on a stretcher and took me away to an ambulance that was parked at the back of the Cusack Stand.

Micky Duffy, who was the father of former GAA Árd Stiurthoir Páraic, was one of the lads over the team. He came running over to assess the damage and so did Jack 'Stookey' Kerr, who was also involved in the backroom. Stookey whispered to Mickey: "Get the jersey off him quick before he goes to hospital..." and that was the last of my contributions to Monaghan that day.

Only no one knew that, except for Mickey, Stookey and, of course, my mother up in the stand. Mackie told me later what happened once I was whisked off in the ambulance. He had been in the stand with the other Monaghan lads who were not playing and was beckoned to come down quietly. There was a member of the clergy also involved with the Monaghan backroom team so Mickey and 'Stookey' didn't want to present him with any moral dilemmas.

Instead, they threw Mackie my shirt and he had his gear with him from the training. As the teams went out for the second half, for all intents and purposes I was back in the No 11 jersey. The boys even went so far as to lightly bandage Mackie's wrist to make it look like the injury wasn't as serious as first thought. In reality, it had gone from hanging off my arm to being a perfect working model again.

My father, who was sitting beside my mother in the stand, didn't notice any shenanigans with his twin sons, neither did our teammates thanks to the way Mickey and 'Stookey' operated surreptitiously in getting Mackie togged out to play the second half in my place.

Mackie's natural position was full-back and with Leitrim on the offensive most of the time, he knew the Monaghan lad on the edge of the square would be better deployed out the field. So after about 10 minutes he went into his own goalmouth and told him to line out at centre-forward, explaining that he himself would replace him in the full-back role.

"But Tommy, aren't you a forward?' the other lad asked more than a little perplexed. This brought home to Mackie how alike physically we both were because not even our teammates could tell us apart. Can you imagine what would have happened if the newspapers or the GAA itself had found out? A twin swapping with his brother in a line-out but no substitution being made through the referee.

As it happened, it took 20 years before anyone spoke of the event nationally – and it was my brother Mackie who 'broke' the story.

In the sixties, RTE did a programme about brothers in the GAA with Michael O'Hehir and Seán Óg Ó Ceallacháin hosting it. The three Rackard brothers from Wexford were on the same night as us and they talked of their time together playing against Christy Ring and the like.

When it came to us, Mackie shocked them all by revealing that one of the great secrets in the GAA took place between the two of us. And he told the nation the story of our swap in Croke Park.

There was another sequel to that game in that the player who accidentally broke my wrist – the Lord have mercy on him he was later killed in a road accident – used to call in to see me any time he was up around Monaghan.

We became friendly and he once confided that Leitrim had six players overage against us that day in 1945. That time it was an honour to have a club player lining out for the county and selectors often overlooked age for the privilege of having one of their own in county colours.

I couldn't really argue back because I knew we too had one player who was overage, though he looked much younger. I suppose it's just the way things were done back then. If you excluded him, and of course Mackie coming on as well, then we were 'legal'.

Under the circumstances though, I don't think we had any right to assume the high moral ground by throwing stones in Leitrim's direction.

*Tommy Moyna is the patriarch of a remarkable Monaghan GAA clan. A former player with Scotstown and his county, he is a retired businessman and has seven adult children. Now in his nineties, he is predeceased by his wife Sheila and his twin brother Mackie.*

# Fallout From War In Bronx Landed Down Under

## Mike Burke

It was the summer of love in 1967 but not on one GAA football pitch on the other side of the Atlantic where blood was shed, thumbs and jaws were broken and, strangely, friendships would later be forged that lasted for decades. Not only that, but the friendship would be televised on a TV show down under many years later.

The year 1967 was arguably the greatest year of all in the annals of New York GAA history. It was the time when the senior footballers showed their true standing by beating the reigning All-Ireland champions of the previous three years, Galway, in a two-legged National League final played at Gaelic Park in successive Sundays in mid-May.

It was also the year that the home team faced up to Meath's and Mayo's conquerors in Ireland... and beat the much-vaunted Aussie Rules team affectionately known as 'The Galahs' in the Bronx.

A man centrally involved in both of these occasions was towering midfielder, Brendan Tumelty, a native of Wicklow who went on to have a stellar career as a detective in the NYPD.

We join the story when the 6'5" star had just announced his retirement from the game. That November Sunday in Gaelic Park, Brendan had joined the thousands of fans going through the turnstiles to watch the famed Aussie team.

Those who arrived early on that sunny fall Sunday gasped as they observed the superbly honed bodies of the visitors making their way into the dressing-rooms for the game.

None was more keen-eyed than the legendary John 'Kerry' O'Donnell, who immediately on witnessing the size of the foe, heard alarm bells ringing in his ears.

"We'll be thrown around like rag dolls against them," he thought as he purposefully made his way over to the stand to converse with Tumelty. Innocently inquiring if he was not togging out, John Kerry was told by Brendan that he had retired three weeks earlier and was enjoying his new role as a spectator.

Not to be deterred, O'Donnell engaged him in conversation about the size of the antipodean group.

"They all look like Mr Universes," he declared.

Tumelty agreed, saying: "They certainly are fine big men."

John Kerry read the situation and saw he was getting nowhere so he pleaded on behalf of the New York faithful by asking the big Wicklow man mountain to move one more time.

"We need you or they'll kill our lads," he stated.

Once Brendan replied: "I have no boots," O'Donnell knew he had his man.

"Don't worry, we'll get a pair for you."

In deference to the fact that he hadn't trained for a few weeks, O'Donnell told Brendan he would pick him on the 'forty' rather than his usual midfield berth. What happened thereafter made headlines around the world and forged a strange kind of friendship between the adversaries lasting down the decades.

Brendan recalled the first half by explaining: "When the game got going, the Aussies were bowling our lads over like tenpins, especially at midfield where I would normally have been playing.

"It was a battlefield out there and how we managed to go in at half-time leading by four points says a lot about the character of our team.

"We were greeted in the dressing-room by a fuming John Kerry, who slammed the door and called for attention. 'Remember what I told you boys about these being guests here? Well forget I ever said that and go back out there and show them how we really play Gaelic football in New York'."

Tumelty switched to midfield for the second half and was told stop the New York players from being bashed around.

"Not too long after the restart I was sandwiched between two of their big boys and when I hit the ground, I had no idea what had happened," he revealed.

"This big Ron Barassi guy was standing over me smiling. I said to him: 'If that's the way you want to play it, then that's fine by me.'

"He made some smart-assed comment back at me, so I just swung and his ass hit the grass. I didn't think I had done much damage to him but it transpired that he suffered a double fracture of the jaw. I didn't get away scot-free either on this occasion as in hitting him, one of my knuckles had shot down to my wrist and I was nursing a seriously broken hand. All I can say is thank God there wasn't any need to throw further punches.

"We both were brought to the medical treatment room but on seeing us the doctor said we needed to go to a nearby hospital. Seemingly, following our departure, both sides really went at it and there were injured bodies lying all over the place. Shortly after I reached the hospital, I was joined by two other New York players and six of the Aussie boys.

"This hospital was run by nuns and we were all told we would have to wait half an hour before we could be seen as they were at vespers. The silence in that room as we all waited together without talking was deafening. While no pleasantries were exchanged, it would have taken very little for all hell to break loose there again."

Perhaps the contest, which New York ended up winning by 4-8 to 0-5, was best summed up by the Aussie Team Manager, Harry Beitzel, who was overheard reporting back to Melbourne from the phone kiosk that used to be in Gaelic Park. 'Yes, we lost the game... and yes, we lost the fight too," he said dejectedly.

Explained Brendan: "Those moments on the pitch and in the hospital were the full extent of my contact with the legendary Ron Barassi until some years later I received a phone call from an Aussie television network. A producer there asked me if I was THE Brendan Tumelty who had played against Australia back in 1967?

"I told him I was one and the same and then he asked me if I would travel to Sydney to appear on a special 'This Is Your Life' show which was featuring Ron Barassi.

"It was a great opportunity and I accepted the invitation even though I'd heard back from some of my army friends who served down there that I wasn't exactly the most popular figure in that country.

"The term 'big Irish donkey detective' reflected my standing among their sports fans and when I arrived, I could detect that I wasn't exactly the most popular guest with the TV crew either.

"When they brought me to the studio where the live broadcast was already in production, I became worried at the negative reaction my appearance was likely to cause. I also wondered how Ron would react to having this guy who broke his jaw, foisted on him in the middle of a programme eulogising him.

"One of the directors saw my unease and kindly offered me a little liquid fortification which I gladly availed of. As I imbibed the local beer, I watched the procession of tough-looking individuals from the Aussie Rules game taking their cue to laud the fearlessness and capabilities which hallmarked Australia's favourite sporting son of the time, Ron Barassi.

"As the show reached its later stages, Ron was asked about the year 1967 when the Aussie Rules team beat All Ireland champions Meath and later Mayo. Then the presenter said: 'You also made a stop in New York before returning to Australia.'

"Ron replied: 'Indeed we did. We played the New York Gaelic footballers in a little dust bowl of an arena in the Bronx where there were trains whizzing right around the ground.'

When asked if they had won the game, he stated: 'No we really got our asses kicked there in every respect.'

The anchor man queried the injury Ron had shipped, to which he replied: 'Yea, I tangled with this big Irish detective Tumelty and came out of the confrontation with a little facial injury...he's not here...is he?'

"The man with the mic said: 'Come in Brendan Tumelty."

Brendan recalled: "A total hush settled on the audience as they looked to the entrance. I was feeling the effects of the few drinks and decided that the best chance I had of breaking the ice was to come into the studio doing the 'Ali Shuffle', as Muhammad Ali was very popular globally at the time.

"Seeing my antics as I shadow-boxed and shuffled my big feet, Ron burst into a fit of laughter and whatever animosity there may have been among the audience before, immediately evaporated. We had great fun for the rest of the show."

On foot of his appearance, Brendan became a much sought after celebrity for the various radio and television shows during the following week as he became one of Australia's most liked foreign sportsmen.

Their time together that week led to a deep and lasting friendship between himself and Ron but then again both were very genuine and fun-loving people who also had a lot in common outside of the sports arena.

A measure of that bond could be seen from the time that the New York hurlers visited Australia in 1973. When Ron heard they were in town, he rushed from his place of work to welcome them, ordering drinks and meals for the entire American party. On leaving them later, he asked them when they got home to extend "my best wishes to Mr Tumelty."

Ron had another link with the Irish later in life when he was directly involved in the so-called 'Irish Experiment' in Melbourne . He was responsible for getting the most famous Irish player of all time to the game down under – the 1991 Brownlow Medallist, Jim Stynes – who sadly died of cancer in his mid-forties in 2012.

Ron still remembers that day in the Bronx. "Four of us, two from each met at the hospital for x-rays, Hass Mann, the champion Melbourne centreman, had a broken jaw. One little red-headed Irishman had cracked ribs. I had a cracked jaw and nose given to me by Brendan, who had a broken thumb from thumping me. At the hospital Brendan took off his coat for the x-ray and there it was – a revolver in his police shoulder holster."

However Barassi's run-in with the other side of the law did little to harm international relations and he believes he made more friends than enemies from that trip. "We became very good friends. I've stayed at his home in New Jersey when I went to visit him some time after Channel Nine had brought him out to Australia in the late 70s."

Unfortunately Brendan, who opened a bar in the Bronx after retiring from the NYPD, passed away in 2014. Ron and he remained firm friends until the day the big Wicklow man moved on and enrolled for the GAA team in the sky.

*Mike Burke is a New York-born Irishman with strong Sligo roots. He moved to live in Ireland in 1973 and played football for Charlestown at underage level in Mayo. He then moved to Tubbercurry in '75 and won an U-21 Sligo football championship medal in '79. After returning to New York he became a legendary figure as a player and mentor with the Sligo senior team. He played in Gaelic Park from the 1960s through to the 2000s and is an honorary president of Sligo in the Big Apple. He also served on the NY GAA board. Mike returned to Ireland 16 years ago, this time to Castleisland, Co Kerry where he lives with his 15-year-old daughter. He also has four daughters and three grandchildren living in the US.*

# Priest's Mass Appeal To End GAA

At the usual weekly meeting of the Holy Family Confraternity in the Roman Catholic Cathedral last Sunday (April 1889), The Rev. Mr Rooney, Assistant Spiritual Director, complained of a falling-off in the attendance and attributed this to the vile system of football playing which had come into vogue on Sundays and which, he said, was the cause of large numbers of men and boys omitting to attend Mass and other devotions on Sundays.

The football playing on Sunday was, he had no doubt, an invention of the devil for the purpose of destroying souls; it was the cause of drunkenness and quarrelling on that day.

The devil had been at the bottom of secret societies such as Fenianism and Ribbonism and when he found those detestable secret societies condemned and stamped out by the Catholic Church, the devil then invented this Sunday kicking, which he knew was doing so much harm.

The reverend speaker implored every man and boy who heard him NOT to take part in these football matches, or even be present at them on Sundays and to do all in their power to put a stop to this vile habit.

*The above was sent to the Hon Sec of the GAA, Mr Michael Cusack, and reported in the Newry Telegraph on April 30, 1889.*

# From World Cup To Eadestown Junior Bs

## Niall Quinn

I made my debut for Eadestown Junior Bs in 2003, the year after the World Cup of 2002 in Japan and Korea and of course Saipan.

I had played on in the Premier League for a few more months into the new season with Sunderland, then retired and came back to live in Kildare after our house was built.

On Easter Sunday we went to Mass in the small country church in Eadestown where the well-known racing priest, Fr. Seán Breen (known as 'The Breener') was the parish priest. I'd known him for years, he was a great friend of my family and naturally I was delighted to meet him that Sunday on his own patch, so to speak.

Seeing as I was now one of his parishioners, he invited me, or maybe more accurately he persuaded me, to play with the local GAA club, Eadestown, the following Tuesday which coincidentally was during the wonderful time that the Special Olympics were held in Ireland.

"The 'Bumble Bees' have an auld match this coming Tuesday, Nially, could you ramble up to the field at seven o'clock and give us a dig out, the lads would love to see you," he said.

I agreed, happy that unlike soccer games I played in, it would be a low-key affair and an opportunity to meet a few neighbours. Also, it was only the Junior B team (affectionately known as The Bumble Bees) and not the Eadestown senior team so it couldn't be that serious.

How wrong I was.

That Tuesday as myself and my young lad, Mikey, made our way up to the pitch, I remarked to him that there must be something really big clashing with the Bumble Bee's match that evening. Everywhere I looked there were cars double-parked along the road for about half a mile before the pitch and I noticed loads of people walking up in the same direction as the two of us.

It was more the numbers you would see going in to a senior county final. As I saw the people going in, it dawned on me that 'Breener' must have done a bit of marketing and I later found out that he had called Kildare FM, the Evening Herald and the local Kildare newspapers to let them know I would be making my club debut. He was a pretty effective club treasurer!

Coming up towards the entrance, I was confronted by a typical looking GAA devotee, a longstanding club stalwart called Pat Doyle who was armed with a bucket in his hand.

"It's €5 entrance fee," said Pat.

"I'm playing myself,' I explained to him, pointing to my gear bag.

"You won't be if you don't put a fiver in the bucket," he gestured, pointing to the bucket.

And, so began my welcome home from the GAA and the new club that I was about to represent. When I went in, the small rural ground was heaving; I was happy to squeeze into the dressing room door along with Mikey. As I began togging out in the corner, I could sense a strange atmosphere that some were pleased to see me... and the other half gave awkward nods, obviously Roy Keane fans I observed.

Like all GAA clubs, there was stuff going on in the background that I knew nothing about. 'The Breener' had sprung my presence and availability on the manager Eddie Dowling who I could tell was none too pleased that he hadn't been consulted. I was relieved when he told me I would be on the bench at the start, or on the ditch, as there was no bench in Eadestown.

Truth is, I would love to have escaped there and then as I felt very uncomfortable and it wouldn't have cost me a thought to miss this particular game against Clogherinkoe.

I watched the match while occasionally hand-passing the ball with the rest of the subs in pedestrian style warm-ups along the sideline. The game was a close affair and about half way through the second half, the crowd began to get restless that I hadn't been given a run. The headlines had lured them there on the strength that I would be playing and now time was ticking by. Fr Breen too could sense the atmosphere and temporarily abandoned his umpiring duties at the far goal to race up the sideline to the manager. In full earshot of both sets of mentors and subs he loudly pleaded:

"You'd better bring Quinner on."

Eddie, without taking his eyes off the game replied just as loud:

"He wasn't at training on Saturday morning Fr Breen and you know the rules, no train, no play".

'The Breener' had a quick look around the ground and said: "Well, if you don't put him on Eddie, there'll be a bloody riot!"

Appearing initially to ignore the PP, some more minutes ticked on before Eddie looked around, rubbed his chin and eventually summoned me to get ready. He put me on for the last seven or eight minutes. I managed to get a few kicks and scored a point before the final whistle sounded that got a loud roar as we held on to win.

Everyone seemed happy enough after the match. I was surprised that members of the national press were in attendance looking for interviews with me after the game.

I would have been quite happy for that cameo to be my first and last game of junior bumble 'B' football, given the hassle my presence had caused. However, by then, we were all on the same side and Eddie quietly told me there would be a starting place for me the following week if I turned up for a grudge 'derby' match against Sallins at home – as long as I made Saturday morning's training!

In the car on the way home I remember Mikey quietly remarking: "They're giving you some welcome home, Dad."

This next match drew another huge crowd and all of the lads on the Eadestown team couldn't have been more welcoming. It was a great match to be involved in. I got a lot of ball played into me on the edge of the square and was fouled three times, resulting in three penalties.

Even I knew it was unusual to get three penalties in GAA but all three were definite fouls. I scored the first two to keep us just ahead in a tight game that had more than its fair share of 'needle.'

For the third penalty I was pulled down by an opponent like he was perfecting a rugby tackle – but not everyone saw it that way.

As the ref pointed to the spot, the nearest umpire (who was from Sallins) threw his green flag at me in exasperation and shouted: "Go back to England, you diving bastard!"

I got up and despite the noise scored my third goal from a penalty on the night. It eased us into the lead and I think we ended up winning by four or five points.

There was a right bit of handbags after the final whistle that I didn't get involved in. While taking the penalties and sizing up the goalkeeper, I noticed that he was a young lad of only about 16 or 17 years of age. Rather than join in the scrimmaging on the way to the dressing rooms, I sought him out to shake his hand and wish him well.

"Hard luck," I said as I held out my hand, "for a second I thought you'd saved the last one."

He kept his eyes firmly on the ground: "Fuck off, you prick, you wouldn't take a penalty when we needed you against Spain."

As some of you may remember that was a reference to the World Cup game in 2002 when Ireland lost on penalties to Spain and yes, I didn't take a spot kick as he rightly said.

The unique thing about the GAA is that let it go long or short, you always bump into opponents in civilian life. Some months later my car got a stone embedded in its windscreen. I phoned a company to come out to fix the problem. Who arrived at the door but the very same young goalkeeper – a little red-faced when he saw who it was but this time, we both laughed loudly, shook hands and that was that. And he did a great job fixing the windscreen.

As things turned out, I went from playing one game for The Breener and his Eadestown team to five years of great enjoyment playing matches all over Kildare with a great bunch of lads.

As I got a bit fitter, I was selected to play at midfield alongside the former Kildare and Offaly star Dave Kavanagh, then a young 45 to my aging 36. We were probably the oldest midfield duo in Gaeldom, but Dave was exceptionally fit and both of us were tall and could more than hold our own in the air.

Sporting achievement is relative but winning that year's junior league and then the junior championship is something I will always cherish.

We won the final after extra time and it was extra sweet for me as two old Kerry pals, the legends 'Bomber' Liston and 'Ogie' Moran, happened to be going up to Dublin and took a detour to watch the game.

Two things stand out about that game – Dave had to go off with cramp late into extra time and his replacement Robbie Smith scored the winning point for us.

The celebrations afterwards went on into the early hours with everyone in great humour – except for Dave, who was clearly upset about something?

I asked Norah, his wife, if he was ok and she answered: "Ah, he hates being taken off but I half-expected it because he ran the Dublin Marathon the other day."

Some man!

While I'll always be grateful for my soccer career both in England and with the Irish international set-up, there was something very special about my time among the Bumble bees and GAA folk in the land of the lilywhites.

*Niall Quinn is a former Dublin minor hurler who played in an All Ireland final before embarking on a star-studded career in professional football in England with Arsenal, Manchester City and Sunderland. During those years, he amassed 92 caps for the Republic of Ireland. Married with two adult children, Niall is now employed in his own business as well as appearing as a soccer pundit on television.*

# 'Yarra' Survived Bloody Sunday Bullet To Star For Dubs

## David Carroll

My grandfather, Christopher 'Yarra' Duffy, was a 15-year-old Bloody Sunday victim who was shot in the neck and seriously wounded while attending the Dublin versus Tipperary game on November 21, 1920 with his older brother Dan.

The nickname 'Yarra' was delivered by his mother because as a small child, her son often played on a boat of the same name tied up in the Dublin docks. The vessel was called after the River Yarra which flows through Victoria in Australia.

In the universal backlash against the British Crown forces for their actions on that fateful day, concentration was mainly and quite rightly focused on Michael Hogan and the 13 others who were murdered during the shooting spree on that tragic day in Irish history.

While there was reference to the scores of other people injured during the indiscriminate firing on that Sunday afternoon, mostly their stories went unrecorded through the decades.

Yarra was one of the wounded who reports at the time felt might not make it, such was the complication of where the bullet, which had splintered in two in his flesh, had lodged at the back of his head.

A newspaper cutting in the Evening Herald of November 24,1920 in the week following the shooting reported on him as follows: "The most critical case is that of the boy Duffy, in whose neck a bullet which had apparently broken in two, has lodged. An X-ray photograph of his injuries was taken today prior to an operation.

"The remains of Michael Hogan, the member of the Tipperary football team who was killed in Croke Park on Sunday, were removed to Clonmel today for interment in Grangemockler on the 9.15 train from Kingsbridge this morning."

So as Mick Hogan journeyed to his final resting place in Tipperary, my grandfather fought for his life on the operating table.

Expanding on the Herald clipping, Yarra was actually shot in the back of the neck at the base of his head just above his spine. We think it was a 0.22 millimetre bullet. We're not absolutely sure what happened after he was shot, but we do know that a neighbour of ours, Mr McCullough, pulled the then 15-year-old boy out of the crowd and brought him to safety. That's a great legacy for the McCullough family because of the big part they played in his survival.

Yarra was brought to Jervis Street Hospital in Dublin's city centre where he was fortunate his condition wasn't severely worsened by the actions of a newspaper photographer in pursuit of getting the perfect photo.

My grandfather recalled lying in the hospital bed when the photographer asked if he could take his picture. Without by or leave, he then proceeded to raise the seriously injured patient by placing several pillows under his head. With a potential spinal injury, this could have had serious repercussions in terms of damage, including paralysis to his body.

Fortunately Yarra's medical consultant saw what was happening and grabbed the camera and the photographer and threw them out the front door. However careless the action was at the time, it provided a picture for posterity that can be seen in the photo sections of this book.

Thankfully for all of us, Yarra had great fighting spirit then, as indeed he had for the rest of his life, and he came through the trauma.

He didn't just survive though; he thrived when he got back to not only walking and working, but playing for both his club and county all through the 1920s and right up to the end of the following decade as well.

And he did it all without bearing grudges. Despite the manner of his shooting, Yarra was never political or sought to use his case for his own benefit. I lived with him for close on 15 years at a time when the Northern troubles were raging in the seventies and eighties and my over-riding memory was his strong anti-violence stance. He believed things could be resolved without killing and I was often amazed at the fact that he harboured no bitterness against the British or their armed forces for what they had done to him.

It was unusual why he became such an avid GAA man, coming from the north inner city of Dublin. Most of his peers would have played soccer but Yarra, born in Sheriff Place off Sheriff Street was GAA to the core from an early age. That's why he and his brother were in the Railway End on Bloody Sunday as they wanted to support The Dubs in the flesh.

He was obsessed with Gaelic football. I think as a person he would admit he didn't have too much time for school but was completely enamoured with his football and this desire spurred him on to become such a significant player later on. Yarra played at midfield for St. Joseph's and was the main man when they won their one and only Dublin SFC title in 1930.

## 'YARRA' SURVIVED BLOODY SUNDAY BULLET TO STAR FOR DUBS

He was six feet tall and while reports suggest he wasn't the fastest specimen on two legs, he was very strong and with a burly figure that could ride tackles and take him past opponents. He was also a good man to get a score for his team and would chip in most days with a point or two from play. One old report of a club game had him kicking the frees on a day when he was responsible for six of the seven points scored in a drawn semi-final with Garda, then one of the top teams in the capital with O'Tooles. The report noted that "Yarra Duffy was the whole (St Joseph's) forward line in himself."

He was a brave footballer and sometimes he could be a bit hot-headed as was instanced in two recorded suspensions for on-field indiscretions. When he felt he was right though, fear didn't enter his mind as was the case when the Garda team 'inadvertently' took the Joe's football into their dressing-room following a match. When no one else dared, Yarra walked into the midst of 25-30 lawmen and retrieved the ball without a punch being thrown.

He went on to win two Leinster senior football championships with Dublin in the early thirties but was beaten in both All Ireland semi-finals by Kerry in '32 and Galway in '33 while he also lost a National League Final.

That was quite successful in that time of the GAA but when you consider that it was achieved against the backdrop of the Bloody Sunday shooting and the time it took him to recover, it was also extraordinary by the sheer longevity of his career.

Yarra seldom, if ever, mentioned his prowess on the field. While sport was always important to him, he also had to earn a living and make his way in life. He started out in the Free State Army around 1923 where he told us he would often be part of patrols guarding the Central Bank and at other state or semi-state building. He then became a stevedore in the mid-thirties on the Northern docks and was really proud of that membership button.

When work dried up significantly there during 'The Emergency', like many others of his time, he went to England to find work and stayed there until the war was over. He had familial responsibilities as he had met and married a Belfast woman, Rosaline Falls, who was known as Lena. My mother Phyllis was their eldest but with another eight mouths to feed as the years went by, Yarra was always working to make ends meet.

He was a very proud man in the nicest way – proud of where he was from, proud of who he was and proud of what achievements came his way.

He moved out to Ballybough House in Ballybough flats with Lena where they brought up their children before moving back to East Wall in the late sixties. Except for the time in England, he lived in that mile-and-a-half or two-mile area from where he was born for the rest of his life.

I admired him because he was very down to earth and played the hand circumstance dealt him. Now and again I'd sense he had regrets over never playing in an All Ireland final. As he got older, two things happened in his GAA world which gave him immense happiness. The first was the arrival of 'Heffo's Army' in 1974 which put Dublin back on the scene after a long lapse. He was overjoyed to see that as it brought back memories of the good old days for him. The two of us would go on Hill 16 to watch the Dubs and he felt a special link with that side when the late Anton O'Toole and a few other Dubs signed one of his Leinster Final programmes from the thirties.

He also got great satisfaction from being recognised by St Joseph's for what he had done for the club as a player. The club had something of a resurgence in the 1980s and he was chuffed when they made him Honorary Life President around that time.

Yarra didn't just stop being active when his playing days ended. Long before sea-swimming was a fad or as popular as it now, he would be out on his bike from April to November every year for his morning dip at the Bull Wall on Dollymount. Any chance I got between the age of seven and 13, I would go out with him. It was a great joy to have that time together and then later he would stop for a few games of cards and a pint in the Wine Lodge, Fairview. He loved to meet up too with his pals in Gaffney's of Fairview and the fact that the club had a St Joseph's team on the wall made it his pub.

From a boy who could have been little more than a Bloody Sunday shooting statistic, Yarra ended up living a full and long life, living a further 71 years after being wounded in Croke Park.

What a blessing for us – and when I say "us", I mean his nine children (four still surviving), his 28 grandchildren and his 48 great-grandchildren and four great-great-grandchildren.

Having been recognised by the centenary of Bloody Sunday last year, we are very happy to have his story recorded in this book, knowing that it will be part of the GAA history for as long as people choose to read. It's unique because in this instance, it's an inner city person leaving a lasting legacy to the GAA.

*David Carroll was born in England but has lived most of his life in Dublin. A father of three, he is currently CEO of Depaul, the cross-border homelessness charity organisation. David would like to acknowledge the work of his nephew Stephen Donnelly in the researching and compilation of facts for this story and is also grateful for the input of journalist John Harrington.*

# Getting A Kick Out Of Football In The Rare Ould Times

## Keith Barr

Often when I tell modern day players that the fun is gone out of the game from the way it used to be, they look at me as if I have two heads.

"It's not about fun, it's about winning," they say and with the way the game has gone, I don't think they are saying a word of a lie.

Still I wish many of those lads could experience what we went through because I think we had a much better balance.

When I mention the word 'fun', it's not that we didn't take our football seriously. We did. In Dublin my generation had to withstand All Ireland final losses against Donegal (1992) and Down (1994) as well as losing to Derry in the 1993 semi-final before we actually brought home Sam Maguire in 1995 against Tyrone.

There was no easy fix for success back then just as there isn't a quick solution today. For me, it only took the sight or the prospect of playing Meath to get myself into top shape. It was the same for all the Dubs, just as it was for the Meath lads when they thought of running out against us in Croke Park.

Meath and Dublin didn't just play a game, we went to war in a way that today's players would never have to worry about because of the change in rules and the strict officiating.

It was the same in every part of the country – Kerry versus Cork; Galway versus Mayo; Derry versus Tyrone or Down versus Armagh – those games were more serous than life itself to the people involved.

I suppose the greatest manifestation of the old standard came for me in that four game saga between Meath and ourselves back in the 1991 Leinster championship. Those games had everything – shuddering physicality, stubborn resistance, amazing athleticism and an abundance of class.

At the end of it all, we held the nation in thrall for a month with all the replays and extra-time played. It was only the first round of the provincial championship but after three replays, both teams got a reception in the Mansion House in Dublin after Meath finally won out.

Long after the roar of the crowd had gone quiet, that series between the most bitter of rivals produced cross-border bonds that have lasted until this day... would you believe the two teams play a golf classic every year there isn't a Covid to recall that special time begun in June and ended on the Saturday, July 6 with Jinksy's (David Beggy's) winning point?

I loved every moment of my Dublin days and the only thing that compared was when I played in the green and black of Erin's Isle, my club.

I tell you we had great fun at club level too. Yes, we were very competitive and won a few county titles and a Leinster championship in my time, but we also had time for devilment and a bit of madness that you don't see anymore.

What I am about to reveal to you happened in my prime when I was a Dublin county player. If it happened today I'd say a tribunal would have to be set up or we would at least have to answer before a Dáil Committee of one hue or another.

We were playing Lucan Sarsfields in a Dublin semi-final. It was a double-bill in Parnell Park and ours was the second game on the list. We arrived over an hour before our throw-in and players from both sides watched the first match lying over the wall just out from the dressing rooms. Earlier each squad had put their gear in the assigned dressing-rooms and then passed the time by watching the other game until we were told by our managers to go in and tog out.

Myself and a few of the boys who shall remain nameless went in to the toilet a little earlier and saw the Lucan dressing-room door open. For a bit of craic, we decided to 'lose' a few sets of our opponents boots. I took Jack Sheedy's out of his bag and the others nabbed two or three pairs as well. Making sure we weren't copped, we threw the boots as far as we could across the ditch into Clontarf Golf club alongside.

Shortly after we all togged out and when the teams took to the pitch, I could see three or four of their lads had runners on their feet. Throughout the match, I couldn't stop laughing as every time one of those boys went for a ball, they ended up slipping and sliding all over the place.

When I think back on it, we could have been suspended if the county board got wind of what had happened. We won the match by five or six points but we might have had to replay it or be thrown out altogether if we were caught.

I was on the Dublin panel with Jack and we were always good friends and still are. However, it took me about two years before I told him what we did that day – and it was at such a remove that the harm had gone out of it. I think he might have ended up calling us "mad Finglas F...ers" which I suppose was a fair call under the circumstances.

The following year we were drawn to play Lucan again but this time the game was played in Fingallians in the quarter-final of the championship.

Lucan were a serious outfit at the time with top players such as Damien O'Brien, Jack and Tommy Carr in their team. They were knocking on the door and we had trained hard to beat them.

My brother Johnny and myself were midfield against, I think from memory, Jack and a towering young Garda who must have been six foot three or four.

It was real championship fare with plenty of verbals and also plenty of tough hitting. Near the end of the first half, Johnny rose high and caught one of our own kick outs and within seconds, the big young lad fouled him. As Johnny was trying to take the free his marker gave him a slap in the Adam's Apple area.

"You dirty bastard," I said shaping up to him.

In fairness to the young lad, he wasn't afraid to give it back.

"That's one Barr done," he shouted pointing at Johnny who was still rubbing his neck. "I'll do another now straight away if you want."

I pretended to walk away by taking a few steps, but I was only setting my 'recoil button.' The young lad dropped his guard. I lunged back at him and buried him somewhere into the middle of next week.

I knew what was coming, and didn't even try to make a case for staying on. I had walked half-way to the dugout before the referee pointed to the line.

Like my own club, Lucan's colours are black and green and it was only a minute or two after I sat down in the dugout that I noticed I was in the middle of their subs and mentors rather than our own. Feeling a little embarrassed I had to stand up and put on a brave face, so I said: "Well lads, who's for it?"

I think they were as shocked as I was seeing me come into their dugout so I got out alive and went back to where the Isles' subs were.

If I was lucky there, it was nothing compared to the day we played Armagh in a league match in Louth.

This was the era when they had the Grimley brothers, John and Paul, playing in their ranks. Big fellas, great footballers and well able to give and take, as was required of top inter-county players at the time.

We had a half-back line of Deego (Mick Deegan) and Eamon Heery on the flanks with myself at centre-back. I loved playing with the two lads because they had everything in their locker. Deego was a great man to anticipate the play and was picking up a load of loose ball when he took a heavy knock from one of the brothers.

If I had thought about it for a second, I might have shouted something at this big opponent and left it at that. Instead I wound up a punch from behind my ears and landed what I considered the best haymaker I ever threw in my life. There was only one problem – whichever Grimley it was took my best shot and I swear it had the same affect on his jaw as if a fly landed there. Other than that he never batted an eyelid, never even slightly wobbled after what had hit him.

"Shit, I'm in deep trouble here," I said to myself because I knew what to expect.

Immediately, I grabbed him by his two arms and wrestled him to the ground. I knew if I did that, others would jump in.

Time slows down in such moments and as I watched, everything appeared in slow motion. I see myself and the Grimley brother at the bottom of a heap of eight or ten players. We were like a rugby scrum that had collapsed on one another. As I looked up, arms are flailing everywhere as I tried to extricate myself from the pile. Just as I freed myself out the back of the scrum, I saw Heery haring in the other side at a hundred miles an hour. As he arrived, he was the subject of a short arm smash to his nose which had him spinning and left him with blood spurting and a massive shiner around one eye.

Eamon has never let me forget the incident to this day. He called me all the names under the sun in the dressing-room afterwards.

"Barr, you're some bastard," he said. "Not a scratch on you after starting the row and the rest of us will have our faces patched up for weeks to come."

*Keith Barr is a former All-Star and All-Ireland medal holder with Dublin. A litigation's manager in the insurance industry, the Erin's Isle clubman is married to Kathleen and they have three grown-up children.*

# Reducing Goalpost Height For Crucial Final

Aonghus Ó Maicín

It was the night before a West Mayo final and the Balla U-12 management team had a problem on their hands. There would be no more training, no more games, no more time to iron out issues. The neighbouring parish were awaiting them in the final and though Balla felt they had the better of their rivals, they had a glaring flaw set to be bitterly exposed.

While Toby McWalter, one of the members of the management team, cannot remember the exact year of the game towards the end of the 1970s, the details of the game and, more significantly, the night before are still fresh in the mind.

"We were picking the team over a pint in Dempsey's in town and one of the selectors along with myself said: 'You know what, we'd win this match only our goalkeeper is too small'."

It was true. The goalkeeper's height, just a couple of inches above five foot, was an obvious problem. Determined not to assume a defeatist attitude before the day of the game even arrived, McWalter and the cohort of selectors devised a plan. Executing it on the other hand would require extraordinary levels of craft and mischief.

The selectors arrived at the conclusion that the crossbar would need to be taken down a few inches. It was introduced as merely a notion – the fact that the game was being held in the neighbouring parish's home ground being just one significant drawback – yet it didn't prevent McWalter and his fellow coaches from attempting to pull off their brazen scheme.

Leaving the dregs in the bottom of their glasses, they jumped off their stools, went to one of their homes where they grabbed a hammer, a pack of nails and a step-ladder. The group then set off into the night, taking the mazy roads out of the parish until they arrived at the pitch.

Surreptitiously, they carried out their work. Slowly, quietly and as meticulously as was possible, they loosened the crossbars on one goal, then the other before refixing them to the goalposts about six inches closer to the earth.

With the job done without alerting a sinner in the area, they furtively tip-toed back to the car before returning to the safety of Balla without arousing even the slightest suspicion along the way.

In all, the covert operation took no longer than an hour, resulting in the selection committee making it back to their stools in Balla for last orders. They enjoyed that final drink of the night as a celebration of what they had achieved before a ball was kicked in the following day's final. Naturally, they could not be sure that their side would win, but they knew for sure that they had succeeded in improving the team's chances of success.

By the following evening, Balla were crowned West Mayo county champions, beating their fierce rivals by just a single point.

"We got one over on them that evening but we deserved to," McWalter explained. "We were playing against some of our own players from our own parish."

The foray to lower the goalposts turned the game in Balla's favour and the management team knew it. In winning they were aware that their short goalkeeper had played brilliantly, saving every shot that came his way and crucially allowing nothing to pass above his head into the net.

As Balla claimed the cup, their custodian was voted man-of-the-match. Only a handful ever knew that night, or indeed for many years afterwards, that he had been given a little help along the way.

*Aonghus Ó Maicín is a sports journalist originally from Balla, Co Mayo. He has written for an array of local and national titles, including the Irish Times, the Western People, Balls.ie among many others. He has been covering Gaelic Games at all levels since 2016.*

# Fine Gael GAA Team's Ambush On Fianna Fáil Hurling Rivals

## Mike Monaghan

It must have been all of 30 years ago when the late Pádraig Dwane told me this story. He was 83 when he died in 2009 and for him the GAA was a major part of his life.

Like many others, he did active service as a player and official. During his time he was our chairman, team selector, trainer, and had the distinction of playing midfield for Cork against Limerick in 1952. However a knee injury at the age of 25 curtailed his playing career.

Every time I met Pádraig he had a story to tell and the one that resonated most with me down the years was his account of how politics entered into a big game played in our neck of the woods some time back in the 1930s.

On the back of the civil war, many parishes were divided for their political alliances. And it ran deep. Our club Kildorrery was no exception – it was called Oldcastletown at the time – but for simplicity sake, we will refer to it as Kildorrery.

The area was predominantly Fianna Fail and the nearest village to us was Shanballymore, which was predominantly Fine Gael. This had a knock-on effect in who played for what club as hurlers from Kildorrery with the Blue Shirts persuasion played with Shanballymore and vice versa.

However one man from our village, Jerry O'Donovan had a small shop there and bucked the trend as a Blue Shirt who threw in his lot with the FF Kildorrery team.

This was quite unusual but not unique. As I did research for this story I contacted my neighbour and good friend Jim Dwane. He told me his father, a Kildorrery man and a Blue Shirt also played for Shanballymore. However when he met his wife who was a staunch Fianna Failer, he had no choice but to change back and play with his own village team.

Back in those day, football or hurling wasn't just about championship and county finals; there were prestigious tournaments run all across the county.

Kildorrery had played in one of these and had made their way to the final. This big match was fixed for Ballyhea, which was situated about 15 miles away. However to get there, the Kildorrery team had to pass through the townland of Doneraile.

Because of his political background, Jerry heard rumours that the Kildorrery team was going to be ambushed on their way to the game by the Shanballymore squad. The purpose of the attack was to delay their political foes long enough so that by the time they got to Ballyhea, it would be too late to start and they would consequently forfeit the match.

Pádraig admitted that it wasn't totally clear what they would do in the ambush to slow them down but assumed they might put a boulder in the middle of the road and then puncture a few of the wheels on the lorry that was taking them to the final.

More importantly, the double agent Jerry listened attentively to the Blue Shirt preparations and found out the exact location where they planned their surprise ambush near Doneraile.

Forewarned is forearmed they say and so when our team left Kildorrery in the back of the lorry, they knew what lay in store. The players were on high alert during the journey and when they came to within a few hundred yards of the attack site, the truck stopped and every member of the team as well as the mentors alighted, armed with their hurleys. They held them high like weapons and walked on both sides of the lorry like army battalions ready and willing to repulse any attack that might come down from the high ground.

The pre-emptive action totally surprised their would-be assailants who decided in that moment that they were better off to keep their powder dry. They knew that capturing the Fianna Failers depended on the element of surprise and any hope of interfering with their transport vehicle was now gone.

As a result, the playing party walked past the ambush area and when there was a no show by the Blue Shirts, they hopped back up into the lorry and arrived in plenty of time for the match. And having achieved victory on the way, there could only be one result when they lined out later that evening in Ballyhea.

*Mike Monaghan is a native of Kildorrery, Co. Cork. He works as a lorry driver and is still driving at the age of 73. Married to Kay, they have six children. A life-long GAA man, pride of place is in his house is his 'Corn Uí Mhuirí' medal won with De La Salle, Waterford in 1965 and two county medals with his own club Kildorrery in 1978 and 1981.*

# Tears That Became Part Of Nicky Rackard's Finest Hour

## Mick Byrne

I was so heartbroken at Wexford losing the All-Ireland hurling final in 1954 that I hid in a reek of hay crying my eyes out that Sunday evening. But there was to be a strange upside to my tears.

Like many young people living in the Ireland of the fifties, the GAA was the one thing that helped us rise above the poverty of the time.

There was little or no money about and in the rural areas, the only enriching moment was when we congregated to play with either a football or a hurl and small ball of some kind.

Croke Park was a far distant Mecca and our only connection with it was when we were allowed to go to a neighbour's house on a Sunday afternoon to hear Michael O'Hehir's commentary on the big match of the day.

I'd never been further than Carnew at the very south of Wicklow at that stage of my life. When I left my family home in north Wexford at the age of six, it was to stay with my aunt and uncle who lived nearby.

We had a cousin who was a priest in our family and out of the blue one day he arrived at the house with the earth-shattering news that he was going to bring my father and myself to the Leinster semi-final of 1954 in Croke Park. I'd never been on a train so the prospect of the journey to Dublin from Gorey on the railway was magical in itself.

Arriving at Croke Park took my breath away as we headed towards the Cusack Stand side. It was very different back then as there were no seats – only standing room.

We approached the turnstile and my father asked the steward: "How much for the chap?"

The kindly man, winking and nodding uttered with a smile: "I can't hear ya."

My father, not copping on, raised his voice which I dare say could have been heard over on the Hogan Stand side.

"How much for the young lad."

Yer man repeated: "I said I can't hear ya."

The priest smiled at the turnstile man, gave him the thumbs up and immediately lifted me across the stile. Then the penny dropped for my father. I was in for free, which was the common practice for youngsters accompanying adults to big matches at that time.

We positioned ourselves down in the front row. I stood at the railing in a trance looking at these great big men out in front of me warming up for battle. I was mesmerised by the whole occasion but as always, wasn't sure which Wexford would turn up as up to then they had been beaten as often as they'd won.

I had no need to worry that day as they hammered Kilkenny by 5-11 to 0-7, Nicky Rackard was unstoppable though he didn't score a goal that day. He was on the Pat 'Diamond' Hayden, who was a great full-back of that era but at 37 was past it at the time. Rackard's strength had Kilkenny in a dither all day and the lads around him ended up feeding off him and getting the goals.

Now Nicky Rackard was our vet at home and I saw at first hand how strong he was dosing bullocks and carrying out other veterinary jobs when he made a call to our place. In this match I remember one stage three defenders were around him, simply trying to stop him bursting past. They were all fouling him but still couldn't pull him down to the ground. He was unmarkable that day as indeed he was most of the time.

Mitchel Cogley in the Irish Independent the following day praised Rackard to high heaven and his verdict overall on the game was – 'twasn't a match, 'twas a massacre.

I had to go back to 'watching' the following matches – the Leinster final against Dublin (Wexford won 8-5 to 1-4) when Rackard scored 5-4 and then the All Ireland semi-final against Antrim on radio. We went up to a neighbour's – McCreas – to hear the commentary. For some unknown reason, I had this dread that Antrim were going to cause a major shock and beat us. To tell you the truth, I was nearly afraid to listen to Michael O'Hehir's broadcast.

I shouldn't have worried. Wexford won 12-17 to 2-3 and Rackard scored 7-7. Despite that performance, they were still underdogs against Cork in the final. This was partly due to the fact that Wexford had been in the All Ireland in 1951 when they were hammered by Tipperary 7-7 to 3-9. There was a feeling that the team had still to prove themselves.

There was a ferocious build up to the final in the county with 'bringing back Liam MacCarthy' the only topic of conversation in every walk of life. We used to get the Echo newspaper locally and it was full of stories about the players and the game. I remember the week before the final, I was helping my uncle on a roof and the weather was scorching.

## TEARS THAT BECAME PART OF NICKY RACKARD'S FINEST HOUR

The newspaper had a full page of pen pictures set out as the players would line out on the pitch with their photos above the information about them. That was my favourite page and I read it over and over again, absorbing every little detail about those heroes. I was totally preoccupied with the Wexford hurling team that time. It was an obsession.

We went up to McCreas to hear the match. And the inferiority complex we feared came to the fore again as Cork emerged victorious by 1-9 to 1-6 in a very low scoring final and one in which Rackard only scored a point.

It was a game Wexford could have won but didn't with Johnny Clifford getting the goal that proved the difference in the end.

I was totally bereft when the match ended. I began crying and couldn't stop. Between the loss and the thoughts of school the next day, it felt like the end of the world. When we got home, I refused to go into the house and hid in a reek of hay that was out in the haggard. My uncle Morgan was trying to coax me back in to the house but I stayed there by myself until well after dark.

My aunt told my uncle not to worry, saying: "he'll come in when he gets hungry," but that wasn't the truth. I finally left the reek because literally, I had cried myself out. I was totally spent.

Some time later Nicky came around the place doing some veterinary work. Morgan started telling him about how I couldn't stop bawling after Wexford lost the game to Cork. I was ashamed that he brought up the subject particularly as I felt Nicky would think that wasn't how a 12-year-old should be carrying on.

My uncle told Rackard that he had been trying to comfort me on the night of the All Ireland. He repeated what he had said then: "I told him 'you're an awful chap to be here crying your heart out and Nicky Rackard and the other boys are up in the Gresham Hotel in Dublin eating and drinking of the best and enjoying themselves'."

What he said stopped Nicky in his tracks. "Listen, we weren't enjoying ourselves at all. I can tell you now I was every bit as upset as this young chap here was. And if you want to know the truth, I haven't got over it yet," he stressed.

As a consolation for me from the story he had just heard, Nicky went over to car and took out a calendar with the Wexford team on it and autographed it for me. He also tossed me a purple and gold hat that he had in the car.

"You know something," he said to my uncle as he cleaned up after finishing his work with us, "when you hear a story where a young chap is crying the whole evening because Wexford got beaten, it makes me even more determined to go out there and win it next year."

"Yes," he repeated looking at me, "it's chaps like you that drives me on and don't worry, we're not finished yet."

I was awestruck that this giant of a man, this son of Cuchulainn, this hurling hero would address me as if I was part of some unwritten plan that he was formulating for himself and Wexford to win an All Ireland.

The great Nicky was true to his word. When Wexford beat Galway 3-13 to 2-8 in the 1955 final and followed it up by beating Cork 2-14 to 1-8 in the 1956 final, my crying game had turned to times of unbridled joy and happiness.

The boys of Wexford delivered not only for us their fellow county men but for GAA people the world over who just loved the style and power play they brought to the game of hurling.

*Mick Byrne is a native of Brideswell, Gorey, Co Wexford. A retired farmer, he is a keen participant in amateur drama and a lifelong GAA fan.*

# Scores To Last A Millennium At 'The Hyde'

## Paddy Joe Burke

It's funny how sometimes you get a flash of inspiration that changes the course of your own version of sporting history. I've been lucky enough for this to happen for two big events in my lifetime.

The first time was when as an avid Roscommon fan, I happened to be watching the 1982 World Cup from Spain on television. I was drinking a cup of tea one evening as Italy were playing Brazil. It was a game when Italian striker Paolo Rossi found his goal touch, a touch that would bring the World Cup back to Rome at the end of the tournament.

It was the name that intrigued me first and foremost – Rossi. I said to myself: "He's a Rossi and maybe followers of our county should be known as 'The Rossies.'"

And in that moment the moniker was born. Kerry are the Kingdom, Offaly are 'The Faithful' and Cork are the Rebels. From then on Roscommon became known as the Rossies.

The next time I went to a Roscommon match, I was in full voice. "Up the Rossies!" I shouted in public for the first time. Before long people around me were doing the same. Then it went viral up and down the terraces. And from that day the term 'The Rossies' caught on.

I'm proud of the fact that I invented the name and am even prouder of my next cathartic moment which happened as the torch was being passed on from the old millennium in the dying embers of 1999 to the new one of 2000.

Where were you that night? I remember where I was as well as if it was yesterday.

During the last hours of the 20th century, I decided I was going to shine a light between the two millennia by entering the most hallowed turf on earth (if you're a Roscommon man or woman that is) and visit Dr Hyde Park.

In our neck of the woods, the weather was unseasonably kind and it turned out to be something of a balmy night across the plains of Roscommon.

I arrived prepared; I had a radio so that I could be sure of the time to sing 'Auld Lang Syne', a torch so I could see where I was and a Size-5 O'Neill's football. I was all set to create history across the globe.

Firstly though, I lit a candle to symbolise the light leaving one millennium and crossing over into another realm of time. Believe it or not, that was quite an emotional moment for me.

Then it was time to create history. Facing into the town end, I put the ball on the penalty spot and with the torch acting as a floodlight scored the first goal of the new millennium in The Hyde as well as anywhere else in the rest of the world for that matter.

It struck me there in the spur of the moment that as a GAA man, I should also kick a point which of course is part and parcel of our games. I went back out to the 14-yard line and kicked one over the lat so that the first point of this new time period could also be recorded.

I did this all against the backdrop of firecrackers from around the town setting the winter sky alight – it also gave the impression that there were invisible fans out there celebrating these unique scores with me.

The flares made it look as if it was still daylight and I celebrated as if I had just scored 1-1 in a real match. I was about to decamp, happy with my night's work when the thought struck me that I should do the same at the other end of the ground – I needed to keep the sporting gods happy all around the greatest stadium on earth after all.

So I jogged down to the far end, scored my penalty as before and then flicked one over the bar – a total of 2-2 scored in less than five minutes. Not too many corner forwards can leave Hyde Park with such a tally after their name in such a short time.

The enormity of it all then hit me that no other human being could even attempt to emulate what I had just done for another 1,000 years. I felt truly grateful in that moment and thanked the man above for giving me the idea of scoring the first goal of the new millennium.

Just like I'd thanked him back in 1962 when I was listening to my first All-Ireland semi-final in the family kitchen with half their neighbours in attendance, as was the norm in rural Ireland.

Our beloved Roscommon were trailing Cavan. Disaster struck when the batteries died temporarily in the radio and the commentary was lost. My mother intervened immediately and told everyone to get on their knees and say the rosary. Such was the power of our prayers that when the rosary was finished not alone was the radio working again but Roscommon had taken what would prove to be a winning lead and won the match.

## SCORES TO LAST A MILLENNIUM AT 'THE HYDE'

I was on a high that evening after that victory, just as I was a happy man walking home that night in the first hour of the new millennium.

*Paddy Joe Burke feels privileged to be a son of Roscommon and loves everything about the county. He drove to and from Páirc Uí Chaoimh in the nineties in one day just so he could see the primrose and blue colours of Tipperary and Clare being raised every time there was a score. He tells his wife: 'I Love the Rossies' many times a day.*

# The Exploits Of Churchill

Robert Bunyan

There is a small GAA club in Kerry called Churchill situated just outside Tralee. It is the home of former Kerry player and Sinn Féin TD Martin Ferris.

One day in a north Kerry national school during a history class, the teacher asked the pupils: "Does anyone know anything about the exploits of Churchill?"

A young lad from the local U-14 team put his hand up and said: "Yes Miss, they beat us by five points in the championship last Friday night."

# Victory Achieved After A Very, Very Short Second-half

### Collette Bonnar

When Anthony Molloy raised the Sam Maguire Cup in Croke Park on September 20, 1992, it was a proud day for the loyal supporters from the Hills of Donegal. The senior team had finally won their first All-Ireland Final.

For my family, it was a particularly poignant occasion. My late father was a staunch GAA man. His lifelong dream was that Donegal would win the All-Ireland. He had a passion for the game that was borderline obsession.

At club level, it was the same and he was heavily involved when Lifford reformed in the 1950s. Unfortunately, despite their best efforts, they were unable to win a match in the early part of their existence.

At that time, it was often the case where teams tossed to see who would take charge of a game if a referee, as was often the case, failed to show up. Luckily, in this case Lifford won the toss of the coin and my father took control of the whistle for the game against Churchill.

At half-time in a keenly contested affair, the scores were level. Then something brilliant happened... about 10 minutes into the second-half, Lifford went into the lead for the first time.

My father became giddy with excitement and couldn't resist the moment. He blew for full-time ... a full 20 minutes early. Lifford had won their first match.

In the Churchill camp, there was anger at what had happened and a general feeling that they should seek immediate revenge. They were planning to block the road out of Churchill and there were fears that not only the referee was going to get lynched but the entire Lifford squad.

Just when it seemed a lynching of some sort was inevitable, my father piped up: "There's free drink for every Churchill player, mentor and supporter on me in the pub so we can sort this problem out."

Peace broke out inside the pub, well at least while everyone was getting the free drink as promised by the stand-in referee. Once the glasses were put down empty on the counter again, the whistler came under renewed pressure from the opposition for what they described as "bare-faced" robbery.

My father again deduced that discretion would be the better part of valour and declared to the barman: "Right, fill them up again."

According to witnesses I spoke to about the occasion of Lifford's strange first victory, my father continued to 'buy' peace until agreement was reached that it was safe for the Lifford players to go home. My father and his buddies left their counterparts in Churchill with no hard feelings. They understood his motives to get a Lifford win after such a long losing sequence but were sore that it was their club which felt the brunt of the chicanery.

For the rest of his life, my father made it his business to do a good turn for anyone from Churchill, especially those involved with the GAA. Anytime he was ever asked about the day's shenanigans down the years, he would smile and say philosophically: "Yes, the game cost me a fortune, but sure it was worth it, didn't we get a win and have a great session, the like of which most clubs would only have if they'd won an All Ireland?"

In recent years, I discovered that one of the Churchill players, Seamus Francis, who was playing that day, remembered the game quite clearly. He's now passed his four score years and has been living in London for most of his life.

My father was chairman of the local Lifford Club for many years. In the mid-sixties, to his great delight, he was elected Eastern Division Selector for the county. On the trips to Dublin for the Croke Park matches, each selector was put in charge of four players on the night before the game to keep them on the straight and narrow.

Daddy was a very outgoing man who liked to socialise. For the four players who were spending the night in his company, it was akin to being with the fox in charge of the hen house! Needless to say, Donegal had no luck that year in bringing Sam to the hills.

In 1966, the Lifford Club needed a new football pitch. The local soccer club also needed a pitch. A suitable field came up for auction and my father volunteered to do the bidding. Finally, the GAA club secured the pitch when the hammer went down on Daddy's bid of £1,000 ... an exorbitant price in those days. When asked afterwards by one of the GAA members how far he would have been prepared to bid, he declared; "Until the River Deele flows up Croaghan Hill."

I remember in the early 1970s when I worked in Dungloe, my mode of transport on Sunday evenings was a lift from the Finn Harps Football grounds in Ballybofey. My brother usually drove me to the game where I

## VICTORY ACHIEVED AFTER A VERY, VERY SHORT SECOND-HALF

would meet the fellows who were giving me the lift. While a great number of my father's friends were soccer supporters, he took the ban on foreign games very seriously. One Sunday, while we were having dinner, Daddy asked me where I was meeting the men who were giving me the lift to Dungloe.

"Is it inside the Finn Harps pitch?" he asked suspiciously.

When I replied in the affirmative, his response was: "If you must attend the soccer game to get your lift, make sure you turn your back on the play."

Such was my father's devotion to GAA at local and county level, the Lifford club named their pitch, Phairc Mhic Diarmáda, in his memory in 2003.

In the summer of 1992, the excitement around the county was at fever pitch as Donegal looked set to finally bring Sam to the hills. Daddy had attended matches in Croke Park for 60 years and rarely missing a Donegal game. On August 1, he passed away peacefully in Lifford Hospital... a mere 50 days before Donegal captured Sam for the first time in Croke Park by beating Dublin.

On that sunny September day, Declan Bonner scored the final point that swept Donegal to victory. The captain of the team, Anthony Molloy, proudly raised the Sam Maguire cup before bringing it back to the hills of Donegal for the first time in GAA sporting history.

Knowing Daddy's form and track record, he would have been looking down from above and true to form would have insisted: "Great stuff lads, the drinks are on me tonight."

*Collette Bonnar is a daughter of the late Barney McDermott and is a former bank official. She is married to Denis and they live in Stranorlar in Donegal. She is a member of the Gateway Writers Group in Lifford. Collette also writes the weekly short story column for the Donegal News and the Strabane Chronicle.*

# Inspirational Manager For Connemara Gaels New York

## Pat Uniacke

During the 1980s in New York, the senior football championship was highly competitive. Most of the senior teams spent large sums of money on players from Ireland in their quest to capture the New York title.

One year the Connemara Gaels had reached the senior football final and had secured the services of two top county players from Galway. Both players had been flown in from Ireland on the Friday evening for the game that was to be played on the Sunday of the same weekend.

The Gaels team were strong favourites but found themselves trailing at half-time. On entering the changing room for the interval, they were met by an irate manager. He berated his team without pause for five minutes. One of the imported Galway players summoned up the courage to respond to his enraged manager's tirade by saying: "Jesus! How could you play football out there when there isn't a blade of grass on the pitch."

The manager quickly shot back, saying: "Did you come out here to graze or play football?"

The Gaels returned to the grassless Gaelic Park for the second-half ... and won the game.

Incidentally, the same manager at half-time in the semi-final the previous week, with his team trailing decided to wait for all his players to enter the changing room before following them in.

As he made his entry he grabbed a nearby hurley. He barged into the dressing room and slammed the door behind him leaving the place in total darkness. He proceeded to rant for several minutes all the while beating the hurl off the table in the middle of the room.

Suddenly someone opened the door and the room lit up. Everyone looked up in total silence... the manager was in the wrong changing room.

*Pat Uniacke is a native of Galway but has lived in San Francisco since 1984. He is a former Chairman of the US GAA.*

# When A Thump Of A Ball Echoes Across The Globe

## Declan Coyle

I write this for the GAA fans at home but even more so for the exiles – many of whom were forced to leave behind their Gaelic paradigm to forge a living in a thousand places across the globe.

I write this because once, many years ago, I was one of that diaspora living in Canada, the Philippines and Taiwan; first as a student and then as a missionary priest. Even now decades later, I can still feel the loss of being away from a football team in Cavan on Sunday afternoons. In those far flung places thousands of miles away from home, I'd suffer withdrawal symptoms when I'd say to myself: "The boys in Mountnugent should be togging out about now for the game."

That would lead to thoughts of my father talking about who was on the 'forty' for the championship, and of the likes of my neighbour Barney Garry capturing in one sentence the great, great hunger that being away from Ireland would pose for me and thousands like me down the decades.

"Isn't that the kind of a morning, you would hear the thump of a ball across the fields, and you'd be gone! You'd drop everything and you'd be gone," he'd say.

And he was right.

Barney's words would give you an ache in the heart. And sometimes a young lad outside in the Far East, who had never heard of the GAA, would evoke the paradise lost in you simply by kicking a ball against the gable end of a makeshift dwelling. The 'thump' would raise up – to stretch W.B. Yeats' language a little – the 'terrible beauty' of missing something you'd love to be doing.

Those wonderful days of a time lost and gone forever. The days of crisp clear blue mornings in Mountnugent when the sound of the thump of a ball called out to us.

On summer evenings too around Dungimmon, there would be magic in the air as we watched Tom Lynch passing down the road with a football on the carrier of his bicycle. You knew where he was headed – to meet up with Oweny and Briany Comiskey to practise down below in the field.

Soon their thumping of the ball could be heard and it would punctuate the August evening like a rustic symphony.

The rhythm of our life cycle was formed in those echoes of the leather. Soon, we too would be senior players like Tom, Oweny, Briany and Barney and we would look forward to making our own music.

If a real leather ball was priceless back then, even more so was a pair of genuine leather football boots. I saw football boots for the first time on Alo Connaughton in Ballinacree school. Not only were they real leather boots, but he had real cogs as well.

Seldom did he get the chance to wear the two together as a mentor would persuade him that he was serving the team better by wearing the right himself and loaning the left for some "citóg" or left-footed player. "The cogs will make a fierce difference," he was told. And good guy that he was, Alo would wear the right boot and his own left shoe so that the team had a better chance of victory.

Gear too was scarce as hens' teeth. Like many of my era, my mother converted a white flour sack into a football togs for us. There were five boys in the family and my sister Kay was our biggest supporter in kitting us out for our days of glory.

In Cavan, gaelic football was the only topic of conversation in those times when the county team was winning or at least contesting All Irelands and Ulster Finals every other year. As youngsters we were serving our time eagerly looking forward to becoming heroes like John Joe, Mick Higgins or Tony Tighe.

Einstein once said: "Logic will get you from A to B. Imagination will take you everywhere." Well, in those mornings, evenings and afternoons around Dungimmon we were John Joe, Mick and Tony. The field in front of the house was Croke Park, and we all heard Michael O'Hehir doing a running commentary in our heads. We pulled some incredible victories "out of the fire" in the last minute.

Our football careers started at under-age when thanks to the commitment of Fr Conor McGreevy, we were driven all around the county for matches. Then in later years, the adrenaline would start on Friday nights when you'd read the Anglo-Celt. "All players gather in Mountnugent at 1.30 sharp to travel to Crosserlough for match at 3pm." Saturday was filled full of anticipation before yielding to a Sunday and the joy of victory; the sorrow of loss was always superseded by the thought that we had another big game the following Sunday.

Because of memories like this, in the years after ordination which was followed by postgraduate studies in Ottawa and then work in the

Philippines and Taiwan, Sundays were always a time of longing. Yes, you had a few hours to yourself on the Sabbath, where in theory you could sit down and read the 'Celt' that my family religiously sent out to me "to keep in touch with what's happening in Cavan".

Looking at reports and fixtures, you'd soon feel the sadness of exclusion – something you'd love to be part of but which could never be because of life choices. The thought of the "thump of a ball" thousands of miles away became an aching thump in the heart.

The 'Celt' was a sort of time-tunnel. It prompted thoughts of Mountnugent and the lads gathering at 1.30 (sharp) to travel to Mullahoran for the 3pm throw-in. Or it might be a county semi-final or final in Breffni Park – the Mecca for all of us either at club or county level. Dreaming the dream as those exemplars in Cavan blue ran out with the captain always giving the ball an almighty thump as he emerged from under the stand as a sort of pre-match warning to the opponents.

Every summer since, the thump of a ball across the fields defines something uniquely ours. Above and beyond the lacing up of the boots, the pep-talk, the clatter of studs on concrete... above and beyond even the roar of the crowd and the action of combat itself, it is the sound of the 'thump of a ball' that will forever epitomise the great legacy Gaelic football has given to Irish people the world over.

*Declan Coyle is an internationally acclaimed author and motivational speaker whose 'Green Platform' concept of living has changed countless lives for the better. A former Columban missionary, he won an Ulster title with Cavan in 1969. Married with three children, he is the author of the best selling books, The Green Platform and Living The Green Platform.*

# Player Sought Free Junket... With Wife

New York clubs used all the powers of persuasion possible during the 1980s to get the top names from Ireland to play for their teams.

It became an industry in itself as Irish-based players hopped across the Atlantic to play in important local games. Monaghan was riding high at that time in New York and their manager Tony McKenna was used to making transatlantic phone calls to get the players he wanted.

There was one player in particular that he wanted to jet over for the following Sunday's championship clash and was delighted when the player was very positive about making the trip.

Just as they were about to finish the conversation, the Irish based player explained to Tony that he had only just got married.

"Oh congratulations," said the official.

"I'll have to take the wife with me," said the player.

"Oh really. And tell me this, what position does she play?" he asked rhetorically, knowing full well that he'd got his point across.

# Memories Of My Dad, Michael O'Hehir

## Tony O'Hehir

For obvious reasons growing up in the O'Hehir household in the 1950s and 1960s meant that sport, especially gaelic football and hurling, was always high on the agenda. The bossman's twin role as a GAA/ Horse Racing commentator saw Saturday as a day at the races while Sunday was all about the match, in Croke Park or in other grounds dotted around the country.

Keeping the scores, watching for substitutes etc in games my father was broadcasting on radio was a role all five of his children filled at different stages, taking over from his long established assistant Tommy O'Reilly, a family friend, who accompanied him to matches from the start of his commentating career in 1938. It meant you had one of the best views in the house and once you did your job and didn't get too engrossed in the ebb and flow of the action, all went well. Reacting too much to a vital Dublin score led in my case to the occasional piercing stare or a briefly raised hand. Distracting the man doing his job as impartially as possible was not tolerated.

A jovial character named Jack Keating, an RTE sound engineer, was a true blue Dub and was on duty one day at Croke Park for a Leinster football game. In his booth alongside but partitioned from the commentary position, Jack erupted when Dublin scored a goal, jumped up and started waving his arms in delight, pulling the microphone lead in the process and almost strangling a startled MOH.

Around 6pm on the Friday before Dublin played Galway in the 1963 All Ireland Football Final, I answered the hall door of our house on Griffith Avenue and spoke with a group of young men on their way home from work who were keen to have a word with: "Micheal O'Hehir, the commentator."

All of them were Dublin supporters and they had a few questions they wanted answers to. Pointing at my father's car parked in the driveway, the conversation went along the lines of: "Mr O'Hehir, are we right in thinking that your are a Dublin man so, if that's the case why are you supporting Galway by driving a maroon coloured car."

The fact that MOH's home telephone number was not ex-directory led to numerous calls, most of them late at night and more often than not from a public house pay phone. Once button A had been pressed and the money had dropped, the questions flowed.

"Who was the best footballer you've seen or the greatest hurler? Who scored the winning goal in a particular match? Name Cork's All Ireland goalkeepers over the past 20 years."

Often the callers wanted bets settled. Many of the questions were straight forward. Others were bizarre and one of the strangest calls of all came around 11.30 one night. Himself had gone to bed. The caller wanted him woken up and was insistent he needed information, claiming there was a lot of money at stake. It was 20 years after Cavan and Meath had met in the National League Final and, bizarrely, the caller wanted to know which team was first out on the pitch for the second half?

Suffice to say he didn't get an answer.

My father had many stock phrases which he frequently used in his match commentaries. "Socks down around his ankle", "He bends, he lifts, he strikes," etc.

Another of them, which he often used in one-sided games, led to him being verbally assaulted by a Cork supporter before a Munster hurling championship game in Thurles. Unless my memory is playing tricks, I think it was a replay between Cork and Tipperary. As was normal practice he arrived at Semple Stadium early and before checking the teams and heading for the commentary box he was approached at the back of the stands by a burly excited son of the Rebel County who wanted "a word."

The Cork fan was in no doubt that it was MOH's fault there was a replay. "If you kept your bloody mouth shut during the drawn game and not said what this game needs is a goal for Tipperary, there would have been no need for a replay..!"

On another Sunday night following a commentary on a Munster hurling game in which the boss, who never believed in being overly critical of any player, referred to a goalkeeper, who was having a nightmare, "having had many better days." Those words provoked an upset member of the goalie's family to phone claiming that the comment had a negative effect on the goalie's confidence ... as if the player concerned was listening to the broadcast as he went about the job.

*Tony O'Hehir is son of the legendary Michael O'Hehir and was himself a top broadcaster specialising in horse racing over the past half century. A legendary figure in racing, he received the 'Contribution to the Industry' Award by Horse Racing Ireland in 2020. He is the father of four grown-up children, three daughters and a son.*

# Legendary Voice Turned Into Medic

## Barney McDonald

I played hurling and football for Monaghan in the 1960s and 1970s. One Sunday, we were playing Fermanagh hurlers in a curtain raiser for an Ulster senior football championship game between the same sides in Clones. Just before half-time one of our players got a very bad cut over his eye.

At the interval our manager was busy attending to the wounded person. He rustled through his little biscuit-tin, which contained sticking plasters and a bottle of iodine. Clearly he was flustered, trying to do too many things in such a short timeframe.

"I'll look after that injury so you can get your lads ready for the second half," said a stranger who had come in and was now standing directly behind the manager in the old dressingrooms at the town goal in Clones.

When I say 'stranger,' he was the best-known man in Ireland at the time… it was none other than the late, great RTÉ commentator, Michael O'Hehir. He had arrived early at the venue to broadcast the football game on Radio Éireann that followed our match.

As it was our first time to see the great man in the flesh, we all stood and watched in awe as he put on as fine a dressing on our injured teammate as any qualified physiotherapist could have done.

*Barney McDonald, Castleblayney, Monaghan*

# Putting The Boot Into Wellingtons

### Martin Fitzpatrick, Mayo

In a junior game played in North Mayo in the early 50s, the match went ahead despite it being a terribly wet day. On top of that, the appointed referee did not turn up. The two clubs decided to toss a coin to see who would nominate a ref.

The chosen man, however, had no football boots. One of the players on the opposing team loaned him a pair of wellington boots.

Thus, the referee clad in his own raincoat, borrowed wellingtons and a club whistle threw in the ball to start proceedings.

As the game unfolded, he was forced into making the difficult decision of sending off the player who had loaned him the wellingtons.

Unhappy with the decision, the quick-thinking player replied: "Right so, I'll take my wellingtons while I'm at it."

The referee decided discretion was the better part of valour and so the game could finish, allowed the player to stay on for the remainder of the match. It wasn't that he got cold feet but he wanted to ensure they stayed dry while he charged up and down the water sodden pitch.

# A Major Challenge... And That Was Just Getting To The Game

Rose Kelly

Urris were sitting third in Division Two of the Donegal league with one match remaining in 1974 and had a chance of going up a division. Their final game was in Glencolmcille against Naomh Columba, who had already won the junior championship, were guaranteed the league title and had remained unbeaten throughout that year in Donegal fare. It meant that if Urris were going to be promoted they would have to earn it playing away to the best outfit in the division.

Ninety-odd miles of hard road separated Urris from Glencolmcille but even that remoteness didn't mean that folk in Urris weren't aware of the existence of Glencolmcille. There were people in every district in Donegal in those days who aspired to what Glencolmcille had achieved as a community... and Urris was no different.

Fr. James McDyer had turned the isolated parish in the far western corner of the county into a model of self-reliance that had inspired people along the entire western seaboard. That genuine admiration didn't extend to standing back and applauding their unbeaten football team though.

Urris would have been in Belfast quicker than the time it took them to reach Glencolmcille but the team and supporters set off optimistic that they could cause a major upset. All climbed on board the bus with the one football the club owned in those days, a ball handed over to us by Master Callaghan at one of our first meetings following the formation of the club in the autumn of 1969.

Vincent Mór was hired for the bus run. Those on the bus had little or no idea where Glencolmcille was and happily settled in for the long haul knowing the navigation was someone else's responsibility.

We had a full team report for duty as the party pulled out of Clonmany and at Cloontagh a tall man from Kildare by the name of John Moore – whom the club was told could play a bit – was picked up. John was married to Susannah McGonigle from Cloontagh and the couple had just returned from England. Now this midlander was on a bus bound for Glencolmcille with a bunch of strangers. They had one thing in common – none of them had made this journey before.

The wagon slowly made progress up the county, hitting Fintown and then onto Glenties before weaving its way through Ardara and up onto the winding heights of the Glenesh Pass which links Ardara and Glencolmcille.

What those on the bus didn't know was that the Glenesh Pass was a pony and trap highway and totally unsuitable for a bus to traverse. It was only when the vehicle was halfway up the pass that those on board became acquainted with this fact. The Urris squad came to a full stop at one particularly sharp turn at a bridge. Looking out of the bus there was plenty of the most breath-taking scenery in view – not to mention a terrifying drop of hundreds of feet on one side.

The situation looked desperate until the driver, Vincent, plucked up remarkable courage and began gingerly reversing the bus towards the aforementioned drop. This was the moment when a football day out turned into a life or death moment. Panic broke out but it was tempered when Rita Friel and the women on board began to recite the rosary.

However, thanks to the driver's amazing skills to negotiate a big awkward bus backwards in the minimum of space, and no doubt fuelled by the prayers storming the Pearly Gates seeking safe delivery, the party slowly but surely inched its way to the top before then descending into the Glen at the other side.

It is said that inhabitants of the area came out of their homes to watch this miracle on the mount for ne'er before had such a big wagon managed to navigate the tight twists and turns leading up to the Glenesh Pass. Some waved, others blessed themselves as if the Urris Bus were ghost riders and not real people. Without kicking a ball, the club made history on that stretch of road that day.

And it was merely the start to what would turn into a very long afternoon. Colm Toland takes up the narrative of what happened next: "The trip had turned into an expedition but finally we arrived at the pitch and togged out. It was a sunny day but there was a strong wind blowing. Glen were on a high after winning the league and championship. It appeared that everyone in the area had come to the match as this was a gala day for the parish. The pitch was lined with cars but there was no fence around it.

The first problem – and not an unusual one at the time – arose when both teams were on the pitch for a considerable time without any sign of a referee turning up. The scarcity of phones in 1970s Ireland was rivalled only by a scarcity of referees for such matches. That presented the makings of a 'hanlin'.

## A MAJOR CHALLENGE... AND THAT WAS JUST GETTING TO THE GAME

The uneasy protocol of the era was that in such a situation, the clubs would toss to see which team would provide the match official. If the opposition won the toss, Urris knew they might as well go home before the ball was thrown in.

And vice versa! If we won the toss, invariably I got the job. Even with the 'best of intentions' it was an utterly impossible task for an official from either club to referee a match to the satisfaction of both sides. Mind you, as I have somewhat sheepishly admitted, I didn't always have the best of intentions.

"The maths were simple – Urris just had to win to get into Division One.

A member of the opposition generously volunteered to take charge of the whistle. Promising to stick by the rules? No chance. The coin was flipped and Urris won the toss. I rolled down my socks and put my trousers inside them. I had a whistle and a watch... and so the momentous occasion began."

As the great Michael O'Hehir was wont to say, this was the proverbial 'match of two halves'. Urris had the benefit of the strong wind in the first half, the highlight of which was a top class goal scored by Neil Doherty. The Kildare man, John Moore, crossed the ball and Neil dived full length to connect with both fists to drive the ball into the back of the net.

That left the half-time score standing at Urris 1-7, Glencolmcille 0-0. So far so good. Back to match referee Colm for an account of a second-half that has gone into the annals of Urris GAA folklore:

"With the aid of the wind, Glencolmcille gradually came back into the game and with about five minutes remaining, the score was 1-7 to 0-9 to us. It was at that time that one of the Glen defenders came storming down the right wing. He had an awkward style of soloing and I counted his steps. FIVE. I blew him up for over-carrying the ball.

"In frustration, he turned around and unable to control his anger at the foul being awarded against him, ballooned the ball away. With the strong breeze behind it, the ball soared high and mighty for a considerable time before disappearing outside the ground.

By the time the locals had scrambled across fences to retrieve it, four minutes had elapsed, meaning there was only (on my watch) one minute left. I didn't allow for time wasted by the opposition. In fact, I warned the player that if he kicked the ball away again, I would blow up the match. As fortune would have it, the same player, who was very athletic, was the one to gain the next possession and once again he sallied forward in search of the equaliser. Once again, in my opinion, he took five steps. I blew him up for another foul. He obviously hadn't learnt his lesson as he again kicked the ball out of play in a fit of pique at my decision. As I had warned, I blew the final whistle. Urris had won by a point!"

A stunned silence momentarily descended over the parish of Glencolmcille before all hell broke loose. The home supporters invaded the pitch, cars drove onto it and scuffles broke out in several parts of the ground.

Luckily, there was a garda patrol car at the match and with the help of some more sensible supporters, calm was eventually restored. Urris retreated to the bus, minus our football which their player had kicked away before I called a halt to proceedings. The Urris party then embarked on their homeward trek, joyful that we had secured the narrowest of one point wins."

◆ ◆ ◆

Urris were promoted on that famous day for the club and Colm Toland entered folklore for the way he turned another team's rash kicking into a positive time wasting tactic for his own team.

The day hasn't quite taken on the legs of where were you when Munster beat the All Blacks in 1978 but in our neck of the woods, let's say the bus could be filled ten times over with people who claim they survived the Glenesh Pass close shave with death... and the famous Glencolmcille win against the odds on that momentous day.

*Rose Kelly is a Donegal native and has been involved with Urris GAA since 1993. A keen music fans and devotee of Bruce Springsteen, she also has a great interest in local history. Rose researched, edited and compiled the club's history 'From Humble Beginnings To Crampsey Park' which was launched by GAA President, John Horan, to coincide with the Club's golden jubilee year in 2019.*

# Cherished Days Together As Father And Daughter

## Rose Maloney Quinn

I slowly opened my eyes and felt Daddy gently shaking me. "Rosemary, Rosemary. C'mon we need to get on with it if we are to be out at the pitch after early Mass," he whispered.

I didn't need coaxing, I leaped out of the bed and quickly got dressed. By the time I got to the kitchen, Daddy was kneeling on the couch by the window murmuring his morning prayers while facing out to our beautiful view of a calm Atlantic Ocean, Easkey village in the distance and Killalla bay.

I noticed his lips were moving much quicker than usual on this fine Sunday morning July 1979... yes, there definitely was a rush on.

Seeing me at the kitchen door, he blessed himself quickly and told me to "put on your Wellies, the dew is heavy this morning."

Without further instructions, I headed down the fields to round up the cows for morning milking. It was a cold, but bright, morning and the birds were chirping loudly. Looking around the surrounding neighbours' fields I knew we were the only house awake. This made me smile and feel somehow important.

The anticipated excitement of a day at the pitch helped me fly through the many jobs I had to do that morning. Before I knew it we were heading to Ballinahincha for the barrels of water for the farm. During it all I never questioned the silence nor did I break it as my dad always had a different urgency about him when jobs had to be done. Finally, all was finished outside and the Maloney clan of five were dressed in our Sunday best and in the car for 8.30 to go to 9.00 Mass in St James Church 1.5 miles away.

Mass dragged that morning like never before; I thought it would never end. In my giddiness I began to twitch and met a stern eye from my mother telling me silently to behave in church.

Mass over (finally), I jumped into the front of the car to go home with Daddy while Mummy and the others went to get the Sunday newspaper and amble home afterwards. She warned us to change out of our good clothes before starting the work on the pitch.

It was action time now as we arrived at the Sea Blues grounds to prepare for the big tournament game we were hosting later that afternoon. Both of us were all chat and smiles as we had the farm work done and looked forward to the GAA time we'd have together. My biggest hope on the way was that I would get a drink of the orange squash in the gallon drum we had brought with us. Daddy seemed to read my mind.

"Sure we better try out this orange first before we raise a hand," he said, smiling and winking. After we had drunk our fill, he put the tasty juice and our box of sandwiches, wrapped in a jumper, under the car to keep the rising heat of the day off them.

Once again he was back in action mode. "Rosemary, sort out the dressing rooms and get the little table out for Martin," he shouted at me as he himself struggled to open the bag of lime to mark the pitch.

"And don't forget the flags Rosemary, you sort the flags too."

He was in a world of his own getting ready to mark the pitch – I knew he'd have every line as a straight as a die because of the big crowd that was expected for the match.

I began sweeping furiously, shoving all the dressing room dirt towards the door like I had been shown while also knocking cobwebs off the bare brick walls.

As I was occupied in getting caked-in muck off the underbelly of the rough benches something glittering nearby caught my attention. To my great surprise, I'd stumbled on two silver coins – two 50 pence pieces.

I held them in the palm of my hand making sure they were real before running across the field to share my good fortune with Daddy. He was absorbed in his own work and jumped with fright when he saw my shadow fall over the line he was making. "Watch yourself or the lime will blind you," he said with a hint of annoyance in his voice.

I came up to him at a different angle and as he slowly stood up and peered down at my now out stretched hand, he asked me where I got the money.

"In the muck under the benches in the dressing-room," I replied.

"Where there's muck, there's luck," he said, a big smile on his face.

"We'll stop off for ice-creams on the way home. Hide them in the car."

After finishing the cleaning in the dressing rooms, I dragged out the little table for the money collection at the gate and then began positioning the flags in their designated holes around the field. Despite the prospects of delicious ice-cream to come, I was careful to concentrate so that the flags were sorted in the right order especially at the goals.

In no time, we had the pitch looking spick and span. Daddy laid his jumper out on the soft grass and we sat down with our sandwiches. Just as we began eating, Martin Connolly arrived on his Honda 50, and almost immediately Dick Jordan joined him as they made their way over to us.

"Look at ye lads coming now the work is done," Daddy teased with a big grin on his face. Dick gave me a slice of shop cake in its own packet wrapping. God I was having one helluva good day on the eating and drinking front!

After our repast, Daddy ordered Martin to get the gate ready. It was still hours to the throw-in but everyone knew my father had to have everything done early.

Martin grabbed the little table and headed towards the gate. I was given the order to bring the small battered biscuit tin which had the float for change and to follow Martin.

The day blurred by in a ray of team colours, banter, shouting and the big hurrah when the cup was handed over to the victorious team. As always as the crowd began to move, I headed back to the pitch to help Daddy gather up the flags. He was now in the middle of a post-match ritual, including talking to everyone he could, before finally arriving back at the car. He was all smiles and energised about the game and the big crowd that paid good money into the club coffers.

We chatted the whole way to the village and, as promised, he pulled in and got us two ice creams out of my luck money. To make sure they were completely gone before we go back to Killeenduff, he took an unusual detour to Easkey Castle, where we pulled in to finish our treats while looking out at the ocean. As he restarted the engine for the journey home, he looked over at me and said: "Remember, Rosemary, not a word."

And I never did tell anyone. This was my most memorable outings out on GAA duty with my dad. I was eight that year.

That innocent first day sharply contrasted to the one 40 years later when we embarked on a very different football journey,

It all started with the fact that Willie, my ageing dad, had decided not to continue his annual All-Ireland final trip because he was no longer able to climb the Croke Park steps.

After our last outing to Croker to watch Donegal beat Kerry in a belter of a match and then a slightly more mundane encounter between Mayo and Meath, we agreed on the drive home that we would go to McHale Park the following week to see Donegal and Mayo in action.

I had the tickets bought by midday the following day. Tickets had always been a precious commodity in our house and once Daddy knew we had them, he relaxed and looked forward to the game.

For the years we travelled far and wide to matches, he would always keep our tickets either in a buttoned back pocket or a buttoned front shirt pocket. He needed to have them on him and it was only at the turnstiles that he'd dispense the precious commodity to others in his travelling party.

This time we had a few other complications. The match was not throwing in till 6pm; gates were not opening until 3pm. My mother put the wind up us by claiming she'd heard on the Donegal grapevine that they were bringing a huge support and would be baying to gain entry to the ground from early in the afternoon.

On hearing this my father decided that I should collect him at 11.30 so that we got there ahead of the posse. My son and myself arrived as ordered and the three of us had a great chat on the road to Castlebar about who would win and if there was any chance Dublin could be beaten that year – or indeed any year.

As we came closer to our destination the rumours my mother had heard seemed to be true – there was a big presence of Donegal registered cars already parked on the various verges. We decided to head for the pitch and pay for parking, which suited Dad's 86 year young legs best in terms of cutting down the walking.

Once that was done, we bumped into a lovely Mayo family and began chatting. They had travelled the relatively short distance from Killala. The banter was good and I was enjoying myself until the Mayo mother happened to pull out their tickets. Immediately, my stomach churned violently and I thought I was either going to faint or get sick.

"Rosemary what's wrong?" my father asked.

Everyone looked at me, awaiting an answer.

"I forgot the tickets," I blurted out as tears streamed down my face.

"What?" shouted my father incredulously, the panic clearly coming across in his tone.

From the first day together to now, more than 40 years later, we had always made sure we had everything ticked off when going on a GAA journey.

My eight-year-old son Oisin tried desperately to unearth them somewhere in the car but they weren't there.

Such was the commotion we were causing that a kindly man from the car park saw how upset I was and told me to relax, that we could work out something.

"I'm afraid not," I told him. "Our tickets are at home in the cupboard above the fish tank."

## CHERISHED DAYS TOGETHER AS FATHER AND DAUGHTER

Dad was now pacing up and down trying to come to terms with the ticket disaster. The couple we had just met tried to comfort him while the man from the car park got on the phone. After a few calls, we had a Plan B ready to spring into operation. A lad from Ballina would drive to meet my friend in Dromore West who would get the tickets from my neighbour, who had just arrived at my house and located the forgotten prized passes to the game. She would hand over the tickets and also send on a photo of them on her iPhone as proof that they were found.

Willie, my beloved dad, was still not convinced but was more placated to hear that the real tickets would be hear by half five.

It was a long and lonely sentry standing aimlessly outside the gates knowing we could not join the growing queue.

"How could you forget the tickets?" Daddy would ask every now and again. I knew his little girl had disappointed him greatly on this occasion.

"You never asked me at Easkey if I had them?" I answered back feeling like the worst daughter in the world. He continued to intermittently shrug his shoulders and shake his head. When my son and his cross-looking grandfather headed for the toilets, tears rolled down my cheeks again.

A lovely Mayo steward in his high viz vest, seeing my distress, kindly asked if he could do anything to help.

"I forgot the tickets," I sobbed.

The man smiled and said: "Is that all?"

I nodded. "I never did this before."

He gently moved me over to where two of his steward comrades were and informed them of my plight. They looked at each other and told me to stop worrying.

"We'll take care of you from now on," they pledged.

As we talked, they told me they were all from North Mayo and had been stewarding for many years. As my father and son returned, they included them in the chat. Then they turned to my Dad and said: "We heard your dilemma. We've sorted it for you."

They brought us into the ground through a gate in one corner. And so there we were, inside the gates after 1.30pm with the pick of the best seats. Oisin piped up, with that great sense of humour he possesses, by teasing: "That worked out well, Mammy, you should forget the tickets more often!"

My father gave me a look that made it perfectly clear that he did not agree. This time there would be no special treat of ice cream for me at the end of the day. Still, when the tickets arrived, when the match was over and when we were on our way back home, we all agreed that despite the problems, we'd had a day that we wouldn't forget in a hurry.

Footnote: That 'ice-cream' day had been our first GAA occasion together as father and daughter; sadly the trip to Mayo was to be our last GAA excursion. My Dad Willie was handed out his wings later that year (2019) and this time he had no need to fret over tickets … the pearly gates were thrown wide open to welcome him into paradise.

*Rosemary (Rose) Maloney Quinn is a native of Easkey but now lives in Coolaney, Co. Sligo and is currently the PRO for Coolaney/Mullinabreena GAA Club. Rose is married to PJ Quinn and the mother of two boys, Oisin 10 and Philip 26. Rose ardently follows her home club Seablues (Easkey), Sligo and parish Club Coolaney-Mullinabreena GAA Club.*

# Lollie, The Subway Kid And Me

## Frank Lynch

Sometimes when I look back I wonder how I could play rugby and Gaelic football side by side. I chuckle at how outrageous this sporting double life actually was.

This was the era of the GAA's notorious 'Vigilante' committees who scoured the country looking for those either attending or playing what was then referred to as 'foreign games'.

In my case, I'm referring to the 1950s when Rule 27, otherwise known as 'The Ban' (it was finally voted out of the rulebook in 1971 at Congress held in Belfast) was arguably the most influential part of off-field GAA activity.

Every day, every week, every month, and every year numerous big names across the country were either unable to play for their club or country because they had been suspended following reports from one or other vigilante circles often operating clandestinely at a sporting function.

My family was steeped in the GAA. I was brought up in Lurgen Green in Dundalk and played minor for St Furseys and senior with Geraldines while I was still going to school.

I cycled the four miles to and from St Mary's Marist School in the town twice a day (I came home for lunch) and was part of one of the strongest ever Co Louth school rugby teams.

We were rubbing shoulders in 1956 and 1957 with the big boys of Leinster senior schools rugby – Blackrock College and Terenure College – and had the legendary Ireland and Lions wing, Tony O'Reilly, training us as we made our way to the semi-finals of that august competition.

All the while I was playing minor and senior with two different clubs while in late '56 the county senior selectors honoured me with a call-up to play at that level as well.

I am now into my eighties and over 60 years from those heady days in my sporting youth. Yet I'm still perplexed at how I got away with playing rugby during the week in one of the biggest competitions that got plenty of local and national newspaper coverage while still playing GAA at the weekends.

The only conclusion I can come to is that it may be due to my nickname.

From an early age I was called 'Lollie' both at home and by my friends at school. I don't know for sure why that was but I have a vague memory that it might be because I liked eating ice-lollies at every turn.

When names appeared in the paper for GAA, that sobriquet was slightly altered to 'Ollie' which meant that Ollie Lynch was the GAA player and Francis Walter Lynch appeared to be a totally different person who played schools rugby.

As I pointed out earlier, those rugby games were covered by the daily newspapers while Louth senior footballers were one of the strongest in the country in 1956 and proved that by winning the All Ireland final against Cork in 1957.

Both teams I played for were high on the publicity list those days and in retrospect I can thank my two names for allowing me to play right up to the Leinster semi-final in rugby and in the All Ireland final at Croke Park against the Rebels in the same year.

I was a hooker in rugby but back then it was the wingers who threw in the ball at lineouts. When Tony O'Reilly came to coach us, he changed my position to No 6 in the backrow. He wanted to use me as a source of lineout possession but he also wanted me to 'hound' Terenure's outhalf, Gerry Tormey, who was their star man.

We ended up losing the match 15-3 but the whole team gave a really good account of ourselves and I was delighted to be subsequently picked on a Leinster Schools Rugby team for that year.

With the rugby season over for me, I was in the twin binoculars of the Louth Junior and Senior GAA teams which were both flying in Leinster that year.

Jim 'Sogger' Quigley had approached me the previous autumn when I was still a minor to tell me he was including me in his plans for the senior team the following year. 'Sogger' was to Louth then what Kevin Heffernan or Mick O'Dwyer would become to Dublin or Kerry respectively. I still firmly hold the view that but for the politicking that went on after we won in 1957, we could have gone on to win two, three or maybe even four Leinsters and maybe another All Ireland or two.

In the early summer of 1957, Louth juniors were advancing step by step and their selectors wanted to hold onto my services. 'Sogger' and the senior management team reluctantly agreed to release me so I didn't get to play the early rounds in Louth senior's successful Leinster year.

I well remember it was FA Cup final day in England between Aston Villa and Manchester United on May 4 when Sogger met me to explain why I wouldn't be playing against Carlow at Navan in the Leinster SF championship the next day, saying the juniors required my services at centrefield alongside Peter Judge. I had no choice in the matter and missed the following games against Wexford and Kildare which saw Louth go through to the Leinster Final.

That was against Dublin. It was assumed that due to an injury reshuffle that I would be brought in at right-half forward and Seamie O'Donnell would revert to wing back.

Once again Jim Cunningham demanded that I stay with his juniors, aware that I would be ineligible once I played even one minute at the higher level.

The best laid plans often turn on their head. Alfie Monks, who was given the nod to play in the half forward line sustained a knock after only 10 minutes or so into the game and was unable to continue.

Brian Reynolds, who was sitting beside me turned to his fellow selectors and said: "Feck that, I've seen enough. Put young Lynch on."

The others agreed.

Once I ran out onto the field I knew immediately that I had relinquished my junior status. Good riddance. I wanted to play senior and now I had my chance. I took it with both hand, doing well and I scored two points as we won by five points 2-9 to 1-7.

I still wasn't sure of my place after the Dubs game but in a few subsequent challenges I did really well and was selected for the All-Ireland semi-final game against Tyrone. We won easily thanks to a virtuoso free-taking performance from Kevin Beahan. We could even afford the luxury of missing a penalty which Stephen White took.

Being retained on the starting 15 for the final was special and I think I repaid the selectors' faith in me by doing well on Paddy Harrington, the father of Pádraig, the three-time golf major champion. Paddy was a really good defender, the teak-tough type who took no prisoners. I had plenty of speed and Paddy gave me a right wallop on the calf after 15 minutes which certainly slowed me down. I got through the game but afterwards I was unable play for a month.

In that final, Seamie O'Donnell played a whale of a game when he was switched to midfield and Kevin Beahan went out to the right wing and also excelled. As forwards, I'd say we had no more than 45 per cent of the play so we were lucky enough to get the win thanks to Sean Cunningham's goal.

We were under terrible pressure near the end as Cork threw the kitchen sink at us. I can remember winning a few vital balls in that time and as the youngest lad on the team was congratulated by the older lads for keeping possession in our hands which was vital as we held onto a slender lead.

Arguably though the biggest regret I have in my GAA lifetime is what happened to 'Sogger' after we won the senior All Ireland title. I emphasise this is just my view, the perfect yet delicate constellation that came together to make Louth football "brilliant" began to lose its lustre all too prematurely as morale and leadership took a nosedive.

The ramifications were far-reaching and soul destroying; so much so that Louth lost out on winning back-to-back titles and indeed realising its true potential as a tour de force that could have been most definitely sustained up to and including 1961 and perhaps beyond.

I admired Sogger so much and was so disappointed when he was axed by the Louth County Board after he, more than anyone, was responsible for bringing Sam Maguire to the Wee County.

As an 18-year old novice, I recall his clarity in explaining to me why my speed on the left wing was an essential component to the team's effectiveness.

Despite his success as trainer coach, and his popularity of heading the voting at the previous year's meeting, he was defeated for the final seat for the upcoming Selection Committee in 1958.

I understand how flawed and easily dented the human ego can be. Having won the All Ireland, I recall the post-victory deluge that descended upon our changing room at Croke Park. Quigley's quick action of slamming the door shut prevented euphoria turning to a chaotic free-for-all. His reaction was the right one. Yet unwittingly, the proverbial closing of the door may have left either an individual or individuals of self-importance feeling left out. In my view, perhaps this did not help or augur well when it came to the proposal not to re-elect the Selection Committee en bloc.

As a momentous year closed, a new year began with a massive void that I felt was tantamount to amputation, with the de-selection of the team's mentor-in-chief.

I remember the shock waves that reverberated among the Louth supporters on hearing the news that Quigley was not to be part of the Selection Committee for 1958 or to go on the New York trip.

Upon arrival in New York the huge welcoming committee from the Louth Society in New York made known their great disappointment that Quigley was not in the group.

This trip is wonderfully imprinted in my memory. I actually ran the proverbial gauntlet down the Brooklyn underground track between Winthrop Street and Church Avenue. I had missed my train stop due to the fact that I was winsomely engaged in conversation with a beautiful, young

American lady. My escapade reached the newspapers and earned me a sort of infamous alias as the "Subway kid!" But that is another story!

My story is a posthumous salute to Jim Quigley: I still savour the experience of Louth's success, but I also need to acknowledge the cutting-short of our potential.

'Sogger', despite the humiliation and hurt he endured, held no grudge and worked tirelessly throughout his entire life for Cumann Lúthchleas Gael until his death on October 4, 2005. To me he was an inspiration and above all, a man of great character and integrity.

◆ ◆ ◆

I regret to say also that my playing days with Geraldine's ended on a sour note in 1973-74. I was on holiday down in Waterford and got news that we were playing in a tournament match so I drove the family back to play in it. During the game I got a very serious injury which, on the day, my great friend and mentor Jimmy Thornton diagnosed as a hamstring pull.

I had never heard of such an injury at the time but it would later be blamed on the use of cars rather than bikes which I grew up with as a means of transport.

Three or four of the team didn't show that day as they were playing soccer for Blackrock. For the next game, I made it known that the lads who had played the previous day should be given starting jerseys for this game. I don't know if that annoyed some of the selectors or not but one of the first players to be substituted that day was my cousin, Michael Lynch.

I was hampered by this new injury and it manifested itself in my inability to kick the ball more than 20 yards where normally I could deliver it 60 yard down the field. The chairman and the selectors must have felt I was acting the maggot in support of my cousin because a few weeks later, they delivered a letter to my wife seriously admonishing me for my conduct.

The letter arrived at the house on Christmas Eve which meant no fuss could be kicked up about it over the holiday period. When the agm was held early the following year, I didn't attend or go near the club after that. Coming up to the time for the first round of the championship in early summer, I was approached to see if I would play. I told them I wouldn't and aside from my later duties as Louth county board chairman, I have never really had any relationship with the club again.

Yes, it was a bad end to an otherwise great association with the club – and all over the fact that they wouldn't believe that the hamstring injury severely restricted my performance, rather than a fit of pique, in that game.

## WAS IT THE GREATEST EVER CROKE PARK SOLO?

Frank Lynch is credited with having produced the longest football solo run in Croke Park. It was against Kildare on June 9, 1963 in the semi-final of the Leinster championship.

Frank recalls: "We were beaten 2-11 to 1-12. I went from our own 21-yard-line to about 10-yards from their goal. As I was about to shoot Pa Connolly hit me with all he had and my shot went over the bar when I was trying for a goal to win the game for us.

The referee Brian Smith took Pa's name but the Kildare defender had done his job in preventing a goal which would have levelled the game.

The late, great, John D Hickey wrote about it in the following day's Irish Independent as follows – "On and on and on he went."

That solo run was on television for two years 64 to 66 on Wednesday night. I have tried to get this and couldn't get it. I think RTE either taped over that game or threw out the recording, instead of having it for posterity.

*Frank Lynch is a Dundalk native who won an All-Ireland SF medal with Louth in 1957. A long standing practising accountant, he is also a well-known businessman and hotelier in the county for over half a century. He is married to Lily and they have four grown-up children and 10 grandchildren. His hobbies include horse-racing and GAA and he is presently on the committee working on the new stadium for Louth.*

# The Long And Short Of My Camogie Dress Dances

Eileen Ludlow

The Naomh Eoin camogie club in Ovens, Co Cork was but a few years in existence. Everything was rough and ready. We were grudgingly allowed to share the training ground with the hurlers of Éire Óg.

The dressing room was state-of-the-art; a wooden railway carriage with doors and windows conspicuous by their absence. This was made up for with fresh air and a view both in and out. There were no steaming showers, just steaming bodies after training or after a game. There were no fancy sports bags or tracksuits, if you were lucky, you had a plastic bag which would carry your jacket and could be tied around the bas of the hurley with your boots.

Cars were scarce among club members and we mostly thumbed to and from the pitch. When it came to away games, we piled into Joan Donovan's minibus to take us to the venue. She was a patient, helpful lady who would drop us all home after the game. In summer we were often invited to a Macra field day to play the village team. These games were usually followed by a dance in the local hall.

Most of the time we would only change our footwear and keep on the sweaty, smelly gear we had played in. A very short miniskirt over black tights ... to say it was short was probably an understatement. There were no changing rooms or showers here either, so we did not have a choice. The local young farmers did not seem to mind and were happy to dance the night away with us. We were excellent for the environment as there was no water wasted in keeping us smelling fresh.

In the late sixties and early seventies clubs used to hold dances as a way of raising money to keep finances in order. On one of those occasions someone came up with the idea of holding a dress dance just before Christmas. We went with the plan, as we all felt we deserved to dress up at least once a year. Since we were accustomed to booking bands and organising dances to raise funds to keep us ticking over, we had some experience of how to tackle this new venture. We set a date and booked a hotel in Blarney and a good local band. When all this was done, we then set about getting the tickets printed as we undertook our selling and marketing of this magical dance.

Our biggest scramble was for dresses – a task that was taken very seriously. Had we concentrated as much at training and playing, we'd have been county champions. In fact, we were more focused on finding the perfect dress than sourcing the perfect escort. Material had to be found somewhere and myself and two pals arranged to visit Mrs Arthur, the local dressmaker. She was a miracle worker as she could produce a dress from a rough drawing. These visits were also sociable occasions where we all discussed with her the lack of escorts and wondered how we could solve the problem. The truth is that myself and others with no man in tow weren't unduly stressed. We knew we could muster up someone who would don a dress-suit for a night as long as we, the girls, paid for the tickets.

Now the idea of a camogie club running a formal dress dance was a bit of a novelty in those days. Dress dances were more for Rotary Clubs and Chambers of Commerce. We knew we were punching well above our weight. Fortunately, when the tickets went on sale we were surprised at the level of demand; seemingly people from far and wide outside the club were also keen on being part of this gala night.

The dresses came together after many late-night fittings, usually after training. The banter included the up-to-the-minute position on our escort situation. The first year was very exciting and in the end, all of us who were single got hitched for the night with someone's brother or cousin.

After the success of the first dress dance, people started asking if we were having another. Immediately, we went into planning phase for the following year. This time we shopped around and eventually decided on the plush surroundings of the Munster Arms Hotel in Bandon as our venue. The date was set in stone for December 2, 1970.

A case of déjà vu as the hunt for the 'gúna' started all over again. There was no way that any self-respecting girl could wear the same dress as the previous time. This time a gaggle of us headed into Cork to source our material. We travelled by bus on out-of-date weekly tickets, trying to save one way what we were splashing out in another… but that is another story.

Then it was back to Mrs Arthur for fittings and adjustments until finally, we were once again happy with the finished article. Unfortunately for me, I still did not have a partner for the big night. I'd had a really unfortunate blind date experience the previous year where I was collected by ambulance and my date, yes the ambulance driver, arrived kitted out for work rather than for a formal dinner dance. To add insult to injury he was seriously lacking in the height department – I'm being charitable when I say the top of his head was somewhere south of my shoulder. Once bitten, twice shy. As result of this quite humbling experience, I put the word out early that I was looking for someone taller than me who might have the inclination to pay for his own ticket. I had no one in mind but one of the girls had sold tickets to a couple who ran a guest house and one of their guests was prepared to come, pay for his ticket and he was tall.

I agreed, and the speculation began, with some teasing that he was approaching 80 among other things. The reality is that I was totally in the dark as to who he was so all I could do was wait. We were so busy putting the final touches to things for the big night that it wasn't foremost in my mind.

Arrangements were made with the guesthouse owners for this mysterious man to pick me up at seven o'clock. I'd made it clear that, as a member of the organising committee, I needed to be there early. However, by eight o'clock no one had shown up and I was considering going solo when a car drove into the yard. It was totally dark outside and I had no way of catching a glimpse of the man beside me in the back of the car. We just introduced ourselves and proceeded to Bandon. As we arrived in the town, I managed to ascertain two things – he was tall and definitely not 80. Other than that, truthfully, I could not have picked him out of a police line up.

He went to the bar with his friends and I took my place at the door. That was the extent of the communication we had in the journey to the dance. Immediately my friends asked me what my escort was like. I giggled and said I wouldn't even recognise him if he walked in this minute.

Once again, the dinner dance drew a huge crowd and before we had time to bless our faces, all the tickets had been collected and the bell for dinner sounded. At last I arrived at our table and got my first good look at my partner for the night.

That was 50 years ago, and he will tell you today that he is still paying the price for that camogie club dress dance. I tell my husband it was the best money he ever spent.

*Eileen Ludlow is a native of Cork who has lived in Drumconrath, Co Meath for over 40 years. Married to Peter with three grown up children, her hobbies include reading, gardening, painting and writing.*

# Pigeons Coming Home To Roost

## Mick Hackett

Living on the border between two counties always leads to great sporting rivalry and the following story is a great example of the Cork and Waterford enmity.

The Mernan twins, Ned and Jim, lived in Villierstown in West Waterford and were tremendous fans of their county and proud of their hurling success in the late 50s and early 60s. They worked at Blackwater Cottons in Youghal (Co. Cork) where they got a lot of 'stick' about which county possessed the better team.

A fellow worker of theirs on the same shift was Bernard Leamy of Mill Road in Youghal who was a fanatical Cork supporter. The twins would give him a drive to work every morning, saving him a two-mile walk, and again they would drop him home in the evening.

Bernard's other great past-time outside of the GAA was homing pigeons. One day he asked Ned and Jim to bring a basket of young pigeons to their home in Villierstown before releasing them to fly back to Youghal. The twins readily agreed to give those young birds their first flight test comprising a ten mile distance.

Away went the birds secure in the basket in the car while Bernard went in home to have his dinner. He estimated that it would be at least a half-hour before any young bird would appear. After finishing his meal, he went outside to watch the sky and wait for his fledglings to arrive.

The half-hour turned into an hour with no sign of wings fluttering in the Youghal skyline. It was a further half-hour, just as he was getting anxious, that he spotted his young birds as they slowly appeared.

They were totally exhausted as they alighted on his perch because onto their legs, the twins had tied little blue and white flags (Waterford colours) and they had flown the 10 miles with these weights attached.

Cork were playing Waterford in Thurles the following Sunday and won the match much to Bernard's delight.

Going into work at Blackwater Cottons on that Monday, the twins saw that attached to the blank walls were the little blue and white flags they had put on the pigeons – with a mournful piece of black cloth on each pennant.

# Stitched Up By A Neighbour's Red Hand

Fionnuala McNicholl

My dearly departed uncle, whose home straddled the Tyrone-Derry border, recalled the great excitement around the parish when Derry made it to the 1993 All-Ireland Football final.

Display shelves in the club lounge had a dusting like never before. After all, if Sam Maguire was coming to perch on a Derry shelf, it would be a polished to perfection shelf. Sam's bottom was not going to be found with a rim of dust as far as the lady club members were concerned. With a few pokes and prods of their male counterparts, they organised the tidy up not only of the pitches but also of the clubhouse.

Every parish within the county would ensure a Derry welcome for the long-awaited Sam Maguire. So it was out with the dusters, paintbrushes, bunting and, of course, flags. There couldn't be any bedraggled, tattered flags gracing poles; therefore, they too would be replaced.

The stalwart mammies, always to the forefront since the days their nimble-footed football geniuses kicked for the under tens, took charge of organising the decoration. The neighbours regularly stood shouting and roaring at the sidelines, until their throats, aching and hoarse, had them fish their pockets for the all-important Throaties and Fisherman's Friends.

Just like the ticket allocation, flags were in high demand for the big day to Dublin. Determined no one worth their salt would arrive in Croke Park without a banner, one of the ladies offered her services to run up a few extra flags just in case any of the local clubs happened to run out. The club coach was delighted. "Don't spare the cloth," he advised as she headed to the town for the essential red and white material.

The lady in question was a dab hand at sewing, having spent her younger days as a factory machinist. She certainly knew her way around a bobbin and spool, doing many alterations for club members, with nips and tucks, trouser hems and shirt-tail trims. "These flags will be top drawer," the coach boasted, at the next club meeting.

"We'll have new flags to hand out to everyone on the bus," he boasted.

At her home, the sewing buff set to work in a spare room, which she had turned into a one-woman manufacturing enterprise. With her pedal-operated Singer Sewer machine whirring for hours, she was happy in the knowledge her friends were getting the youth of the parish to give a fresh coat of red and white paint to every feasible surface. Grazing sheep didn't even escape as their woolly fleeces too, had a red and white spray.

As the big September weekend approached, the parish swamped in a sea of scarlet and white, as banners, flags and bunting flew from every lamp post and home. All-Ireland day arrived with a bus and cavalcade of supporters assembling at the club grounds. The coach himself was travelling by bus and had his seat reserved upfront to keep the singing and chanting alive as they negotiated the long rocky road to Dublin. With palpable enthusiasm, supporters boarded the bus, some already with their flags while others were awaiting the fresh creations.

The coach was fussing around, on and off the bus umpteen times, scratching his head and ticking off the names of the pre-booked enthusiastic supporters as they boarded the bus.

"I made a special extra-large flag for you," the machinist called to the coach from the bottom of the steps after her husband had left the boxes of precious flags on board. "See you all in Monaghan," she called, with a wide wry grin and wave as she returned to join her sons waiting in the car.

As the bus pulled away from the club grounds, the driver hooted and honked the horn, while passengers waved and cheered to a group of well-wishers gathered to see the supporters on their merry way.

"Bring back Sam," the fans shouted, while the team coach, like a child on Christmas morning, pulled the tape from a cardboard box with his name scrawled in big black marker writing. Smiling from ear to ear, he began unfurling his red and white pride and joy.

"Three cheers for Derry," he shouted at the top of his voice, throwing open the silky flag from his outstretched hand.

With bewildering laughter, boos and a few expletives, he took a second look and before his disbelieving eyes, he saw the red hand of the Tyrone County GAA motto span the centre of the flag. Duped by his old friend and neighbour he stood not knowing where to look, his face, lobster red, wondering whether he could risk opening the other three boxes.

For years, the coach and his machinist neighbour, in good humour bantered about their county allegiances. However, in all his excitement of Derry reaching the All-Ireland final, it slipped his mind that she was a Tyrone woman. He'd often joke with her as only being an honorary Derry supporter.

There was even more ribbing when they all met at a Monaghan hotel for breakfast. Eventually seeing the funny side, he was ever thankful upon opening the other boxes to find as he described them, "the best-stitched Derry flags flying at Croke Park," with only the one 'joke' flag on top of the box designed to give him the shock of his life.

The machinist's family couldn't believe either that she had carried out such a prank on a man, who the world knew wasn't, to put it mildly, a fan of Tyrone when it came to football.

On Hill 16 however, as the game unfurled, he noticed that the hard-working machinist cheered until hoarse for her adopted county as Henry Downey lifted the Sam Maguire for the first and only time (so far) in their football history.

*Fionnuala McNicholl is a Co. Tyrone native who now lives with her husband in Co. Derry. A retired nurse, she has had several stories published in various magazines. In 2019, Fionnuala won Ireland's Own memoir writing competition.*

# Derry Game Records New Score

Seamus McRory

Derry legend and 1958 All-Ireland final captain and first winner of the Footballer of the Year Caltex award, Jim McKeever, was a genius on the pitch. He was able to relate a top class tale off it when the occasion demanded.

My team, Ballymaguigan were playing Coleraine in a club game at Coleraine in the early sixties. One of our best players, Michael Young (brother of future Roscommon manager and Boyle Bank manager Seán), did not want to play as he had hay ready for baling and the weather forecast in this particularly rainy season was not good.

However, he was persuaded to line out. The pitch was not well marked. There were no nets and at one end a thick rope served as a crossbar. Halfway through the second half, a Coleraine player shot towards the Ballymaguigan goals with the roped crossbar. The ball went through with one umpire giving the shot as a goal, the other awarding a point.

Our umpire had magnanimously given the decision against his own team and said that it was a goal. The Coleraine umpire had incredibly done likewise and said that it was a point.

For several minutes total confusion reigned as both sides debated the merits and demerits of the conflicting opinions of the umpires. Eventually the normally mild-mannered Michael Young went up to the referee and told him that he should hurry up and make a decision because he had a field of meadow ready for baling and rain was on the way!

The referee realised that both umpires had made honest decisions, so he used common sense and awarded two points for the score. Both sides gracefully accepted the decision as that wonderful servant of Ballymaguigan, Michael Young, raced back to take up his position in the centre of the field!"

*'The Voice From The Sideline'* – Seamus McRory

# A Different View Of The 1996 Meath-Mayo Fracas

### Seán Boylan

It was 27 seconds of madness but the 1996 All Ireland final between Meath and Mayo is forever remembered as if the melee was something premeditated and orchestrated... with yours truly mostly to blame according to some critics.

It occurred in the replay after we had fought back to snatch a draw the first day in the most dramatic of circumstances on a Meath 0-12, Mayo 1-9 scoreline.

That was a pulsating game as we overturned a six-point deficit after Ray Dempsey scored a Mayo goal. It took a long-range point from Colm Coyle to secure the replay. His long-range kick bounced over to equalise.

Mayo were the better team on the day and I suppose I was relieved that we had got out of the game with the opportunity to put things right the next day. The replay was just as close and we squeezed through to win in the end by a point 2-9 to 1-11. Trevor Giles from a penalty and Tommy Dowd scored our two goals and Brendan O'Reilly elegantly left-footed a point from an acute angle that was as fitting a winning score as any to adorn such a big occasion.

Yet that wasn't the centre of conversation that evening or for the following week after the replay. All people talked about and indeed to this day the focus remains on the so-called 'brawl' that lasted less than half a minute.

It was front-page news... and back. Even as the week went on the 'brawl' continued to dominate, so much so that by the Thursday, I had it up to my eyes and said to my wife Tina: "Let's go somewhere for a drive and a meal to get away from all this nonsense."

As most of the national media was located in Dublin, she came up with a number of suggestions as to where we might go down the country. She felt that was our best chance to get some peace.

When I suggested Dublin she said: "You must be mad to think of going there."

This was an age when there were no cameras on phones or twitter or Facebook so I felt we had a better chance of being anonymous somewhere in Dublin than if I pulled into some town down the country. Every town is a small town and you'd be sussed much quicker in Westmeath or Longford that you would in Dublin.

Reluctantly she agreed and we set out for the capital on a lovely fine evening. I had no intention of going to O'Connell St or anywhere near it. My intention was to drive the car to the north of the county.

Eventually we decided we'd head for Howth and when we arrived at the harbour, we got out of the car with the intention of stretching our legs and taking the salt air for a few minutes.

No sooner had we done so, who should pull in right alongside our car than the great Dublin star of the sixties, Lar Foley and his wife Jo.

I knew and admired Lar for years as a hurling fan and remember him and his brother Des playing for Dublin when the county last appeared in an All Ireland final in 1961 when they lost by a point to Tipperary.

It was great to see a friendly face and even better that in congratulating us on winning against Mayo, Lar never once referred to the row.

We must have stood at our cars talking for the best part of an hour about every subject under the sun. Although a Dublin person by birth and allegiance, Lar was also a countryman. He farmed in North County Dublin and had more in common with how country people thought and operated as he too was working with cattle, driving tractors and using machinery all his life.

Eventually it was getting to the time when we would part so I got around to telling him why Tina and myself had decided to head for Howth. "The All Ireland melee is all over the airwaves every time we turn the radio or television on. There are journalists ringing every five minutes looking for quotes so we thought we'd get away from it all for a few hours."

Lar listened to what I was saying and screwed up his face as I mentioned the fisticuffs breakout.

"Jesus Christ almighty, I don't know what that crowd is talking about," he said as he lifted up his cap to scratch his head as if totally perplexed by the media.

"You know Seán the truth of it is, I often saw more jostling at last mass on a Sunday with the people going up and coming back from Communion than I saw in Croke Park!"

*Sean Boylan is a former Meath hurler and manager who shot to national prominence by managing the Meath footballers to glory during his 23 years at the helm from 1982 to 2005 – winning four All Irelands, eight Leinster championships and three league titles. Married to Tina, they have six children. The Dunboyne herbalist was conferred with the title Freeman of Co Meath in 2006 – the first to hold such a title.*

# Fans Protest As Payne Stewart And I Shoot The Breeze In Croker

### Brian Jaffray

Offaly gaels worth their salt have a story to tell about the day Jimmy Cooney blew up early. They were all there. And weren't they all at the vanguard as they stormed the pitch to demand a replay.

As the years progress and the myths magnify, the numbers from the Faithful county who proclaim to have been on the hallowed Croke Park turf grow by the day and by the telling of the yarns. You're nothing in Offaly gaeldom if you don't have an "I was there" story.

It's a bit like the day the county hurlers made the breakthrough in that glorious summer of 1980 when All Ireland champions Kilkenny were dethroned and Offaly won the Leinster title for the first time.

Sure, thousands from the hurling heartlands of Birr, Kilcormac, Banagher and Kinnitty can claim they were on the pitch as Pádraig Horan lifted the Bob O'Keeffe Cup in the Hogan stand.

Throw in the multitudes of Gaels from the football end of the county like Tullamore, Clara, Daingean and Edenderry who also assert to have been there and the few that were left behind in Offaly were either footing turf or milking the cows. The fact that the official attendance was 9,613 is neither here nor there.

With Scottish Presbyterian heritage running in my blood but 100 percent born and bred in Offaly, it would be stretching it to claim I'm a 'fíor Gael', as genuine Gaels like to profess themselves. You know the type. The lad who has all the lingo and knows all the All Stars from the year dot and who played where, in what position, and who didn't. The bore on the high stool with all the questions and the answers.

I consider myself more of a gentle breeze than a Gael and to my chagrin I can never boast to have played "a bit of minor with the county" or caught the eye with any nippy corner-forward moves. Indeed, it would be fair to say that most of my work on the playing fields went completely unnoticed.

# GRASSROOTS

Still, owing to my profession as a journalist I've been lucky to have witnessed most of Offaly's great days. Martin Furlong lived down the road from our house in Tullamore and, as a nipper, I travelled to Offaly games with his parents Tom and Margaret, his brother John, his uncle Seamus Morris and his son Dermot. The late, great Paddy Fenning was a family friend. I was there in Croke Park with my Dad in 1971 and 1972.

I was under shelter from the rain for the Seamus Darby goal (or as we in Offaly like to call it the 'AE2' final) and crammed into the Canal End as Johnny Flaherty broke Galway hearts, the previous year. And work afforded me the opportunity to witness the great Offaly hurling victories in 1985, 1994 and 1998 from the comfort of the press box.

And what about the infamous Jimmy Cooney game against Clare? The match was on a glorious Saturday afternoon in late August. Over 90 tall ships were in Dublin Port at the end of the Cutty Sark Tall Ships race.

Dublin was thronged. Such was the traffic that the Offaly team bus was late getting to Croke Park. An ecumenical service was held prior to the game as a mark of respect for the victims of the Omagh bombing. It was a day that lives in the memory.

Clare led by 10 points at half-time and Offaly looked dead and buried. Billy Dooley and Joe Errity raised green flags and with it Offaly's hopes and before you could say "we'll leave now to beat the traffic and stop in Kinnegad for a mixed-grill" Offaly were right back in the game. Then Jimmy blew his whistle and the rest has gone down in GAA folklore.

Cue bedlam and pandemonium. Poor Jimmy had to be escorted off the pitch. Offaly fans staged a sit-in demanding a replay. Those of us up in the stands watched in amazement at the unfolding scenes on the hallowed Croke Park turf. It took some time for the pitch to be cleared. The Faithful gaels had made their point. Fair play, replay.

As Jimmy's famous shrill of the whistle was writing its own headlines, and away from the madding crowd, one of the world's most famous sports stars, US golfer Payne Stewart, was totally anonymous to most as he queued for the grey dank toilets under the Hogan Stand. The glamour of it all.

With his red tab Levi 501s, white cotton teeshirt and docksiders he could well have been the visiting American relative waiting in line to get into Spiders nightclub in Tullamore.

The only thing that made him stand out was his deep tan, blonde streaked hair and muscular body. You knew this guy was fit, athletic and an outdoor type and definitely never thinned beet or cut silage in his life.

In his working gear he dressed to thrill and was golf royalty. Immaculately decked out in his NFL inspired uniform of plus fours, neck tie and cardigan, Scally cap and gold toed golf spikes, Stewart was your classic flamboyant in-your-face type of American sports jock. His face adorned billboards, newspapers and glossy magazines around the globe. His character transcended the golfing world.

Brashness and perceived arrogance were adjectives that were never far away when his name came up in conversion. He inhabited a world in the 1990s where first-class travel, five-star hotels and red-carpet treatments was the norm.

However, in the 'Seomra Fir' under Michael Hogan's stand he was just an ordinary guy waiting his turn to do what a man needed to do. Together we stood, side by side. He caught my eye and knew instinctively that "I knew that he knew that I knew who he was" if you get my drift.

"Are you Payne Stewart?" I enquired wearing my Irish Independent journalist's hat. "Yes, sir," replied my new acquaintance politely without a hint of arrogance or hubris. So much for brashness and arrogance.

Sure enough Payne (we were on first name terms by now) should have been at the K Club as he was in Ireland to play the European Open at the Co Kildare venue. He was the star attraction. He was a two-time major champion having won the PGA at Kemper Lakes and the 1991 US Open at Hazeltine.

Unfortunately, for the organisers and Irish golf fans, Payne never read the script and missed the cut and had the weekend off. With nothing else to do and plenty of time on his hands, what else would he be at but heading to Croke Park for the hurling?

We talked and walked together as we made our way up Jones' Road towards Mountjoy Square. He was ever so charming and engaging. He was accompanied by his friend and host for his Irish visit, JP McManus.

Offaly gaels of my acquaintance, on their way to the county's branch office in Bermingham's pub on Dorset Street, looked on in amusement as I strolled along my new friend Payne on that glorious Saturday evening in 1998.

A year and a few months later on October 25th, a few months after he won his third major at the US Open in Pinehurst and mere weeks after helping the US to victory over Europe in the infamous 'Battle of Brookline' Ryder Cup, Payne Stewart and four other passengers were killed after his Learjet crashed in a pasture in South Dakota.

The plane suffered a catastrophic pressurisation fault at about 40,000 feet. It flew halfway across the United States on autopilot as the pilot, Payne Stewart and his fellow passengers aboard lay unconscious. His final hours were beamed live on TV across the world.

## GRASSROOTS

The day Jimmy Cooney blew up early still lives long in the memory for Offaly gaels. Some memories are much more personal than others.

As the years go by and the day's momentous events are recalled in homes and pubs where the Faithful gather, my anecdote is less about the protest and instead about the precious window of time I shared with an iconic world sporting figure. Payne Stewart, the pleasure was all mine.

*Brian Jaffray is a native of Tullamore. As a journalist he worked with the Westmeath/Offaly Independent, Offaly Express, Sunday Tribune and the Irish Independent. Married to Caroline, they have three grown up sons, Daniel, Eoin and Andrew. Brian is a fan of all sports and also enjoys playing golf and travelling. He still keeps a close eye on Offaly's travails.*

# Gate Opening That Cost Carlow Thousands

Tommy Murphy

Dr. Cullen Park in Carlow was opened on August 9, 1936 and has hosted a huge amount of Gaelic games ever since. The Dr. Cullen Park committee were continuously carrying out improvements to the grounds and in 1960 they erected new entrances and gate ways at the Castledermot Road end (Dublin Road end).

Eight new turnstile entrances were built along with two wide exits to greatly enhance access to the ground and an aid to crowd control. Up to then there was only one entrance to the grounds from the Oak Park Road side.

The whole project turnstiles, exit and gates was almost completed very late on Saturday evening August 13th 1960. The workmanship looked excellent from the outside. However, one job that remained to be done was to secure proper lock bolts on the inside of the two large exit doors. With daylight fading fast, it was decided that a couple of large stones against the doors would suffice until the job could be finished properly on the Monday.

On that Sunday Carlow hurlers were playing Down in the All-Ireland junior hurling championship semi-final in the same Dr Cullen Park. The resurgence in Carlow hurling had led to exceptionally large crowds supporting them. Down had caused an upset by beating a fancied Antrim team and this added to the attractiveness of the occasion.

Locally, there was a lot of talk about this game from all parts especially the hurling strongholds. It meant that people were going to travel to the game by any means possible, whether that was bicycle, motor bike, or car, which were scarce on the ground at that time.

Our story starts with four friends, who lived high up on the hills over the village of Myshall. The father, Andy and his son, Mick had a blue van used mostly for carrying sheep. This particular Sunday, they were also bringing two neighbours, Pat and Neddy. All the arrangements were made mid-week and the job was sound.

However, business was always part of work and play and the two neighbours had recently done work for Andy and were owed for their labours. There was no problem there other than the fact that this father and son were known to be tighter than a duck's rectum when it came to parting with money.

Notwithstanding this background, all four were on their way to the game on the Sunday in a happy-go-lucky state of mind. Approaching Myshall village from the Croppy Rd, at the entrance to the Naomh Eoin GAA club, the van chugged violently and came to a shuddering halt at the side of the road.

The son, who was driving, was in foul mood with his father and glared at him in the front passenger's seat.

"I thought I told you to put petrol in the van," he said angrily as he banged the palms of his hands against the steering wheel in total frustration.

"I did. As God be my judge, I put a full porter bottle of petrol in before we left," the father said in his defence, not seeing the mirth it was causing the two passengers in the back.

They had no choice but to disembark and push the vehicle to the petrol pumps which luckily were only four or five hundred yards away. Once they had the motor ticking over again, the mood changed, though it isn't known for sure who paid for the petrol.

The general conversation was slowly steered around to the work the two men had done but they were now fairly sure from the responses that all accounts would be settled up on the way home, possibly in the famed Fighting Cocks pub. This was a great half-way house for the weary traveller, and the hope was that if Carlow won, spirits would be high and purse strings might be loosened, however slightly.

Sunday August 14th was a day of bright sunshine and all was ready for the big occasion with stewards in place and the crowd pouring in from an early hour. All of what followed it must be remembered occurred because stewards were manning these new fangled turnstile gadgets for the first time, with very little briefing on how they worked.

From the beginning, red flags were raised as the operators found all sorts of problems. For instance admission to the game was two shillings, which could be presented in a number of ways... and yes, the halfpenny was still legal currency at that time.

The slowest was when a person produced 24 old pennies. This took an age to count out and then there might be arguments that there were only 23 pennies so a recount was necessary. Even the presentation of a shilling, a few thrupenny bits and the rest in coppers (pennies) significantly slowed the progress of people getting into the ground.

Other problems emerged. The odd person presented either a lovely red crispy ten shilling note or a one pound note. This took an inordinate amount of counting to give those people the exact change back. Time was being eaten up and the queues were growing at an alarming rate.

Making matters worse was the fact that there was the odd con man or two in the crowd who had their halfpennies wrapped with silver paper and pressed tightly giving it the look of a shilling. One mechanical washer also covered with silver paper was presented while the rush was on, and the poor person on the turnstile pressed the pedal and the customer was gone through in a flash, never to be found again.

Frustration was setting in as the snake-like queue of fans moved slowly. This feeling of annoyance increased significantly when a huge roar went up inside the grounds signalling that Carlow hurlers had come out on the field at about a quarter to three. As the minutes ticked down to the 3pm throw in, it became patently clear to the crowd that they were not going to see the full game unless something radically happened.

Then there was complete silence inside as the band struck up 'Faith of our Fathers' then further silence as 'Amhrán na bhFiann' was played.

The roar of the crowd inside led to an explosion of anger outside with a chorus of 'Open the Gates, Open the Gates' being chanted by annoyed supporters.

Our four amigos from Myshall were part of that group now numbering thousands who were patiently hoping for entry to see the game in its entirety.

The father, Andy, was always the resourceful type. He was one of those fellas who found a solution to the biggest of problems. Lo and behold if it wasn't the same Andy who found a solution to this threat of revolt outside Dr Cullen Park.

While waiting in the queue close to the aforementioned 'locked doors,' Andy decided to see if he could get the massive portals to slide back. To his surprise and delight – and let it be said the same emotions for thousands of others – the doors divided in a flash and in less than two minutes an estimated 4,000 fans burst into the grounds, eschewing the slower turnstiles' route.

After gaining entry, Andy quickly gathered his wits and fuelled by the fear of being seen as the perpetrator of the mass free entry brigade, he made a beeline to the far end of the ground. He kept his head down so that no one could pin the blame on him and left the others in his wake. When it came to the threat of parting with money, Andy decided it was a case of 'every man for himself' as others too gleefully scattered to all parts of the ground. He needn't have worried about being fingered as the game was already under way and all eyes were on the action.

Once in the blue van and out of Carlow town past Wall's Forge on the way home, Andy was like one of the brave heroes of old. He now believed that his actions gave him great bargaining leverage, repeating that it was great that his two friends, Pat and Neddy and his son Mick had got into the match free – not to mention the 4,000 others. He was of the opinion that all financial accounts against him from those within the van should be summarily dismissed.

"After all didn't ye get to see a top class match as Carlow reached an All-Ireland junior hurling final. If ye search your pockets, you'll all have the two shillings in your pockets that should have gone to the county board."

Andy had a phrase of his own... "By damn but... it's true lads."

As the van chugged along, he declared: "By damn but of all the bad things that has happened to me, that was one of the best outcomes," he said gleefully.

Thanks to a slow turnstile and a faulty pair of gates, he had cost the county board hundreds of pounds but more importantly from his own view, his son and himself had got in free and the debt with their neighbours had been written off.

I was there myself as a 12-year-old that day and remember the commotion after the throw in when the dam burst and a flood of free entries swelled the ground to capacity. Since that Sunday some 60 years ago, I've met hundreds of people who were part of that queue. On man told me years later: "Not alone did I see a great match but I had another two bob to put with the one I saved for spending. I had a great night's dancing and was able to buy two minerals. It was definitely one of the great days and nights."

*Tommy Murphy is a native of Lismaconly, Myshall in Co Carlow. A member of Naomh Eoin GAA club, he served as PRO for the Carlow Co Board for 33 years. A former employee of Keenans of Bagenalstown, he enjoyed traversing across Leinster erecting farm and industrial buildings and making friends with fellow gaels. He is married to Mary and they have two grown up sons, Gary and Brian.*

# I Was A Sixties 'Wag' – And Proud Of It

## Joan Cleere

Croke Park on All-Ireland Day brings back many memories and I thought it would be nice to wander down memory lane recalling the good times I had as a 'Sixties Wag.'

WAG for the uninitiated stands for 'wives and girlfriends' in the sporting world. There was a great bunch of girls on the scene in that era and we all enjoyed the attention and excitement associated with the games and the dinners and functions afterwards.

My first All-Ireland was in 1963. It was very special because my husband, then my boyfriend, Seamus Cleere, was captain of the Kilkenny team that year. In those times sponsorship didn't play such a prominent part as it does nowadays. Players weren't kitted out as well as those of today.

Tracksuits had yet to make an appearance; likewise the team jerseys favoured by today's fans were not in vogue. The battered suitcase which held Seamie's gear was a direct contrast to the colourful sports bags carried by today's players. Team members wore their own clothes to receptions and presentations. Sometimes shirts were sponsored by local businesses.

Players were transported to matches in hackney cars. Occasionally Seamie brought some of the players and if there was room I travelled with them. For important matches we travelled on the train or hired buses.

My first impression on meeting officials and their wives was positive and girlfriends of players were made to feel welcome. A number of people stand out in my memory, including the late Maureen Grace – wife of Paddy Grace, secretary of the Kilkenny County Board for many years – both now gone to their eternal reward. Jimmy Brophy and his wife from Piltown also come to mind and Olive Walsh (Ollie's wife).

Following the All-Ireland, the team and officials visited Players cigarette factory and the Guinness Brewery. At the Player's factory they were given presentation boxes of cigarettes (Seamie's box was later given to my father, Michael O'Neill, a hurler of some note himself, with a London team and Thomastown).

The celebrations following the 1963 win went on for some time as each village was visited by the team for the traditional filling of the MacCarthy Cup. Each club would organise a meal in the local hall for the hurlers, officials, wives and girlfriends. The evening invariably ended up in the pub where sing songs were part of the ritual.

The year was important for another reason as Seamie won the Caltex Hurler of the Year Award. The ceremony in the Gresham Hotel was a huge occasion, bringing together the elite of the sporting world.

One of the regular stopping places on the way home from Dublin after a match was Eddie Marum's pub in Naas. We had some great sessions there in the company of such characters as Chew Leahy, a great friend of Kilkenny GAA and Paddy Grace. Ollie Walsh would always sing his party piece, 'The Green, Green, Grass of Home,' which Tom Jones had made famous.

Friendships made during these years endured and when reunions take place from time to time we all enjoy reminiscing over old times. Sadly some of the hurling stalwarts of that era have passed on, including Ollie Walsh, Ted Carroll, Cha Whelan and Pa Dillon.

As girlfriends and wives of the hurlers, we attracted a certain amount of attention as we circulated at dances and functions. It was great to be part of it all.

Some of the hotels frequented during that time were Barry's and The Hollybrook in Clontarf. Both places hold good memories. The staff were always very attentive and the activity before and after the matches was always interesting as fans would be hanging around to get the views of the lads about their chances in the game and autographs were much in demand.

One particular night stands out in my memory. It was after an All-Ireland and we had driven to the reception at the Hollybrook. When we returned to our friend's car, he took a length of rope from the boot and started twirling it. Before long we had an impromptu skipping session with everyone vying for their turn as boys and girls danced in and out with great agility.

As All-Ireland hurlers, the lads were often invited to appear at fetes and presentations. The Kilkenny Beer Festival was in full swing at that time and some of the hurlers were asked to the Gala Dinner held in Kilkenny Castle to welcome the guests and dignitaries.

On one occasion, Seamie was asked to judge the "Miss Iverk" competition at the Piltown Show with Larry Gogan (RTE). The "paparazzi" were much in evidence at these events and photographs appeared regularly in the local papers.

The hurlers were generous with their time and their appearances in matches throughout the country helped to raise funds to build churches and community halls in many parishes. Tournaments in Dunhill, Co Waterford and Bansha, Co Tipperary attracted huge crowds. Prizes for the winners were suit lengths and gold watches in some cases.

In 1967, Kilkenny beat Tipperary in the All-Ireland final and Seamie and I were married. The opportunity arose for me to travel to New York with the Kilkenny team and friends. This was a brilliant experience and one which I treasure. We stayed in the Manhattan Hotel on 42nd Street and had a really great time. The Irish people in New York gave us a tremendous welcome and showed us all the sights. We were invited into their homes and they organised parties and barbeques for us.

Gaelic Park was the venue for some of the matches and I remember watching one of the games in the company of the late Bishop Peter Birch and Seamus Pattison, who was Mayor of Kilkenny at the time. They had travelled to New York with the team and friends.

When the team was invited to play a game in Chicago which hadn't been on the schedule, the hurlers got together and made it possible for me to travel. This was a very generous gesture on their part and one which Seamie and I appreciated very much.

Some of the Irish people in New York who I remember taking us around were Lily Ryan, Billy Dobbyn, Brid Walsh, Matty Maher, Dick Buggy and Roddy Butler.

One of the bars frequented by the lads was McSorley's Old Alehouse. This was a popular "watering hole", but it had one drawback where I was concerned, women weren't allowed in. I think this policy has changed now.

I was privileged to be a part of the GAA scene in the sixties and nearly 60 years later am still enjoying a little bit of celebrity status.

*Joan Cleere is a native of Thomastown, Co Kilkenny and has been living in Bennettsbridge for over 50 years. Married to Seamie, they have five children, Tony, Ray, Catriona, Brendan and Jonnie. Joan is a member of Bennettsbridge Art/Writers Group and is local correspondent for Kilkenny People for 37 years.*

# My Father The Ref Saved By Honest Kicker

### George Murphy

My father Willie Murphy was a well-known referee back the years in Derry. One day he was officiating at a match between two bitter neighbouring rivals in the championship, Ballerin and Glenullen. They were evenly matched. The game was played on a small pitch. The goalposts were much shorter than they are now. As a result, when the ball was kicked very high in the air, it was difficult to establish if the shot was a point or a wide ball.

In those days, umpires were not neutral and normally one umpire from each club stood at the goalposts. The game was level on 0-12 each with only a minute left to play. Dermot Mullen had an educated left foot and played left-half forward for Ballerin. When he took a shot, he always kicked the ball as high as he could in the air. Any passing aircraft was in danger of being brought down by his shooting.

As the seconds ticked down to the final whistle, Dermot gained possession on his side of the field. He took aim and let fly with a shot 30 yards out from the Glenullen goal. The ball sailed skywards in the direction of the goalposts. It looked like a point but you couldn't be sure. Naturally, the Ballerin umpire raised the white flag to indicate a score, while true to tradition, the Glenullen umpire waved the ball wide.

From where my father was standing on the pitch, he found it impossible to tell. His verdict would be crucial; it would decide whether he would actually walk off the pitch or leave it in a coffin.

Would Ballerin advance or would a replay have to be organised?

He saw only one way out of his dilemma. He ran across to the player who had taken the shot and said: "Dermot, you can either save my life here or sink me out of sight. Was that ball inside the post or was it wide?"

To his eternal credit, Dermot immediately responded: "Willie, that ball was a foot wide."

He could so easily have said what most players would say in his position... that it was a point. My father flagged a wide and sounded the final whistle. The game went to a replay. My father lived to see another 15 years, thanks be to God... and, yes of course, thanks to Dermot Mullen too.

# Deireadh Seachtaine Na Síob – Cluiche Ceannais Peile

Brian Mac Lochlainn

Sa bhliain 1970, d'fhreastail mé ar mo chéad Chluiche Ceannais Peile Uile-Éireann agus a bhuíochas sin do go leor daoine.

Bhí mo dheirfiúr Nóirín agus mé féin ag obair i mBaile Átha Cliath an t-am sin. Bhí Nóirín ina cónaí ar Shráid Dorset, cóngarach do Pháirc an Chrócaigh, i dtuaisceart chathair Bhaile Átha Cliath ag an am agus bhí mé féin i mo chónaí i Ráth Maonais i ndeisceart na cathrach. Bhí ár gcol ceathrair Micheál ina chónaí agus ag iascaireacht sna Dúnaibh ar leithinis Ros Goill i dtuaisceart Dhún na nGall. Bhí suim againn uilig sna cluichí Gaelacha agus is iomaí tráthnóna samhraidh a chuir muid tharainn thíos ar An Dumhaigh, taobh le Trá na Rosann, áit a bhfuil léana cothrom le cleachtadh a dhéanamh ar na scileanna peile nó iománaíochta.

Bhí an t-airgead gann san am sin, cosúil leis an lá inniu, cha raibh gluaisteán ag duine ar bith sa teach s'againne agus bhí sé de nós ag Nóirín agus agam féin a dhul ar an ordóg agus síob a fháil achan deireadh seachtaine ó Bhaile Átha Cliath go dtí Na Dúnaibh. D'imigh muid abhaile chomh minic sin de bharr bhás ár n-athar, Padaí Bhrianaí Mac Lochlainn, agus bhí muid ag iarraidh cuideachta a thabhairt dár máthair. Bhí daoine flaithiúla ag tabhairt síobanna dúinn i gcónaí, agus níor theip orainn riamh ár gceann scríbe a bhaint amach.

Deireadh seachtaine amháin luath i Meán Fómhair na bliana 1970, shocraigh mé féin agus mo chol ceathrair Micheál go ndéanfaimis iarracht a dhul chuig Cluiche Ceannais Uile-Éireann. Leag muid amach plean taistil leis seo a chur i gcrích. Cheapfaí go raibh muid as ár gciall. A' dhul ó Bhaile Átha Cliath go Tír Chonaill agus ar ais faoi dhó in aon deireadh seachtaine amháin. Caithfidh tú a shamhlú go raibh muid óg, ligthe, lúfar san am sin. Faoi mar a dúirt Pádraig Ó Conaire ina ghearrscéal M'Asal Beag Dubh, 'Ní raibh aird againn ar an saol ná ag an saol orainn.'

Tháinig tráthnóna Dé hAoine, 25ú Meán Fómhair agus chas mé féin agus Nóirín ar a chéile i Sráid Uí Chonaill. Ar aghaidh linn ar bhus Uimhir 40 agus amach linn go Fionnghlas, nach raibh ann ach baile beag tuaithe taobh ó thuaidh den chathair san am sin. Scilling amháin an luach a bhí ar an turas seo. Ní raibh i bhfad go bhfuair muid síob go Carraig Mhachaire Rois. I ndiaidh béile bhreá, rinne muid ár mbealach go himeall an bhaile. Bhí muid tamall beag ansin go dtí go bhfuair muid síob go Leifear. Bhí muid inár gcontae féin ansin. Síob eile ó Leifear go Leitir Ceanainn, chomh fada leis an áit a bhfuil Timpeallán an Polestar ann. Chas fear áitiúil orainn agus fuair muid síob ghasta le hAnton Mhicí Sophie go dtí baile fearainn Cheann a' Leargaí sna Dúnaibh. Bhí muid chóir a bheith sa bhaile agus de bharr an dorchadais lean Anton leis dár dtiomáint go dtí ár mbaile fearainn féin. Faoi mar a deirtear fá Ros Goill, bhí muid "landáilte".

Is gearr an tréimhse a chaith mé sa bhaile. Lá arna mhárach, d'imigh Micheál agus mé féin ar an ordóg. Shroich muid árasán Nóirín i mBaile Átha Cliath thart fá am tae. Bhí sé doiligh in amanna síob mhaith a fháil ó Bhaile na Deora mar nach raibh mórán carranna thart fán áit ach bhí eolas intuigthe againn go mbeadh daoine a' dhul ag siopadóireacht go Carraig Airt fá choinne fheoil an Domhnaigh agus a leithéidí sin. Mar sin, d'fhág muid thart fán deich ar maidin mar gur seo an t-am ba ghnách seo a dhéanamh. Bhí cúpla deoch againn sa Big Tree i nDroim Conrach Oíche Dé Sathairn agus chodail muid go suaimhneach go dtí maidin Dé Domhnaigh. Shiúil muid isteach go lár na cathrach agus bhí béile breá blasta againn i mbialann Síneach The Luna trasna ón GPO. Bhí sé de nós ag daoine béile a bheith acu in Óstán an Chaisleáin ach bhí an áit sin pacáilte nuair a chuaigh muid thairis. Rinne muid ár mbealach ansin go Páirc an Chrócaigh thart fán haon a chlog. Shocraigh muid a dhul isteach sa Canal End mar, ag an am sin, ní raibh gá ticéad a cheannacht roimh ré.

Bhí an áit dubh le daoine. Chuir sé i gcuimhne domh na Monster Meetings ar thagair múinteor liom, Micheál Mac Aoidh, dóibh agus é ag múineadh stair na hÉireann dúinn. Chan fhaca aon duine den bheirt againn Páirc an Chrócaigh riamh agus chan fhaca muid é ar an teilifís ach an oiread. Sin ráite sheas muid go cróga ag amharc ar ár gcluiche náisiúnta, ar lá a raibh an bua ag Ciarraí ar fhoireann na Mí 2-19 le 0-18.

I ndiaidh an chluiche, léim muid ar bhus 40 agus amach go Fionnghlas linn. Chuaigh muid ar an ordóg ar ais ó Bhaile Átha Cliath go Ros Goill. Caithfidh tú smaoineamh gur seo tráthnóna Dé Domhnaigh agus go raibh an chuid is mó den trácht ag teacht i dtreo Bhaile Átha Cliath, 'sé sin daoine a chuaigh amach faoin tír ag pilleadh ar an ardchathair le dhul ag obair arís maidin Dé Luain. Mar sin féin, fuair muid síob díreach go Muineachán. Bhí sé chóir a bheith dorcha faoin am seo ach bhí an t-ádh dearg orainn mar go bhfuair muid síob díreach ó Mhuineachán go Leitir

Ceanainn. Bhí a fhios againn go raibh damhsa na Ceathrú Caoile ar siúl agus shocraigh muid a dhul ansin mar bhí a fhios againn go mbeadh baicle as na Dúnaibh ann agus go dtabharfadh duine acu sin síob abhaile dúinn. Landáil muid ag an halla damhsa ag a haon déag a chlog, dhamsaigh muid ár sáith go dtí an dó a chlog ar maidin agus fuair muid síob abhaile le Hughie Fina. Bhí seisean cineálta san am sin agus d'fhág sé Micheál agus mé féin ag geafta an tí s'againne. Cha raibh iomrá ar bith ar fhón póca san am sin le hinseacht dóibh sa bhaile cá raibh muid.

Tháinig maidin Dé Luain go tobann, d'ith mé féin agus Nóirín ár mbricfeasta agus bhain muid cúpla iomaire préataí dár máthair. D'fhág an bheirt againn slán ag Baile na Deora agus d'imigh ar ais arís ar an ordóg go Baile Átha Cliath. Bhí Nóirín i gcónaí glic agus shocraigh sí an deireadh seachtaine sin cárta thart fá 8 X 10 n-orlach a phéinteáil dubh, ansin phéinteáil sí na focla i mbán Donegal ar thaobh amháin agus Dublin ar an taobh eile. Char inis sí riamh domh cá bhfuair an phéint! Anois bhí gléas againn le hinsint do na daoine cá raibh muid a' dhul. Thóg sí amach an cárta don chéad uair agus diabhail i bhfad go raibh an bheirt againn inár suí istigh i gcúl Renault 16 agus muid ar ár mbealach go dtí An Ómaigh.

Bhí na Trioblaidí a' dhul ar aghaidh sna Sé Chontae fán am seo. Shiúil muid go himeall na hÓmaí agus creid é nó ná creid fuair muid síob ar an lá sin ón Ómaigh go timpeallán Bhaile Uí Dhálaigh ar chúl jeep de chuid Arm na Breataine. Léim muid isteach sa jeep. Cha raibh mórán áite le suí agus mar sin shuigh muid ar na boscaí a raibh na piléir iontu. D'oscail mé féin ceann acu agus bhí sé lán go béal le piléir fá choinne raidhfilí Lee Enfield. Bhí lear mór trealaimh eile agus gunnaí ina luí thart ar urlár an jeep fosta. Cha raibh muid ábalta teagmháil súl a dhéanamh leis na saighdiúirí agus nuair a stad siad ag timpeallán Bhaile Uí Dhálaigh léim duine acu amach agus dúirt,

"Are you alright here mate, this is as far as we can bring you?"

Sheas muid ansin ar feadh tamaill agus fuair muid síob díreach go Muineachán. Suas linn go dtí an Ardeaglais, amach leis an chárta arís. Stad carr láithreach agus bhí an bheirt againn istigh i suíochán cúl Ford Cortina a raibh an gear leaver ar an column. Nuair a thosaigh muid ag caint, d'amharc bean an fhir a bhí ag tiomáint thart orainn agus iontas mór uirthi. Shíl sise go raibh muid balbh agus gurbh é sin an fáth a raibh an cárta linn leis an fhocal Dublin air. Go cinnte bhí siad a' dhul i rith an bhealaigh go Droim Conrach in aice leis an áit a raibh an t-arasán ag Nóirín. Nuair a landáil muid ansin rinne Nóirín tae agus ceapairí domh. Nach orm a bhí an bród as an éacht a bhí déanta agam. Nach iontach gur fear a bhí san arásán liom an t-am sin i 1970 a fuair ticéid domh blianta fada ina dhiaidh sin fá choinne an Chluiche Ceannais i 1992 nuair a bhí an bua ag Dún na nGall ar na Dubs. Rotha móra an tsaoil ag casadh de shíor agus rotha na ngluaisteán ag casadh gan staonadh an deireadh seachtaine sin.

*Rugadh Brian Mac Lochlainn i leithinis Ros Goill, áit a raibh an Ghaeilge go smior sa cheantar. Chaith sé seal sa Státseirbhís i mBaile Átha Cliath agus seal ag tiomáint leoraithe do thógálaithe ansin fosta. Tá sé ag cur faoi in Inbhear, i ndeisceart Thír Chonaill lena theaghlach, áit a mbíonn sé ag tiomáint busanna do Bhus Éireann ó Ghleann Cholm Cille go Baile Dhún na nGall.*

# Michael Hogan's Girlfriend On Bloody Sunday Was...?

Oliver McMahon

It was sometime in the early 1990s, over 70 years after the atrocities of Bloody Sunday in Croke Park, that I learned for the first time that my mother Margaret (Peg) McMahon, nee Walsh, was in the stadium when the British forces opened fire indiscriminately on the players and spectators alike.

My mother, who was 16 years old at the time, had gone to Croke Park to see her boyfriend Michael (Mick) Hogan play for Tipperary against Dublin.

Her family, the Walshs were farmers in Tipperary and the name of the farm was known as Gleann na Gcunna near Nine Mile House which is not far from Grangemockler. She came from a family of five and had three sisters and a brother.

The conversation arose as my then 85-year-old mother and I watched a programme on RTE's Nationwide about the rebuilding of what would become the new and modern Croke Park. The programme also dwelt on the historical artefacts contained in the GAA museum.

"You know Ollie I was there on Bloody Sunday," she said quietly out of the blue.

I am the youngest of 12 children and I'd not heard her mention this incident before. I told her this was part of history and it should be recorded, but she explained that it was something she seldom if ever spoke of without actually telling me why. I suspect though it was a painful part of her life and experience and it was something she preferred to forget.

Which is why decades later, instead of embellishing one of the most iconic historical moments in Irish history, she told me instead the story of her involvement in a handful of sentences.

"Mick (Hogan) was my boyfriend. I went up to school in Eccles Street in Dublin that September as a boarder. He sent word that he would be playing for Tipperary footballers in a game against Dublin so I arranged with a friend to go along to see him play in Croke Park.

"Not long after the game started, the British forces came in and began shooting. I crawled to safety out of the place on my hands and knees, hoping I would not be spotted."

Unfortunately, Mick was not so lucky on that day November 21, 1920.

He too had tried to escape by crouching low during the shooting but was hit by a bullet in the back and was one of 14 people killed that day. The young Tipperary corner back was the only player to die, though a Wexford youth Tom Ryan, who went on to the pitch to pray beside the wounded Hogan, also died later in hospital, having been fatally shot while beside Hogan.

My mother also told me that afterwards she made her way to O'Sheas in Clonskeagh where some of the Tipperary supporters met up after matches in the city.

It was there she learned that Mick was one of those shot dead.

I pressed my mother later that evening for more details but she was loath to continue and dismissed the incident as something that had happened long ago.

I felt it was wrong to intrude further as this memory was obviously deeply painful for her, even at this remove.

However, I confirmed the story she had just recounted to me a while later with some of my older siblings. One of the bits of information that came back from Tipp first hand was the fact that the Walsh family would often refer to Peg and Mick and the atrocity of Bloody Sunday for years after the shooting.

It was some three years later in 1923 when my mother met my father, George, while training to be a chemist in Dublin. The initial contact came through their love of ballroom dancing when both attended the same dancing function.

My father came from Crossmaglen in south Armagh. My mother and himself set up home on the Kilkenny Road outside Carlow town. They had 12 children all of whom went to boarding school, the boys to the Cistercian College in Roscrea and the girls to the FCJ in Bunclody. The only exception to this was the youngest – me.

I went to Willow Park and then on to Blackrock in Dublin as I was too young to board in Roscrea.

Consequently, I didn't play GAA at school, as Blackrock was and still is a predominantly rugby school, so I had very little involvement with the organisation.

The memory of Bloody Sunday must have been horrendous for a young schoolgirl and I can only now understand, having recently seen the documentary based on Michael Foley's book 'The Bloodied Field', why my mother was unwilling to recall that fateful day.

## MICHAEL HOGAN'S GIRLFRIEND ON BLOODY SUNDAY WAS...?

However, I often think of her part in this story – probably the saddest single day in the history of the GAA – and wonder just what feelings of love and loss, pain and heartache, that must have been part of her other life which we, her children, knew so little about.

*Oliver McMahon is a former head of catering and corporate entertainment at AIB. He is married with three grown up children and lives with his wife Susan in Mount Merrion, Dublin. His greatest sporting memory was being present at Croke Park when Ireland beat the England rugby team in 2007.*

# Still Playing... After All Those Years

## John Arnold

It's always a question in every community: Who is the oldest person to have played a match for your club?

New York remembers the dark years of the Second World War when, because of lack of movement, the ages of some of those were in the high fifties who lined out – with others in their sixties.

The year 1960 produced a man in his seventies playing for the Clare hurlers when they faced Waterford in a league tie. With the team shipping a lot of scores, the manager beckoned to 70-year-old Jim O'Donnell to go on as a sub. Jim was unable to stem the tide but he performed well and kept the leakage to the minimum for the rest of the game. From the Kilbane club in Clare, he arrived in the Big Apple in 1914 and continued to play at the top level for four decades.

# Sons Starred For Kildare But Mother Only Had Eyes For Páidí

John Kelly

Back in the late seventies, my parents Seán and Esther built a new bungalow on our farm just outside Castledermot in Co Kildare.

It was a fine-sized house and the kitchen in particular was built to accommodate the nine children and two adults in the house.

Like every other house in the country, the picture of the Sacred Heart looked down on us from one wall while my mother had a huge picture of Páidí Ó Sé, resplendent in his Kerry colours, looking down on us from the opposite side.

In a GAA-mad house, the pictures were a good combination – God and Páidí.

No doubt due to my mother's influence we all had a soft spot for the Kingdom legend and sometimes it was hard to know which of the pair on the wall was revered the more by the Kelly clan.

Kerry were the football kingpins of the time, having more or less dominated the football world at national level from the mid-seventies with Dublin.

While we hadn't that much to shout about at inter-county level in Kildare, locally we were always either playing games for the club or school and were well versed in the standards of Wicklow, Laois and Carlow as well.

The thoughts of some day making a Lilywhites team that played in Leinster against our neighbouring counties drove us on as we went up through school competitions and through the juvenile and minor ranks with our clubs.

And then finally the week arrived in 1980 when my brother Paul was picked to play midfield with myself, John 'Boots' Kelly, named at full-forward for the Kildare senior team in the National Football League.

Adding to the value in our household was the fact that we were both picked to play at home in Newbridge against none other than Páidí and Kerry.

Such was the excitement and anticipation in our house during that week that it was more like the countdown to An Ireland Final. The fact that the two of us were starting against the Sam Maguire holders was a huge honour. Of course it also brought added pressure on Paul and myself to make sure we performed well now that we had been given our chance on the big stage.

St Conleth's Park was heaving on the Sunday as the ball was thrown in. Kildare might have fallen short on the pitch over the years since last winning the All Ireland under the captaincy of Larry Stanley in 1928 but our fans have always proven themselves to be the best in the country. Despite once again turning out in large numbers that Sunday, few gave the young and up-and-coming home team a chance against the might of the green and gold.

However, we played out of our skins on the day and ended up beating the legends by a point.

The throaty roar of the crowd that greeted the final whistle had to be experienced to be believed. All our players were on a high and the Kerry lads as always were gracious in shaking our hands and saying "well done."

I was delighted to have the honour of marking John O'Keeffe that day and when I scored a goal early on in the game, it was more than I could have dreamed of. My brother Paul also had one of those days in midfield where he seemed to catch everything and was the most influential player in that sector.

As we savoured the atmosphere in the immediate aftermath of the game, we knew our parents would be immensely proud of the pair of us. Daddy seldom came to watch the big matches, preferring to keep the farm work ticking over while listening to the game on the radio. We knew he'd be heading out after the match to look at the cattle with a lighter heart than usual.

Mother was different; she had to be with us at every game as we grew up and was never far from the action. We knew too that she'd be delighted that we'd beaten Kerry on this Sunday.

Once the game was over, a large section of the crowd spilled onto the pitch to salute their heroes.

I made my way to Paul on the pitch to give him a hug and celebrate what I knew would be one of the great sporting memories in our lifetime.

As we embraced, we could see Mammy coming in from the terrace boundary and heading in our direction. In her delight she was running like a young one, her face totally concentrated.

Just as Paul and myself were about to put out our arms to greet her, we noticed her attention was not focused on us, her sons at all, but on someone else behind where we stood.

## SONS STARRED FOR KILDARE BUT MOTHER ONLY HAD EYES FOR PÁIDÍ

She continued running for another 20 yards or so before grabbing a firm hold of Páidí and giving him a big hug.

What could we do but laugh as we saw the pair of them chatting together as if they were old friends. While she was talking to him, she saw us a little away and we could hear her telling her hero: "Those two lads over there are my sons. They played against you today, but you're the best of the lot."

We could hear her tell the Kerry defender too that "you were always a big hero of mine" as she departed and Páidí, despite the defeat, was just lovely to Mam the way he gave her his time without trying to run away and then gave her the biggest of hugs as they parted.

When she came over to us we teased her that she'd forgotten her own. "Oh yea, we're only your sons...sure it's more important to talk to the Kerry big shots."

She was beside herself with joy on the way home and all that evening telling Dad how lovely a fella Páidí was.

Paul and myself kept the mock-hurt up but Mum knew us too well. And why wouldn't she? From the time we could kick a ball out of our way, we knew she was there for us through club and Kildare minors, U-21 and senior.

Mum never had to make excuses to any of us. We were her family and she gave us everything, but Páidí was her knight in shining Kerry armour – and when she got a chance to tell him, well, there was no stopping her.

Now 84 years young and still going strong, this mother of nine loves the GAA more than ever, though it nearly broke her heart when Kildare lost the 1998 All Ireland final against Galway.

*John Kelly is a proud Kildare man now farming and working in sales in the concrete and quarry business near Horse And Jockey, Thurles, Co Tipperary. A father of three grown up daughters, John also played club football in Dublin with Cuala and rugby and football in Tipperary.*

# The Referee Sorted The Problem

### Seán Nugent

A championship match took place back in the sixties between two neighbouring clubs. Now as we know there can be a lot of tension and rivalry between neighbouring clubs.

Everyone wants to beat their neighbour. In some cases years ago anyway, it was nearly more important to beat your neighbour than to win the championship. This game however was mild in terms of such games at that time.

The referee did not have much difficulty controlling the game except for one offender who continually questioned his decisions.

The referee warned him but to no avail so the official decided that the next time it happened he would deal with it… and he did. The offender rushed up again to the referee uttering abusive language. The knight of the whistle delivered a left hook that sent the offender spinning to the ground. That was the end of the matter.

When submitting his report to the local board, the referee wrote: "It was a fine sporting game and a pleasure to referee except for one problem which I promptly sorted out myself."

# Scaling New Heights In Gaelic Park

## Liam Fardy

As a young goalkeeper growing up in Wexford where I played underage for my club Gusserane and also for St Peter's College, sometimes during games I would look up and wonder how high I could jump to save shots going over the crossbar.

By the time I had hit my mid-teens I had grown to over six feet tall and with a long arm stretch I found I could at times maybe prevent certain points by timing my jump and reaching to a foot or so above the bar.

While I spent much of my time as a Gaelic footballer playing inside the box, the lonely life of a goalie got me used to thinking outside of the box.

"What if I could do this?" or "what would happen if I dared to push the boundaries?"

It was while playing a game for Sligo in the New York championship in the early eighties against a Frank McGuigan-inspired Tyrone that I decided it was time to put my theories to the test.

Only by now I was a big 6' 2" and 14-and-a-half stone fullback instead of a custodian. That change of position was due to another spur of the moment situation in my life; my first week at Thomond College in Limerick as part of the PE degree course in the early seventies.

I arrived for the first training session and it was a virtual 'Who's Who' of top class GAA talent in the country. I recognised Brian Mullins and Fran Ryder as Dubs, Johnny Tobin and Brian Talty (both Galway) while Hugo Clerkin (Monaghan) and Joe Mulligan (Offaly) were also in the circle. When the guy next to me was asked to say who he was and what team he played for he said: "Teddy Owens, Cork and Arsenal youth's goalkeeper."

Wow!

A nobody from Wexford was certain to become a backup to that sort of GAA and soccer pedigree for the duration of his studies – instantly I decided to change position.

When it came to my turn to introduce myself, I was ready: "Liam Fardy, Wexford fullback."

Little publicity was given to our county's senior footballers in that era that I got away with it. Except it turned out to be the truth as I subsequently played for over a decade at the edge of the square for the Wexford seniors before transferring to Waterford and playing full-back for the Deise for another three seasons.

Which brings me back to Frank McGuigan and New York. The Sligo team had played its heart out on this particular day to go head-to-head with the highly fancied Red Hand outfit.

Then with time almost up, the referee blew his whistle and pointed for a free against us – about 35 yards out and dead straight in front of our goal. The way Frank had been kicking, and remember it was off the ground at that time, I knew he could slot this free over in his sleep.

I had to give him something to think about so I turned to our goalkeeper and said: "Give me a leg up. I want to climb onto the crossbar."

The goalie asked me if I was mad and I answered: "I'll show you in a minute."

As Frank was lining up to take the free, I levered myself up with reluctant support from our keeper and by holding the upright with one hand, I was able to stand straight up and balance myself.

My plan was to see where Frank's kick was going and if possible to manoeuvre myself along the crossbar to divert it.

Everyone began shouting at me to get down, especially my own teammates. The Tyrone players were also annoyed and told me I was out of order. Then the ref, who had taken up a position half way between the free kick placement and the goal-line, blew his whistle to admonish me, signalling that I should come back to earth.

"You are not allowed do that," he said, obviously baffled like everyone else because he had never encountered a man standing on top of the goals in a GAA match before.

I wasn't for turning though.

"Where does it say in the GAA rulebook that I can't get up here?" I asked, with an air of conviction that put him on the back foot.

"You just can't," he added.

"Yes I can and I'm staying until the free is taken," I informed everyone.

My antics led to a long delay as both my own players and the opposition, plus the umpires and a good section of the crowd once again started roaring at me to get down.

I didn't budge.

In the end, the ref told Frank to go ahead as the free was the last kick of the match. I think he hoped to get out of the mess I had caused by blowing the final whistle and getting off the pitch as quickly as he could.

Frank must have been put off by the delay. Would you believe it, he pulled his effort well wide of the posts. I didn't even have to leave the sentry position I had taken up to stop it.

Delighted that we had secured a draw, I shouted: "Right, I'll get down now."

Looking back on the incident now, it was a hair-brained thing to do and it was also potentially very dangerous. But such is the impetuosity of youth.

I suppose there was an element of karma involved too because while we celebrated getting another bite at the cherry, we were beaten in the replay by two or three points.

I saw a few years ago that Kerry were wondering if they could, rugby style, get two players either side of another player to lift him well over the crossbar if they wanted to prevent conceding a late point, but it never came to pass.

I still think you can get away with it, except maybe the ref might give you a card for 'ungentlemanly conduct' and could send you off if you persisted in defying his orders to come down.

Following the crossbar incident against Tyrone, the local Irish New York newspaper, The Irish Echo, put a heading up which stated: 'Sligo Player Scales New Heights In Gaelic Park.'

I got to know Frank by marking him in both those matches and afterwards in the bar. I regret that I never got around to taking him up on his invitation to visit his pub in Tyrone.

I actually loved New York and would probably have stayed there except my then girlfriend and now wife, Carmel, insisted that we go back to Ireland to live.

I was a teacher when I went to work for the summer and through a former college friend from St Peter's College, Phil Kennedy, I got in with Sligo. The head of the carpenters' union in the city was a Sligo man named Jim Nicholson. When Phil proposed me as a top-line recruit for the summer, it cut little ice with Jim because Wexford footballers weren't exactly premium currency.

On the Saturday night before the Sligo juniors were playing in a final on my first weekend there, Phil marked my card: "Fardy, you'll have to play out of your skin tomorrow to get a carpenter's job with this man."

They picked me in midfield and that suited my game on the day. I had the height to go up and catch a ball and while running wouldn't have been my forte, I found my eye was in with long range kicking and I scored 10 points, including a free from 70 yards. Talk about fluking an exam.

The next morning when I went down to sign on for work, I decided that discretion might be the better part of valour and told the lad checking me in: "I'm a third year apprentice carpenter I think."

The guy looked at me and said: "Lee (they never called me Liam for some reason out there). Aren't you the big guy who scored 10 points yesterday, right?"

I nodded.

"Mr Nicholson has you down here as a qualified carpenter earning the top rate of pay," he stressed.

For once I had nothing to say but just between us I can confirm I earned a stack of money that summer.

*Former school principal and Wexford and Waterford footballer Liam Fardy hails from Gusserane. He is married to Carmel and they have three grown up children Eoghan, Emer and Brian. He is also a former handball champion.*

# The Clash Of The Ash

## Joe Kearney

It is with justification that envy is named as one of the seven deadly sins. I know this for a fact. When I broke the shaft of my juvenile camán stick it coincided with my best friend Mickey Finn sporting a brand new hurl.

This acquisition followed his appearance on Paddy Crosbie's 'School Around the Corner' on RTE television. How I coveted the bone-white perfection of his prize. I wondered at its flexible bend and its grain as true as a schoolboy's conscience escaping through the confession-box door.

It fitted against Mickey's hip and when he connected with a sailing sliotar it resonated with a muted "thuck" that told you the small ball would find a home either above or below the crossbar.

Over the following weeks I moaned, nagged and complained to anyone who would listen about my hurling hardship. Eventually, it was our neighbor Joe, who either through genuine sympathy or just plain boredom with listening, promised that he would make me my very own tailor-made hurley stick.

Now, like a Saville Row suit, my camán required that I present myself for periodic fittings. On my first such visit, disappointment reigned when I saw the crude lump of ash tree that leaned against Joe's workbench. It was as far from the perfection of Mickey's white stick as a block of crudely quarried stone is from Michelangelo's David.

Joe explained that the ash had come from a tree on a ditch in the town land of Ballinashig. He coaxingly expanded the background by pointing out how the bas would be fashioned from the tree trunk where it bent towards the root. I remained unconvinced, particularly when I tried to lift the unwieldy block of unplaned and uncut timber.

I knew that the game of hurling is a sport of gods played by mortals but even the superhero Setanta would have had trouble wielding this monstrous weapon.

Joe assured me that all would be well but I knew him to be a hopeless optimist. He was a man, I heard it said, who would compliment the devil on the quality of his fire should he ever find himself in hell and knowing the ditch that this particular stump had been dug from seemed singularly unimportant to me.

Fraxinus Excelsior, or the common ash grows particularly well in the deep fertile limestone soil of Kilkenny. Because of its high flexibility and resilience to splitting, ash is the traditional wood used for sporting equipment, tool handles, and even weapons such as bows and arrows.

Indeed, the word ash has its etymology in the Old English or Norse word "aesc" meaning, spear. In 1366, the Statutes of Kilkenny were drafted in an attempt to restore, what was deemed to be, proper English conduct amongst the iniquitous native Irish and their Norman colonisers.

Some of the laws passed proscribed certain social activities. One such activity was hurling. The following is an extract from the Statutes: "Do not, henceforth, use the plays which men call horlings, with great sticks and a ball upon the ground, from which great evils and maims have arisen...."

The legislators would have believed their ban to be justified if they could only have seen Joe's unfinished weapon. However, true to his word, within a week a supreme metamorphosis occurred; I got the call to collect my bespoke camán... and I could have wept for joy when I saw it.

I had, at last, a stick that could compete with Mickey's, one that fitted my hand like an extension of my own limb and for weeks it rested beside my bed, within arms reach, like a comfort blanket. In the half-acre field at the back of our house, we replayed great finals of the past and invented titan games of the future. In all of these matches we were the forwards who saved the day with a fury of mighty last-minute goals driven into the opponent's quivering net.

In those far removed times, after milking time in the soft swallow dip of late summer, it was not unusual to hear on the darkening air the cries from neighbouring fields as young lads devised impromptu hurling matches.

In my memory their shouts rise up like flocks of blackened crows across fields of amber stubble. And there amongst the triumphal cheers is that one singular inimitable sound, the one that is as compelling as church bells... the mighty clash of the ash, the resonance that echoes down the centuries.

And now that I had my very own specially designed camán which surpassed even the spanking new Mickey Finn model imported from afar, I was sure that I too would in time turn out and pay proper homage to the ancient wondrous game designed for the gods but played by mortals.

*Dr Joe Kearney is a native of Callan, Co Kilkenny. A retired oil industry executive, Joe is an award-winning documentary maker for RTE and has written a number of published collections. He is married and lives in Co Wicklow.*

# The Magnificent Seven Who Went To Jail For Playing GAA

## Michael Commins

They were the GAA's version of the 'Magnificent Seven.' As famous in the folklore of Garrymore GAA culture in Co Mayo as the western film that was later to imprint itself on the mind of the Wild West frontier culture.

Today, they are all gone to meet their maker but some years ago I was fortunate enough to interview the last remaining member of that famous band who, in 1940, laid the foundation for what many believe is still inherent in the Garrymore psyche.

Garrymore native Paddy Prendergast was that last member of a group of seven young lads aged between 15 and 17 who spent a week in Sligo jail back in 1940 after contesting their right to kick a football on a playing field.

Legendary Garrymore footballer, Billy Fitzpatrick, who also interviewed Paddy and his brother Martin for a special programme on Claremorris Community Radio, believes that the 1940 episode is at the very heart of the Garrymore 'spirit'.

Billy says: "Those seven young lads laid down a marker for the generations that were to follow. The pride, spirit, passion, loyalty, the never-say-die attitude of Garrymore, may well have come from the actions of those seven men. It became part of our upbringing."

That's a powerful statement from one of Garrymore's most famous sons. The fact that it is so close to the truth makes it very special. Paddy Prendergast told me what had happened in those far-off days of 1940.

"The trouble started when there was a change of ownership of land in our area in 1939. We used to kick football in a corner of a large field. After being warned that we were trespassing, we eventually found ourselves before the court. The seven consisted of Tony O'Toole, Gabriel Heaney, Joe Prendergast, Sonny Commins and my brothers Seán and Tom Prendergast and myself. We got the summonses by post. The court was held in Claremorris. We had no one to represent us. We were fined nine shillings in total or seven days in prison.

"From the first day we decided we wouldn't pay any fine. Gabe Heaney,

Tony O'Toole – whose son Anton won All-Ireland medals with Dublin in the 1970s – and Joe Prendergast were the first to be brought away to Sligo jail. They were escorted there on Christmas Eve. They then came for the three of us and Sonny Commins on December 29. It was terrible for our parents seeing the Ballindine guards coming in the dark winter's morning. We walked to Ballindine. Fair play to Mrs Burbridge, wife of the guard, she fed us all day with tea and ham sandwiches. At one stage she said to her husband: 'For God's sake, what are they but children'. I never forgot her for that.

"We left Ballindine at night for Sligo in Mick Waldron's car, accompanied by two guards. We were told to strip off and marched down to the bathroom tub. We were awakened early the next morning to be fitted out for the prison clothes.

"The food was woeful, the meat was tough. We were put chopping timber outside during the day. They knew us as the footballers during our few days in Sligo. Allowing for the day going and the day coming back, we spent five full days in Sligo jail.

"We came back on the train and the four of us had to walk home from Claremorris. There was a big bonfire up the road and great celebrations. They came from all around to welcome us home and we had a mighty night. We were treated like heroes. But we were also marked men for a while after that by the authorities. We found that strange as we never did anything wrong in our lives."

Paddy's brother Tom, who lived in Sylane for many years and who died about a decade ago, never held any grudge against the gardaí who brought them to Sligo. Indeed, the opposite was the case.

In a lovely article published in 'The Garrymore Story' in 1984, he wrote: "I pray that the Lord rewards Sgt. Burbridge and Garda McKenna for their kindness to us all day, both in our homes and in the barracks and the journey to the jail. I still recall the way they went to each of us in turn, shook our hands and wished us well as they left the jail. I would like to remember the kindness of Mrs Burbridge in Ballindine for catering for us at her own expense, for giving us the run of her kitchen and for serving two meals."

Martin Prendergast (brother of Paddy) from Garrymore, who resided in Galway for years, recalled the early times when the club that was later to become Garrymore had its origins out in Ballyglass. "My first memories go back to around 1936. There was Jack Gill, a big strong defender, and others like Murty Farragher, Fred Culkeen, Paddy Murphy, Paddy Joe Heaney, Alo Heaney and Mick Heaney. Alo later played for Galway and marked Jack

Lynch (who went on to become Taoiseach) of Cork in Croke Park. Gerald Heaney broke a leg around that time. He was a fine player too."

"Malachy Forde's (Hollybrook) was a great football field in later times. Petie Toole used to bring the goalposts down in an ass and cart and lime the pitch. He was a great referee too, very fair and respected by all. Paddy Murphy and Paddy Joe Heaney were very good players. The Co Board didn't think much of footballers from south Mayo at the time; Henry Dixon was one of the first to make that breakthrough in the 1950s when he won All-Ireland medals with Mayo."

Emigration was rampant. Eight of the Fitzpatrick family from the Ballyglass area went to America. Jimmy and John Joe Feerick from Carras went too, as did Sean and Pete Tierney and Jimmy Joyce from Carras. Four of the McHughs left Garrymore – Mike, Jimmy, Bertie and Peggy – and four of the Prendergasts – Colm, Raymond, Jimmy and Dan.

Paddy and Martin Prendergast fondly remembered the people who were at the heart of the Garrymore club. "Tom Murphy was excellent. His life revolved around the club. 'Come on Garry, mark up' was his call as he was up and down the sideline. He did so much for the club. He cycled to Shrule one evening to get a set of jerseys for the lads. He kept the whole thing going. Petie Toole from The Heath was a great footballer. He knew how to put the ball over the bar. 'Pass it to Petie' was the call back then.

"It was the Carras team that really started a lot of the good things that were to follow for Garrymore.

They were very good lads and built up a good junior team. They went on to win the intermediate county final and then Garrymore hit the golden years when winning six county senior titles in the 1970s and '80s while reaching an All-Ireland club final on the way.

"The Heaneys of Ballyglass, Paul and Paddy, were good corner backs. Paul was captain of the Carras minor team that beat Belmullet in 1956. Pete Fallon from Ballindine and Vince Nally were fine players of that era."

The role of Jim Mannion in the development of Garrymore was fondly remembered by the Prendergast brothers. "Jim [from Roscommon] was the best thing that every came to Garrymore. He was able to speak up and prove his point at a county board meeting. Larry McGovern from Newport said Jim Mannion was a brilliant man to put his point across.

"Mick Heaney was the master of the dressing room. While Jim would go down on his knees and say the prayer, Mick would then get up and give some real instructions. The tradition of saying the three Hail Marys so that no one would get hurt was started by Jim Mannion and became a great tradition in the Garrymore club."

And no one can overlook the role of Bertie McHugh either. "Bertie was the driving force behind much of the development at Garrymore. The club is indebted to Bertie and others of his era for their huge contribution to Garrymore over many years."

Paddy Prendergast was the keeper of the flame of the Magnificent Seven and the great Garrymore tradition. It remained a club close to his heart with what happened in 1940 defining its core value.

*Michael Commins is a native of Claremorris, Co Mayo. He is a leading broadcaster and journalist both locally and nationally with Midwest Radio, Sky 365 Spotlight Country channel and The Mayo News. He is married with two daughters and two sons. His passions include hurling and Gaelic football and country music as well as a fondness for regional and international radio and current affairs.*

# When Football's Loss Was Tug-Of-War's Gain

## Tom Lynch

During the hungry 1930s, interest in football in Kerry was at an all time high, mainly due to the fact that the county team won six All-Ireland finals between 1924 and 1932.

Enthusiasm for the game was particularly keen in the Dingle area, where John Street (Sráid Eoin), The Quay and Grey's Lane fielded strong teams of fine luathfear men, as did Lispole, a few miles east of the town.

Sandwiched between the town and Lispole was a group of rural townlands or villages as they are known in West Kerry. This district comprising of Garfiney, Ballinvounig, Ballybowler, Flemingstown, Ballintaggart, Beenbawn and Dún Síon provided some players, mainly to the John Street team.

The area was described as "a majestic spot, where the birds whistle and the bees make music" by John Street publican Michael O'Sullivan. This narrative was often repeated by locals.

Jobs and money were scarce in that era. Farms were modest and opportunities for work limited. Open hare coursing, football and card playing were the primary recreations. The weekly toil was eased by visits to local rambling houses, the consumption of a few pints of stout on a Sunday night and smoking the odd Woodbine, if funds allowed.

Tough times!

As the middle of the decade approached, the young men in this farming community discussed the prospects of forming a football team. They envisaged one that would equal the town teams and surpass Lispole. They would be hailed as heroes. Glory beckoned.

*Níor chaill fear a mhisnigh riamh é.*

This was their moment of opportunity, when they could take on neighbouring teams, beat them and perhaps enter and win the West Kerry League. The sky was the limit. There would be no holding back. They had the men to do it.

A few training sessions were held in a sloping field near Garfiney Cross. Some players were skillful, others showed promise and more had notions.

The spine of a team was provisionally selected. Soundings were made with the Lispole team who were more than willing to take on the challenge. The men from the East (Lispole) versus the men from Nomansland.

The next task was to find a field for the clash of titans. Various venues were proposed. Some farmers refused as they did not wish their good grass to be trampled on by young men full of teaspach and foolish enough to chase after a bag of air. Other fields were deemed too rough or having too much of an incline. Eventually a suitable venue on Higgins' farm at Ballinetig was sourced. The field was generously provided by its owner and was aptly positioned between the Townlands and Lispole.

On the appointed Sunday in early July, goalposts were hastily erected. The straightest lengths of timber to be found in the locality were used. Some of these were almost certainly washed ashore at nearby Trabeg or were left over from a recent house build. By today's standards they might be deemed a bit crooked but beggars could not be choosers. Without doubt, the field had cowpats, hidden in tufts of grass, along with thistles and ragwort. Nobody cared.

*Bhí an lá tagtha agus bhí gach éinne ullamh.*

With the Garfiney River flowing gently to the east, the Dingle to Tralee narrow guage railway line to the north, the birthplace of patriot Tomás Ághas looking down on páirc na himeartha from the south and Dingle Race Course to the west, the scene was set. As yellowhammers sang their little-bit-of-bread-and-no-cheese song from the top of furze bushes, the teams and their supporters arrived at Ballinetig.

*Bhí an ghrian ag scoilteadh na gcloch and excitement... and expectation filled the air.*

Maurice Neligan, a star player on the Townlands team, was unable to line out due to an ankle injury. He reluctantly agreed to referee the game. Apart from blowing for half-time and full-time, his whistle was as silent as Brian Cody's at a Kilkenny training session.

The Townlands team entered the field wearing various coloured shirts and long-legged trousers. A few had football boots. More wore hobnail boots and others a pair of soft shoes. Lispole took to the field looking dapper by comparison, wearing a set of jerseys, proper togs and football boots to the cheers of "Go on Lispole."

*"Mo ghraidhin go deo sibh".*

To the neutral observer, the signs were ominous even before the ball was thrown in. However, little separated the teams for most of the first half. Jimmy Kennedy drew the Townlands level with his second point with a few minutes remaining in the half. Game on.

## WHEN FOOTBALL'S LOSS WAS TUG-OF-WAR'S GAIN

It was then that man of the match, Dan Griffin, struck for Lispole. Dan pounced on a hopping ball, easily rounded his marker and sent a daisy cutter past the Townlands goalie.

Though small in stature, he was skilful, determined and packed with energy. To the cheers of "I wouldn't doubt you, Dan," he scored three excellent points to extend his sides advantage during the second half.

Two further goals from Lispole during this period ended the game as a contest. The opposition managed to raise two white handkerchiefs which put some cruth on the score. It was of little consolation that one of those points was the score of the day.

Jimmy Kennedy advanced towards the Lispole goal. He rounded his marker but was pulled by the tail of his shirt as he was about to kick the ball. As he fell backwards his right leg made graceful contact with the pigskin and it skimmed over the Lispole crossbar. Even the Lispole supporters acknowledged it. As the game drew to a close, a kick out from Paddy Johnson, the Townlands goalkeeper, drifted towards the nearby ditch. A Lispole supporter shouted "Tis out."

Townlands midfielder Patrick Lynch met the heavy brown leather football with a mighty belt of his fist and sent it half way across the next field. "Tis out now," he shouted. Time wasting was in vogue in 1935 also.

Shortly afterwards, the long whistle sounded leaving the final score, Lispole 3-5, The Townlands 0-4. Handshakes were exchanged. Loud cheers could be heard from the Lispole supporters as they headed east to milk the cows. Some of them were probably reciting a verse from The Champions of the West 1929.

*For Lispole had won honours*
*In no uncertain way*
*And no wonder we'd be proud of them*
*For the game they played that day.*

As the lads from the Townlands team ambled home, the post-mortem and recriminations began. The dream of entering a team in the West Kerry League was in tatters.

*B'shin sin. Bheadh lá eile ag an bPaorach. B'fhéidir?*
To live is to dream.

All agreed that goalkeeper Johnson could not be faulted for the three shots that swept past him. Indeed were it not for his four brilliant saves, the margin of defeat would have been embarrassing.

Full back, Tomáisín Kennedy remarked to his neighbour Jimmy Kennedy: "You weren't great over there today, with all your experience playing for John Street."

Jimmy replied: "And what about yourself, letting a slip of a garsún in under your legs to score two goals?"

Tomáisín who was a tall, lanky, strong man responded: "Ah sure, what could I do with him unless I jumped on him and killed him."

Thankfully he didn't, because he would have denied Kerry one of its great centre half backs. The 'slip of a garsún' was none other than the famous Bill Casey who went on to win four All-Ireland medals with Kerry and six county championships with Dingle.

The finger was also pointed at Mago Sheehy, Ballintaggart who at the time was home on holidays with college football experience. A disgruntled supporter muttered: "You didn't do much either."

Mago pointed to his new shiny shoes saying: "How could I play well with them?" He neglected to bring his boots from his Alma Mater.

After milking the cows, a dejected number of players and followers strolled to Michael O'Sullivan's pub in John Street. Of course some of the Townies settled by the counter had heard news of the match. Comments like "stick to thinning turnips, lads" quickly raised tempers. One word led to another and a nasty row was on the cusp of commencing when the publican intervened. "Easy now, lads. Simmer down. Sure it was a first day out for the boys."

*Bíonn gach tosnú lag.*

At closing time the mood was lighter as more relaxed kindred left the pub. As the Townlands residents walked the mile and a half or so to their homes, the match was debated again. A rematch was mentioned. After the few pints, some thought it might be a good idea. Wiser heads thought differently.

As the days passed, the truth of Ernest Hemingway's one-liner – "enthusiasm isn't enough" – slowly sank in among the players and supporters of the gallant Townlands team. No further challenges were issued. The hay was saved with little difficulty and everyone headed to the nearby Racecourse in early August.

Some paid at the gate. Others entered on a nod and a wink and more just jumped over the ditch from one of the surrounding fields. The atmosphere was mighty. A few chanced their luck, trying to hit Sammy-in-the-Barrel with wooden blocks, purchased for a penny.

Children put a few pence on the roulette known as a penny on the black and the red. The hawkers shouted: "Too late, too late will be the cry as flying quick silver will pass you by" to encourage race goers to part with their hard-earned money. Those interested in the horses bet a few bob on ponies in the Barony and the Derby. Most of the men sought out the tents where they drank "cold black dirty porter" as some described it or "a pint of the best" as O'Sullivan the publican defined it in his tent. Conversation flowed as pints were lowered.

A local character from the Townlands nicknamed Geknobs overheard a group of young lads talking excitedly about an upcoming Sport's Day to be held in Lispole in early September. He cocked his ear when they said it would end with a tug-o-war and the prize for the winners would be a pound, no small sum of money back then.

Geknobs quickly made his way to O'Sullivan's porter tent where most of his neighbours had gathered. He told them his news! "Do ye want to get revenge? If ye do, get a rope and start practicing." Men looked at one another and smiled. The rematch was on but without the ball.

A few days after the races a stout rope was purchased in Atkins Hardware Shop and the task of picking and training eight strong men plus two subs began in Cahalane's field near the Cross. Geknobs appointed himself, manager, coach and selector. He assumed this role due to his experience in the British Army prior to World War 1. Wasn't he lucky to leave the Army in time? Some said he went AWOL as his return home almost coincided with the commencement of hostilities.

Eventually ten fine fámaires of men were chosen to represent the Townlands. Some of the light, handy footballers were not considered. Horses for courses.

Height and strength were the deciding factors on who was selected and who didn't cut the mustard. The cynics said that with Geknobs in charge, the team was doomed to failure. Many thought he was nothing but an amadán at the best of times.

It was decided that the team would be called 'Garfiney' after the old civil parish which was merged with Dingle parish since the mid-nineteenth century. All the Townlands were within this old parish, so the name found approval.

Geknob's team had a secret weapon in their anchor man, Kenny Kelleher. He was the sage in the community who could turn his hand to anything and solve most problems. Indeed he had electric power in his house long before the ESB came west of Tralee. He was over six foot tall with two hands like shovels, a giant of a man... fathach fir. He inspired confidence in the team. He had the temperament, stamina, brawn, toughness and backbone for this game.

Sports Day Sunday dawned bright and clear. In the early afternoon, the Garfiney team and their supporters, women and men, headed east along the sun-drenched Mail Road to Lispole. Arriving at the fuchsia hedgerow field near Garrynadur, they sat and watched the various events. Sprint races followed the mile race, three-legged race, long jump, high jump, tossing the sheaves, a bicycle race and the spud-and-spoon race. It was a mighty Sports Day with tremendous, hardy athletes.

Eventually the final event of the day was called... the Tug-o-War. Four teams competed for the pound, Ballinclare from Annascaul, Cuas from west of Dingle, Lispole and Garfiney.

The draw was made, Ballinclare versus Lispole and Cuas v Garfiney. Nothing would be won easily here.

Lispole overcame Ballinclare with little difficulty. Only two pulls were needed to decide the best of three. Garfiney won the first pull against Cuas but lost the second. It was do or die on the third pull. After a tough struggle which lasted over 10 minutes, Garfiney prevailed.

Then for the final.

Doubts began to creep in. Had the tough pull against Cuas taken too much out of the team? Did Lispole get it too easy and anyway, they would be fresher as they had the benefit of a long rest?

The Townsland boys eyed up the Lispolians with trepidation.

The two teams were called to "take the rope."

Geknobs did his best to inspire his team.

"'Tis now or never lads."

*Anois nó riamh.*

"Never say your mother reared a weakling. Win this one for yourselves and... me." He even invoked the John Street Wren motto: "We never died a winter yet and the devil wouldn't kill us in the summer."

Each team member dug six inch holes in the dry sward with the heel of his hobnail boots. A good foothold would ensure no slipping or sliding. The judge called out ..."Take the strain."

When the red marker on the rope was directly over the centre line, he shouted: "Pull."

Lispole won the first pull fairly easily but Garfiney fought back gamely to win the second. It all hinged on the third and final round. Whatever team tugged the other from the red mark to the white mark on the rope would be the victors. Thirteen feet between Garfiney and glory.

The fact that both teams sought early advantage led to two false starts. Finally the judge's roar of "Pull" was heard above the cheers of the crowd. Lispole gave a mighty heave and dragged their opponents within inches of the centre line. Geknobs was going berserk, waving his hands, screaming: "Hold them, lads, in the name of all that is sacred, will ye hold them?'

The rope steadied.

## WHEN FOOTBALL'S LOSS WAS TUG-OF-WAR'S GAIN

Both teams held.

The markers on the rope did not move for a number of minutes. Geknobs eyed his own team and the team at the other end of the rope. Noticing a moment of weakness there, he gave a mighty leap into the air and ordered like never before: "Pull... Pull... Pull!"

Kenny Kelleher at the back of the rope felt more grip come to him and slowly eased it through his hands. After a few more tugs the red marker rested over the centre line. At this point one of the Lispole team lost his grip and slipped.

Geknobs roared like never before: "Now, pull, pull, ye hoors."

His team dragged, jerked and yanked until the white marker on the Lispole side of the rope crossed the centre line.

Champions!

The Garfiney supporters threw their caps in the air and acclaimed their heroes. Geknobs was shouldered around the field waving his hands in victory as if he was an All Ireland winning captain.

"Only for Kenny and myself they had us. Jesus the sweat is rolling off me. Me back is stuck to me shirt," he explained in a cart-before-horse manner as he basked in a rare hot-bubble moment of victory.

Kenny and his team lay back on the ground totally spent but basking too in their moment of high achievement.

The pound note was collected and the Garfiney people hurried home to milk the cows. There was a pep in their step. They couldn't wait to get to O'Sullivan's in town and stick out their chests that night.

Shortly before eight o'clock the townies propping up the counter were delighted to see members of the victorious team and their lucht leanúna march down John Street.

"We never doubted ye lads. We knew it was in ye."

*"Hay and oats for the Lispole goats,*
*Eggs and rashers for the Garfiney slashers."*

Truly, victory has a thousand fathers.

The pound was added to and O'Sullivan was told to tap a barrel. As the creamy pints of stout were handed round, the compliments and laudations increased. Tadhg Lynch played a few polkas brilliantly on his melodeon. It heightened the exhilaration of achievement during the evening.

"Ye'll bate them at the football next year," a man by his side roared, intoxicated on free porter and the hallucinogenic rapture of the oompahs.

Whatever about that, pride had been restored and no one would ever again doubt the courage, might, power and muscle of the men of the Townlands. And just as importantly, it meant that pulling mangolds and turnips out of muddy, stony ground would be a lot easier in the weeks that followed.

Or as one local put it: "They slept happily under Coneen Donoghue's slated roofs that winter and not a slate has stirred off anyone of them to this day."

*Tom Lynch was born in Garfiney, Dingle, Co. Kerry. The retired primary teacher is married to Nuala and they have two daughters Aileen and Caoimhe. He is a staunch supporter of Dingle GAA Club and Kerry. Tom served as treasurer of Cumann na mBunscol an Chláir from 1992-1997 and also as PRO of Cumann na mBunscol na Mumhan.*

# Black '47 In Ireland Became A 'Golden Year' In Cavan

Pat Lynch

Some years are defined and remembered by natural weather phenomena such as 1946, the wettest year on record, but then 1947 arrived and its ferocity wiped '46 clear off the map. In early January 1947, a severe frost gripped the country and lasted for several months. Near our home in Cavan, Kearneys' lochaun froze solid, as did the Cullens' one alongside, except at its centre, where a deep spring bubbled up, providing fresh water for the resident mute swan, the passing mallards and other water-fowl present.

Towards the middle of January, the first heavy snow fell and remained on the ground until a second big fall arrived towards the end of February. It snowed non-stop for 36 hours, and as it was accompanied by a bitter east wind, there was widespread drifting with large accumulations.

Some amount of snow fell almost every day for the following month and with school suspended, this, for a lad who had yet to reach his 11th birthday, was the next thing to heaven. As all the animals on the farm were housed and the haggard had sufficient fodder to last some months and the turf house was nearly full, our thoughts turned to helping the neighbours, some of whom were quite distressed.

All able-bodied men were mobilised to clear pathways to isolated houses and to rescue animals lost in the blizzards. The remains of a lady who had died, were eventually carried miles across fields to Ballynarry Church, at the other end of our parish. People walked miles to get provisions in shops, and food was shared out among neighbours.

The snow and frost lasted until the second week of April, and only then could the ploughing and crop sowing commence. The big thaw had made conditions very difficult, and potato planting could only begin during the month of May. Some people were still setting the potatoes in June, a task usually completed in early April. As the weather improved, we were treated to one of the warmest and longest summers on record and the harvest yielded great returns.

Early in June a letter arrived at our door from America. Our uncle, the Monsignor, a PP in Carrol, Iowa, was returning for "an extended vacation" and explained he would have the use of a hired car from Dublin. We couldn't wait and as planned he arrived towards the end of June. My older brother David set out to meet him, and after an epic journey by bus to Dublin and then Shannon, met up with Fr. Pat and escorted him back to Dublin, where they acquired a hired car. David described hair-raising moments on the journey home when the car spent most of its time being driven on the wrong side of the road.

Fr. Pat, a renowned poet, loved his music and sport, so we anticipated lots of parties and fun and he delivered handsomely. I had the task of serving Mass for him in the local church each morning for which I received a little present, but of more significance, he taught me an appreciation of nature as we walked to and from the church. He attended the Ulster final in Clones on the Sunday July 3, where Cavan defeated Antrim by four points. He then made his way to Killenummery Drumahair, where his brother Canon Hugh was parish priest, and remained there until he took the train from Sligo to Dublin for the semi-final against Roscommon. Here, as arranged, he met up with Canon Hamilton, a friend from his early days and the man largely responsible for taking the final of that year to New York.

On his return, he regaled us with stories from the match, and his plans to attend the final in the Polo Grounds on returning to America, to meet-up with the Cavan team and Canon Hamilton there. He fulfilled that promise.

Meanwhile at home, excitement was building towards the final, fixed for September 14. It was the chief topic of conversation in our school and all around the country. The weather had held up, the crops were saved and had yielded really well, the hay was in and the haggard was nearly full again. As confidence was high, we spent all day Saturday, the eve of the match, gathering firewood for a huge bonfire to celebrate victory. We carried this firewood to the top of Carrick rock, a vantage point visible in every direction for miles around, with a few of the neighbours chipping in with turf and sticks.

Fr. Butler, a Leitrim man, wished the team well after the Mass sermon. Afterwards, outside the chapel, arrangements were being made by the local lads to meet up at John Reynold's house to listen to the match later that evening. Electricity was still a figment of the imagination in our part of the country and even battery powered radios were very rare.

Only three existed in our end of the parish, the other two were the property of Fr Butler and Master Timoney. I listened outside the church as the discussion ranged around the composition of the Kerry team, and the names invoked awe and wonder, such names as Gega O'Connor, Jackie and Dinny Lyne, Paddy Bawn, Joe Keohane, Danno, Bill Casey and Teddy O'Sullivan. I was awe-struck. Kerry seemed so far away and so powerful.

Most families in our part of the world were affectionately known by their nicknames, and all young men played at some stage for the parish. We played with enthusiasm but with little success. At that time Pat the Yankee was our captain and he was the first to arrive to hear the match was due to start at 8.30pm. I arrived with my brother David and took my place near the fire, sitting on a little three-legged stool.

Next in was Jimmy the Lamb who was the official statistician. Jimmy completed his formal education at the age of 13 but he was highly read and one of the most intelligent men I ever met. He covered every angle of the match for later discussion, and sat next to me. Tommy D was next in. He was our goalkeeper, the best around. He always wore a hat while playing and also wore his ordinary working pants during the match. Pat the Nut, along with his friend, Pee the Black arrived, and then came Joe the Duck on his bike. Harry Plunkett, the only man from the parish to represent Cavan up until then, was there along with Neddy the Lamb and Mikey the Fall.

The kitchen was full and soon the yard outside filled up with all the other neighbours arriving. A big cheer went up as the match began with shouts of 'Up Cavan' all around. Then shock set in. Kerry totally dominated the first 20 minutes of play, and the goals rained in. Luckily two of them were disallowed. Jimmy announced that Cavan had switched the midfield pairing just as someone in the yard shouted 'where's the Gunner?' and Cavan came to life and took over. A few quick points and two marvellous goals propelled Cavan into the lead by half-time and the mood of those present had changed dramatically.

The second half was a rollercoaster as every Cavan score was greeted by loud and prolonged cheering. Near the end O'Hehir feared the broadcast would be cut off before the match ended and as he pleaded with invisible technicians not to unplug the over-running broadcast, we too were on tenterhooks. Fortunately as it turned out just as the final whistle blew, the commentary ended abruptly. The place erupted as Cavan had won by four points.

When sanity returned, John Reynolds produced a can of paraffin oil and we all headed off to our bonfire on the top of the rock. I can still hear the cheering all those years later as the blaze erupted and then other bonfires appeared at various points across the horizon.

We were in heaven and that night has sustained me through all the years since. They called it 'Black 47' in the rest of Ireland but for Cavan, it was truly a 'golden year.'

*Pat Lynch is from Cavan and qualified as a veterinary surgeon in 1959, working across a variety of private and state bodies for over 40 years. An avid GAA fan all his life, he also has serious interests in mountaineering, tennis and horseracing.*

# A Royal Tale Of Two Patrick Rattys

Michael O'Brien

Where would the GAA be without its long and chequered history of objections? Clubs were forever objecting about the smallest of things – a name or a cheque not written as Gaeilge, not to mention a surfeit of overage players, illegal players and 50 shades of other types of illicit team selection activity.

The objecting pandemic often times spilled over to inter-county fare where the modus operandi normally was for a county to put its rival on notice that all was not well in their line-up and they would fulfil the fixture under protest though warning that they would be going the 'objection' route thereafter.

Back in the 1920s, Longford failed to give such advance warning that they had reservations about Meath's team. They lost the game when it was played in January of 1925 and afterwards objected to the Royals being awarded the Leinster junior football championship. This was done on the grounds that one of their players, Patrick Ratty, had already played in the senior championship against Dublin in Navan.

The Meath delegates argued that the charge was not in order as Longford did not lodge their protest prior to the match as required by rule. The referee stated that the Longford captain had mentioned to him before the throw-in that Meath had senior players on their team. However, they did not lodge any written or formal protest at the time.

The chairman of the Leinster Council, Bob O'Keeffe, ruled that the skipper's protest against illegal players on the Meath team was sufficient for him to declare that the Longford objection was in order and should be heard.

Longford then provided evidence to prove that Patrick Ratty, who took part in the junior final, had played senior with Meath in Navan. Meath delegates didn't try to make a defence on this issue but instead explained that there were two Patrick Rattys playing for the county. The chairman then adjourned the case to give Meath time to present the two Rattys at the next meeting of the council.

The next meeting of the council was held in Croke Park after the annual convention. Both Patrick Rattys appeared before the meeting with the required certificates. The Meath representatives held that the elder of the two was the senior player who had taken part in the match against Dublin while the younger man played for the victorious Meath juniors.

Longford had prepared themselves for the hearing by bringing forward a witness named Mr. Durkin. He stated that he knew the younger Ratty and witnessed him play in both the senior inter-county match between Meath and Dublin and subsequently in Mullingar in the junior final on January 25, 1925. This was a major blow to the Meath case but their delegation held firm and denied the claim, repeating that it was the elder Ratty who lined out in the Navan match.

To their credit Longford had undertaken serious sleuth work between the original hearing and this second meeting. Considering the era, they did exceptionally well to track down and produce a photograph of the Meath senior team from their match against Kilkenny which showed the younger Ratty in the team photo.

Meath's argument was now starting to buckle before their eyes but they came back with one last retort – they explained that the junior Ratty only stood in for the photograph because the senior Ratty was delayed by a breakdown to the car in which he was travelling and only arrived in the grounds fully togged out seconds before the throw-in.

The chairman put the question to the meeting and the vote resulted, 13-5 in favour of the objection. Accordingly, the junior title was awarded to Longford.

Meath weren't done yet and appealed their case to the Central Council. When the birth certificates were produced for the two Patrick Rattys, it was discovered that one was aged 27 and Patrick senior was in fact 47 years old. It was claimed by Meath that the 47-year-old played in the senior championship clash with Dublin. If true, Patrick Ratty senior must surely be one of the oldest men, if not the oldest, to have played senior inter-county football.

The Central Council threw out the case and that was the end of the 'tale of two Rattys.'

*Michael O'Brien is a native of Johnstown, Co Meath and was a member of the 1967 All-Ireland SFC winning Meath squad. He also coached the Royal County to win a National Football League title in 1975 and Walterstown to five Meath SFC successes between 1978 and 1984 and two All-Ireland Club SFC final appearances. A noted historian, he has published three books – 'Perseverance Brings Success – a history of Walterstown GFC', 'The Struggle for Pairc Tailteann' and 'Royal & Loyal – a history of the first 50 years of the GAA in Meath'. He is currently an Honorary President of Meath GAA.*

# What Happened Next After Ref Sent Me Off

John Lynch

Tyrone players in the seventies and eighties looked forward to the Ulster championship every year, but in the knock out days, often it would be a long, long summer away from the inter county front if we were beaten in the earlier rounds.

In such situations, you would find a huge number of big names relocating to play in New York, Boston or San Francisco for the summer.

The likes of Frank McGuigan, Patsy Kernan, Gerry Taggart and the late Dominick Daly lit up many a Sunday in Gaelic Park, New York and won several championships there with the local Tyrone team.

Those guys were heroes at home so when they came back and recounted the great time there was to be had in the States, it got us younger lads thinking we might give it a try if our club team went out early in the county championship. I stayed at home during my younger years but when I was in my thirties, I began to cross the Atlantic regularly when the opportunity arose.

In one particular year – 1997 – I got an offer to go to Boston to play there with Notre Dame, an Armagh club for the summer. Now it fitted in perfectly as I was studying at the time and my course ended the day before I flew out to the USA.

I was very keen on qualifying as a sports injury specialist and part of getting insurance to practise meant I had to study for an intense first aid course to get certification.

I arrived in Boston on the Saturday delighted to be finished with the books and looking forward to a summer of football. I was told that we had a big game on the following day against Shannon Blues, a Galway Exiles side in Dilboy Field out in Somerville part of the city.

The teams there would know each other well and would also be aware of who was 'imported' from Ireland to bolster their bid to win championships.

Those players would be marked men and they would go through a softening up process during those initial games to see what they were made of.

Now I was never a shrinking violet when it came to the physical stuff but I had no intention of throwing my weight around either.

There were a few handbag incidents over the opening 20 minutes and then the ref caught me throwing a punch at my opponent near the end of the first half.

It was a lovely warm summer's Sunday but I was boiling inside more as I trundled off because I knew I wasn't much use to my teammates if I was sitting on the sideline for the rest of the game.

A few scuffles broke out after that but all seemed to calm down again when the ref – Pat Bligh from Roscommon – blew for half-time. Both teams went into separate huddles on opposite sides of the pitch as the selectors handed out bottles of liquid refreshments to cool us down and restore our energy.

Just as we were passing the water around, one of our lads came up to me and said: "Hard luck John on the sending off."

After taking a swig out of the bottle as he looked across the field from the sideline, he pointed his finger excitedly and said: "Jesus, one of their lads must have decked the ref – look he's stretched out over there."

We all looked over to where he was pointing and sure enough, the ref was flat out on his back near the halfway line. Initially, we presumed he must have got a box from one of our opponents but then something inside told me to go over and investigate further.

I ran across and as I got nearer I could see that his complexion had turned purple. Immediately, I got to work on him, using all the knowledge that I had acquired studying first aid from the previous weeks.

I didn't need any doctor to tell me Pat had suffered a massive heart attack. I called out to the others to ring for an ambulance as I began to administer cardiopulmonary resuscitation (CPR). I couldn't find a pulse when I checked and I was a bit worried that he might be already gone. I decided to keep working on him and went into automatic drive knowing that it was better than just giving up.

It felt like an eternity but I suppose it was only 10 or 15 minutes before I heard the Fire Brigade's siren arriving into the stadium. They rushed over to me and were immediately able to take over and provide a superior form of resuscitation with their equipment.

Shortly after that an ambulance arrived and Pat was rushed to hospital where he successfully underwent a quadruple bypass.

He was detained in hospital for some time but recovered to full health again and in fact lived to the age of 78.

I have two great memories arising out of that game. Somehow it came to the Massachusetts Governor's attention that an Irish player had saved a referee by keeping him alive while the emergency services arrived to take over. Some time later in September of that year, I was invited by the Massachusetts House of Representatives to the State House in Boston where the Speaker Of The House, Thomas M Finneran (a politician of Irish descent) presented me with a certification for valour.

That was a really memorable day and very nice to get but it was nothing compared to the way the Bligh family treated me. I was lucky to have just completed the First Aid course and I suppose it was lucky for Pat too. His brother had a number of pubs around Boston including 'The Corrib' and we had some good nights there.

Pat would always remember the incident by saying when he met someone he knew in my company: "Let me introduce you to the Tyrone man I sent off in a football match and who luckily for me came back onto the pitch to save my life a few minutes later."

*John 'Tar' Lynch is a former Tyrone player, who broke his leg against Kerry in the second half of the 1986 All Ireland final. A former GAA Allstar, he works in construction and runs his own moulding company – Derg Ornamental. John is married to the former well-known athlete Christine Gallen from Donegal's Finn Valley club.*

# Refereeing To Sound Of A Train

## John Arnold

Dick Doocey did a bit of refereeing during and after his playing days. His life-long friend Ollie Wilkinson described his refereeing style in one word – " unique."

Dick explained that further when describing how once he reffed a game in a certain town in West Waterford. During the first half, which had started at seven o'clock, his stopwatch failed – at the time watches were scarce.

He knew that at 7.30pm a train would be leaving the nearby station and the driver always gave a 'hoot, hoot' when pulling out. Dick played on until he heard the hoots and, in his own words: "Fellas were saying to me, 'God – Doocey that was a long half hour.'"

Dick said nothing but during the interval, he managed to get the watch going. The second half lasted about 33 minutes and there was no complaints about it.

However Dick later discovered that the train had set out a full quarter of an hour later that evening than usual. That meant he had presided over a 78-minute game which was meant to last 60 minutes. A man ahead of his time in West Waterford in 1959.

# Germans Invading... Stop... Can't Fulfil Fixture... Stop...

### Pádraig MacMathúna

Every Co Board official will tell you he or she could write a book about the various excuses clubs put forward when seeking the postponement of a game.

Death in a family of one of the players is undoubtedly the most common reason proffered but arguably the most ingenious one, citing current mitigating factors, was thought up in Clare during the Emergency years of World War Two.

In 'The Crooked Ash' book which is the Scariff club's history, the difficulty in fielding a team during that period was highlighted.

The man in charge of ensuring his club played that weekend was Vincent McInerney, a good club hurler of his time who was then in charge of his team.

He was the brother of the famed Dan McInerney, an outstanding county hurler, who lived to 93 years of age. In his time serving Clare through a long career, Dan proved himself a match for the best, including Christy Ring, Nicky Rackard and Mick Mackey.

His brother Vincent took over teams after hanging up his hurl and in this instance had a Sunday fixture to fulfil. However he knew that there was no chance of getting a postponement from the fixtures' man in charge, so he didn't seek a deferral days in advance but instead left it to the last minute of the Sunday morning.

He then sent a message asking for a postponement arising from a possible issue of war. He contended that German forces seeking to surprise the British had parachuted onto the west coast of Ireland and had progressed as far as Holy Island, which was close to his club.

He said that most of his team, who were members of the Local Defence Force (LDF), felt they had no choice on this occasion but to put their country first before the GAA.

They were granted the postponement on the day but sometime later when the word got back to Canon Hamilton that this request had more basis in creative fabrication than truth, he had a few hard things to say to the Scariff club, claiming they would find it very tough to get another postponement under his watch.

Whitegate had lined out to play a Camogie fixture when a problem was signalled by the referee before he threw in the ball.

The official said he would not go ahead with the game as the Whitegate girls didn't have black tights as part of their attire, which was under the rules of the Camogie Association at the time.

He pointed to his watch and said he would give the club a short period of time to rectify the matter. This led to supporters running down to the local shops looking for black tights but alas there was none in stock.

They came back long-faced but another local man, Jim Kelly, came up with an ingenious way of passing the ref's strict leg colourings.

He sourced the biggest tin of black polish in the district and administered it across the brown tights the girls were wearing – turning them into de facto black tights.

The fastidious ref inspected the girls after they received their coat of paint and proclaimed himself totally happy that the game could go ahead.

And regardless of the result, it was one occasion where an entire team could be said to have delivered a 'polished performance.'

◆ ◆ ◆

Looking back at the minutes of GAA meetings from the past in Clare throws up some happenings that can only be described as hilarious when judged from the perspective of the present time.

For instance there was a Minor B Final between Ennistymon and Coolmeen in the 1940s which had a series of objections and counter objections, ultimately leading to a decision that saw both clubs disqualified from the competition.

This sanction was taken when it became understood that of the 30 players due to start the encounter, only one was sufficiently under-age to legally play in the grade.

There was a story of a similar nature about a juvenile game which I retrieved from Shannon Gaels GAA history.

The then chairman of Gaels, Vincent McGarry, observed the arrival of the Quilty players, their opponents in the game.

Stroking his chin as was his wont, he remarked with a heavy degree of understatement on their age: "They are indeed fine strong boys."

Then turning to his own team, which incidentally didn't contain one juvenile, he added: "we have a fine strong group of boys ourselves."

## GERMANS INVADING... STOP... CAN'T FULFIL FIXTURE... STOP...

The two teams went out and played their match which the Gaels won... and needless to say, there was no objection from Quilty.

My own club, Cooraclare, also known as The Milesians, travelled to Coolmeen to play the Juvenile final against Kildysart only to discover no one was expecting us there... and besides there was no actual playing field to stage the encounter.

You'd think that would be the end of the matter with the game being refixed for another venue the following week. Instead, a man called Tommy Hanrahan and a few other locals sprung into action.

They brought the two teams down into a big field where they proceeded to work feverishly; cutting bushes, digging holes, erecting poles, and tying ropes for crossbars. They then used the cut whitethorns and other bushes as sideline 'flags'.

A little later than the (not) advertised time, the 1948 juvenile final got underway. I was playing myself. We won it very easily and we were particularly proud that we achieved the win – as we only had a couple of overage players!

That may sound a strange thing to say but the reality of the situation was our opponents had many more ineligible players than us. The player I marked that day became a friend of mine when we grew into manhood. I asked him one time if he was overage for that occasion and he said: "Not by much, only three years."

There are stories that linger in the background of local GAA affairs, some because they happened and others because they might not have taken place at all.

The story I'm about to relate falls into the latter category... word of mouth says it was a junior football game, but I can't remember which teams were involved in the encounter from the late thirties or early forties.

Not unusual for that period in history, the referee turned up but had no watch in his possession to check the timing of the two halves. When he enquired if anyone had a timepiece, he was disappointed to find that none existed among the supporters or mentors.

Some local then suggested that the pub across the road called Downe's Pub had an eight-day clock. To enable the match to go ahead – and everyone present wanted that to happen – one volunteer was given the job of going into the public house where he was detailed to take note of the time and come back out to the pitch once half an hour had elapsed.

That plan went ok for the first half but by the end of the second half, the man in question had imbibed a lot of liquor, and also had become engrossed with the singing and craic that had risen up inside the hostelry.

As the referee felt the second half was going on much longer than the first, he kept glancing across to the pub door hoping to see the time-man emerge so that he could signal the end of the game.

He had no choice but to ask another person to enter the pub and see what the problem was. The other man saw the original timekeeper was approaching inebriation and had no recall of his time mission, never mind how long the half had gone on.

When the second man reported back to the ref, the man in the middle himself felt it was at least three-quarters of an hour since the second half had commenced… and blew the final whistle, much to the delight of the exhausted players.

As I say, the reported timing of a game from a public house has long since been denied as pure fabrication… but it's so long ago that you'd never know if it happened or not. Indeed another version I heard was that the official in charge went into the pub and borrowed the clock which was brought out onto the sideline for the duration of the game. Whatever about the first story, I can't see an owner letting his prized clock go out of his possession.

*Pádraig MacMathúna is a native of Cooraclare and turned 87 in June this year (2021). He spent all his working life in Ennis with Clare Co Council. He attended his first football game in 1942 and still remembers it clearly. Pádraig has served as President and Irish Officer for Clare Co Board and was a long-serving editor of the annual Clare GAA book.*

# Arnotts And Dublin Break New Ground In GAA Sponsorship

## Bill Kelly

My love affair with Dublin GAA began as a six or seven year old when my dad would bring me to Croke Park to watch the senior footballers and hurlers play.

I was more of a hurling man and was delighted to play at minor and U-21 level in hurling for Dublin while using my skills from that game to play hockey with St Ita's Portrane and Glennane.

Then my world changed dramatically when as a 17-year-old both my parents died within six months of each another. I had to grow up and enter the real world. I started working in Arnotts as a sales person and had to put my sports career to one side.

It would be some time but Dublin GAA would come back to play a huge part in my life as Arnotts not only entered the sports sponsorship world but blazed a trail across the Gaelic Athletic Association beginning in the 1990s.

In the subsequent two decades, I had the opportunity to be central to one of the most exciting times in the development of Arnotts and Dublin GAA as the two became synonymous in the public perception.

Through it all I have two extraneous forces to thank for allowing this symbiosis to flower to the extent it did. One was a soccer giant – Manchester United, the other a rabid Kildare man, Tom Toner, who also happened to be the chairman of the Arnotts company.

It was sometime in the nineties that I went to Old Trafford to see a United match. On the morning of the game, I strolled into the gift store and was knocked sideway with what I saw. There was frenetic buying as fathers bagged clocks, jerseys, tracksuits, bed covers, pens and other paraphernalia to bring back to their children.

I stood back in awe watching this up close. Within a few weeks of that experience, I read an article in the Sunday Independent saying that United would soon open its first overseas shop – in Belfast.

I was intrigued, so much so that I went up north to see the place. It was not in a fashionable area of the city yet the same merchandise... clock, pens, kits were flying out the door.

I knew then we had to grab a piece of the action. On the Monday I rang Old Trafford and it took several phone calls and many days of probing before I got a name and a number to ring.

Ron Wood had won the franchise and lived in Bury where he had built up a huge birthday greeting card business called 'Birthdays'. He was a hard man to track down. It got to the stage where his secretary confided that Mr Wood just didn't return calls to people.

I said: "Tell him if he wants to make a million to give me a call back. If not don't bother." I also added that Kevin Moran would vouch for my bona fides as a Dublin businessman.

A few days later the phone rang in Arnotts and the man on the other end said: "You're a persistent bugger, aren't you. Now about that million?"

I had him hooked and when I told him I'd gone to Belfast to see how his shop was doing, he was impressed. I invited him over to Dublin for a pint and when he said he liked Dublin, I knew the door was opening up.

When I met him, I was struck by how similar in looks he was to Mal Donaghy, who played for United in the late eighties. Ron and myself hit it off straight away to the extent that we are still good friends.

I brought him around our premises and told him I envisaged a 1,000 square feet Man United shop at the back of our sports shop which at the time was in Liffey Street.

We took in a million quid in the first year and Arnotts took an agreed percentage of that amount. We got a few great years out of the enterprise before United decided to run their own shop in Dublin at O'Connell Bridge between D'Olier and Westmorland Street that looked good visually but had little footfall because of traffic.

They thought I was being a sore loser when I told them the location wouldn't work... within 18 months they closed the shop.

By that time Ron had sold his extensive business for £90 million, bought a jet and decided to follow United around the world in comfort.

The United experience had got me into sponsorship mode. As a GAA fan I knew the association was starting to think along those lines. People think Arnotts became the first Dublin sponsorship but it was Kaliber, the non-alcoholic beer, who signed up first but only for one match and left it at that.

The way I looked at it Dublin was the Manchester United of the GAA and I told Tom Toner, my chairman, that we should consider sponsoring them.

He directed me to go and talk to them. I visited their then HQ in North Great George's St where I met Con Clarke, who was Chairman, Jim King, the

## ARNOTTS AND DUBLIN BREAK NEW GROUND IN GAA SPONSORSHIP

Secretary and Donal Hickey, who also worked in the office. From memory I think the late Eddie Toman from Erin's Isle was also at the meeting.

And this is where my GAA past came in to help me break the ice.

"You're that Bill Kelly from the underage hurling teams," Jim said as I sat down opposite them.

So we spoke of days gone by – of people who played with me like Leslie Deegan and Harry Dalton, of going to my first All Ireland in 1961 between Dublin and Tipperary, of watching the two Boothmans – Achill and Bernard, who were from my club and were my heroes. After half an hour of shooting the breeze, we did the business end very quickly.

It was a simple equation – the lads wanted Arnotts to pay an upfront annual payment to the county board with a performance related stipend for every win the senior footballers achieved after that. In other words, we might have to top up with four or five extra payments if Dublin reached the Leinster final and All Ireland senior final in any of those years.

Between the annual down payment and potential add-ons, the sum jumped up to over £50,000 – a lot of money over 40 years ago.

I had two problems now – getting Tom and company at Arnotts to agree but more pressingly, I realised I'd forgotten about the hurlers and the other football grades.

So I huffed and puffed a little in front of the boys about the cost of such a sponsorship and then mentioned the other teams.

"We'll throw the rest in if you agree those figures," they said.

When I reported back to Tom Toner and Seamus Duignan, they were the ones doing the huffing and puffing.

Tom had a classic line in such circumstances that he never failed to ask. "Bill, if it was your money, would you give it to them?"

Without hesitation I said "yes" and then pointed to the huge opportunity we had. I also made the point that if we were the sponsors, none of our competitors would get the chance. I underlined the business potential, basing my optimism on our United experience. Tom put up his hand to stop me in midstream and said: "This is definitely a case of a man's heart ruling his head."

However, seconds later after chiding me, he directed me to make the arrangement with Dublin Co Board. They did the contract and we signed it little knowing that 1991 would be the year of the great Dublin-Meath saga. What a way to start our relationship.

At that time, I was only interested in the clothing aspect of the sponsorship but I got O'Neills, after our Manchester United experience, to design various tops – rugby and golf shirts as well as jerseys. Paula Lee, who worked in the Co Board, had designed the original Dubs pale blue top and navy trunks and I asked O'Neills to do a reversal of that kit with navy tops just to see how they would go.

Napoleon loved a lucky general and that year I could understand why. The four game saga of June-July 1991 gripped the interest of the whole country, even those who weren't GAA fans.

Week after week our shop was full as thousands of Dubs went to Croke Park bedecked in the various Dub tops with the Arnotts logo on every one of them.

Such was the excitement that I brought my son out to see the Dubs training and sometimes there would be A versus B games. The As had an ancient set of jerseys while the Bs were kitted out in old itchy woolly jersies that were affectionately known as the 'Bumble Bees' kit. Every time you washed them, they shrunk. That night I went to Pat O'Neill and Paddy Cullen and told them I'd get a proper set if they weren't offended.

They were delighted. I asked Tony Towell in O'Neills to design this second set in reverse colours to the normal Dublin kit. They were so popular that the night I delivered the 30 jersies, 27 of them disappeared. I knew straight away I had a market for this line of Dub jersey which incidentally is the one Stephen Cluxton still wears in goals for Dublin. Great but cheap marketing research.

During the games in 1991, Arnotts name across the chest of the jersey could hardly be seen because of the restrictions the GAA had come up with for size of sponsors' logos. Until this changed we used block letters across the middle of the jersey in white out of navy so the name Arnotts could be clearly seen.

I pointed to the unprecedented sales levels and told Tom and the board that it didn't real matter as the venture was a massive success.

The players too appreciated the human touch; we had specially embroidered American jackets which they loved and we also tried to look after their wives and girlfriends. For instance, after the four game series, we gave all the panel cufflinks and the ladies got pendants and cut glass vases as a memento of the saga.

When Dublin finally lost out to Meath on Saturday July 6th, the word went around the following weeks that the county board had made a fortune out of the agreement with Arnotts. Con Clarke invited me to lunch in the Gresham Hotel one day shortly afterwards and I knew only too well what the conversation would be about.

Before going up to the hotel, I went into Tom and told him I wanted us to give Dublin an extra ten grand as a gesture of our appreciation. "Oh you're a generous fella?" he said when I mentioned the amount.

## ARNOTTS AND DUBLIN BREAK NEW GROUND IN GAA SPONSORSHIP

I suppose that would be something akin to giving them £100,000 now but I sold it as a great building block with the Dublin brand.

At lunch I told Con I was in a hurry back to the office and after a little beating around the bush, he brought up the subject of further payments.

"Con," I said, "we have given you all that you are contractually obliged to get as you won no championship game this year."

I could tell Con was dreading having to face a county executive meeting that night with no further money forthcoming from Arnotts.

So before I left, I slipped the ten grand cheque into his breast pocket and when he opened the envelope, I've seldom seen a happier man. He now had something extra to keep the members happy.

I'm convinced that out of that meeting, the goodwill that was always the bedrock of Dublin GAA and Arnotts relationship not only grew but prospered for some 20 years.

By now we had expanded the Dublin range to include the Man United model – dugout jackets, rugby shirts, golf shirts, rain jackets, pens, clocks, mugs, quilts and watches. And of course jerseys, which were now termed 'home' and 'away' by the fans. Once the rugby and golf tops were done tastefully, they sold well.

As time went by we also introduced a kiddies range for jersey but noticed that because they were smaller, the fashion conscious ladies were buying those to wear themselves rather than the larger, less figure hugging adult ones. That inspired us to introduce ladies jerseys.

Tom Lehman, the great American golfer, was to give me an understanding of the tourist market that I had overlooked. I was pally with Donal Bollard of Allianz who is also a great Dub fan. He rang me shortly after Tom had won his only major – the British Open – in 1996 to say Tom was looking for a Dublin top. He had seen the Dubs play on television and although it was nearly 6pm on a Saturday he asked if I could bring one down to the K Club where Lehman was playing with Paul McGinley.

As it happened my son and his pal had gone down to watch the golfing exhibition and I said I'd collect them. I picked the pair up at the gate on a wet evening. The gateman didn't believe my story about "having a present for Mr Lehman" initially until I showed him the jersey. When I went in to reception, the lady rang down to Tom's chalet. He was delighted to hear about the jersey and invited us in.

As I presented the jersey to him, his face fell as he asked me what 'Atha Cliath' meant?

I told him it was the Irish for Dublin but that didn't cut any ice with him. He then looked across at my son who was wearing his bigger brother's rain jacket. It had the word Dublin and Arnotts on it and asked if he could take that instead. Here was a multi-millionaire golfer who was a major holder with all his clothing sponsored, eagerly pursuing a second-hand raincoat with the Dublin name on it.

After that, despite resistance from some people in the GAA, I knew that our range of clothing had to resonate with people visiting our city from abroad, so Atha Cliath and Dublin had to go on whatever item we sold.

The other big project Arnotts became involved in without too many knowing about it was the redevelopment of Parnell Park. By this time the late John Bailey had taken over from Con and was busily trying to raise money for the £3 million plus development. Bertie Ahern as Minister for Finance and later Taoiseach had promised to get money from state coffers while the Leinster council coughed up half a million and the GAA itself provided a similar amount. Clubs also had contributed by selling season tickets to help repay the loans.

John wasn't everyone's cup of tea but I liked him and I knew he had Dublin at heart. He wanted to get Dublin GAA away from the corrugated dressing-rooms era and provide it with a spanking new stadium. When it came to looking for something, he certainly wasn't the retiring sort. Indeed, he would often pass by our outer ring of receptionists and secretaries in Arnotts and walk into my office unannounced if he wanted something. And at a time when such a big undertaking was going on, the county board was invariably stuck for money.

One Friday evening at three o'clock, I was looking forward to getting home early and maybe getting out for a few holes of golf in Newlands Golf Club near where I live.

I heard a commotion outside and as I looked up from my desk, the door opened and Bailey walked in. Normally, despite his habit of talking through gritted teeth, he'd have a wry smile or a positive vibe about him as he made eye contact. On this afternoon, he looked drawn and ashen-faced.

I asked him if everything was okay and he shook his head. He proceeded to tell me that the builders on the Parnell Park site were threatening to pull out the next day unless he could come up with the final financial instalment.

That put him in a bind because if they left it would take 40 or 50 grand for them to get all their equipment back into the place. And that was on top of what was still outstanding.

I felt very sorry for him but asked him, maybe quite innocently: "John, why are you telling me all this?"

"I was hoping Arnotts might give us a loan to keep them in," he said.

Only a man with a hard neck could come looking as John had done. The amount involved was several hundred thousand – probably the equivalent of a million and a half in today's money.

He pulled out a piece of paper, about six by four inches, and on it he had all these figures which he'd obviously gone through with the site foreman before coming in to see me.

"You're not asking for much," I said sardonically but as I did so, something flashed through my head.

Although we had just extended our contract with the Dubs a short time before, I took my courage in my hands and walked over to Tom's office. Seamus was in with him and I told them the story.

Toner as always had a few choice things to say. "That effer has the hand out looking for money every time he comes in here," he said colourfully.

Behind his gruffness though, Tom had a brilliant mind. He oversaw the whole Arnotts re-development at our main store and behind his bluster he could see the opportunity of being involved long-term with the Dubs.

"If it was your money, would you give it to him?" he asked me, not for the first time?"

I tried to show him that my heart was not ruling my head every time there was a Dublin issue. I pointed out the benefits of a long-term involvement with a team that had been in All Ireland semi-finals or finals on a consistent basis and also stressed that if we were locked in, it ruled out our competitors trying to gazump us at some stage. "And that's not factoring in the fact that we'll get between half and three quarters of the money back from our sponsorship deal, not to mention the clothing sales."

We made the decision there and then and I went across to our finance head who got weak when I told him what I wanted but eventually he wrote out the large cheque.

Bailey was a man transformed when I handed him the cheque. He said Dublin would never forget that only for Arnotts, the Parnell Park project would not have been finished for years. As he was leaving I told him it was the last time I wanted to see him in my office unless he was bringing good news.

In fairness to him, no project of this magnitude is ever as straightforward as it appears to the ordinary supporter. No sooner had he put out the finance fire than he was faced with another problem which potentially could have scuttled the whole redevelopment.

Just as John thought he was sailing in clear blue water, the fire officer told him there wasn't sufficient space for crowd safety at one exit. That looked like his project had hit the rocks but he had remarkable resources in getting around obstacles. He went down to have a look at the exit area one day by himself and seeing the woman from the last residence, he struck up a chat with her.

Noting that the grass in the garden was just about kept in check, he asked if she was a good Dub follower. She nodded and he said he was too, in fact he told her he worked with the county board without saying he was chairman.

"I'd say your husband has a pain cutting all the grass," he said.

"He hates doing it," the woman replied.

"What would you say if I took that chore away from him and built a little kitchen extension for you – would you give Dublin GAA a swipe of the garden because we need it to expand the exit?"

And so John is back smiling at my receptionist and opening my door a short time after getting the big cheque.

"How much is a fridge, a cooker, tables and chair and micro-wave for a small kitchen?" he asked me without even saying hello as part of the small talk?

"How the hell do I know?" I replied.

He then told me about the deal he'd struck to get more land and how he needed to finish it off with good kitchen implements and furniture from our stores.

I got one of our floor managers to bring him around and after he got all the fittings and furniture sorted, he told me it would make a great impression for an Arnotts lorry to deliver it to the house. Never a man to take 'no' for an answer, we did as he asked.

I'd like to think that we did well out of the Dublin sponsorship deal over the years with Arnotts brand recognition while enriching the GAA in the capital at the same time. It was a helluva roller-coaster ride but what a joy it was to be part of the first draft of history being written on sponsorship in Irish sport and business at the same time. Above all though, it was a labour of love.

*Bill Kelly is a former Sales and Marketing Director and CEO of Arnotts. Married to Una, he is father of three grown up children. As well as being an avid Dublin fan, Bill likes to keep active in his retirement with a round of golf at Newlands and also enjoys reading and travelling.*

# Pushing Myself To Beat Christy Ring

## James Power

Who was the last Waterford man to go head-to-head with Christy Ring in a competitive game? That's the question I ask my family when I'm in the mood for a bit of fun.

The answer of course is me, James Power, a nothing hurler and I'd go so far as to say I'm also a failed footballer back in the day when I tried to play with Kilrossanty at underage level.

So how did I manage that unique feat of literally facing off against the man many consider the greatest hurler of all time?

Oh sorry, I forgot to mention that it was in the mercurial game of Push Penny that Christy and myself regularly crossed swords.

That was back in the early seventies when I worked in Roadstone at Carrolls Cross, Kilmacthomas and we had a big shiny table in our office. It was the perfect surface for Push Penny and hardly a day went by without myself and my former colleague, Eddie Rowe from New Ross, using up part of our lunch hour playing a few games.

We had two old English pennies which were the players if you like and a 'thrupenny' bit which acted as the ball.

At the time Christy worked as an oil salesman around Waterford and would call every so often to fill orders. He used to come into us regularly at one stage and watching Eddie and myself go at it stoked the competitive nature in him.

"Any chance I could try my hand at that for a while, boys?" he asked us one day. Ever the gentleman, my colleague Eddie allowed him to take over his penny.

"Now there are rules and regulations," I told him half-jokingly, "and if you don't follow them, you could be sent off."

Christy enjoyed the banter but once the whistle was blown, so to speak, he was deadly in earnest. There was only one thing on his mind – winning.

Eddie and I were far more practised in the art of pushing pennies than our Rebel friend, but it wasn't long before he had the measure of us. He had great hand to eye co-ordination and that was only to be expected when you consider what he could do – and did – out on the hurling field.

We played against Christy several times and every time I felt it was a privilege to be in the great man's company. My only regret is that I didn't get a picture of the three of us together – in today's world with iPhones and modern gadgets, the photo would have been instantly posted around the globe.

Back then, even if you had a camera, you'd be shy about asking a famous person to stand into a photo. I suppose I always thought I'd meet up with him sometime again. The world was much younger then in our eyes.

It certainly was a sad day when I learned that Christy was found dead of a heart attack later that decade at the young age of 58.

He may be long gone but for this old timer now in his 80s, the memory of those days with the great Cloyne clubman and genuine ordinary person will live on until I draw my last breath.

*James Power is a native of Kilrossanty in Waterford and is married with three grown-up children. A former employee of Queally Quarries and later Roadstone in Waterford, he has a lifelong interest in both Gaelic football and hurling.*

# About A Boy Who Played Camogie

## Dermot Gilleece

There was no hint of any profound, emotional release, of some great weight being lifted from his shoulders. Indeed the more he talked about the events of 1964, the more he seemed to be enjoying the memories.

Like Thady Quill, the exploits of PJ Reynolds have become the stuff of legend. And poetry. As in the verse: "For sports star of 1964... No need to take a vote... Salute the him, the camogie Jim... Who won the cup in Moate."

When I visited him nearly a decade ago at his home in Mullingar, PJ was ready to talk. Yes, it was true that he played in a Westmeath camogie final, as a member of the winning team. And it was also a fact that his duplicity led to a high-speed cross county border chase from Moate in Westmeath towards Clara in Offaly, after a car-switch to elude outraged pursuers from Tang, Cullion's opponents in the final.

On his RTE morning radio show in 1984, Gay Byrne was reading headlines from the newspapers of 20 years previously. One of them, from the Irish Press, posed the question "Was the she a he?" The country's most celebrated broadcaster of all time had a special interest in the story, having failed in two attempts to get the individual involved onto the 'The Late, Late Show.'

"I wonder where this camogie player is now?" mused Byrne with a chuckle.

"Hey P J, come down and listen to this," Marie Reynolds shouted up the stairs to her husband, who at the time was in bed with 'flu. He was too ill to be interested.

A short time before I interviewed him, Reynolds, who ran his own electrical contracting business, was in Mullingar Hospital for a minor operation to have a cyst removed from his nose. "Careful nurse," cautioned the surgeon. "We've got a cross-dresser here." And not for the first time, PJ shared a joke about his past.

Back at home, where his wife and their twin sons, Paul and Denis, waited eagerly for him to bare his soul for the first time in public, a crucial question had to be asked. "Why do it now, after so many decades of silence?"

It happened through the persuasive powers of a mutual friend, the late Michael Duffy, whom I knew as a past captain of Mullingar GC and who was a neighbour of PJ's for years. "Anyway, I think the mystery has been dragged out long enough," he suggested.

So, Reynolds began his tale of a county camogie final in which his local club, Cullion, met Tang from Ballymore, near Athlone. And how Cullion had surmounted formidable odds by forcing a draw with six unfit players in their side.

That was what prompted a cunning plan whereby a ringer would be introduced for the replay, which was fixed for Moate. Though he grew to over six feet tall and weighed up to 16 stones, Reynolds was only a whippet of a lad back in 1964, when he was targeted for the deception. Remember, this was the time of Beatlemania, when long hair had become a male fashion statement, making it easy for a fresh-faced lad to pass as a member of the opposite sex.

"It happened in October 1964," he began, "when I was 14 and a schoolboy at St Mary's, Mullingar. We had to attend school for a half-day on Saturday and on my way home, I was approached by Pauline Delamere, one of the girls involved with the Cullion camogie team."

Visibly warming to the memory, Reynolds went on: "When she asked me if I would line out in the replay of the final the following day, I thought it was a bit of a joke, so I said: "Sure."

The idea was that I'd dress up in my own football togs and jersey and then wear the team's maroon and white gym-slip over everything. And I would be given a coat belonging to a sister of Mary McCabe, the camogie club secretary.

"I can only guess that they chose me because I was slim, athletic and a useful hurler with one of the Cullion under-age teams. Anyway, I expected her to call back later and say it was all a gag. But I began to get worried when I hadn't heard from her by the following morning.

"By then, everything began happening so fast that I hadn't time to protest. As far as I could gather, none of our players knew what was going on. In fact Mary McCabe wasn't told until shortly before the throw in."

"The pitch was about a mile outside Moate and just before the team were about to go out on the field, I was brought into the dressing-room and introduced as Kathleen Corcoran. Since the rest of the players said nothing to me, I can only assume they had been told all about the situation before I arrived. Anyway, none of them seemed surprised.

"So I trotted out onto the park as a midfielder, with the number eight on my back. And when the whistle went, I got right into it, just as if I was playing a hurling match for the club. But I soon became aware of minor disturbances among the spectators. I learned later that the girl I replaced on the team wasn't too happy and was crying and creating a bit of a rumpus."

And what was the age profile of the side? "Oh they ranged from my age up to 30 and over," he replied. "In fact there was one lady on the team, a great Westmeath camogie player and she could have been nearly 40." With that, he let out another of his frequent laughs: "Yes, there were ladies on the team who were old enough to be my mother."

Though Reynolds knew nothing of it, it seems the opposition had become highly suspicious of the fleet-footed midfielder with dark, curly hair. According to the piece in the now defunct 'Irish Press,' one of Tang's best players expressed the view to colleagues that the player marking her was going in far too hard to be a girl.

The upshot was that Tang officials decided that a half-time visit to the Cullion dressing-room might be in order. But Cullion were already a move ahead. "They told me I was being taken off at half time," said Reynolds. "So I made a quick visit to the dressing-room, put on a girl's coat over the gym-slip and was whisked away by Mary McCabe into a waiting car.

"I was then driven from the pitch to the convent in Moate by the late Tony Nangle, who was married to one of the Ling camogie players from Kilkenny. Mary McCabe knew the run of the convent, where her sister was studying for the Leaving Certificate, and after taking me in one side of the building in my camogie gear, I was brought out the back entrance in my football gear.

"They knew the Tang people had given chase, so we switched cars and Mick Power, the local hurling secretary, took off at high speed out the Clara road. Sitting in the back seat, I could see there was a car in hot pursuit, but Mick was a right man to drive.

"With his boot to the floor, he put a fair bit of distance between us and our pursuers. Then, when we went round a sharp corner in the road he stopped the car and told me to hop out. And as I slipped through a hedge into a field, he was already way down the road.

"Unaware of what had happened, the Tang car kept chasing Mick while I was in a field, dressed in my white tee-shirt and white shorts. And with a herd of bullocks surrounding me, I stood there for about two hours, shivering with the cold, waiting on Mick to come back for me.

"I heard later that he had no problem in losing the Tang lads. Meanwhile, the match was continuing in Moate, with all sorts of rumblings about the mysterious, young midfielder in the Cullion team. And to prove how easy it is to deceive people, there were many who swore I was on the pitch right to the finish. Eventually, I was picked up and told on my way home that Cullion had won the match by three goals to two."

What he wasn't told about was the second-half scuffles in which a Mullingar butcher got a black eye after going onto the pitch to bring away his two daughters, who were in the Cullion team.

According to an observer at the time: "During the second half, the Tang crowd kept shouting from the sideline 'There he is', 'No! There he is.' They couldn't seem to make up their minds which was the lassie they thought was a gosoon."

As Bernard Shaw's Major Barbara might have told them: "Like all young men, you greatly exaggerate the difference between one young woman and another."

Meanwhile, these outrageous claims were emphatically rejected by the Cullion hurling secretary, Power, who told the Irish Press: "The whole thing is only hearsay. In the first game, six of our players had been ill and only got up to play the match. With our full team on Sunday, Tang couldn't understand why they were being beaten and they began to say we had a gosoon playing for us."

Power concluded: "There will be no protest from Tang. They have nothing to protest about. There was no gosoon in the team."

As it happened, Tang had no need to take action. After the presentation of a cup and medals to the Cullion team, all of the silverware was recalled by the county board and given later to a football team. But according to Reynolds, one medal survived. "Mary McCabe has it," he said. "It was considered worthless at the time because of a mistake in the inscription on the back. She was asked to give it to me but I didn't want it."

Reynolds, who crossed hurleys with the great Jobber McGrath, went on to have a successful career with the Cullion club, playing until he was 43. And was he ever ribbed about his cross-dressing? "No," he replied with a quiet smile. "But that was probably because I had a reputation for being able to take care of myself."

He continued: "I knew of another man, since dead, who played camogie for a team in Delvin. But to be honest, I don't think it was worth their while playing me that day. And it certainly wasn't worth all the trouble that came afterwards. There was a lot of stuff written about it and the story went on for months, even years."

Is he sorry he did it? "Oh no," he replied with some emphasis. "Though I've never really admitted it until now, I got great craic out of it, particularly from lads working on building sites."

Then, his sense of fun coming to the fore once more, Reynolds concluded: "It's become a part of my life. And you know, it's not every camogie player who makes the national papers."

*Dermot Gilleece is widely-regarded as one of Ireland's most authoritative sports writers over a number of decades. Having worked initially with The Irish Press and the Daily Mail, he joined The Irish Times as golf correspondent in 1981. He has been a golf columnist with the Sunday Independent since 2002. He lives in Sutton, Dublin, with his wife, Kathy, and they have two married children, Tara and Mark. For relaxation, he plays poor golf as a member of Clontarf GC.*

# The Only Radio In The Parish

Robin O'Connell

My uncle's house in Co Clare was the home of the only radio in our parish. He had a dry battery radio that usually would last about three months. Every Sunday a large group of people from the parish gathered in my uncle's house.

There were often 50 people gathered around his radio. In 1951, Tipperary played Wexford in the All-Ireland hurling final. Michael O'Hehir, who was doing the commentary said: "It's a 21-yard free for Wexford. Nicky Rackard bends, lifts and strikes."

Just as the word "strike" left his lips, the radio blew up.

A fella arrived late to listen to the match but my uncle quickly turned him away: "You may go home. Nicky Rackard is after busting the radio."

Another man present in the kitchen was searching for something around the fireplace.

"What are you doing?" asked my uncle.

"I'm looking for the sliotar," he said, convinced that it had come through the radio and landed near the hearth.

# Ecstasy And Agony Following The Banner In The Mid-Fifties

John Ryan

For a few Cooleycasey youngsters, the Oireachtas Final and replay between Clare and Wexford in late 1954 in Croke Park was all consuming, before, during and after, and is still memorable 66 years on.

As an aperitif, Gerry Egan and Rodgie Liddane seemed knowledgeable on the team and tactics, while Jimmy Stephans, John Liddane (RIP), JJ and Thos Ryan listened enthralled and were well briefed in advance.

We were glued to the only pre-electric wireless in the place for both games. It was our first experience of the new magic, while our hosts John and Paddy Begley were equally hooked. With the commentary as Gaeilge by a youthful Mícheál Ó Muircheartaigh, every word was absorbed and digested by the pupils of the famed Derrynaveigh (Oatfield) National School academy.

The final was a draw with a month's anticipation to the replay and a Banner win by three points, supposedly with an attendance of 80,000. So we heard. No towering stands, corporate boxes or social spacing then. On match commentary conclusion, no analysis or interviews, the wireless was switched off promptly, saving the wet and dry batteries for the equally important news and weather.

While the marvels of the 'new' technology gave us garsúns our match fix, some more mature Oatfield gaels travelled all the way to Croke Park. They likely included Mick O'Grady, Dave O'Grady, Bob Tynan, Timmy Ryan, Mick Keogh and Eddie Brandon. Tom Cullinan represented Cooleycasey. Reports from Croke Park informed us that the Oatfields shouldered Jimmy Smyth round the pitch. In a frenzy of ecstasy Tom Cullinan threw his new overcoat skywards but it failed to return, to Tom anyway.

Hats and caps took a celestial trip also.

The great Wexford full-forward Nicky Rackard, complained to the great Clare full-back, Dan McInerney, about his difficulty in securing the sliotar. Whereupon, Dan advised him to call to Woolworths for a rubber ball.

These 'takes' added to the victory and assumed legendary status in our formative minds. Two mighty teams full of household names. Some weeks earlier, Wexford were All Ireland runners-up to Cork. No slouches, then or later, the boys of Wexford, winning back-to-back All-Irelands and Oireachtas titles in '55 and '56. It was awesome. What an appetiser for the 1955 Munster championship, a mere seven months on from the Oireachtas glory. Following a week of bog purgatory with hay-knife and wooden wheelbarrow, my 'spartóg' partner, Jimmy Mason proposed we'd go to Thurles, by train from Sixmilebridge (SMB), for the game against Cork.

Oh the ecstasy. 'Twas worth the penance. Cork were champions of Munster and Ireland ... and going for four-in-a-row. No backdoor then. A Jimmy Smyth pile-driver skimmed the crossbar in the first half; no back netting then either. The brown sliotar must have cleared the Killinan embankment end. Kilkishen native, with Cooleycasey roots, Noel Deasy, at wing back was marking the Rebel genius Christy Ring. A lasting memory late in the game with Clare leading by a point; Ringy 'fell' on the edge of the square... a free in? Christy at least would score the equaliser, if not his traditional trademark goal.

The tension for thousands of Banner and Rebel supporters resulted in a claustrophobic silence. The ref pointed ... a free out. A mind-enhancing Banner win, the first such over the Rebels since the 1932 Munster final. A very sweet one – we were on our way. Fág an bealach!

The return train to SMB, with official and unofficial stoppages along the way, and bikes uphill home, was on board cloud nine. Glory be. Five weeks short of my second teen birthday, I was amongst the youngest Banner supporters in far-off Thurles on that mind-blowing day.

Next up was the Premier County, the reigning National League champions, in Limerick. Up and over the windy gap with Dad on bikes. Another point win. Our time had finally come. Enormous crowd mostly on grass banks, moving imperceptibly along as the crowd pushed in from access points. One exit was down a bottleneck steep incline to the Ennis Road. Those who can now recall, still wonder how some were not suffocated in those years.

Met up with the Gleann na gCross Spaights, Snr. and two sons, post-match. Had a few 'sergeants' and lemonades, to tackle the homeward climb on bike power. We had now accounted for 'three majors' and only the Treaty boys stood between us and Munster and possibly All-Ireland glory. We even played them at home, down the road in our former Thomond territory, no travelling expense to a neutral venue, get on with it.

Booked as jarvey for that Sunday to ferry Mam and some siblings by 'dolly' and trap to her sister's family, the Woulfs in Concilrea, Truagh. For some reason I was not unhappy at missing the title encounter. Weren't we racing certainties – beidh lá eile ag an mBratach, in Croke Park.

## ECSTASY AND AGONY FOLLOWING THE BANNER IN THE MID-FIFTIES

Towards evening, both sets of cousins got the match result from a passing cyclist. No wireless over there. It was not believable, Clare well beaten, a nine point defeat. Perhaps the result should be reversed, our reporter was having us on. Confirmation came all too soon, 2-15 to 2-6. The result has remained unchanged from that day to this. For those still left and can recall, it remains unexplainable, searing the Banner hurling psyche, taking 40 years to return the compliment. 1995 certainly assuaged but did not expunge the Munster wounds of '55.

The slackish Banner support in Thurles in '95 may have reflected the trauma of four Munster final defeats by Limerick – '55, '74, '81 and '94. Theories surfaced for the shock '55 humiliation. Some Clare players subsequently gave interviews which boiled down to a few simple contributory factors. Clare were entitled to be confident, whatever about over-confidence.

There were no pre-match celebrations or in-house antipathy. July 10th 1955 was a blisteringly hot day, one of the few that year. The Dal gCais were red hot also. As the result was a foregone conclusion, many Treaty supporters headed west to Clare beaches. Tap water was supposedly on sale for parched supporters in the Gaelic Grounds by an enterprising entrepreneur. The day suited a young, light, fit team – Mackey's greyhounds – more so than their heavier, stronger opponents. And Dermot Kelly's tally of 1-12 meant Limerick were Munster Champions.

Next up was the All-Ireland semi-final between the Shannonsiders and the Slaneysiders. It was of huge Clare interest. Wexford were now our bankers. It was devastating to miss the 'live' wireless on same, with honorary Bannerman Michael O'Hehir on the mike. I was mandated to escort a cow to the local bull, an Irish mile or so distant, on that very day of all days. No transport boxes then to speed up matters.

On entering the field our bovine host trotted over to greet his visitor. He was light on his legs, a distant cousin of the modern behemoth, which can hardly walk let alone perform as nature intended. Watching a snorting, focused bull lining up the bovine visitor on lower ground was a terrifying experience for a novice teen in short pants. It seemed as if every youth in the place was scared stiff of bulls, or what they thought were bulls.

Wexford winning the semi-final and final that year and the following, plus two Oireachtas titles, just emphasised how near the Banner came to stardom in that era. We waited over 20 years for league success, which was ecstatic, and nearly as long again for Munster and All-Ireland glory.

Undimmed memories of '54 and '55 – ecstasy and agony, seared and sealed in the mortal psyche as in an eternal time capsule. What an emotional roller-coaster with the 'trimmings' of first inter-county games and travel, the crowds, the unforgettable three wins and one defeat, betting and winning, the wireless and the famine school, the birds and bees, the 'Bridge first Clare Cup. In a few more years, those still left to recall those halcyon hurling days will be themselves but memories.

It's possible that come 2060, some elderly Banner supporter will again pen youthful memories of the nineties roller coaster. These memories will remain embedded forever in the psyche too.

## POSTSCRIPT

Despite annual honest endeavour, it took Clare 63 years to bridge the provincial gap from '32 to '95 and 81 years to win a second senior All-Ireland – 1914 to 1995. One wonders how the perennial triumvirate who have garnered most of the hurling honours since 1887, might have fared had their return in honours been as bare?

That trio have amassed 94 All-Ireland senior titles, while nine more counties and London, claim 39 between them. Limerick now with nine, lead the long charge for equality. It seems that, it's the Clares of the GAA world in football and hurling, who have kept the prairie fires burning with very little fuel, or allowance for county populations, club numbers, county board income, dual codes etc. Could positive discrimination be applied for the serial 'also rans' as suggested by Donal Óg Cusack?

Witness the countrywide joy when one of the annual hopefuls achieve some success, emphasised recently when Tipperary and Cavan were crowned with provincial football honours.

While saluting Dublin, national rejoicing is unlikely following their 10 Leinster and six 'Sams' in a row. Even the Dubs, 'in the mix for six', may be getting bored, never mind '7th heaven'. The enforced Covid-19 extended club space, for the vast majority and the tighter schedule for the elite may engender a fixtures realignment.

Concluding this article coincided with some noteworthy GAA milestones, 1) Centenary of Christy Ring's birth, 2) Fluorescent sliotars, 3) Bamboo hurleys, 4) Water/Tactics breaks, 5) Record hurling championship points, 6) Pre-Christmas All Irelands, 7) Camogie and Peil na mBan joining and enhancing the GAA family 8) Virtual club/county conventions, 9) Election of Cratloe stalwart – Jack Chaplin, as Chairman of Clare Co. Board GAA, 10) Bloody Sunday commemoration.

I've often wondered, re latter, if the 14 who shared a common Croke Park destiny resulting in death should be commemorated by a group/collective name for the Hogan Stand by 2026? At this remove, do the player, nine men, three children and bride-to-be merit equality... eight of whom lay forgotten in unmarked graves until recent years?

Might the Premier County form the van, confirming the Thomas Davis adage: "Where Tipperary leads, Ireland follows?"

*John Ryan is a native of Cooleycasey, Sixmilebridge. Living in neighbouring Cratloe parish since his marriage in 1968 to Kitty Mullane, a Camogie star with Truagh (Clonlara), they have six grown up children. He is a former employee of Shannon Airport (Sales & Catering /Aer Rianta) where he had a service record of nearly 48¾ years between 1958 and 2006. John has held several positions at club and county level, including chairman of Cratloe club and Co Board treasurer.*

## One Free In Entire Game

This story takes some beating when it comes to a referee's use of the whistle. In April, 1935 Tipperary hurlers beat Cork senior hurlers in an important New York championship fixture. In a keenly contested encounter, the man in the middle, Gus Fitzpatrick, blew only once for a free in the course of the hour. Remarkable in any game that a ref blew so little and yet kept full control of the game.

# A Place Apart – And Yet Just Like Any Other

## Declan Bogue

He would have his favourite seat in our house. This gentle, elderly man would park his Fedora hat atop the fridge and freezer stack right beside the back door and make himself comfortable in an armchair set against the low radiator, looking out onto the lawn.

Granda O'Connor. Eddie O'Connor. Though he didn't always get that. A lot of the time, the family were referred to as 'Connors', in a manner similar to how Kerry folk drop the 'O' with the likes of Micko and Páidí as 'Dwyer' or 'Sé'.

Every week, you would be urged to go out there and show your progress with the solo run. On fine days, you wore shorts. On wet days, denim jeans with your football shorts and socks worn over them. A few laps of the garden soloing a soccer ball and then back in for the verdict.

On the days you didn't drop a single ball. On the days you managed it off both feet. On the days you couldn't get it right at all and fell over in the attempt.

"Keep at it."

Later on a Sunday, with Mass attended – the O'Connors were without fail the last group of people left in the car park of Cradien Chapel, sucking the last goodness out of the morning – and the early dinner eaten, there would be a game. Somewhere, anywhere in the county.

Before the rush of clubs in the '90s to build a stand at every venue, there was a tradition of parking on the banks and watching the game from the comfort of a car seat. The radiator made a sauna for all inside. Goals and points were greeted with a sharp parp of the car horn.

There is a great yarn of a school game once in Ulster refereed by an official from the safety/comfort of his car, positioned on the halfway line. He blew the horn for a foul, then used his car indicator to show what direction the free was.

Eddie hated dirty play. It was an undisputed fact that one or two of his sons were renowned exponents of the dark arts. He wasn't thrilled by that.

Back when he would watch them, the mood could be black when they returned home. As mild-mannered as he could be, he had no problem confronting a lack of sportsmanship.

When a bit of digging would break out in a televised match, my mother's immediate reaction would question what her father, God rest him, would have thought of it all?

All those thoughts and memories came flooding back recently when an old photo captured on a mobile phone circulated through family WhatsApp groups. It was of a Cavanacross Gaelic football team from 1939. It was familiar because the same picture hung in the kitchen of Eddie and Eileen O'Connor's little bungalow, just above where Eddie would rest his left arm on the table and pack his pipe with tobacco.

Seeing the picture again? It's like Neil Young's opening lines of 'Distant Camera';

*'The flash of a distant camera,*
*Reconnecting thoughts and actions,*
*Fragments of our missing dreams...'*

And it's like I'm right there. My grandmother is sitting in the living room. Snooker or wrestling is on the television and she's making a bold declaration that someone should be hung, drawn and quartered while her husband laughs softly to himself, a picture of contentment.

Rediscovering the picture prompted some obsessive researching of the Cavanacross club of this period.

The primary source material of the time are the microfilm issues of The Fermanagh Herald. And this is where happenstance kicks in; one of the prominent Cavanacross players was Seamus Kelly who despite his youth, served as Co Board Secretary at the time. It could be no more than a logical bet, but this junior club's activities seemed to be better documented than most others.

Eddie would have been 29 by the time of the picture. He holds the ball in the front row which would indicate he was the team captain. Their jerseys are remarkably uniform and tidy by the standards of the time.

Most of the players have just one glove on, the theory being you matched your glove hand with the foot you kicked off.

Alongside him in a black jersey looking like Lev Yashin is Johnny McCaffery. The Herald would lavish praise on him and he became a regular county goalkeeper.

The names resonate down through the generations. Johnny Cleary was a county minor and by all accounts a remarkable stylist. I grew up with his grand-nephew Hugh. We were in the same class in primary school. The very house I sit in now was built by his hands.

## A PLACE APART – AND YET JUST LIKE ANY OTHER

Next-door neighbour Owenie Kelly was a county minor and a regular goalscorer in the reports.

Cavanacross is a particularly rural part of Fermanagh. It's steeped in a pagan sensibility, evidenced in a series of wedge tombs, stone circle and stone alignments from 4,000 years ago around the fields. The greatest concentration of prehistoric monuments in the county is right here.

Various activities flourish in the area including the Cavanacarragh Pipe Band, the Topped Mountain Historical Society, a strong amateur dramatic tradition, all based around Cavanacarragh Hall. Just above it is the home grounds of Lisbellaw St Patrick's hurling club.

With such a strong local identity, little wonder that despite few numbers, there was a constant effort in the area to field a team of their own.

What mattered was that they played at all. The realities of their lives weren't simple.

Eddie O'Connor was sold into labour as a young man. He slept where he could, many years later recalling in a local history book that he made a hay loft his bed on many occasions.

Most families did not permit their sons and daughter to play sport, it being seen as a distraction from labour-intensive farming before the introduction of machinery.

So when they played, it was a mini holiday. To get to an away game might involve a 40-mile round trip on a bicycle. Dressing rooms were a whin bush. An argument might break out for an hour prior to throw-in concerning the eligibility of some players and reports of games from this time would readily attest to competitors returning to their communities with a black eye or worse.

When you have nothing, it doesn't take much for entertainment. It is well documented how a county like Mayo suffered during the Famine, for example, losing 29 per cent of her people.

And yet, the population of Fermanagh in 1841 was 156,481. At the last census, it was recorded at 62,527.

As much as the Famine decimated communities and townlands, partition was a cruel joke for those along the border.

As a farm labourer, Eddie O'Connor's prospects were limited. As a farm labourer with nine children, his resources were put to the test.

But he and Eileen were made of stern stuff. She was a camogie player of renown, playing for Cavanacross and Fermanagh. In time, he would gain a caretaking job. They kept pigs and chickens in the house they eventually built. The livestock was Eileen's responsibility. They had to be self-sufficient.

Peader Livingstone notes in 'The Fermanagh Story' of the years 1929 to 1940; 'Work of any kind was scarce. Even in the towns, conditions were not good by modern standards. Shop assistants had usually to pay a fee when they became apprentices... Domestic servants were often domestic slaves. In the circumstances thousands of young Fermanagh people abandoned the county and sought their fortunes elsewhere.'

Throughout the ten years from 1930 to 1939, the annual unemployment rate never fell below 20 per cent and averaged 25 per cent. Income per head was little more than half the average for the kingdom.

The Fermanagh Civil Rights Association published a booklet in the late '60s that exposed widespread Unionist gerrymandering of votes, where electoral wards were drawn up to maximise areas where Catholics were in a narrow minority, in order to 'waste' as many votes as possible.

A forensic detailing of Governmental positions was extremely damning. Across 24 county officer jobs, only two were held by Catholics.

Across all civil servant jobs, 32 were held by Catholics and 338 by Protestants. It wasn't that this prejudice was confined behind closed doors either.

Two famous quotes from this time portray the attitudes, forged in English Public Schools and prevalent in the Ulster Unionist Party. Those in power would give free expression to the prejudices during their 12th of July addresses.

Senator John Porter-Porter proclaimed at 'The 12th' in Lisnaskea in 1931; 'The Northern Government is a Protestant Government, put into power by Protestants and the welfare and safety of the Protestants should be its' first consideration.'

Two years later, Sir Basil Brooke went further in his address in Newtownbutler, stating, 'Many in this audience employ Catholics, but I have not one about my place. Catholics are out to destroy Ulster...If we in Ulster allow Roman Catholics to work on our farms we are traitors to Ulster... I would appeal to loyalists, therefore, wherever possible, to employ good Protestant lads and lassies.'

And still, pockets of places such as Cavanacross held people together and allowed them to play games that weren't long established in Ireland at that point, but had spread like the 'prairie fire' of Michael Cusack's description.

The football team played at a variety of venues; McMulkin's, Cox's or Gavin's fields.

A few hundred yards from any of these venues was Garvary Wood. In 1847, The Erne Packet newspaper reported that amid the Famine, hundreds of corpses were buried in a pit there, the victims of cholera, 'their relatives too weak to carry them to the graveyard.'

And so when they were able, they played their games.

They played camogie. In December 1932 they began Irish classes, which along with their other activities earned them the warm praise of, 'They will then be the foremost Irish-Ireland GAA club in the county' in the Fermanagh Herald.

For a time, they held Irish dancing classes in their community centre. There was an amusing line in a report on this, commending the club for steering the youth of the area away from the Jazz music that was gaining a foothold at the time, imported by the American GIs stationed in Fermanagh.

How good were they? Records are sketchy and there was a preoccupation for the 'With The Gaels' GAA column in the Herald to recount long, lengthy accounts of county and provincial board meetings rather than the meat and drink of domestic affairs. But they fielded at Junior level.

How good was he as a player?

He gains mentions in dispatches as a commanding figure. One report is particularly pleasing when they went to play Tyrone club Dromore.

Without a regular programme of games, challenge matches and Carnival events took on as much importance as any others and it was noted, 'It was generally thought that Dromore would prove too strong for the Fermanagh Junior team but Cavanacross, displaying the sparkling form which has been characteristic of their league matches this season, sprang a surprise by scoring a well merited victory over the Tyrone team.

'In E Connors they had the best all round player on the two teams – his brainy football paving the way for most of the winners' scores.'

In 1941, they won the Junior Championship. We say won, but there is more to it than that. They were leading Irvinestown in the county final, when the ball burst. So they collected the trophy.

The year after, they wrapped up a Junior League.

And then?

Nothing. They literally slip off the pages.

There may be a curious reason for this. Around this time, a breakaway league was formed and various clubs joined 'The Erne League.' Perhaps wishing to curry favour with the establishment, the activities of The Erne League were not reported or recorded for the short period in operation.

Bit by bit, their players drifted away. Eddie's brother Vincie was a dominant figure of the team and mentioned constantly in the match reports. Economic necessity took him to Barrow-on-Furness and the smoke stack chimneys of the north of England. He reared a family over there and never returned aside from holidays.

The local village of Tempo finally got around to organising themselves properly with the Maguires club, named after the local Chieftains. Most of the best talent went there; the Doherty brothers Eddie and Tommy. Johnny Cleary the flying forward. The Curran brothers, Jim and Tom.

Seamus Kelly began a long association with Enniskillen Gaels and Cavanacross petered out.

Eddie O'Connor would later serve as Chairman of Tempo Maguires in the early 50s', but maybe his heart wasn't in it.

With four sons of his own, there were further Cavanacross teams formed at underage. A picture of a successful Juvenile team from the early 60's featuring three of his younger sons hung on another wall in his home.

Occasionally, he would gather up a team for a sports day, call it Cavanacross, or Mountdrum – a neighbouring townland – and play in Sevens' tournaments.

He and Eileen formed a new camogie club and named it St Matthew's. My mother would be a mainstay in their green and gold jerseys, green skirts and gold socks. Even though they hadn't much, they put up the money for the Fermanagh camogie Championship trophy. It was called 'The O'Connor Cup.'

The demise of Cavanacross is a tale that would be repeated right across Ireland. GAA clubs formed in a blaze of enthusiasm. The embers burning bright for a time, the traditions were established. Then reality would bite.

The connections echo through the generations however.

Seamus Kelly formed strong connections with Enniskillen Gaels. His son, Dr Gregory Kelly is the current Fermanagh county board Chairman.

The goalkeeper Johnny McCaffrey married Eddie's sister Rose.

The young men of the area play football for a variety of teams now, Coa O'Dwyers, Enniskillen Gaels and Tempo Maguires, depending on what way their parents blew in. But mostly, they play hurling for Lisbellaw St Patrick's, the only hurling club in the county, standing defiant on a lane past Cavanacarragh Hall.

A place apart. And yet, just like any other in Ireland.

*Declan Bogue is from Garvary in Co Fermanagh. He grew up playing football for Tempo Maguires and hurling for Lisbellaw St Patrick's and has worked as a sports journalist for national newspapers in Ireland and England. His book 'This Is Our Year' which chronicled the 2011 Ulster Championship is acknowledged as one of the best books ever written on the GAA. He is married to Ciara and they have three children; Thomas, Lily and Ruairí.*

# How We Played Hurling In Canada – Without Hurleys

Bernie Comaskey

It was the summer of 1967. In England, the Beatles were singing about 'Penny Lane.' In Canadian bush-camps we were feasting on Merle Haggard and Hank Snow. Friends holidaying in Ireland returned with records of 'The Black Velvet Band', 'The Boston Burglar' and Joe Dolan's 'The House with the Whitewashed Gable'. It was the 'Summer of Love' in San Francisco; but I tell you, there wasn't much love of any kind where I found myself in 1967.

I was one of more than 2,000 underground miners extracting nickel from the bowels of the bush-covered wastelands of northern Manitoba in Canada. We were centred around a town (made a city in 1970) called Thompson. Of the miners working for Inco, more than a 100 were young Irish guys like myself while as many more worked on surface jobs.

The year 1967 was an important one in Canada, as the nation celebrated a hundred years of confederation. There were all sorts of festival celebrations organised across the country – and Thompson was determined to do its bit for the cause. This was easy because there is nothing that thirsty miners like more than a party.

The main celebration in Thompson was centred over one long weekend. It was called 'Astum Pema Waka' – which is Cree Indian, now 'First Nation' translated as 'Come and have Fun'.

As part of the many diverse, cultural and social events on show, the Irish Canadian Club offered to stage an exhibition hurling match on the Sunday afternoon. This got a lot of advance publicity.

I loved hurling from the first day I attended primary school. Growing up in the 1950s, hurling was our only escapism from a dreary, grey era. In the school playground we were all Nicky Rackards and Christy Rings – as well as our own local Westmeath and Leinster hurler, 'Jobber' McGrath. I did score 3-2 in a schools championship final victory in 1957 – but that was to be as good as it got. That was the only hurling medal I ever won ... but now, 10 years later, here I was with a golden opportunity to make a name for myself on the international stage.

There were lots of hurlers and footballers in Thompson that year. A hurley was a most prized possession – especially as they seemed to break easier in the Canadian climate. There was no football where I came from in north Westmeath, so I had never played football back home.

This exhibition match generated exceptional banter and excitement in the build-up to the event. Nothing was left to chance. There were trial matches to pick the teams and The Irish Canadian Club gave a 'grant' towards ordering 50 new hurls from Ireland.

Paddy Flanagan, the then secretary of Westmeath GAA County Board, sent our team out a set of maroon jerseys – thus ensuring we would be the 'best dressed' team on the day. Incidentally, the team was captained by my late brother, Willie (Bill) who remained in Thompson and went on to become the longest serving mayor of the city. He was a great hurler lost to emigration. He won the Thompson Open Racquetball tournament and held the Thompson Golf course record for some years.

We got into some 'serious training' for the big event. This was hard on our diminishing cache of hurls. Another factor was that underground hard-rock miners looked down on surface workers. This too was a reason why the time was hard on hurls.

I was picked as a forward and was marked by a tall, athletic-looking, soft-spoken Kerryman. We didn't know John all that well, because he wasn't long in town and didn't work in mining. He was employed in the meat department at the Safeway Store downtown, and to us, he simply went by 'John the Butcher' – as there were a lot of Johns around.

One thing was clear; John loved everything GAA, but had told me he played very little hurling. His enthusiasm and the fact that he was such a nice guy had got him a 'start' on the other team. The week leading up to the match, I would idle up to his meat counter and remind him he was lucky he was used to the sight of blood. John just put on his 'shop face' and smiled.

But a catastrophe was looming. Those in charge were trying to conceal their anxiety. The hurls hadn't arrived from Ireland by the Wednesday of 'Astum Pema Waka' week. Frantic phone calls were made home twice a day.

"They were shipped in loads of time."

"They are on the way."

"They should be in Canada now."

"Don't worry, you will have them by Sunday."

Right up until the throw-in, we were promised the hurleys would be with us. Then the bombshell was dropped; the hurls were lost somewhere at Winnipeg Airport.

I had arrived early at the sports arena ... a little hung-over. There were already 700 spectators present. The 'Thompson Citizen' newspaper had

# HOW WE PLAYED HURLING IN CANADA – WITHOUT HURLEYS

sent a reporter and photographer, and a popular radio celebrity was floating around doing random interviews.

Behind the scenes, the blame-game was being hotly played out. Brothers and close friends were being torn apart and even the good name of a couple of girlfriends came up for discussion. Panic and wholesale splits erupted in the camp. John Deveroux, president of the Irish Canadian Club, tried to be the voice of reason. "We have to do something," he suggested.

It was almost agreed that we would play seven-a-side, with "as many subs as you like". But that plan came a cropper because nobody wanted to give their hurl to anyone else! "If this hurl is going to be broke today, I'll break it myself!"

"Well, we have to do something…"

Then a snap decision was made. We would have to play a football game instead. The pitch was rock-hard and without a blade of grass. I know this for a fact, because I spent most of the hour eyeing it up from a horizontal position. The modest, soft-spoken Kerryman, had neglected to mention that he played senior football back home. I somehow got the ball in my hands once during the entire match. In my anxiety to avoid the next 'dunt', I hastily attempted a fisted pass to… anywhere. John the Butcher nonchalantly intercepted my pass and I can still hear the thud of leather upon leather as his size 11 boot left the ball at the other end of the field. Worse still… before John kicked the ball, he had time to turn to me, put on his 'shop face' and smile.

The long whistle ended my misery. As my marker and I shook hands I said to him: "I thought you were called 'John the Butcher' because you worked in a butcher shop."

Two lessons to be learned here: (A) don't go to play a hurling match without a hurl; (B) keep your mouth shut until the job is done. Oh yes … 1967 was quite the year alright, the year a hurling match became a football game. I think many of the Canadians present are still scratching their heads trying to work out what happened.

*Bernie Comaskey lives in Delvin, Co Westmeath, with his wife of 50 years, Pamela. They have two adult children and six grandchildren. Bernie has published four books, is a longtime columnist with the 'Westmeath Examiner' and a contributor to several other publications. As well as the stint in mining, Bernie has been a farmer, publican, retailer, and sports-centre owner. He is an overall sports enthusiast – but his greatest passion is reserved for GAA.*

# Young Ring Fan Vs Major Star

## Barrie Henriques

Ah yes, the 1952 All Ireland Final between Cork and Dublin... this 12-year-old was at his first final with his dad, a native Corkonian.

At last the boy would get to see his hero – Christy Ring – in the flesh. My father paid a shilling to get in and 3d for his match programme. I was lifted over the barrier to get to the sideline seats along the front of the old Cusack Stand. Those seats were made of railway sleepers with concrete supports. The place was packed.

A man arrived beside us looking for a seat. It was a lost cause until my Dad piped up: "Here's a seat for you" while simultaneously telling me to make space for the stranger as he put me kneeling between his legs.

The man was thrilled to get a spot and thanked my father profusely.

The game started and this young lad went wild, roaring his head off every time Ringey went near the ball. Christy was then accused of making an error of judgement by the man who was sitting in the boy's seat. The boy was not happy.

Boy: "Hey Mister, (in an ill-mannered attitude), you better not be talking about Ringey like that."

As was the norm in that era, the Dad administered a stinging clip to the left ear of the boy.

Boy: "Ow, what was that for?"

Dad: "Mind your manners, young fella. Do you know who you are talking to?"

Boy (still hurting from smack): "I don't but I'll tell you Dad, he knows nothing about hurling."

Dad (leaning towards the man): "Sorry about that Mick, he can't see any wrong from Christy."

Boy (whispering): "Who is he anyway?"

Dad: "That is Mick Mackey."

◆ ◆ ◆

As the match finished the man gave the boy a "tanner" – 6d!

# Milk Truck Expedition To Thurles That Turned Sour In Victory

Donal Herlihy

It was an uncomfortable trip in an old lorry to see Cork play at Thurles but the antics around the epic foray still stir fond memories. It all started with the unalienable fact that Cork were in another Munster Final in 1946. They were up against their arch-rivals of the time, Limerick, who were backboned by the legendary Mick Mackey and his brother John, the Herberts and the Cregans.

Cork had Jack Lynch, Alan Lofty, the Riordan brothers, Gerry and Mossy, and of course, the one and only Christy Ring.

Two evenly matched teams boasting some of the greatest hurlers in the game and the match fixed for Thurles in high summer. Everyone wanted to be there to see these stars in the flesh but how could a bunch of lads from around Kindale manage it.

In 1946, war time restrictions were still in place and with the scarcity of petrol, travel was very, very difficult. Our pub was packed on the Sunday night Cork won their semi-final game and the principal talking point on everyone's lips was how to makes the 200 miles round trip three weeks down the road.

Bicycles were suggested and discounted. Similarly the pony and trap was ruled out. Sonny Canty then said he would walk it if he had to but one thing for sure... he wasn't going to miss this battle of the Titans.

Pete Crowley arrived in for a late pint after the pictures and after some persuasion, emerged as our saviour and hero. He had an old Morris truck which was used for collecting milk from the farmers of the locality for delivery to the local creamery.

After some arm-twisting, he agreed to undertake the trip but warned those wanting to travel that reliability wasn't guaranteed. He said his old jalopy could only take a maximum of 20 supporters but they would have to pay ten bob (shillings) a head before setting out.

Names and fares were given to my father, who agreed to be our travel agent, saying bookings would be done on a first paid up basis. He had a full list before my mother let the last customer out the back door that night.

With excitement building towards the big day, everyone went on a saving spree. Back then Thurles was so distant it might as well have been in outer space. Most had never been outside the county. For others, Cork city would have been the limit and quite a few never went further than Belgooly or Riverstick to a hurling match.

A man needed a fair few bob in his pocket travelling all the way to Thurles for a Munster final. For those following weeks the pounds, shillings and pennies were saved in every manner. Newspapers were scanned daily for up to date news on the teams and how they were doing in training. Word had gone around the town that Pete's lorry was making the trip and requests for places came thick and fast. The list though was full and those on it looked forward with eager anticipation to a great day's drinking to go with a Cork win.

The day finally arrived and in our house in the Glen we were up bright and early at six o'clock for a hearty breakfast. I was going, along with my brother Michael and my sister Eily, who being Pete's girlfriend, was 'upgraded' to travel in the cab with her pal Kitty Kelly. The start time was set for 7am. With a lorry capable of a speed of no more than 30 miles per hour at very best, and with a stop for Mass and other emergencies thrown in, Pete estimated it would take up to six hours for the trip to Thurles.

The assembly point was our pub. The first to arrive was Jim Gillen and his pal Harry Connors. They were no sooner in the door when they asked for two pints, just to get the day off on the right note at 6.30. Eily reluctantly gave them two bottles of stout, saying there was a long day's drinking ahead of them.

The rest arrived shortly afterwards as did Pete, who got a loud cheer as he parked outside our front door. Unfortunately, the day was very overcast and already a heavy drizzle was falling. Pete unfolded a heavily mildewed tarpaulin cover which smelt to high heaven of sour milk. This then had to be propped up to give some head room.

Jim Donovan suggested the old furniture which my mother had stored down in the garage, having considered it too old fashioned to use. Legs were broken off solid mahogany tables, chairs and beds, furniture which would now be worth a small fortune. Had my father been present watching us breaking the legs off what could have been a Queen Anne dining table I fancy he would have said: "Serves her (the Queen) right, the ould B."

These legs were fitted to the sides of the lorry so that they would hold up the canvas. Two of the legs were nailed together and fitted in the centre

# MILK TRUCK EXPEDITION TO THURLES THAT TURNED SOUR IN VICTORY

like a tent pole. Long wooden benches from the bar, bottle crates and butter boxes were used for seating. We all piled in and on the dot of seven we headed down the Glen for Thurles.

The plan was to try to make eight o'clock mass in Fermoy. We hadn't travelled the first mile up the Eastern Road when it became obvious that this was not on. Pete already had his boot to the board and we were crawling at about 30 miles an hour on the flat.

Paddy Reilly, who was sitting on a butter box up near the cab, made a suggestion to the girls and Pete that maybe we could skip the mass if we all said the rosary in the back. He was turned down flat, although he had full backing from the crowd in the rear.

The accommodation in the back was pretty uncomfortable to put it mildly. Lads who were lucky enough to have a seat on the pub benches kept sliding back and forth as Pete braked, with the fellow at the end sometimes falling on top of the lads who were sitting on the floor. In the stuffy atmosphere the smell of sour milk was vile and with the drizzle persisting outside, rain dripped through from the numerous holes in the tarpaulin cover. Failing to make mass in Fermoy was only one of our many problems.

We were on schedule for nine o'clock in Mitchelstown... but for the law intervening. As we entered the town the lorry was halted and Pete could be heard talking to someone and then the canvas flap at the back was lifted and this red-faced guard with rain dripping from his cap peered in.

The look of delight on his face said it all. Compared with the bicycle lights, and dog licence summonses he had in his book, this was super league stuff.

For the third town in a row Mass was again missed – this time in Cahir. Requests that we pay a visit to a pub instead was turned down flat. We pressed on and near Boherlain at about 11.30 we came to a small country church. Pete pulled in across the road and after the girls had checked there was mass at midday they ordered everyone out and into the church.

A large, elderly grey-haired priest shuffled onto the altar with two altar boys, both of them were wearing hob nailed boots. "Please God, if this man has hurling blood in him he'll hurry things up," we prayed. No such luck. He entered the pulpit and began his sermon. On and on he droned, 10,15,20 minutes to the sound of traffic flying past outside.

As our nerves became strained, a low murmur began among us at the back. The man in the pulpit looked startled at such effrontery but never broke his stride. The murmur grew louder and then with an exclamation never before heard in a church, Petie Bollard charged for the door.

Sonny Canty bolted in like fashion. Within minutes we were all tumbling out the door, piling into the lorry and with smoke belching from the exhaust, we headed out of the village.

It took another hour or so to reach Thurles. The narrow country roads were by this stage packed with pony and traps, bicycles and people walking to the match. The mood in the lorry was turning very aggressive.

Some had brought sandwiches. Paddy Reilly had a dozen packets of Rolos under his seat on a butter box. But the anger was mostly coming from the majority who had money burning holes in their pockets. Nearly seven hours on the road and not a drop of drink as yet.

At about one o'clock Pete parked the lorry in a side-street just off The Square. Before anyone could move he laid down hard and fast rules about the return journey. Everyone was to come straight back to the lorry after the game. He would then get us out of the town fast and we could stop at a country pub, where we could then celebrate a Cork victory.

There was to be no exceptions. If anyone broke the rule there would be no stop on the journey home. All agreed.

Through throngs of supporters wearing the red and white and the green and white of the two counties, we made our way to the ground. Buskers, colour sellers and the usual scattering of three card trick men were everywhere. The ground was packed. Scattering to different stiles, a bunch of us managed to squeeze in to a mass of bodies on the bank behind the town end.

Waterford played Tipp in the minor match. Sean and Paddy Kenny were on the Tipp team as was John Doyle, who was playing full back. John cleared every ball that came into the square but what I vividly remember was the way he cleared every Waterford forward who dared even approach the square. Even then in his youth, he was a big man, and twas no wonder he went on to win eight All Ireland medals in his long career. Tipp won handily.

Cork and Limerick took the field and after parading around the pitch behind the Moykarkey pipe band, the ball was thrown in and the game was on. In no time the sparks were flying. Mick Mackey was at centre forward on the Limerick team and his brother John was at full. Limerick was awarded a seventy. John took up a position outside the 21-yard-line and faced the Cork goal. When the ball was struck John, ignoring its flight, raised his hurley like a cleaver and tore into the Cork goalmouth.

As the two Murphys, Con and Billy, and Din Joe Buckley watched the flight of the ball, Mackey raced into the square and buried Tom Mulcahy in the back of the net. A Limerick free not long after and John repeated

## MILK TRUCK EXPEDITION TO THURLES THAT TURNED SOUR IN VICTORY

his act. Racing in to the Cork goal with hurley raised, he again bundled Mulcahy into the net.

The Murphys and Din Joe went into a quick huddle as the ball was being pucked out. Some time later Limerick were awarded another seventy. Mackey took up his position outside the 21, hurley raised and his eyes fixed on Mulcahy once more. John made his charge as soon as he heard the whistle, unaware that this time the Cork backs had their own trap set. Ignoring the ball, which was going wide, the defenders suddenly stepped aside as John made his charge, Mulcahy stepped out of the goal, and with all three pulling the flat of their hurleys across his shoulders, back and backside, Mackey was helped into the net with Billy, Con and Din Joe piling in on top of him.

What followed resembled the bunt of a net with four or five large salmon threshing around trying to escape capture. Eventually Mackey minor crawled out battered and bruised but to his credit, being a Mackey, unbowed. It was noticeable however that he kept his eye on the ball instead of Tom Mulcahy for the rest of the game.

The game ended with Cork winning well by 2-12 to 1-7. We filed out of the ground on cloud nine and headed for the lorry, eager to be off and into that country pub to guzzle down pints and celebrate our great victory. The lads arrived back in twos and threes, much to Pete's delight, and even the most seasoned elbow-benders arrived without glancing at a pub.

Pete did a quick head count. Seventeen. Three missing. Billy Kidney, Ritchie Healy and a farmer from Summercove called Coughlan. Three quiet types who would arrive shortly. Half an hour passed and then an hour. The rain was again coming down and the mood in the back of the lorry was getting ugly.

Pete stood guard at the back to make sure no one escaped to the pubs. Jim Gillen moaned he had a pocket full of money, hard saved during the previous three weeks and apart from a lousy bottle of stout that morning at 6 o'clock, not a drop had passed his lips. At around seven o'clock with the crowds around the square thinning out, Billy and Ritchie arrived at the motor to be met with howls of abuse. They were dragged on board, lucky to avoid physical violence. Eight o'clock and Coughlan was still missing.

The mood was now approaching mutiny and Pete had to act. Coughlan was abandoned and with 19 angry passengers on board, finally we pulled out of Thurles. Just outside the town a stop was made so that a load of hay could be acquired from a field to ease the plight of those without seating.

As we were about to pull away, four Cork women from the north side rushed up and begged us for a lift back to the city. They were in Thurles since morning with stalls selling apples and oranges and had missed the last train. Before Pete could even voice an objection, they were eagerly hauled in over the tailboard. With a whole day without drink, this chance of a bit of fun as consolation wasn't going to be passed up.

The situation in the back of the lorry was now a shambles. The carved solid mahogany table legs acting as tent poles had collapsed, pouring a deluge on to the occupants. The tarpaulin was sagging in the middle creating two sections. One in the rear half and one at the front. Being only in my early teen years, I was squeezed into the front part, as the four women together with perhaps a half dozen or so of our more youthful passengers occupied the rear. I wished I could have been at the back. The noises from there suggested they were having great sport with the women.

With the rain pouring down and dusk setting in, the long awaited stop for drink was out of the question. A few cries of protest were heard as Pete, with his foot to the board, passed the pub at his top speed of 30 miles an hour. The majority though were by now too sore, wet and tired to object. Billy Kidney, being one of the only two on board to have enjoyed a few pints, was being given a hard time. Tedso Tisdall, who had seen action with the Royal Navy at the battle of the River Plate, shouted to Pete in the cab that he saw Billy drinking sea water and suggested throwing him overboard as he was going insane.

We joked, talked and nodded off as best we could in the wet and cramped conditions as we crawled south through Cahir and on towards Cashel. Pete was persuaded to make a stop in Cashel but efforts to get food or drink failed. The town was like a graveyard. Mitchelstown, which we reached sometime around midnight, was the same but as we passed through, someone noticed a light in a small shop window at the top of the square. Pete pulled over and those who were able, crawled out and crowded into the shop.

Apart from a few bars of chocolate, some sorrowful looking apples and bananas, and some large bottles of Little Norah red lemonade, the shop was bare. What that little old lady was doing having that shop open at that hour I'll never know but her entire stock was bought up within minutes with a mad scramble for the bottles of lemonade.

The four Coal Quay passengers, looking very dishevelled, were cast ashore in Cork city and we rolled up to our pub in the Glen nearly 24 hours after leaving it, with the first light of Monday showing in the sky.

Jim Gillen, with over three weeks spending money in his pocket, had disposed of a total of one and six on two bottles of stout the morning of the previous day and ninepence on the bottle of lemonade in Mitchelstown which he had to fight hard for.

## MILK TRUCK EXPEDITION TO THURLES THAT TURNED SOUR IN VICTORY

The man who had been abandoned in Thurles arrived back in Kinsale three days later to be told he was sacked from his job as a gardener. All the following week the local guards carried out an intensive investigation into the serious crime of carrying passengers unlawfully to Thurles in a lorry.

One by one we were called to the Barracks to be interrogated. "How many travelled in the lorry."

"I dunno."

"Did you pay money to the driver?"

"No."

"Were you asked to pay any money?"

"No."

"Did you see anyone paying money?"

"No"

"Are you related to the lorry owner?"

"Yes."

The law didn't accept the evidence that Pete had taken relatives to Thurles all for free. A month later he was up in court in Mitchelstown charged with unlawfully carrying passengers in his lorry.

His fine of £30 was scant reward for his heroism in allowing us witness one of the great day's in Cork's hurling history.

As it transpired, most of us who travelled that day ended up following Cork as they contested and won many Munster and All Ireland titles in the decades that followed. Journeys to and from those occasions certainly were more comfortable but lacked the epic nature of the expedition to Thurles on the back of Pete Crowley's milk truck back in 1946.

*Donal Herlihy was born into a family of nine children in Kinsale in 1929. At the time of the story he was 16. He spent most of his working life in the technical department in RTE in Dublin. Married with four children, Donal passed away in 2018 at the age of 88. Additional information for this story was provided by his grandnephew, Colm O'Donovan.*

# Brexy The One-Handed Wonder

### Gerry Tolan, Dublin

In June 1957, as part of an effort to raise money for Ardee's parochial fund, a 7-a-side inter-county Gaelic football tournament was run involving teams from across the north east.

The Balbriggan Pioneers found themselves in the final after winning three tightly contested matches. The extraordinary thing about the young Pioneers team was that their star player, Tony "Brexy" Gildea, had been born with only one hand.

Despite his birth defect, he was not impaired in his fielding, speed, soloing or kicking accuracy. His talents stood out among the other players and drew hordes to support his team and ultimately led his team to victory in the competition.

After the final, the Balbriggan boys gathered in the marquee for the presentation of the prizes. It was to their great surprise and amusement that the club's chairman was not presented with a cup, plaque or even medals but instead with tailored suits. The suits were all of various lengths, patterns and colours.

It was later revealed that the attendance at the tournament had far exceeded the parish's expectations. To express their gratitude, it was decided that a substantial prize was in order.

As a result, the Balbriggan Pioneers were blessed and dressed with the most unique of GAA prizes.

# Player Sent Off Twice In Different Countries In The One Day

### Gerry McLaughlin

This story ended up as a GAA exclusive on the front page of the Irish News newspaper in 1992. It was about a player who was unlucky enough to get sent off twice in the one day – in two different countries.

Eddie Duffy was always a larger than life character. He was one of the mainstays of the Omagh St Enda's GAA team when they won a county title in 1988.

He was playing as a 'banger' for a team in London against Tir Conaill Gaels in the London Championship on a fine summer's afternoon. But Big Eddie had a major problem as he was also due to line out against Omagh's bitter rivals, Ardboe, in the Tyrone championship later that evening. Time was passing and Eddie would need to rush if he was to catch a flight to Aldergrove.

According to an eye-witness Eddie, to give himself sufficient time to get home, apologised in advance to one of the opposition before committing an act that ensured he was immediately sent off.

Having successfully negotiated an early walk to the dressing room, he gathered his things and rushed to the airport to catch the flight. He was the last man on board, and only barely made it despite a mad dash through the airport to the gate from which the plane was departing.

Fortunately, the flight went like clockwork and he landed in and was out the front door of Aldergrove in no time. When he came through the door, a number of friends were in a car with the engine running, ready to bring him to Pomeroy for the match against Ardboe.

This game didn't need further fuel to rouse the dander in both sets of players but with all the rushing and the memory of an earlier sending off, Eddie was supercharged for battle.

From the throw-in, it was hot and heavy with plenty of hard hitting and melees breaking out every so often. Eddie was never far from the action, so much so that he caught the eye of the referee and was invited to take an early shower for the second time that afternoon-evening.

When I was first told about the story, I found it hard to believe despite the fact that it had come from excellent sources in London and in East Tyrone. Copies of the referees' reports on the games backed up the story. Eddie had managed to break a number of rules, from playing illegally in London to playing again only hours after he had been sent off.

Under rule, he faced a suspension of a year and his club would have been thrown out of the Tyrone senior championship in a year when they had a real good team. Naturally St Enda's appealed the case to the Ulster Council but there was strong documentary evidence against them.

When the story appeared on the front page, there was a huge reaction with many expressing anger because we published it in the first place, notwithstanding that the article was correct.

The upshot saw Omagh thrown out of the Tyrone SFC, Eddie was suspended and under rule, the club secretary and chairman should have been suspended too, but that did not happen.

Like all good stories, there was another twist in the tale. Some locals were not amused and sent me a fake report concerning a melee at another match.

Presumably, they hoped I would print it and get into trouble because if they could prove what I published was untrue in that incident, it would cast doubt on the validity of my other account about the double sending off in the one day.

In fact even years later I know there are GAA people who hold it against me that I wrote that story. Of course, it was journalistic gold dust and any penman worth his salt would have no option but to run with it.

There are always players who line out in London and other areas playing as 'bangers' but this was the first time that it was uncovered in such unique circumstances.

*Journalist Gerry McLaughlin is a native of Meenaleck, The Rosses in Donegal. He is married to Agnes Kelm, a member of a famed Fermanagh GAA family. Although neither was born in the county, Gerry and his brother Liam both captained Fermanagh senior teams, with Liam leading the footballers to a NFL quarter-final in 1980 and Gerry skipper of the senior hurlers in the early eighties.*

# Ag Bualadh Báire Leis Na Síoga

Lá amháin sa bhliain AD 1800 d'fhág Ned Mistéil a chábán in aice le Cnoc Tua, Contae na Gaillimhe. Bhí a laí ar a ghualainn aige agus é ag dul ag baint fataí sa ghort. Bhí sé díreach tar éis tosú nuair a tháinig sí gaoithe a bhain a chaipín de agus a scuab léi é. Leag Ned a laí uaidh agus rith sé i ndiaidh a chaipín ach bhí an caipín ag imeacht uaidh. Lean sé air ag rith go dtí gur laghdaigh an ghaoth.

Ag an am seo bhí sé leath bealaigh suas Cnoc Meá. Rug sé greim ar a chaipín agus chuir sé ar ais ar a cheann é. Lig sé a scíth ar chloch mhór. Go tobann tháinig fear os a chomhair. D'iarr Ned air cé as a dtáinig sé chomh sciobtha sin. "Bí socair anois," arsa an strainséir, "ba mhaith liom cúpla focal a bheith agam leat," agus chuir sé é féin in aithne do Ned, ag rá gur Finnbhearra an t-ainm a bhí air.

D'inis Finnbhearra dó go raibh comórtas báire socraithe idir Shióga Chnoc Meá, Contae na Gaillimhe, a fhoireann, agus Síoga Bhearnán Éile, Contae Thiobraid Árann. Bhí sé cloiste ag Finnbhearra go raibh an t-iománaí is fearr i gCúige Laighean le bheith ar fhoireann Bhearnán Éile.

D'iarr Finnbhearra ar Ned dul ag bualadh báire ar a fhoireann mar go raibh cáil Neid mar fhear camáin cloiste aige. Dúirt Ned go n-imreodh sé agus chuaigh sé abhaile chun a chamán a fháil.

Dúirt sé lena bhean gan a bheith ag súil leis abhaile an oíche sin ach níor inis sé di cén fáth. Bhí sé faoi mhionn ag Finnbhearra gan aon rud a rá faoin gcluiche. Ag an am a bhí socraithe thosaigh an cluiche ar pháirc an bháire i gCnoc Mheá. Bhí seaimpín Chúige Laighean ag imirt ar fud na páirce. Bhí buaille thar cionn aige agus ní raibh aoinne in ann dúshlán a thabhairt dó.

Bhí Ned ina chúl báire ach nuair a chonaic sé céard a bhí ag tarlú chuir sé síóg sa chúl agus chuaigh sé féin amach in agaidh an churaidh. Bhí na coimhlintí idir an bheirt go han-ghéar agus amanta bhí sé brúidiúil. Bhí splancanna le feiceáil ag teacht ó na camáin. Rith na fir chróga seo suas síos an pháirc. Bhí an bheirt i ngleic lena chéile go minic. Ag deireadh an chluiche bhí an sliotar ag teacht i dtreo na beirte go hard sa spéir. Léim seaimpín Laighean ar dtús. Agus é ag léim thug Ned buille sa bhrollach dó agus leag sé amach é. Bhí sé gan aithne, gan urlabhra agus b'in deireadh leis sa chluiche. Gan ach cúpla orlach fágtha ar chamán Neid chuir sé an sliotar idir na cúilíní agus bhí an bua ag foireann Chnoc Meá.

Nuair a bhí an cluiche thart d'ardaigh na sióga Ned ar a nguaillí agus mháirseáil siad timpeall na páirce leis. Bhí ríméad ar an lucht leanúna. Tugadh go dtí an pálás faoi Chnoc Meá é agus chaith sé oíche iontach leis na sióga draíochta. Bhí an ghrian ag dul faoi agus é ag déanamh a bhealaigh abhaile an tráthnóna ina dhiaidh sin. Bhí sé tuirseach traochta agus nuair a shroich sé a theach chuaigh sé díreach a chodladh gan leithscéal a ghabháil lena bhean chéile nuair a d'iarr sí air cá raibh sé.

An mhaidin dár gcionn d'éirigh a bhean ar dtús agus chuaigh sí go dtí an chistin. Baineadh geit aisti nuair a chonaic sí bó iontach ag féachaint uirthi tríd an bhfuinneog. D'oscail sí an doras agus shiúil an bhó díreach isteach sa chistin. Rith sí go dtí an seomra leapa agus d'iarr sí ar Ned teacht go bhfeicfeadh sé an bhó a bhí sa chistin.

Nuair a tháinig an bheirt ar ais bhí bó agus lao ann. Bhí a fhios ag Ned gur bronntanais ó na sióga a bhí aige. Bhí Finnbhearra go maith do dhaoine a chabhraigh leis.

*Story sourced by William Henry and translated by Mary McGrath*

# A Scór Night Of Error When Robert Emmet Captained Kerry

## Joe Hunt

When Scór was in its infancy in the early 1970s, the adjudication system wasn't of the high standard that generally we find today.

For example when Westmeath's Séamus Ó Faoláin contacted Longford official Jimmy Fox requesting "good adjudicators" for a Westmeath semi-final in Castletown-Geoghegan, there seemed to be no problem. Jim organised his groups of priests from St Mel's College and nuns from the town's Convent of Mercy.

Nothing was left to chance and nothing could go wrong – or could it? As zero hour approached, Mr Fox found to his dismay that like the gospel story, none of those invited could come. He was forced to travel with a much-depleted team of Tommy Nevin and Paddy Doris. With due respect this trio would hardly regard themselves as competent judges regarding the finer points on Rince Fóirne or Rince Seit.

On arrival at a packed hall, they were asked by Seamus if the other adjudicators were travelling separately and if so, would they arrive imminently?

"You're looking at them all," Jimmy confessed.

Seamus almost conked out and contemplated calling the whole show off. But other counsels prevailed and competitions began.

Contrary to his expectations, the Rince Fóirne presented no problems as one particular group were clearly superior and nailed on winners. Just like with all the other disciplines except for the Rince Seit. The Downs club and the home club were obviously very evenly matched with both setting an extremely high standard.

The adjudicators were in trouble and they knew it – and only a miracle could save them. Then they got it when one of the girls at the back had a flapping lace. This was seen by the eagle-eyed Doris and when mentioned was like manna from heaven for his colleagues who immediately gave the thumbs up to the other team. Saved by a shoelace but honour in tact nonetheless.

Afterwards Séamus shepherded the trio out a side door and down the street to this home where they were wined and dined by his late mother.

"Lads, ye did a great job but never do that to me again," Seamus said as he waved goodbye to the Longford car in the wee hours as they headed for home.

Seán Donnolly, Longford full-forward on the 1968 Leinster title-winning team was also a Scór adjudicator of some ability. In the early seventies, Seán took a team of competent adjudicators, competent that is in disciplines other than dancing and instrumental music to a Munster semi-final. Moltóirí from elsewhere would judge music and dancing, they were told in advance.

Those judges never turned up however and the Longford quartet was foisted with the added responsibility. In the circumstances, Solomon could have done little better. In both Rincí competitions, two groups were nominated to advance to the Munster finals while the toss of a coin decided the Ceol Uirlise winners.

Unorthodox adjudication is by no means confined to specific competitions or decades of time. For example, a Longford quizmaster was once in charge of the Roscommon Tráth na gCeist Final. There were six clubs, 18 individuals in all on stage that night in the Dr Hyde Centre. All went well until the round of general knowledge was reached. A slight problem presented itself as there were no questions prepared due to an oversight. The forgetful quizmaster showed no reaction and kept his cool by drawing on his own experience and asking questions from memory while staring at a blank page. With the exception of the scorekeeper and timekeeper, no one on stage noticed anything amiss.

The incident of the carbon copy quiz happened in Longford in the very first Scór of 1969. Four semi-finals were held at different venues on the one night. Entrusted with supplying questions and answers for the Tráth na gCeist final, the county secretary hit on the idea of using carbon sheets to provide identical sets at all venues. One particular quizmaster emphasised the questions weren't his and accordingly he would have to accept the answers supplied from "headquarters" as he said.

However, in the process of doing the carbon copying, one sheet slipped resulting in the answering sequence being transposed. The first question of the night asked the name of that year's Kerry football captain. Without hesitation the contestant correctly answered: "Johnny Culloty."

"Sorry," responded the quizmaster, "the answer is Robert Emmet."

A closer scrutiny revealed that the history answers had been supplied for the GAA questions and vice versa.

1947

Right: Tommy junior and Dr Niall Moyna, with their dad, Tommy senior (92), outside the family premises in Scotstown last summer (2020) and, above, Tommy (left) and his identical twin Mackie in 1947.
See 'The Phantom Croke Park Sub', Page 17

Mike Burke with Gary Allen in New York jerseys.
See 'Fallout From War In Bronx Landed Down Under', Page 23

Niall Quinn, swapping the Republic of Ireland and Sunderland shirts for the Eadestown colours in 2003.
*See 'From World Cup To Eadestown Junior Bs', Page 29*

'Yarra' Duffy pictured in hospital recovering after being shot as a 16-year-old in Croke Park on Bloody Sunday. Right: an admission ticket for Croke Park on Bloody Sunday.
*See 'Yarra Survived Bloody Sunday Bullet To Star For Dubs', Page 33*

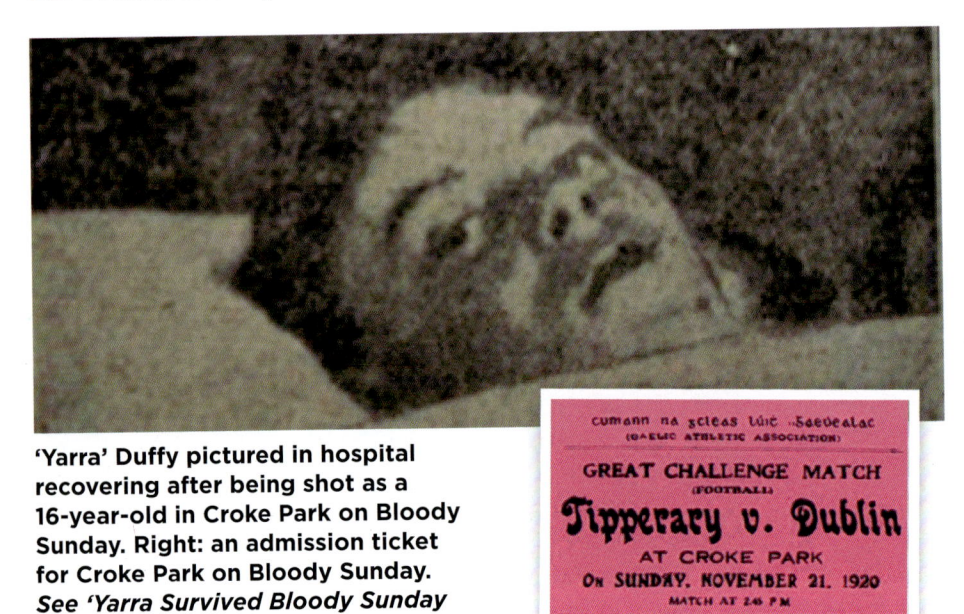

cumann na gcleas lúit ṡaeḋealac
(GAELIC ATHLETIC ASSOCIATION)

GREAT CHALLENGE MATCH
(FOOTBALL)
Tipperary v. Dublin
AT CROKE PARK
On SUNDAY, NOVEMBER 21, 1920
MATCH AT 2.45 P.M.

ADMISSION                    1/-

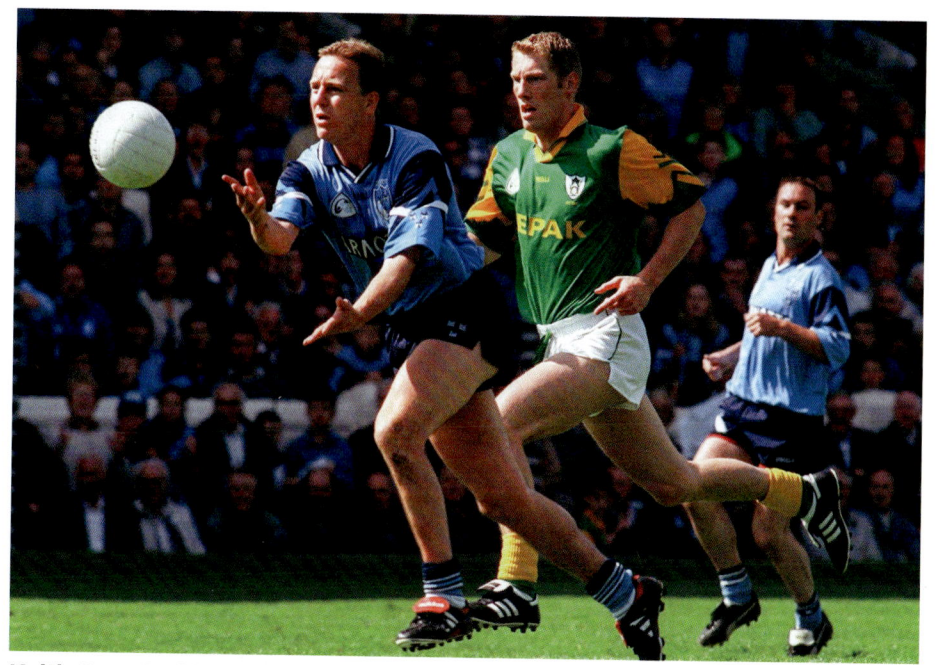

Keith Barr (Dublin) in action against Meath's Graham Geraghty in the Leinster championship of 1997. *See 'Getting A Kick Out Of Football In The Rare Ould Times Page 37*

Nicky Rackard, the hurling giant from Wexford. *See 'Tears That Became Part Of Nicky Rackard's Finest Hour', Page 45*

**Michael O'Hehir's enduring legacy is mirrored in the fact that he is the most often mentioned name in this collection. He is also the subject of two stories.** *See 'Memories Of My Dad, Michael O'Hehir', Page 61, and 'Legendary Voice Turned Into Medic', Page 63*

Seán Boylan transformed Meath during his 23 years in charge.
See 'A Different View Of The 1996 Meath-Mayo Fracas', Page 89

Dr Cullen Park today but back in 1960 it was attempting to modernise. See 'Gate Opening That Cost Carlow Thousands', Page 95

Actor Barry John Kinsella poses as Michael (Mick) Hogan who was one of the 14 victims of Bloody Sunday in Croke Park. *See 'Michael Hogan's Girlfriend On Bloody Sunday Was...?', Page 107*

Seamus Cleere and his bride Joan on their wedding day in 1967 with Kilkenny players forming a hurling guard of honour.
They are (l-r): Paddy Moran, Fr Tommy Murphy 1963 team, Liam Cleere, 1957 team, Larry Cleere, Sam Carroll, Jim Treacy.
*See 'I Was A Sixties 'Wag' – And Proud Of It', Page 99*

John Kelly scores for Kildare against Kerry in Newbridge 1980.
*See 'Sons Starred For Kildare But Mother Only Had Eyes For Páidí', Page 111*

**Re-united:** Former classmates at Thomond College, Limerick get together many years later. They are (l-r): Hugo Clerkin (Monaghan), Joe Mulligan (Offaly), Brian Mullins (Dublin), Liam Fardy (Wexford), Larry McCarthy (Cork and current GAA President), Fran Ryder (Dublin) and Teddy Owens (Cork). *See Liam Fardy's story 'Scaling New Heights In New York', Page 115*

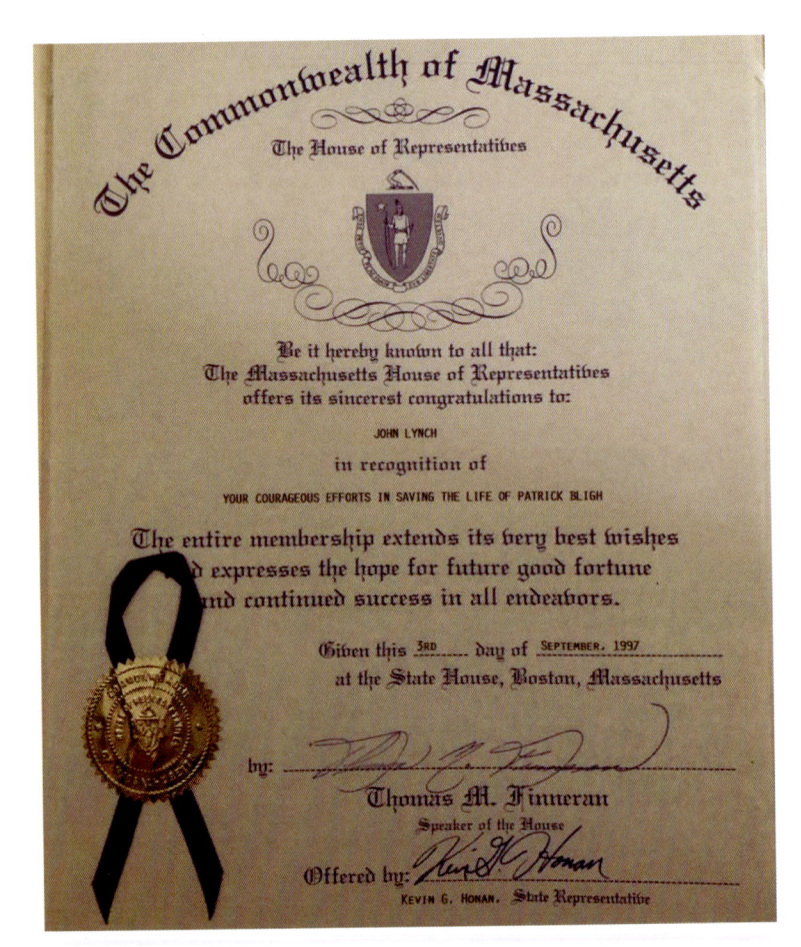

A 'Citation of Bravery' for Tyrone's John Lynch. *See 'What Happened Next After Ref Sent Me Off', Page 139*

Christy Ring – the central character in many stories in this book, and not always playing hurling.
*See 'Pushing Myself To Beat Christy Ring',
Page 155*

## CAMOGIE GAME ALLEGATIONS LEAD TO OFFICIAL INQUIRY

Westmeath Camogie Board officials are to hold an investigation into the Co. Westmeath junior camogie final between Tang and Cullion in an effort to discover whether or not a boy dressed up as a girl had played on the winning Cullion team. The match was played in Moate at the end of October.

The decision to hold the investigation came after a meeting of the board in Mullingar. Mr. Larry Coughlan, the Tang delegate, alleged that during the first half of the game the Cullion team included a boy dressed a' a girl and said that he was easily noticeable by his good hurling and running.

Mr. Coughlan said that they had tried to get into the Cullion dressing-room at half-time, but were refused. Later some of the Tang officials saw a man and what appeared to be three women leave the dressing room and travel by car along the Tullamore road. They followed and the car turned back into Moate. He alleged that the three people who appeared to be women went up a laneway. One of the ladies took off her coat and gave it to a person dressed as a player. There was something wrong when that was going on, he said.

Mr. Coughlan siad that he saw another girl come on in the second half, but the person whom they alleged was a boy did not come back on after half-time.

His allegation was that the boy dressed as a girl changed and the uniform was given to a girl who was then brought into the game.

Nan Rabbitte, a Tang player, said that she was playing at centre field and saw the particular player, whose headscarf blew up revealing a boy's haircut. She also saw the player fall on the ground and then became satisfied that it was a boy.

Mr. M. Power, Cullion, said that if Tang felt they had a grievance they should have approached the Chairman and secretary of the board, who were at the game, and the matter could be investigated there and then. A ladies dressing room, however, was no place for men to try and enter.

Mr. Coughlan said that the girl who was "playing on the player" was detailed to examine the player when the whistle went, but the player immediately ran to the dressing room at half-time.

Commdt. D. O'Callaghan, chairman of Westmeath G.A.A. County Board, said this matter should be investigated in fairness to both sides. If what was alleged had happened it was a despicable thing and something should be done about it and if it did not happen Cullion should be fully cleared.

Bernard Flynn of Meath in action against Dublin in the Leinster championship at Croke Park in 1991. Photo by David Maher/Sportsfile.
See 'Breaking In To Local Hospital After Our Daughter's Birth', Page 195

Left: The 'Leitrim Observer' newspaper carries a report on a camogie game where a male played in a Westmeath final.
See 'About A Boy Who Played Camogie', Page 157

Author, columnist and Listowel publican Billy Keane with his son John supporting Kerry against Dublin in 2013.
*See 'Writing The History Of Phantom Pregnancy Final', Page 217*

Michael Duignan, seen here in action against Cork's Brian Corcoran in 2000, is now a voice of the GAA and Offaly Co Board Chairman.
*See 'Memories Of Unbelievable Coincidence And An Action-Packed Day', Page 233*

Joe Connolly, lifting the Liam MacCarthy Cup. *See 'Forgetting My "Name" While Playing Féile Illegally In Roscommon', Page 271*

Nudie Hughes pictured playing against Kerry in the All Ireland semi-final of 1985. See 'Fun And Games On And Off The Field', See Page 289

Micheál Ó Muircheartaigh is a great GAA ambassador.
See 'Micheál's Voice Transported Us To The Land Of Tír Na nÓg', Page 319

Kilmore captain Jimmy Connellan is presented with the Fahey Cup by Roscommon County Chairman Micheál O'Callaghan following Kilmore's historic SF Championship victory in 1983.
*See 'Whatever Happened To The Fahey Cup?', Page 321*

Senator Bobby Kennedy shakes hands with Louth's Frank Lynch before the Cardinal Cushing game in Gaelic Park, New York in 1965. See Frank's story Page 75. The man in the middle with the whistle is referee on the day Peter Nolan, the famed Offaly and New York defender.
*See 'By The Way, You Wouldn't Be Anything To...?', Page 323*

Armagh manager Joe Kernan celebrates following his side's 2003 All-Ireland Final victory over Kerry at Croke Park. See 'Inch By Inch, Row By Row', Page 327

George Cartwright on Cavan's feud of the last century.
See 'Winners Forged From Feuding Cornafean-Slashers' Rivalry', Page 357

Paddy McFlynn, the former GAA President seen here with former Taoiseach Garret Fitzgerald, got into hot water as a player.
See 'Chairman Sends Off County Secretary And Future GAA President', Page 391

## A SCÓR NIGHT OF ERROR WHEN ROBERT EMMET CAPTAINED KERRY

Times have changed and the rules governing adjudication have been amended and updated over the years. Transparency is now essential and judges must submit written comments justifying their decisions.

Marking systems are clearly defined under different headings and the book of guidelines and rules caters for almost every eventuality.

This professional approach is essential if Scór is to survive successfully through this century. But some of us still look back nostalgically to the days and nights when a decision hinged on a loose shoe lace or the toss of a coin or to Robert Emmet captaining Kerry.

*Joe Hunt is a retired national school principal who lives near Ardagh in Co Longford. The Ballinahown, Co Offaly native has particular interests in the GAA, bridge and history. He is also a quiz enthusiast and has won many major competitions, including two All-Ireland Tráth na gCeist titles.*

# Paddy Writes His Own Long John Story

Jamesie Murphy

In the Kilkenny junior football championship of 1928, there was indeed a strange occurrence. Barrow Rovers faced Glory Rovers of Dunamaggin at Mullinavat in an eagerly awaited semi-final.

The Glory Rovers team were on the field when news came that the creamery lorry conveying some of the Barrow Rovers players had broken down. Panic set in when the latter found they had only the bare 15 players. Further panic ensued when it was discovered one player had forgotten his togs.

The Rovers were prepared to field with 14 when the said player, the bold Paddy G piped up: "I won't let ye down." He then proceeded to pull down his trousers, roll up the legs of his Long Johns and prepared himself for action.

A right good match he played too in this unique lower body strip, as he helped his team to victory. Further success awaited him and his comrades when Barrow Rovers won the Kilkenny final beating Cloneen 1-3 to 1-1 later on that year – and this time he had a proper togs on.

# 'Breaking In' To Local Hospital After Our Daughter's Birth

## Bernard Flynn

You remember the build up to important firsts in your life but in my case the arrival of my first child also had me in deep trouble

Jessie was born on April 30, 1995 in Mullingar General Hospital. I had just pulled down the curtain on my inter-county career with Meath a few months beforehand, but on the local front the Shamrocks club had a good senior football team and were on a roll. We had completed a three-in-a-row of Westmeath senior titles and were going for a fourth successive championship.

Eddie Casey was a teammate during that time and was and is a very good friend of mine. He is also a good businessman and ran the successful nightclub called 'The Final Fence' at the time.

Everyone in the squad knew Madeleine and I were about to become parents and when the word got out that our daughter Jessie had arrived, I got a huge amount of congratulatory texts and phone calls.

It had been a long and hard labour on Madeleine and I headed away from the hospital at about half seven in the evening because she was exhausted and needed to sleep.

I was on such a high and so proud that at 30 years of age, I was a father. I wanted to go out to celebrate the occasion. Eddie was of like mind and so were my two pals, Mick King and James Tormey.

We went on a right tear for the night and then when the pubs closed, Eddie said he had arranged a spot for us to continue our celebrations at his nightclub out the road.

By the time they were clearing up after the night there at about half three, I was "well on it" as they say. The drink had brought out the romantic in me and I told the boys that even though it was a crazy thought, I wanted to go back up to the hospital to kiss Madeleine good night and tell her I loved her.

James had the jeep outside and said himself and Mick would go up with me and wait while I went inside. Even in my half-inebriated state, I knew the security people or staff wouldn't let me in at that hour of the night, so

I directed James to go around to a side door which was near to the ward Madeleine was in two floors up.

What followed was a bad attempt to replicate a Mission Impossible scene as James reversed the vehicle up to the door, Mick opened it and I did a Tom Cruise impression by shuffling across the floor on my knees in order to avoid any CCTV cameras.

I tiptoed up the stairs and when I got to the nurses station, I was back in Cruise mode dropping to the floor and sashaying on my knees past the medical point and into the ward. I knew Madeleine was in on the right side so once I opened the door, I was confident of the geography of the room.

I was feeling really proud at how well I had penetrated the hospital without anyone seeing me as I gently rose up onto the bed, put my arm around my wife and told her how much I loved her.

My words were met with an ear-splitting scream that shook the stillness of the night. Immediately, I could hear feet running along the corridors towards the room and lights came on everywhere in the ward, along the corridors and even outside.

Fortunately a number of the nurses who ran to the ward to check what was happening were well-known to me – at the time we had a shop called Albany Home Décor in the middle of the town and they were very good customers of ours.

"Bernard Flynn, what are you doing here in the middle of the night?" one of them asked.

I tried to explain that I had gone out for a few drinks and just wanted to give Madeleine a hug before I went home. I now looked at the woman in the bed beside me and I noticed for the first time that it was not my wife who I had just hugged and kissed.

Naturally, the lady in question was upset which, under the bizarre circumstances, was totally understandable. There was absolute bedlam in the ward and I was in a state of confusion as the nurses led me outside to their station.

There they explained that Madeleine had felt very hot after I left and asked to be moved to the window bed, so the nurses swopped her over. They told me that the other woman had later given birth to her child and was put into the original Madeleine bed after delivery. The nurses also had given Madeleine a few tablets to help her sleep and luckily for me she slept through the whole fracas I caused when I went back in.

With a full lockdown in operation following my 'break in,' the nurses suggested that the best thing would be for me to make myself scarce as quickly as possible.

## 'BREAKING IN' TO LOCAL HOSPITAL AFTER OUR DAUGHTER'S BIRTH

Outside at the side entrance we must have resembled something akin to the Keystone Cops as James revved the jeep, Mick flung me into the back seat and we headed down the town like a group in a bank robbery getaway car.

It was now way past five o'clock and for someone who had a 'skinful' of drink that night, I was as sober as a judge. I couldn't sleep a wink and decided that I had to go back up first thing in the morning to apologise to the woman and the nurses.

I arrived back up around half eight and rather sheepishly made my way towards the ward. As I approached the entrance, I got the fright of my life when six or seven of the nurses at the station had big smiles on their faces and began clapping as I walked through.

Seemingly in the few hours since my 'break in' the story had gone viral around the hospital. The nurses told Madeleine when she woke up what had happened while she was sleeping.

I should have been in serious trouble for my antics but I knew from Madeleine's face when I approached her bed beside the window that she wasn't going to give me a hard time.

What I was far less sure of was how the woman I had hugged and kissed would take the strange events of the night. Once more I was blessed that the particular lady involved was and is a great GAA woman and because of that connection, she was more inclined to forgive my indiscretion.

Aileen Lawlor was a GAA referee and later went on to become the 29th President of the Camogie Association. A true Dub from a great family of hurling sisters, she had relocated to Westmeath where she lived with her husband Donal.

Of course, I apologised profusely to both of them. I was mortified to tell you the truth but they were both good sports in every sense.

Madeleine later told me she was initially embarrassed when Aileen recounted the story. As the hours passed that morning, they all seemed to see the funny side and I was extremely lucky that the sheer terror I had caused was seen as a slapdash comical moment by yours truly.

The nurses too were great – they saw that I was the worse for wear that morning and gave me a few tablets which had me feeling fine by the time I left the ward.

As I went outside who should I bump into but the best man at my wedding, Mick Dempsey, who people will remember as Brian Cody's right hand man during the recent years of Kilkenny hurling domination.

Mick was delighted to hear the news of Jessie's arrival and insisted that we celebrate with a wet lunch. That evening we ended up in Dublin and by the time I got back to see Madeleine 24 hours later, I knew that this time there would be no round of applause as I went into the ward to see her. I would have to face the music on my own.

*Bernard Flynn is a former All Ireland winning forward in '87 and '88 with Meath and was honoured twice by the All Star selectors. Married to Madeleine, they have three grown-up children and live in Mullingar, Co Westmeath. As well as running his own businesses, Bernard has worked for RTE for over two decades as a commentator and is a widely read columnist with the Irish Mirror newspaper.*

# Putting Unholy Order Into My Banger Days

Ricey Scully

Sundays in the sixties were normally a case of what to do after Mass if you were a young GAA player whether your team was still involved in championships or not.

Most counties ran their championships on a knockout basis which meant that if you lost in the first or second rounds, you would end up playing mostly in local tournaments or gold medal competitions.

The particular year and the Sunday I'm writing about was one such year. Offaly had gone out of Leinster, Clara had gone out of Offaly and all the young twentysomethings had to look forward to was a Mill House Cup tournament in our own town every couple of weeks.

Sometimes in the GAA, it can be either a feast or a famine. The particular Sunday, when our game against Daingean was fixed for half seven throw in that evening, was one such occasion.

On that day I was also booked to play in two other counties, starting with a game of hurling in Dublin with Patrick Morans, now known as Geraldine P Morans (where there was an 11.0am throw in against, I think from memory, Clanna Gael in Ringsend). After that, it was a case of switching province and heading for Ulster to tog out for Blacklion in the Cavan junior football championship at 3.30, before making a bee-line home to play in the Sportsfield, in time for the 7.30 throw in.

These opportunities to play were commonplace in the Ireland of that era. The ban was still in vogue and with most people unrecognised outside of their own locality, it meant that the use of illegal players (called bangers or ringers in different parts of the country) was rife.

The trick on the day you were impersonating someone else on the pitch was to keep a low profile so that you didn't get in trouble. You also had to keep it quiet at home because if your own club chairman or county secretary heard what you were up to, it could lead to a suspension and unwarranted headlines from a county board or club meeting where such shenanigans would be adjudicated on.

We were wanted for the early hurling match in Dublin because a Clara native, Hughie Ennis, was deeply involved with the Patrick Moran's club. A renowned Blacklion native Tommy Dolan came to live in Clara in the fifties and immediately immersed himself into our local club. But his heart was also with his native heath in West Cavan where emigration had robbed the area of many good footballers.

Anxious to keep the club going, it was through his organisation that the Clara carload often headed north on summer Sundays. It got so regular at one stage that the reporter in the local newspaper up there, the Anglo-Celt, described 'The Black' team as they were known as "the club of many accents!"

On this particular Sunday it was a case of getting our timing right. Jimmy 'Baney' Roche, who was a nephew of Hughie Ennis, picked me up outside Tom Naughton's shop in Clara at 9am sharp for the first leg to Dublin. 'Baney' had to be back in Clara for a family occasion in the afternoon so he wasn't pencilled in for the Cavan trip.

Tommy Dolan was bringing his load of players, Noel O'Brien, Joe McGrath and Peter Tuohey on later and the plan was that they would drive to Dublin, pick me up after the Patrick Morans game and head north for Cavan.

Unlike officials down the country where games would often run later than advertised, the refs in Dublin were punctual and by the time we arrived at the pitch around quarter to eleven, he was already togged out and checking the goalposts.

That match was a pleasure to play in and because both 'Baney' and I myself had played a bit of hurling with Offaly, we found the standard in terms of skill maybe better but in terms of aggression something less than we were used to on home terrain.

However, although there was no skin and hair flying, the fact that no one wore helmets then meant you were liable to pick up an injury from a loose pull. That is exactly what happened to me near the end of the game that left me needing stitches.

Fortunately, there was a doctor attending the game so as I got togged in with the Cavan car revving outside and Tommy Dolan pointing at his wrist watch, the doctor inserted two or three stitches in my forehead and put a loose plaster over it as I told him I had another match to play in the afternoon.

The medical treatment slowed down our planned departure as it was close to one o'clock before we headed across the Liffey. Luckily while the roads weren't the best then, there were very few cars out on a Sunday and we made great time, pulling up at the hotel at 2.45 where we got our first bit to eat since leaving the midlands.

## PUTTING UNHOLY ORDER INTO MY BANGER DAYS

We then met up with our teammates for the afternoon game, were given our new names for the day (Peter Tuohey wrote his name on his hand so he wouldn't forget it in the heat of battle) and ran out to uphold the honour of Dolan's local club.

We always enjoyed the games up there – they were played with a passion and you could tell what winning meant to their supporters. We won on that particular day – that made it two wins out of two. It was now approaching five o'clock in the afternoon and the boys wanted to have a few pints after the game, which meant that I, as the resident pioneer in the group, had to drive the car back. Mind you, I was used to it because on the days we had no late match to worry about, we'd go back to Tommie's cousin Jimmy Dolan's where you seldom had to put your hand in your pocket, and it would often be the early hours before we loaded up for home with me in charge of the vehicle.

We had one run of games in Cavan where the word got around in Offaly that the Clara lads were gone every other week. I was particularly friendly with John Dowling, the Tullamore man who was Offaly county secretary at the time and later would go on to become President of the GAA.

John bumped into me in O'Connor Square, Tullamore one day and asked where I had been the previous two Sundays. As I mumbled some gibberish in place of a truthful answer, he said: "You want to be careful. I hear you and a few of the lads are playing so well at the moment that you might be called into the Cavan panel for the National League."

John would pull a pretend cross face and then burst out laughing. "Anyway," he went on, "it won't be happening again. I was onto the Cavan secretary and we agreed to fix Clara matches at the same time as the club you are playing with up there from now on."

That ended those northern trips for us and as a footnote, I was sad to learn that a short time later the Blacklion club as was, ceased to exist and later became part of Shannon Gaels, which incorporated a wider district in that area.

At this remove, readers are entitled to ask how we got away with what we did? After all opponents would have known what we were up to. The answer was: 'Let him who has not sinned cast the first stone' for as sure as apples are apples, if there were four Clara lads lining out for Blacklion, there was as many, if not more, lining out for our opponents on any given day.

My 'banger' days came to an end following a scary experience I had playing in Tipperary. My link with a club down there came about through a man named Paddy Maher who was from that part of the world but was working on the Ballycumber water scheme a few miles from Clara.

Paddy and I became friends over the time he was in and around Offaly and one day he asked me if I would play a championship football match for Rockwell Rovers down in Golden. He told me that I'd have to go in under the guise of being from the nearby Rockwell College where coincidentally, a Kenneth Scully was a priest.

I had played a match down in Limerick for Tournafulla earlier that summer and the experience there was less than memorable, though it was of our own making. A Clara player with me who normally excelled in defence was asked if he wouldn't mind playing in goal as their usual goalkeeper was injured.

Within ten minutes, we were three goals behind and my townsman wasn't exactly covering himself in glory. It didn't help that I ran half the field to shout: "You've a better chance of saving the shot if you dive before the ball is in the back of the net."

I'm sure the locals were bemused to see what happened next as the makeshift 'keeper and my travelling companion ran out of goal in hot pursuit of my head. He would have killed me if he caught me, I'd say. Frank McLoughlin, the Garda sergeant in Tournafulla, who won Offaly championships with me, was mortified at our behaviour and was as good as his word when he told us he'd never ask us to play for him again.

So when the Tipperary offer came up, I was a bit reluctant at first to accede to Paddy's request to show up at Golden for the 3.0pm throw-in at a match which the great referee, Johnny Moloney, officiated. As far as I can remember, it was the Junior A championship and the night before I embarked on the drive south, I called over to the then St Anthony's Franciscan Novitiate in Clara and one of the brothers there gave me an ecclesiastical collar and clerical shirt in case I needed to become Fr. Scully for the day.

I arrived in Tipp in my civvies to meet my new teammates in the dressing-room and once the game started, all the play was directed towards me. I know this sounds a bit far-fetched but I can sum up the outcome of the hour's football like this – we won 0-10 to 0-9, I scored the ten points and I even got into the goal in the last minute to save a penalty.

It was to be expected then that when the losing team were looking for someone to vent their frustration on, they didn't have to look beyond me, especially after I saved the penalty.

They smelled a rat over my bone fides and were baying for blood shortly after Johnny Moloney sounded the final whistle. Immediately I too smelled danger and knew the longer I stayed around, the greater chance I had of landing myself in deep, deep trouble.

## PUTTING UNHOLY ORDER INTO MY BANGER DAYS

I sprinted towards my car outside the pitch and when I noticed that a fair few vociferous fans of the other team followed me, my fears were confirmed.

I had left the car unlocked but unfortunately had put the ignition key in my trousers pocket so it meant I couldn't just jump into the driver's seat and speed away. Which is what I wanted to do.

As I opened the boot to get the ignition key, I saw the clerical collar and black ecclesiastical regalia beside my clothes. I took the Rockwell jersey off and immediately put the white collar around my neck and the black shirt which was latched onto it.

When I turned around the mob, which was forming a semi-circle around the back of the car, recoiled like Dracula after being confronted with a crucifix.

"Oh Father," one of them said, "We didn't know you were from the college."

Then a priest, obviously believing the ruse of my holy background, stepped forward and invited me back up for Sunday tea to the college.

"God bless you all," I said, "but I've an urgent errand to run to save a man's life."

And that was the truth because I was referring to myself and I knew that if anyone twigged as to who I really was, I'd be lynched.

Seemingly in the aftermath, there was a right furore over who the 'disappearing priest' actually was, so much so that Paddy told me the Tipp GAA authorities had launched an inquiry into the game before opting to stage a replay.

"It's on next Sunday," Paddy revealed when I met him a few weeks after the first game. "I don't suppose you'd be available to play again, would you?"

*Eamon 'Ricey' Scully is a native of Clara and a former Offaly hurler and footballer. Well-known as a radio presenter and a band leader on the music circuit, he is now retired. He is married with four adult children.*

# Minor's March Of Time On Sideline

Sean Nugent

Tipp and Cork were playing a Munster minor hurling championship match in Páirc Uí Chaoimh. It was a great game with little or nothing between the sides.

There was great excitement as play swung from side to side. Patrons were very impressed with the level of skill shown by the young players.

It was noticed that Cork had a sub warming up on the line and it looked like he was coming on but then he went back to his place on the subs' bench.

This was repeated for quite some time as the same player warmed up, looked like coming on but was sent back to the bench once more.

With 10 minutes to go he appears again to do his warm-up routine. A frustrated Rebel fan in a strong Cork accent shouted: "For God's sake, lads, put him on or he will be overage."

# The Great St Mel's College Breakout Of 1963

## Denis Glennon

'*It is not the literal past, the 'facts' of history, that shape us, but images of the past embodied in language*" – Translations by Brian Friel

Like all schools with an exceptional sporting history, St. Mel's College, Longford is justly proud of its record in Gaelic football, winning four All-Ireland Hogan Cup titles, 29 Leinster senior colleges titles, 15 Leinster junior colleges successes and four U-14 Leinster titles since the school first entered competitive football in 1928.

The students of each successful sporting era have their own special memories of great players, scoring deeds, powerful defenders, exceptional fielders, valiant foes and lucky breaks.

One event holds a unique place in the annals of the college and is recorded for posterity in two books on the history of St. Mel's. The first called 'St. Mel's of Longford a History 1865-1990' published in 1996 by the late Eugene McGee, (journalist, newspaper editor and All-Ireland winning football manager with Offaly 1982). The second book was by me called 'Selected Memories St. Mel's College 1865-2015' to celebrate the 150th anniversary of the school.

The 1960s saw the school reach its sporting zenith when winning two All Ireland titles after reaching four successive finals. In that golden era, five Leinster senior titles and five Leinster junior successes were also celebrated.

To be allowed out to attend a Leinster or All-Ireland final was an occasion to be savoured by boarders, even by those with little interest in sport, as in all boarding schools at the time they were not allowed home during school term. Before big matches there was always an atmosphere of great excitement in the college with chanting and singing in anticipation of the match and the hoped for victory.

St. Mel's had won the All Ireland title in 1962 and were on course for back-to-back Hogan cups. Football fever was running high even among the non-participating students who were looking forward to attending the game and cheering on the team.

The mischievous gods, however, were about to put a spoke in the wheel of the excited boarders who planned to attend the final. They were informed by the president, Fr. Lennon (RIP) that they would not be allowed to attend the All Ireland final against St. Brendan's Killarney.

He had previously refused the standard request of the prefects on behalf of the boarders to go to the semi-final game against St. Colman's, Newry, which was played in Kells.

The story around what became known as the St Mel's breakout was provided by the late Dr. Peter Heraty, a senior student at the time. "For the All-Ireland semi-final, the prefects made the usual request to the president to attend the game. In previous years this request was no more than a formality and therefore we were all dumbfounded when Fr. Lennon said, 'No'.

"When pressed for a reason for his refusal, he claimed that it was because some expensive chairs had been broken in the college parlour the night of the Leinster final and also it was reported that some non-playing seniors had been 'drinking'. Some players were said to have had a celebratory drink after the Leinster Final. We asked what the damage was and he said it amounted to £15.

"We knew that the president had a soft spot for the African missions so we organised a whiparound among the students and collected £20 . We went to the president and gave him the £20 which he accepted for the missions but he still said 'No'."

The semi-final ban was reluctantly adhered to and St. Mel's beat St Colman's without any boarders among the supporters. Now for the final against St. Brendan's Killarney.

The ban by the president on attending the final was a bridge too far for the students. Desperate situations demanded desperate remedies as far as the pupils were concerned. They defied the president and organised a mass breakout on the Sunday morning in time to catch the 10.25am train from Longford station to Dublin. In Peter Heraty's words: "A military style operation was put in place by the seniors for 90 boarders to break out and travel to Croke Park by train. Considered too young, the first years were excluded from the plan."

It was agreed that 10 seniors, who were not prefects, would act as group leaders, with each taking responsibility for nine students, collecting the ticket money of a £1 per head and the purchase of train tickets with the help of dayboys. The fare was actually 17 shillings and six pence with the first leader of a group of nine to reach the station receiving a free ticket.

It was normal on Sunday mornings for the students to have a prayer meditation period in the college chapel at 10.0am and a bell was rung to announce the start of this service. On the morning of the final, it was arranged that the bell would not be rung until 10.10am and this acted as the signal for the 'escapees' to dash across the senior field onto the Bishop's Road (also known as the Ballinalee Road) and then run the short journey to the railway station.

All 10 groups raced across the senior field, the only physical obstacle being the college boundary hedge all along the Ballinalee Road (also Bishop's Road). It was a sight to behold the mass of students emerging through every gap onto the Ballinalee Road to board the train at the station.

A delayed departure caused great anxiety with prayers invoked that school authorities were not somehow putting an end to the adventure before it had begun. Tension mounted by the minute as rumours spread that the president was on his way to the station to order the students back into the college. Obviously the prayers were answered as the train pulled out of the station, but it was only after it had sped through Mostrim Station that the escapees relaxed.

This escapade had all the hallmarks of a great adventure, with a mixture of youthful enthusiasm, the fear of being discovered and the prospect of watching their own college team win in Croke Park, all adding to the excitement of the day.

The responsibilities of the senior organisers were greater than, perhaps, even they fully appreciated as they had all the worries, concerns and fears which are normally the lot of teachers accompanying students. Fortunately from the organisers point of view, the escapade went off without consequence until they arrived back in Longford.

That night, the team was paraded through Longford on the back of Glennon's Timber lorry and down the college avenue with the intention of observing the traditional celebration and speeches from the college balcony.

The President announced that there would be no celebrations to honour the victory. He asked the team trainer Fr. Jimmy McKeon (RIP) to tell the public to go away but the trainer replied that since he had not asked them to come in to the college grounds, he would not tell them to go away. Finally, at the behest of the president, the crowd drifted away to celebrate elsewhere in the town.

There was an air of unreality for several days afterwards in the college as tension and expectation mounted that something dramatic was about to happen. Then it emerged that the dean of the college, Fr. Peter Bohan (RIP) and Fr. Jimmy McKeon (RIP) had been summoned to Bishop McNamee's residence on the Monday after the game. The president considered the breach of discipline to be so serious that he felt it was a matter for the bishop to adjudicate upon.

Fr. Bohan went in first to speak to his lordship, who was dressed in his full ceremonial robes. Then Fr. McKeon followed and was told: "I couldn't congratulate you even if you had won the championship of Europe."

Fr. McKeon was expecting the worst but was surprised when the conversation drifted into pleasantries such as where the team dined in Dublin. Bishop McNamee was old and infirm at that time and the consensus was that he agreed to go through the motions of appearing to back up the president.

The writer of this account was a second year day student at the time and ended up in Longford County Hospital (The Infirmary) in the week after the final with a broken ankle after being injured in the school Prep leagues (for first and second years).

In the hospital at the same time was the well-known local solicitor, P. M. Farrell (RIP) who had suffered a heart attack amid all the excitement at the final in Croke Park.

PM was on the first St. Mel's team to win the Leinster Senior title in 1928. I made frequent visits up from my ward to the hospital's only private room where he was recuperating. I listened in awe and wonder to this great raconteur giving me his unique and humorous take on life.

A familiar sound near the hospital was the repeated rat-tat-tat of gunfire coming from soldiers shooting in the adjacent Sean Connelly Army Barracks during regular rifle practice. It was a sound familiar to all Longford people at that time.

Humorously PM informed me that I was hearing the senior students involved in the break out being shot in batches at the back handball alleys of the school!

*Denis Glennon is a former pupil and principal of St Mel's College, Longford. Married with three grown up children and three grandchildren, among his many interests are gaelic games and sport generally, an Gaeilge, theatre, reading, community involvement, DIY and gardening. Denis would like to acknowledge the research of Eugene McGee in the compilation of this article. He also wants to highlight the fact that Fr. Lennon was a well-liked teacher and despite this episode, normal friendly relations were resumed within a short period of time.*

# All-Ireland Final Fever Hits The Equator

## Norman Freeman

Nowadays, the All Ireland hurling final can be seen by Irish people all over the world. There will be cheerful and cheering gatherings in front of big television screens in cities and towns on all five continents. Thanks to the internet, to communications satellites circling the globe and astonishing advances in information technology Irish people can see the All-Ireland on their laptops, tablets, PC's, and even mobile phones from Alaska to Zanzibar. During the game itself, excited viewers and listeners from all over the globe can call home, can talk to those actually at the game in Croke Park.

What a change from 50 or 60 years ago. Many of the huge Irish diaspora in all continents came from a background where the Gaelic games were part of daily life and conversation. They longed for news of the All Ireland championship and especially the finals. Some who lived on the western areas of England hoisted aerials onto rooftops to try to pick up Radio Eireann on its medium wave transmission from Athlone. For all others scattered around the world there was no possibility of hearing the big games.

However, people in RTE knew how much it might mean to exiles to hear the All Ireland commentary. The station did not have a global shortwave radio service but in the 1950s an arrangement was made with the colonial authorities in the French Congo to have the match re-broadcast over the powerful shortwave transmitter Radio Brazzaville. The time and the radio frequencies were published in the Irish newspapers. Letters were sent worldwide to men working on oil rigs off the coast of Borneo, round-the-year painters on Brooklyn Bridge, women and men in Australia and Argentina, missionaries living within sight of Mount Kilimanjaro or in Nigeria and the Philippines.

It was great news to people like myself. It was 1956 and I was one of several Irish marine radio officers attached to the Marconi office in the great port city of Mumbai on the west coast of India. We served on ships that stayed east of Suez and many had not been home for a few years.

I was second Radio Officer on a deck-passenger ship that plied between Mumbai and the East African ports of Mombasa, Dar es Salaam and Zanzibar. My boss, the Chief R/O was Irish too but he had been on Eastern Service so long that he knew little about the hurling championship. I told him about the Cork side, powered by players like Christy Ring, Willie John Daly and Josie Hartnett who would be facing a great Wexford team backboned by the Rackard brothers and hurlers like Ned Wheeler and Tim Flood.

Our ship was ploughing across the Arabian Sea towards Africa on the night of the re-broadcast. We sat in the sweltering radio room in our shorts. The equatorial heat was claustrophobic.

We had difficulty finding Brazzaville, despite having the benefit of a powerful marine receiver. The Chief used his tapering nail-bitten fingers to rotate the tuning control. He was in a bad temper. He had been severely reprimanded by the captain for unseemly behaviour with a lady passenger in the first-class bar. In a rage he had flung things about in his cabin and in doing so lost his full set of dentures. His mouth on his gin-soaked face was a sunken slot.

Suddenly he shouted; "Hold on, hold on."

Then, like the genie out of the bottle, the familiar voice of Michael O'Hehir cascaded into the radio room. It was a heart-stirring moment. Our shouts rang out in the tropic night. When the Artane Boys finished playing the national anthem, the roar of over 80,000 spectators came pouring out of the receiver in a landslide of sound. A Lascar seaman, padding barefooted past the door, glanced in with curious eyes.

As the game got under way the rapid-fire commentary evoked the shoulder to shoulder races for the ball, the swing of hurleys, the sliotar soaring through the air with the packed stands as background.

Just after Christy Ring scored a goal from a 21-yard free, the radio room was invaded by several large locust-like creatures that had been blown out into the Indian Ocean from the nearby coast of Somalia. They buzzed about infuriatingly and we cursed as we swatted at them, using the radio log book and the radio message receipt book as implements until we drove them away.

We sat transfixed listening to the great battle for supremacy. The climax was the great save by the Wexford goalkeeper, Art Foley, from a hard shot by Christy Ring and the thundering goal from Nicky Rackard that sealed the game for Wexford.

When Michael O'Hehir signed off and the broadcast ended, we were limp. We both suffered an attack of homesickness. The Chief, who had downed more than several gin and tonics, became tearful. I suppressed some tears myself in case the captain should walk in and think we were both drunk.

*Norman Freeman has published two books on hurling and two based on his seafaring experiences. He is a regular contributor to the Irishman's Diary column in the The Irish Times.*

# Tullogher Rose From Dead To Meet Challenge

Jamesie Murphy

In the 1903 Kilkenny senior football semi-final, a huge attendance descended on the Rower Village to see the action between Tullogher and Glenmore who were age-old rivals. It is recorded that these two teams played 'Cad' long before the advent of Gaelic football.

The Glenmore team and some supporters arrived at the Rower in two Charabangs, long horse-drawn carts with seats. On the tailboard of each they had rather arrogantly painted in large white letters "R.I.P Tullogher". This spurred on the Tullogher boys and their captain, Mickey Neill, in his pre-match address, laid it on the line for his team. "Never mind the Rest in Peace, Tullogher, go out now and Rip into them, Tullogher."

And the team duly carried out the rallying call of their skipper to the full and ended up winning the game 0-7 to 0-3. Incidentally, the self-same war-cry has lasted from 1903 with teams from the parish right down to the present day.

# Award For The Man Who Hated Players

Larry McGann

I had a rule of thumb during my 48 years as secretary of Knocknavanna Gaels GAA club never to talk to journalists other than Eugene McGee, Lord have mercy on him, who I knew had GAA blood in his veins.

The rest of them couldn't be trusted, whether it was the correspondents in Dublin thinking they were important figures in our games because of their power with the pen, or the local alicadoos, who could read the Koran backways quicker than they could decipher how a match was going on before their eyes.

Those boyos were forever looking for team lists which baffled me because by and large it was the same faces playing every year in club junior and senior championship and they never knew who most of them were.

My philosophy from an early stage in my GAA life was to give those buckos as wide a berth as possible. It was the same within the club and county board structures which were largely filled with whippersnappers looking for something for nothing... or something that required little or no dedication.

I admired the handful I met over the years who were in the GAA for the love of it – not for what they get out of it. And I can assure you right now that only for them draconian libel laws out there, I'd love to name you dozens of the lazy robbers who have made up the latter lot since they gave up playing. Professional GAA politicians is what I call them.

I knew one in particular with whom I served on the provincial council back in the sixties and he believed the GAA would be a perfect organisation... if there were no players involved. Always busy in the committee room, he seemed to lose his will for life when he heard the sound of studs on concrete leaving dressing rooms and the roar of the crowd greeting the real stars of the association in the public eye.

That was at total variance with 'Your Man's' own view of GAA life. In it, he was the important one and the players were only pawns to his knight.

Yet, 'Your Man' had the ears of provincial chairmen and GAA presidents down the decades and nothing ever happened in the county without his say-so.

Now as people who used to read the Eugene McGee column in the Independent would know, I was never a great lover of the GPA crowd since they came into existence 20 or 30 years ago.

In fact if I'm being truthful, the only saving grace I could get out of their existence at all was how it used to drive 'Your Man' semi-apoplectic at the mere mention of the organisation's name in his company. Which was one of the reasons why I'd never fail to bring them 'innocently' into whatever conversation we might be having.

Reading McGee every Monday as all GAA people did at that time, 'Your Man' knew where I stood on the issue of the GPA. Eugene quoted me one time as saying: "The best news I heard in 2009 was when the GAA put a halter on that GPA crowd and made sure they would have to toe the line like the rest of us and I have to compliment that Cork man Christy Cooney because he had the cuteness to get it done.

"All the rows and disputes in Cork, Offaly, Clare, Limerick and Cavan over the years were a disgrace to the GAA, but it should be a thing of the past now with the GPA having to obey the same rules as the rest of us. It was nearly worth all the money they got from Croke Park to rein them in and let county boards run county teams like they always did.

"The top players are doing well at the minute and I even see a couple of county lads here in my own place with free sponsored cars for the last two years, even though the county team never threatened much in championship football.

"I was told once that the Dublin footballers did not get meals after games in Croke Park during their glorious days in the 1970s, but divil a harm it did them," I concluded.

After that article appeared, 'Your Man' actually went so far as to ring up the house here one Monday morning to say I was the only one that was standing up for the true principles of the association, claiming – wait for it – that players cared about nobody but themselves.

"They think they are the heart and soul of the GAA but where would they be without the volunteers at grassroots level and the likes of me and you at committee and board level giving endless hours fixing matches and appointing referees and officials so that games could be played?" he said.

I could hardly wait to get off the phone and talk to Rose Ellen, the wife, about what 'Your Man' had just said.

"I don't think the word 'hypocrite' does him justice," I said to her later as I sat down – just as the Radio Eireann news at one o'clock came on – for my dinner of bacon and cabbage.

## AWARD FOR THE MAN WHO HATED PLAYERS

"You'd need to put a fair few other descriptions in there to get half way close to the sort of jennet that he is."

As I was thinking through words over the dinner, the wife started laughing as I came up with the following – hunker-slider, sleeveen and above all disloyal schemer.

"You've narrowed it down to about a thousand GAA officials. Sure he is no worse or no better than a lot of them," she said.

"You're not wrong that a lot of them have one or two of those traits but no one other than your man has them all," I replied.

I then had an idea. There was only one trait I had left out and which I hoped would be the most important one in getting 'Your Man' to show once and for all that he was the biggest shyster in the history of the GAA.

The previous week I read in a small column in one of the Sunday papers that the players' group were holding an awards night before Christmas with something about candidates being inducted into the hall of fame for their service to the GAA.

So, and God forgive me for this, without ever telling them, I wrote to the organisers using and forging the signature of Eugene as well as Liam Mulvihill and four or five other lads I knew up the ladder in the provinces. I put forward 'Your Man' in their names. The reason I (they) gave was "for a lifetime of unfaltering belief in how player power had affected the GAA and for his forthright views on where players stood in importance within the association."

As someone without Sky television and still using a Nokia phone instead of those new-fangled iPhones or androids, I'm not as up-to-date as the young bucks as to what is happening in Croke Park or in Dublin. Seemingly nowadays you find out what happens in a meeting during it, never mind having to wait a week or fortnight for a report like used to happen when I was growing up.

This may partly go to explain the reason 'Your Man' blanked me totally at the following club and county board meetings, both of which were held in the last week of January of that year.

It was only when I bought the local paper the following week that the penny dropped as to what had happened and why he was indeed suiting himself once more.

On the front page of the sports section of the now tabloid edition – something incidentally I hate as I preferred the bigger pages – there was a big picture of him and the former inter-county star player up on a stage at a 'do' in Dublin. The heading over the accompanying article underneath the photo read: "Players reward stalwart for fighting their cause".

Never was a truer sentence uttered, I thought, only exactly the opposite meaning to what the headline writer thought he was writing.

I nearly choked laughing as I read down the article which stated that 'Your Man' had "been a universal choice for this coveted award" with many outstanding figures in the GAA backing his candidature.

"What's so funny?" herself asked.

"Do you remember the day I spoke about 'Your Man?'" I asked.

She nodded. "Well, he's graduated with flying colours."

I passed her over the sports section and her giggles as she read down meant that truly the dart had hit the bulls-eye.

The man who hated players more than anyone I ever met in the GAA, had just got a life-time achievement from the players' group.

And it had proven to me that aside from being hunker-sliding, a two-faced sleeveen and disloyal schemer, he had an ego that would stop at nothing when it came to giving him column inches and public notoriety.

"Is that why he isn't talking to you any more? You'll see him for the hypocrite that he is," she enquired further.

"No," I said, "it's because I now have proof of it."

*Larry McGann was an outspoken official who became visible as the alter ego of the late Eugene McGee, revered GAA manager, writer and journalist. McGee's idea was to use Larry as a conscience of old decency within the association. The ubiquitous official was therefore a native of every county and a member of every club. And still is.*

# Writing The History Of Phantom Pregnancy Final

## Billy Keane

The 'phantom pregnancy' final was the cause of the forever enmity between the twin parishes of Glen Lallyduff Upper and Glen Lallyduff lower.

I was working as bar man in the pub still known as John B's back in the days when there were pubs in Ireland.

It was the graveyard shift. A Monday afternoon it was and it was then I was given the true story of the phantom pregnancy final of 1822.

An old timer told me his version. Whether it's true or not, I will leave it for you to decide. Please take in to account the old timer who was fast approaching his 103rd year was a Timmy Tom Pat and a Glen Lallyduff lower man. But my back up research suggests his account seems accurate enough and he proved here history is not always written by the winners.

Here are his exact words as told to me. "My great great grandfather would be one of the Timmy Tom Pats. There is no doubt that Theresa, the star of the phantom pregnancy final was a Timmy Tom Pats, even though the other septs have tried to claim her intermittently. Why else would she have been called Theresa Timmy Tom Pat?"

The Timmy Tom Pats, according to the old timer, were his mother's people, and he said "every one of them was a giant of a man, even when they were women. "

He ascribed his own smallness to the fact that his mother married his smaller father, who after giving the marriage his full attention for six months left for England.

The old timer was bitter. "What with the bit of size in the mother's family, I could have won six or seven All Ireland's for Kerry if I had a bigger father. I was handy you know. A dinger with two legs and I feared no man."

But that's a tale for another day, and we would respectfully suggest the next volume of GAA stories should be kept for the what might have beens. The tome would run in to thousands of pages.

But the story of the phantom pregnancy final is what concerns us here.

The game itself was played nearly two centuries ago but the legend of Theresa Timmy Tom Pats lives on. The old boy was proud of his distaff ancestor. "Theresa", he said, "is rightly lauded as a feminist icon as she was as good as any man, and better."

The 102-year-old man took a sip from his pint and continued with the story of family glory.

"Theresa's father Pat Timmy Tom Pats stood three inches taller than the famed Kelly the boy from Killane in County Wexford. I checked out on Kelly's height from the song of the same name. The song goes, 'Seven feet was his height with some inches to spare, and he looked like a king in command'."

The man sang the song with some gusto before taking up the story after downing the last dregs of his seventh pint.

"So if we take it then that Pat was taller than Kelly, well then he must have been about seven feet seven inches, which was a good size even back then when giants roamed Ireland. Theresa was his eldest and a noted athlete and that it was an awful pity there wasn't basketball back then, as she was nearly as tall as a her father."

The game played then was called Caid. Gaelic football as we know it now evolved from Caid.

The object of the game of caid was to get the inflated pig's bladder over the line at all costs. The goal line could be five miles or more distant from the throw in.

Every kind of trick was used. There was subterfuge. There was violence. There was name-calling. There was skill as well, but not much. There could have been a thousand players on each side.

The game was never considered to be anywhere near exciting back in those days unless at least two or three of the players were killed and several more carted off by donkey and cart to the local infirmary or the faith healers mud cabin.

Glenlallyduff lower hadn't won the local cup for a good many years. There was hardly a day passed by where they were not taunted by the Uppers on the way to mass or at the fair or even just passing by at the street.

The old timer told me the Timmy Tom Pats took these six years of taunting very much to heart. "Our family motto is, 'we are a breed of men that don't fit in', but we had to take our beating when the Upper boys won six-in-a-row."

The parish priests of both parishes urged the Uppers and the lowers to be kind and to treat each and every opponent as if he was one of God's children, or even Christ himself. So it was that the parish priest blessed each player and gave the more advanced the last rites.

The cup was presented by the local landlord Lord Alphonsus De Lire Ponsonby KBE. His lordship knew that if the annual game between the two parishes went ahead, there would be blood and murder and this internecine strife would deflect the locals from agrarian unrest and violent uprisings. The White Boys and the Moonlighters were dead against the landlords who treated the tenants badly, for the most part. Lord Ponsonby presented the cup and there was also a prize of a guinea for the player who carried the ball over the finish line.

The old boy was growing excited now when he came to the game itself. He rose off his stool and shouted out: "Glory to the lowers." I will hand you back to him now.

"The game went on at death speed after the parish priest threw the ball in. The Upper boys, as usual, took control. They played a possession game on the dangerous and boggy terrain with huge bog holes you could drop a man into and he would never be seen again. The beating went on and the fighting and lower were being hammered sick. Old Timmy Pat Tim, my three times great grandfather was coming to his seventy seventh year at the time and while he was still a fine figure of a man, he didn't have the same speed or endurance he had when he was in his sixties.

His daughter Theresa was always the apple of his eye. She came along as a spectator and her father told her to stand in an area where she wouldn't get hurt. But then in the middle of the fray, when the bladder was dropped into a bog hole, Theresa came into her own.

The bladder had been washed downstream by a fast flowing current, which is unusual in bogs but many said afterwards that it was some sort of a miracle. The spring sprung up and just vanished the ball into the next bog hole.

Only Theresa noticed this. She discarded her clothing and dived into the bog hole when no one was looking as she was a modest girl.

She retrieved the ball bladder from the murky waters, put her clothes back on, and placed the bladder inside her blouse. She walked along a mile or so before anyone noticed. The two sides were batin' each other sick. The ball was an irrelevance.

The lower parish priest who was busy anointing the stricken when he saw Theresa: "Oh, don't tell me Theresa, you're after getting into the family way. And you named after a saint."

Theresa blushed, lowered her head to the ground and said: "Bless me father." The priest accordingly said: "You must be married tomorrow, who is the perpetrator of this disgusting and evil crime? I hope he is not an Upper man."

"Oh," said Theresa, "I'll talk to you tomorrow, Father," and she kept on walking.

Lord Ponsonby who was nearby was said to have uttered: "Tut-tut, disgraceful behaviour Padre, what?"

But Theresa did not respond, for she was made of firmer stuff. Theresa was on a mission.

Before long, what with her long stride, Theresa found herself within four hundred yards of the goal line. (There were no metres back then.)

Now word had got out from a careless whisper that Theresa had indeed taken possession of the bladder on behalf of her team. The Upper boys proceeded with full haste and tried to catch Theresa. But she was a noble athlete and changed the casual walk she took on so as to not arouse suspicion, into a full sprint.

The Uppers team threw shillelaghs like boomerangs. Rocks, stones and a lasso were flung at her. The Upper boys were barely missing her. It was only a matter of time before Theresa would be downed or drowned.

There was a rare sort in the Upper ranks. He was a chivalrous corner back, still rare even in today's game. "Stop lads, will we stop?" he shouted. She must be six months gone or even more. Will ye look at that bump on her, will ye?"

Whereupon they all stopped immediately. That gave Theresa a little more time. But what happened when Theresa turned round to thank the Upper boys for their kindness, only didn't the full bladder fall out from under her snow-white blouse and on to the brown bog below.

It was then the Upper realised there was a subterfuge and a phantom pregnancy. Theresa galloped on and fell into a bog hole but swam across to the other side. Theresa would have been the first ever Irish triathlete, if bikes had been invented at that time.

Theresa stumbled again, but this time she kept on going. The Upper boys were after her with pitchforks, scythes, knives and a sacred sword that was said to have belonged to Red Hugh. Missiles flew over and near her. A gunshot was heard.

Theresa made it over the goal line in the nick of time. She took the bladder out from underneath her blouse and shouted: "Lower Abu. We have won the Ponsonby Cup. I claim victory and a guinea."

The cheers went up from the ranks of the two thousand strong lower team. Her father was emotional: "Oh, I was so wrong, Theresa. You have done us proud. You have brought back the cup to your father's and grandfather's people. You will forever be known as Theresa Bladder."

Most historians agree that this heroic feat carried out by Theresa was the beginning of the playing of football by women in the GAA.

Upper objected. They argued it was unjust and illegal that women pretending to be pregnant should be allowed play in the Ponsonby cup final. The matter was referred to the lower parish priest for adjudication, who said he could see nothing wrong with Theresa winning the cup, as it was a great relief of all concerned, she was not with a child.

Lord Ponsonby declared that Theresa could not be allowed win on behalf of her team because she was a woman. Then the cup was presented to the Upper captain but it was no good to them as it was forever known as Theresa Bladder's cup. The Upper people hid the cup all that year because they were ashamed of what had happened. "

The rules of the game were changed in the 1820's and women were allowed play caid but only if they promised not to stick the ball up their jumper.

Theresa played on every year after that until she really became pregnant, and indeed lifted the Ponsonby Cup as captain when she made a comeback after the birth of her 14th child."

The old boy was in tears by then. To console himself he drank another pint which brought his total up to the gallon.

I filled one for myself. "To Theresa cried the old boy". We lifted our glasses in unison. "To Theresa," I replied.

"Do you know who she married?" asked the 102-year-old Gael.

"No," I replied.

The old boy gave out a wry smile. And then he told me.

"It was the chivalrous cornerback from Glenlallyduff Upper."

*Billy Keane is a Listowel native with a great fondness for Kerry football and Munster rugby. The well-known publican is also a leading newspaper columnist with the Irish Independent. Married with four children, Billy is the author of a number of best-selling books including his novel, 'The Last Of The Heroes.'*

# Wexford And I Ripped To Pieces

Tim Horgan

For any 13-year-old Cork boy to see Christy Ring scoring 6-4 against the mighty Wexford would be something to cherish for a lifetime. Yet on a mild November evening when the two teams met at the old Athletic Grounds and Christy was in his usual stupendous form, the occasion proved a total disaster for me.

"Take me in, in front of ya, sir," was the usual way youngsters gained free access to matches. Unfortunately, I had grown a little too tall to be taken through the turnstile by an accommodating adult. An alternative ploy was required.

We had discovered a gap in the wire between the cheap part of the ground and the expensive seats side by the river. It was perfect for slipping into the more select section of the park.

The day of the game, I walked down with my pal, Ken O'Connell, who got in "with a man" as he was still short enough. I had to pay 3d to enter the schoolboys gate. We'd arranged to meet inside by the fence. We scrambled through and the two of us made our way to the seating. It was then my delight at this cheap entry was shattered.

"Look at his pants!" shouted a boy behind us. Gingerly I felt behind for the damage. To my horror, I discovered a huge L-shaped tear. The wire had cut right through and it was literally a case where I didn't have an arse in my trousers.

Thereafter the noise and the match were a blur. When half-time came I told Ken I was leaving. To the amazement of the turnstile attendant, I asked to be let out. I must have cut a pitiful figure walking as fast as I could, with my hands tightly holding up the torn part of my trousers as best they could to cover my modesty.

I made it home. I waited in dread for the inevitable "killing" I'd get for ruining my Sunday suit. To my amazement when the family arrived back from the match, everybody was in great form, delighted with Cork's win and Christy's magnificent display. My mother told me off, of course, more through obligation than anger. The pants were duly stitched and the matter eventually forgotten. I was never more thankful to Ringey than I was that evening.

# Bobby Charlton In Genuine Awe Of Hurlers

Gerry McGrath

I'll never forget the day I met England World Cup winner Bobby Charlton – and believe it or not, it was he who insisted on getting my autograph after I had asked him for his. Let me explain how it happened.

I was born in Portaferry, County Down and have been steeped in hurling and the GAA from early childhood. I played for Down minor hurlers in 1972/73 when we were drawn away to Kildare in an All Ireland minor championship game in the days when it was an open draw.

We travelled to Naas and I lined out at centre-forward that particular day. In hurling, centre-half backs always carry a fearless reputation and are the mainstay of most teams.

The guy I was marking was no exception. A very tough and tight hurling duel ensued. The game finished in a bruising draw. Extra-time followed and fortunately we won by five points.

I felt bruised and battered afterwards but there also was a sense of achievement and reward leaving Naas that evening. On the bus home the team management congratulated us and announced that they were bringing us to the Imperial Hotel in Dundalk for a bite to eat.

It had the trappings of a banquet as we ate and discussed the game. We were all on a high as we poured back out in to the foyer area of the hotel with glasses of coca-cola, orange or whatever else we were allowed.

We were relaxing with our soft drinks in one hand and our hurls in the other. Yes, that was the way of the world then – your hurl never left your sight. You nearly took it to bed with you there was so much passion for the sport in our neck of the woods.

Then something happened which forced all of the squad gathered together to do a double take. I still couldn't believe my eyes as I saw this pair of sporting icons nonchalantly enter the hotel.

Someone behind me asked: "Who is it?"

"It's Bobby Charlton… and Nobby Stiles is coming in directly behind him," I explained to the non-soccer follower in our midst.

In those days I also played a lot of soccer and, of course, followed world football and other sports. I made a speedy bee-line to Bobby and shook his hand saying that it was great to see him.

"Do you mind me asking you why you're in Dundalk?" I queried.

Bobby laughed and looking down at my hurl, he responded: "Never mind about me, what are you doing?" he asked.

I explained that we were returning from a hurling game in Kildare.

He smiled and asked if my team won. I told him that we had to go to extra-time but emerged victorious in the end.

At that point he flummoxed me.

"Can I shake your hand?" he asked.

I found this particularly strange as I had already shaken his hand and said so. He swatted away my remark by stating: "Any man who plays that game, I want to shake his hand because it frightens the life out of me. I wouldn't play that game for a pension," he joked.

He then revealed that he had watched the All Ireland Final on the television in the UK, adding that was the closest he was happy to get to such a robust game. He really was in awe of the skill shown but fearful of the belts that players got and gave in the course of a game.

It was at this point as I am listening to a World Cup and European Cup winner and former captain of Manchester United that it dawns on me that I am the one who should feel overawed – not him.

After I told him that hurling was a really enjoyable game to play, I asked if he would give me his autograph?

He didn't answer straight away but looked thoughtful for a second before saying: "Of course I will, but only on one condition."

I looked at him wondering what that condition was.

"You have to give me your autograph first."

For a second I thought that he was winding me up and having a bit of fun at my expense.

Nevertheless I didn't care what he was trying to do. I told him to stay where he was as I bolted across to the hotel reception desk and asked for a blank A4 sheet of paper and a marker.

I wrote out my name and handed my own autograph over to Bobby.

"Now," I said, "Can I have yours?"

He said: "Certainly, it would be my pleasure."

I asked him to also sign my hurl and he duly obliged. Before saying goodbye, I felt a little cheeky and reminded him that he hadn't told me why he was in Dundalk.

"Oh, Nobby and I are guesting for Preston North End in a pre-season friendly up at Oriel Park."

What a serendipitous moment in a young sport follower's life to meet a giant of global sport – and have such a genuinely interesting conversation.

As we shook hands again and said our goodbyes, I realised the reason Bobby was such a sporting icon was because he was also humble and kind. Someone who had time to be interested in a young lad's game as if it was more important than anything else in his world at that moment. What a gift.

My story doesn't quite finish there either and in truth what I am about to tell you calls my judgement into question.

When I arrived home I related the story to my parents. My father as a hobby used to do some craftwork. He regularly stitched hurling balls for me when they were in need of repair. That night he decided to use a hot needle and he went over the signed name of Bobby Charlton on my hurl so that it stayed there permanently.

This was a stellar hurl already treated by steeping it in water, drying out before being covered in linseed oil. I swore that I would never use it and that it would be kept for posterity.

At the start of a senior hurling season in those days, players bought one hurl and got one for free. After that, all hurls had to be bought. Normally, two hurls would be made to last a season... and often longer.

However, in the early 70s Portaferry had a particularly tough start in Division One of the Antrim League, where we competed so that we could experience a higher standard of hurling.

So, after a particularly gruelling couple of matches against Ballycastle and Dunloy, my two hurls were lying in pieces on the battle zones. This is where the folly of being young comes into play. With little funds available to pay out on another hurl, I began using the 'Bobby Charlton' hurl.

I played a few matches with it and all went well. Then in the Down Feis at St Patrick's Park, Bryansford in Newcastle, Portaferry reached the 7-a-side hurling final against old rivals Ballycran. I was playing midfield and during the play, I hooked an opposing player. Whatever way the connection was made, my prized hurl crumbled in bits before my very eyes.

I arrived home after winning the tournament and will never forget the look on my father's face and his reaction.

"Where's the Bobby Charlton hurl?"

I explained that it was lying in bits back on the Bryansford pitch.

"You bloody eejit, you should have brought it home and I would have glued it together," he chided

Of course he was right. I never should have used the hurl in the first place and now as a broken object, it wasn't even in my possession anymore.

Nearly half a century on, wouldn't it be a prized possession to have today?

*Gerard (Gerry) McGrath lives in Belfast with his wife of 37 years. Despite losing his most precious camán, he is still an avid hurling fan.*

# Last Charge Of The Bike Brigade

## Michael McDonnell

When Gaelic scribes recount great games, invariably they refer to those fabled encounters played at Thurles, during or shortly after World War Two.

At that particular time luxury items were in short supply, petrol was scarce and cars were only for the rich. The popular modes of transport were the steam train or bicycle. The masses of people who made the journey to the likes of Thurles and other Gaelic venues on two wheels were to become known as the 'bicycle brigade.'

My first trip to Thurles or for that matter, my first intercounty game outside Limerick, was as a young member of this brigade. The occasion was the Munster championship game between Cork and Limerick in Thurles in 1946. The build up for the match at that time occurred at the crossroads where we gathered each evening.

There was no big preview for the game on television because it didn't exist. No interviews with players, selectors or coaches. Still the stories of deeds past and of great things to come made for fireside chats or crossroad meetings... and how they stirred the spirits. Then, the pros and cons of going to Thurles by train or bicycle were discussed at length.

For some reason, still not clear to me, many decided not to let CIE do the driving but to pedal all the way themselves. As time went by and the day of the big game approached, some of my older friends said that they would be part of the bicycle brigade.

Why shouldn't I go too? After all I was a big lad of 15 and a proud owner of a girl's bicycle. Firstly, I had to convince my mother that it was only 55 miles each way. Then I checked the bicycle that was to transport me to this faraway place. Tyres and brakes were inspected and the saddlebag was filled with a new 'outfit,' a few inches of valve rubber, patches and two large spoons, all necessary for mending punctures.

The spoons were used for removing the tyres from the wheel rim, something akin to modern tyre levers in the event of getting a puncture. Well equipped with an LDF cape and a large bag of sandwiches, four of us set out for Limerick and arrived in good time for eight o'clock Mass in the Augustinian Church in O'Connell Street. Having observed one of the main precepts of the church, we set out for Thurles, some four hour journey away via the Dublin road. After passing Annacotty, we swung right for Newport and headed into the hills.

We were only outside Newport when it started to rain...the downpour lasted about an hour. It was then that I appreciated the usefulness of the cape. While wearing capes slowed our progress at least we were dry. On we cycled past Rearcross to Milestone. At each crossroads we met up with a number of fellow travellers, and gradually our group numbered at least 20 as we approached Thurles.

The journey was shortened by singing songs such as 'The Wild Colonial Boy' and other popular numbers of the time. Some Corkonians in the group contributed a few lines of 'The Banks' which were interspersed with shouts of "Come on Limerick" from our supporters. Then a few swears coloured the air as one of our crew discovered he had a puncture.

Everyone stopped to lend a hand. One fella offered a pump, another patches etc. while others used it as a chance to have a rest and sample the sandwiches. The speed with which repairs were carried out would do justice to present day pit stops in Formula One racing. The remainder of the journey was uneventful and so at about 2pm the town of Thurles was in sight.

The view of the Sugar Factory in the distance was the signal for a big cheer. We were all delighted to have achieved a portion of our task. As we had some time to spare before the big game, some wise guy suggested that we should cycle up town into the square and do a few laps before going to the game.

Accompanied by the ringing of bicycle bells we did no fewer than four laps of the famous square and also stopped to admire Hayes Hotel where the GAA was founded. By this time we were ready to go back towards the field and park the bicycles with thousands of others at a cost of 3d (three old pence) each.

Like all of his seed and breed, the park attendant promised solemnly to protect each bicycle with his life and to be on hand after the game to see that we all got our own bicycles back. This guy could sell oil to an Arab but there are no marks for guessing what happened. After the game the man was long, long gone with all our thrupenny bits and not a care what happened to our bicycles.

And what of the game? Many accounts have been written but no words of mine can properly describe the excitement of being present at such a thrilling contest. Even though the result was not what I would have wished, I savoured every moment of the occasion. All the big names were there on the day. The Cork team included such talented players as Din Joe Buckley, The Murphys, Jack Lynch and a young Christy Ring.

Playing for Limerick were the unforgettable figures of the Mackeys, Paddy Fitzgerald, Peter Cregan, Jackie Power, Derry McCarthy, Dr Dick Stokes and Dr Jim McCarthy. When the game was over the long road home was not a very exciting prospect.

The remaining sandwiches were quickly eaten, the party assembled, and we set out for home. Like the wise men of old, we journeyed home another way. We arrived in Limerick saddle-sore and weary – which was remedied by a good meal and a long night's sleep.

Looking back on that adventure and cycling with the 'brigade' I'm glad I had that experience, as when the 1950s dawned, no more were hurling enthusiasts willing to make those long journeys by bicycle.

*Michael McDonnell is a native of Croom, Co Limerick. Married to Eileen, they have two children, Mary and John and four grandchildren. A former District Inspector with the Office Of Public works, Michael has served the GAA in many capacities both as a player and administrator with his club and county since 1949.*

# Family Warning For Phil 'The Gunner'

## Paul Fitzpatrick

It's July, 1950 and New York are in town for a National League final. Croke Park is rocking and rolling but, on the field favourites Cavan are sending out distress flares. At that time, the format was a 'home' final before New York would fly in and take on the Irish champions in the final proper.

Ten of the Cavanmen had featured in the Polo Grounds three years earlier but that famous welcome seemed like a faint memory as a New York team, led by Roscommon's Bill Carlos, just keeps on coming. Twenty-five minutes in and Cavan's Tony Tighe is upended. There is sorting out to be done and Cavan look to their full-back, Phil 'The Gunner' Brady to do it.

Now, there's a back story here. As it happened, the Gunner's sister Rose was living in the city at the time and doing a line with a strapping Mayo man called Tom Gallagher, a member of the New York panel.

She knew the combative Phil's form and keen that big brother wouldn't scupper the embryonic romance, had taken out her pen a couple of weeks earlier. "Whatever you do," she wrote to her mother in Mullahoran, "don't let Phil start fighting with Tom."

The rest of the story writes itself. Tom and Phil collide at full tilt and the ref quickly points to the line. The story goes that the pair walked off arm in arm, laughing at the good of it.

New York won the match, 2-8 to 0-12, but the lads got over it. Rose later married Pat White. Rose White (nee Brady) passed away in New York in March 2020 aged 90.

There was another interesting denouement to the tale. It was presumed that Cavan would win the match so, as a memento for the exiles, beautiful gold medals in the shape of a map of Ireland were struck up for the losing side.

New York, though, hadn't read the script and ended up winners, picking up instead base medals. And the members of the losing side were left with beautiful reminders of a very disappointing defeat! The great Tony Tighe's late wife Betty wore her husband's on a necklace right up until her passing in 2016.

# GAA's Own Case Of 'Sudden Death'

## Jackie Napier

One particularly memorable occasion that stands out in my mind was the All-Ireland Junior Hurling Final of 1971 when Wicklow played Hertfordshire. The contest took three outings to complete satisfactorily.

After the sides had ended level in the first match in Aughrim with Wicklow on 2-12 to their opponents 3-9 on October 10, the replay was fixed for Sundown Park, Luton. The Wicklow team travelled across the Irish Sea in a confident mood, but the replay turned out to be one of the most controversial on record.

No fault could be placed on the two teams involved for the controversy. When the time had elapsed, the referee, Donal Doody of Dublin, did not change the sides around for extra-time but instead decided to play on until the next score, without informing the teams involved.

There were roars of "time up ref" aplenty but the knight of the whistle refused to blow. Wicklow were dominant at this time late in the game but they sent wide after wide as the minutes ticked by and it looked like they were throwing away their chance of collecting the Celtic Crosses.

Ten minutes beyond the hour and the official still didn't look at his watch but enthusiastically continued to wave play on. Then with 12 minutes overtime played, Herts foraged up the field and showing much greater economy than their opponents, scored a point.

Immediately, the official blew the long whistle and recorded that Herts had won by 4-9 to 3-11.

It was the first "sudden death" in GAA history. The referee would not allow the ball to be pucked out much to the consternation of the visitors. The Michael Cusack Cup was presented to the Hertfordshire captain and it looked as if Wicklow would return home empty-handed.

However, on consideration of the match report the following week, the Central Council of the GAA decided that the referee had erred in his application of "sudden death." It was ruled that the sides should meet for a third time as there was no provision in the rulebook for a 'golden score.'

Wicklow prevailed by a single point on this occasion on November 28 at Croke Park on a scoreline of 4-6 to 3-8.

The referee was seemingly given the plane tickets to travel by a Croke Park official he was told to make sure to play the game to a finish.

The whistler interpreted this to mean if it was level at full time to play on until either side scored but of course this was not the rule. The referee was assaulted after the game by a Wicklow official who was later suspended for 12 months.

That wasn't all that happened in the game. Wicklow emerged victorious by the minimum of margins but their opponents immediately lodged an objection claiming that one of their players, Eamon Murray, who played at full-forward, was not properly qualified to play for his native county.

They alleged, quite correctly, that he had played in the London Senior League. At a lengthy hearing in the council chambers in Croke Park, Murray admitted the charge. However, he was pronounced legal to participate in that London game as he had commenced the competition on a date before transferring to his club of Avoca. Therefore, the GAA executive committee ruled, he was fully entitled to go back and finish a competition which he had started before his transfer home.

Ironically, if Wicklow had lost, they too would have had an avenue into the Croke Park committee rooms as Hertfordshire used four substitutes in the third game between the sides. And it would have resulted in the Garden County being given the game or, spare the thought, a third replay.

It was less than a month before Christmas but the players enjoyed coming out on top given that they had to play in three All Irelands finals to win one. So for the rest of the long winter nights, they enjoyed the celebrations at club level before they were properly feted as a group the following February when they were presented with their All Ireland medals at the long since departed International Hotel in Bray.

*Jackie Napier is a native of Bray, Co Wicklow and is a lifelong member of Bray Emmets. A former letter press and litho printer, he is married to Josie for 51 years and have a grown up son and daughter. His major interest is hurling and has been with Wicklow teams in every county in Ireland bar Cavan.*

# Memories Of Unbelievable Coincidence And An Action-Packed Day

## Michael Duignan

Whenever I press the rewind button on a whistle stop tour of my time in the GAA to date, it surprises me where my memories end up taking me.

Yes, I have been fortunate enough to play in Croke Park on All-Ireland winning days and they are standout moments in any player's lifetime for sure.

Yet the older I get, the moments that linger longest with me are far away from the big crowds and big days. In my case, the spotlight focuses on my Féile to Minor days when something so coincidental happened that I still have to double check that it is true.

As I moved into senior ranks with the county as a dual player, there is also one jam-packed day that stands out like no other – even at this remove of over three decades.

First to the Féile story which began for me in Kilkenny in 1979. I was lucky to play as an 11, 12, 13 and 14 year old in this competition for St Rynaghs but it is our time in Mooncoin that I remember most clearly.

I was a slip of a lad at 11, just about holding my own as a corner back to be on the team. I was lucky that my school pal and nearest neighbour Roy Mannion was there with me every step of the way. In fact, Roy is a significant part of this first Féile tale.

As those who have ever gone to this great GAA competition knows, one county hosts the hurling Féile every year. Visiting county winners are put up in different clubs and we were fortunate as Offaly's representatives to be hosted by Mooncoin.

The detail is that the local club will try to ensure that young lads on the panel like Roy and myself are housed for the weekend with a family who have young players of the same age.

We had a great weekend with the Murphys on their farm just outside the village. Joe and Tom were our minders for the few days and they did a great job. Before I left Banagher, my mother had slipped £2 into my pocket with the express order that I treat the lads I was staying with.

That was a year before Offaly seniors made the big breakthrough by beating Kilkenny in the Leinster final of 1980. The win was all I needed to start dreaming of playing for the county and I knew Roy shared my ambition.

By the time we had a good minor team together in 1986, the Offaly seniors had reached even higher peaks by bringing home the Liam MacCarthy cup in 1981 and again in 1985. Mannion and myself were seldom seen without a hurl in our hand at that stage. We wanted to be part of history as Offaly had never won a Leinster minor hurling title up to that time.

There was a good reason for that – a team called Kilkenny. And it was the black and amber we were drawn against on May 24, 1986 in Portlaoise. A huge crowd witnessed a pulsating game on this Saturday evening and while it ended in a draw, Kilkenny had shot the last two or three points to level the game.

The consensus was that we had let our chance slip and the Cats wouldn't be as accommodating the following Saturday.

Once again the huge crowd got great value for their money as the intensity from the first day increased with each passing puck. For much of the game it looked like the familiar Offaly 'hard luck' refrain as Kilkenny managed to keep their noses in front. Into the last minute they were still two points ahead when Declan Pilkington moved across the goal to drive home the winner on a 3-9 to 4-5 score-line.

That win catapulted Offaly minors into the big time. We went on to win the All Ireland in three out of the following four years but away from the dizzy heights of glory and celebration was what must be one the greatest coincidences in the long and varied GAA history.

Roy played the two games at full-back marking Tommy Murphy who was full-forward for Kilkenny. I lined out in both games at full-forward for Offaly and Joe Murphy was my direct opponent at full back for Kilkenny.

Seven years previously on that blissful Féile Sunday morning, we had walked the road from the shop in Mooncoin to their farm eating ice-creams from the 'treat money' my mother had given me, talking hurling and wondering if we would ever go on to wear our respective county jerseys? What an answer the hand of fate threw us by pitting the Féile visitors against their hosts.

My second day of memory has stuck in the reel of my playback years simply because it was so full of activity. I was in my early twenties, living in

## MEMORIES OF UNBELIEVABLE COINCIDENCE AND AN ACTION-PACKED DAY

Dublin, working in AIB and playing with the Offaly footballers and hurlers, both of whom were showing serious promise of revival at the time.

The previous month, I had opted to play with the footballers in the National League quarter-final where we put it up before losing narrowly to a Donegal team who would go on to win the All Ireland a little over a year down the line. The hurlers had beaten Waterford and were looking to win their first league title too.

On this Wednesday in May, I was due to play an inter-banks final in Parnell Park on Dublin's north side in the afternoon. I rang my Offaly football manager Brendan Hackett about getting a lift but the timing didn't suit as he had to go down early to have everything ready for our challenge match against Kerry in Birr.

"I tell you what," he said, "I'll go down with Gerry McDermott (RIP) who is doing the stats tonight and I'll leave my car at the Spa Hotel in Lucan. If you get a taxi there, you can drive yourself to Birr."

I can't tell you whether we won or lost the game in Parnell Park but I remember drinking plenty of water as it was a hot day and now I had another 70 minutes in front of me. The taxi man collected me as arranged and knew short cuts to get me over to Lucan away from the afternoon gridlock of the time.

I hadn't a chance to change in the dressing room and was still in my football togs and socks as the taxi dropped me off beside a spanking new Mercedes which Brendan had left for me to collect in the hotel car park.

Although I was well able to drive, I couldn't afford a car of my own at the time so I felt a bit at sea because I had never driven such a big and powerful model as this one.

By the time I got to Kinnegad I was getting the hang of it and was starting to enjoy myself. That was until I turned a corner and the long arm of the law beckoned me to pull in to the side of the road.

I could see by the expression on this guard's face that he wasn't having a great day at the office. I knew I was in for a right grilling. He came over to the driver's side and as I rolled down the window, he looked at the cut of me with the togs and football socks still on. Then he rubbed the roof of the Merc and said: "This must have cost you an arm and a leg."

I knew I had to give as good as I got back to him so I said: "Aye, and you should see what it takes to tax and insure her as well." I spoke as if I knew what I was talking about.

My tactic must have surprised him as he didn't look for a driver's licence or any documentation and instead grunted something about watching the speed limit and waved me on.

What a relief to talk myself out of that. It was a pleasant shock as I was sure I was done for but now I had to focus as I was up against clock to be in Birr for the 7.30 throw in.

The referee was blowing his whistle to start the game when I pulled into St Brendan's Park. Already togged out, I tied up my boots, was given a No 8 jersey for midfield as I threw the keys at Hackett and straight away the game was on. No stretching, no sprints, no warm up except for a 130 kilometre mad dash from Lucan to Birr.

Whether I was fired up by the events of the day or whether it was just one of those early jousts you sometimes surprisingly get between players in challenge games, I don't know for sure but within 10 minutes of the throw in, the referee was pointing to the touchline and sending me off for hitting my direct opponent a slap in the face.

I said: "You can't do that, I have a league semi-final to play for the hurlers next Sunday."

Initially, he wasn't for moving but when my midfield partner Padraig 'Podge' Dunne, – in his own inimitable way it must be said – put his arm firmly around him and explained how important it was for Offaly that I could play, the referee reluctantly changed his mind and gave me a stern verbal warning but allowed me to stay on to play the rest of the game.

Afterwards, I got a lift back with two of the panel. From the luxury of a new Merc, I was now travelling to Dublin via Kinnitty with Mick Casey and Mike Devine. Mick was driving the two-seater van which meant I was 'sitting' on my knees in the back talking to the two of them in front of me.

As we turned a corner near the village, a car came around on the wrong side of the road, forcing Mick to swerve violently to prevent a head-on collision.

That didn't stop yours truly being thrown forward between the two boys where I cracked my head against the windscreen. As we got out, I had a few bumps and cuts and was trying to get my bearings while the lads were surveying the damage done to the van.

Out of the blue a car came along and stopped. It was my uncle from Dublin who had been in Tipperary. It was another great coincidence and a good one for us. He brought us back to my parents' house in Banagher where my mother bandaged me up and my father fed us all a few brandies to get over the shock of the ordeal.

They insisted that we should all stay in the house that night and my mother promised she would have us up at six o'clock the following morning to ensure we got to our desks in Dublin in time for our day jobs.

## MEMORIES OF UNBELIEVABLE COINCIDENCE AND AN ACTION-PACKED DAY

As we were leaving at that ungodly hour, she turned to me and asked: "When will you be down again, Michael?"

I looked at my watch and replied: "In about 12 hours, Mam. I've training with the hurlers in Tullamore tonight."

*Michel Duignan is a former Offaly dual player who won two All Ireland SH medals and a National Hurling League title and was also honoured by the All-Star selectors. The current Offaly Co Board chairman is also a highly-regarded RTE hurling commentator and analyst. Predeceased by his wife Edel, he has two grown up sons and is a self-employed businessman.*

# 'Cabbage' Failed To Bring Home The Bacon

Jim Brophy

There were characters in most clubs who specialised in defending or supporting objections. One of the greatest was a fella they called Paddy 'Cabbage' in Wicklow. He was stuck with this name because he used to smell distinctly like cabbage plants. He was known to have played a few "bangers" himself from time to time. This time, however, he was caught and in serious trouble. However, he had a suspicion that the opposition had a couple of wrong ones too.

They were a good bit away though and he had no way of getting a line on them. Eventually, he decided to dress up as a tramp and do some investigating. He got a loan of an old rimrock of a car and headed off across the mountains to West Wicklow.

'Cabbage' believed they were all mad around the hills so he dressed up in some well-worn clothes not to stand out before he set out on his task. The first woman he asked gave him tuppence and a mug of tea but said she knew nothing at all about football. He went into another house where the man said he hated the sight of the GAA because all he ever got out of it was a bad knee from his playing days.

Says he: "I was playing in Knockananna one day and a savage with the nickname 'Cabbage' ran into me and the knee has never been right since. I'd tear him apart this minute if I could lay my hands on him," he added.

There was worse to come. Apparently, there had been a robbery in the area the night before and the word had gone around that it was a traveller who had done the job. As a result they were all watching 'Cabbage.'

Someone saw him and sent for the guards and the long and short of it was that 'Cabbage' had to clear out of the area as fast as his ould jalopy could carry him. The next day two members of the police force arrived at Paddy's house and but for the fact that one of them was a club member and knew what he had been up to, he would have been arrested.

So much for going undercover as Paddy lost the match, got a 12-month suspension and of course lost his standing as a 'fixer' in the club.

# Croats, Serbs And The Fighting Irish

## Ciarán Macken

I had the pleasure of spending over a decade-and-a-half in Australia and like thousands of other Irish people, can't thank the GAA enough for how it helped sustain my own sense of Irishness while I was thousands of miles away from home.

In fact with 40 first cousins, four sisters and a brother still living in Australia with their families, I am reminded constantly in our Skype calls and other correspondences just how vital a role the GAA plays in their daily lives.

It was ever thus, even to the pioneer Irish who arrived there in the early 1800s with little more than a faded photo of Robert Emmet and the Sacred Heart to remind them of their Irish upbringing.

We underestimate the bond between Australia and Gaelic games as the Irish emigrating as far back as the 1820s were seriously influential on how sport was played there. In fact, each generation who emigrated helped evolve Australian sport while cementing the bond between them and those already settled there for 100 years and more.

Playing Gaelic games was particularly prevalent around Melbourne and The Snowy Mountains, which was possibly the biggest engineering scheme ever undertaken in the country – and which attracted thousands of people to work there.

I didn't see it myself but my friend Paddy Fitzgerald told me he was often amazed at seeing 30 men come off a grassless field after playing a game of hurling covered head to toe in red dust from the earth they played on.

This wasn't anything out of the ordinary as hurling had been played by Australians in the towns of Bungaree and Ballarat for years before the GAA was officially formed down under in 1948. It was in the area and around Bendigo, about 100 kilometres west of Melbourne, that Australian Rules football was born out of a strong Irish influence.

The Irish miners working there used their spare time at weekends and evenings to play Peil with a pigskin ball just like they did at home before they set sail for Australia in the 1800s.

Ironically, Aussie Rules today holds onto some of the old set-ups and rules of the original Irish Peil better than the GAA. This is because in Ireland, there was a drive to change away from any anglicised influence in sporting pursuits. More than any other countries, the Aussies and ourselves wanted to deliberately create national games that was different to those that the English had developed.

'Footy' is now regarded as genuinely Australian as the boomerang or the kangaroo while the Irish nationalist of the late 19th century ensured that our hurling was different than cricket and our gaelic football was totally distinctive from the likes of rugby or soccer.

Originally if you attended a Peil game in Jones Road in Dublin, there were four upright posts at either end and while that was dropped by Michael Cusack et al in the run up to founding the GAA, the Australian game held onto them and they are still very much part of that set up today. There is also the two-score method in both games, goals and points in GAA and goal (six) and a behind (one) in Aussie Rules, which was at variance with any England-centred games of that time or even to this day.

On a similar 'hand-me-down' from old Peil where games involved 200-a-side and the intention was to drive your opponents back to their own village, there was the description of 'following' the game. The term 'follower' is still pertinent in Aussie Rules with the ruckman, ruck rover and rover assigned this appellation. They are called 'followers' because traditionally they are deployed to follow the ball around the ground in contrast to playing in a set defensive or attacking position.

Personally, as I look back now in that period from the sixties and seventies, I still carry various snapshots that both amuse and enrich from my involvement with this most significant of Irish cultures in Australia.

As soon as the GAA began to put down official roots, it led to a serious growth in clubs, particularly in Victoria. One memory stands out when clubs were encouraged to stage exhibition games in hurling and football all across county towns in the province. As a game was progressing in Geelong, and to the amusement of players and spectators alike, a kangaroo wandered onto the pitch and stopped play. It led to a succession of funny quips from the usual wags on the sideline, with one shouting: "What county is he from?" with a quick quip saying: "He looks like he might be related to their full-back." All harmless fun with only the deadpan kangaroo failing to see the funny side as he was directed back into the bush.

The gods of sport weren't with us when we held the first Australian GAA championship finals in Adelaide in the early seventies.

I had the honour of refereeing that game on a weekend when between

3,000-4,000 people attended the tournament. However, on the day of the final, the heavens opened and what we first hoped would be a prolonged shower turned into a total deluge.

It was the proverbial day you wouldn't put a cat or a dog out in – but we had no choice but to play on as people had travelled hundreds and thousands of miles to be in Adelaide that weekend.

Adelaide and Sydney qualified for the final and I remember predicting that there wouldn't be too many scores from play. Each side had accurate place kickers and it ended 0-8 to 0-7 in favour of the hosts.

Of the 15 scores, 13 came from frees with just one from play from either side. Yes, the first occasion was a damp squib but only in terms of the weather. The spirit of the Irish was burning bright and continues to do so. I was astounded when I returned to Australia in 2018 to see that the event had grown into a five-day extravaganza to include junior camogie and ladies football as well as the usual men's games.

Mostly the GAA has acted as a positive catalyst within Irish communities and the Gaelic Centre in Keysborough in Melbourne with its 23 acres makes it probably the biggest GAA headquarters in any country in the world.

Like everything else in life, there is always the odd time where the exuberance of teams and fans left those overseeing competitions slightly embarrassed. One such moment happened in 1969 at a Victorian GAA championship game at Parkville in Melbourne.

By coincidence, there was a big soccer match arranged at the exact same time between Croatian and Serbian teams in an adjacent pitch within the park complex. This had been widely advertised and the local police chiefs, mindful of the historical enmity between those two races, sent a large force to the game in the hope that their presence would quell any violent outbreak.

They were indeed successful in dealing with the soccer game where the match was run off without incident. Unfortunately in the hurling match, there was no such calm as tempers became increasingly frayed during the game.

This led to an invasion by supporters onto the pitch, where the proverbial 'free for all' broke out between both sides. The police moved quickly from the soccer pitch to disperse the warring Irish factions and, in fairness to them, they restored order within minutes. Following the melee the police decided to stay on the sideline, as they were fearful of a renewal of hostilities during or immediately when the match was over.

Typically, once the bit of bad blood had been drawn, the two Irish teams showed wonderful Corinthian spirit and sportsmanship and gave an exhibition of all the finer arts of the wonderful of game during the remaining time. They left the pitch at the end, arm-in-arm, much to the bafflement and bemusement of the watching police officers.

During my time residing in Australia, arguably the most poignant moment I recall was seeing the reverence with which an elderly man held a hurley which had been kept hidden as a treasure. This man wasn't Irish but an Australian and in that moment of total respect – for what and for whom the hurl represented – is a memory forever engrained in my mind's eye. The historic nature of the hurl, which wasn't made from ash but a timber remarkably like it, is that it may have been around for 40 or 50 years.

*Ciaran Macken is a native of Dunboyne, Co Meath. He emigrated to Australia in 1966 and returned home in 1983. Married to Marie, with two sons Kevin & Eoin. Now retired, still interested in GAA & History.*

# Ghost Train Into The Past

Seán O'Grady

The man's grandson was my companion on a journey to Co. Mayo. He carried the legacy of storytelling, with wit and smart answers unequalled in the county of Kerry and beyond. It was he who told me the story of the ghost train of 1955 to the famous All Ireland final between Kerry and Dublin, even though he was only a six year old that year.

The train left Killarney station somewhere between 11.30pm and midnight. On board for that great encounter was a particular party of four from the town, amongst many others. Though Dublin were the firm favourites, the four were steeped in Kerry tradition and held notions that Kerry could win.

What better way to demonstrate that belief than to leave bed, house and home, girlfriend or wife behind, to sit in a train that would take six or seven hours to reach its destination, with the only consolation being a sandwich, a deck of cards and a few cases of porter.

The four Killarney men were Mickey Costigan, who had a close relative playing on the team, Danno Keegan who had played Kerry junior in his day, Shamus Mahoney, a good oarsman and a great follower of sports of all hues and Michaleen Greaney, small in stature barely turned 18, going off to his second All Ireland and the first without his father.

He had been present in Croke Park two years earlier when Kerry beat Armagh in the final. All four were followers of my football club, the Legion. Three were excellent club players. The cards and the porter were unleashed as soon as the train pulled away from the platform. By the time they reached Dublin the porter was long gone, and the moustache was almost worn off the joker.

Mass was the first port of call on the quays and after they adjourned to some hostelry or other for a few more sandwiches and porter until the time came to make off for the field. By this time Michaleen was fast asleep over in the corner, not being used to staying up all night or indeed drinking with the men.

Shamus, seeing the condition of Michaleen, asked the others what they should do with him.

Mickey Costigan turning around and scratching his backside at the same time (a habit of his), to view the spectacle said: "Yerra, he'll be all right there 'till we get back."

"Well now," said Danno, "he won't. We'll take a taxi. We all have seats near each other, and we'll put him in his seat, and we'll all be together."

This was agreed and so it was done. When the match was over and Kerry had won, the four made off for Kingsbridge Station, as it was known then, and all got home safely.

The homecoming to Killarney was on the following evening and our group of followers together with those who didn't or weren't able to travel, gathered in their usual haunt, Marie's, or to strangers, the Ross Hotel, to play the game over and over again.

The craic was mighty.

The feel-good factor was at its highest when Michaleen began to relate to the assembly about the great point that Tadhgie Lyne had scored from near the centre of the field just after the ball was thrown in.

"Without doubt," says Michaleen, "no footballer before kicked a point from such a huge distance."

Mickey, with all the indignation he could muster in the midst of such a powerful conviviality, remarked: "It was one of the best ever scored but for God's sake, Michaleen, will you be quiet. There was only two men, ever, in the history of Croke Park, who were conveyed to their seats, De Valera because he was blind and yourself because you were blind drunk and neither of you saw any part of the match, so shut the f*** up."

There was no coming back from that, as the whole pub erupted in prolonged bouts of laughter and the throng went out into the night to the railway station to welcome back the heroes.

*Sean O'Grady was born in Killarney in 1945 and has worked as a fitter/turner, Insurance agent and company director while also giving 40 years of service as a public representative. A former chairman and secretary of his own club, Killarney Legion, his book 'The Wonderful Life of a Councillor' was received to critical acclaim after being launched in 2019.*

# The Game That Never Finished

## Peter Gordon

On a sunny Sunday afternoon in 1964, our local football team Mohill travelled to play a junior championship game against Gortletteragh, our neighbouring rivals. The venue was known as Fox's of Tooman, so called after a famous local hostelry. We travelled with our loyal supporters. By 3.25pm both teams were ready for the battle of the Titans but not unusual for the time, it was realised that the appointed referee had not arrived.

There was a rule in Leitrim which stated that if the appointed referee did not arrive, the away team could supply the person to take charge of the game. As it happened the manager of our team had made a bold decision to omit any player aged 28 or over for his selection. I was one of three established players dropped under his new policy and was thus approached to referee the game. This did not trouble me unduly as I had been refereeing underage matches for a year or two by then.

Before I threw in the ball I gave a little pep talk, the gist of which was that if I saw anyone throw a punch, the culprit would be sent straight to the line, thereby getting at least a month's suspension from the County Board.

Within five minutes I realised that my pre-match warning had fallen on deaf ears. Our corner back and their corner forward started punching one another. There were no such thing as yellow cards in those days so all I could say was: " Now lads, there is no need for any of that."

In a community like ours in south Leitrim, everybody knows everybody else. I knew the two lads very well. To compound my problem our player was a work colleague. In addition to having the "chat" with the players, I also appointed my linesmen and umpires. In the interest of balance and fair play, I appointed men from each club. On one side of the pitch, the Rynn River flows gently. Gortlettragh employed a young fellow equipped with a long pole to retrieve the ball from the river in case of some mis-kicking. It was certainly very prescient of them in hindsight as the young fellow was to have a busy afternoon.

It was, as I mentioned earlier, a lovely sunny day. When the ball went into the river, as it did so many times, the players would lie down on the pitch sunning themselves until hostilities resumed. These lads did not bother with sunblock or suntan lotion but decided to soak whatever rays came their way. I do not know what all the fighting was about as neither team had much hope of progressing to the business end of the championship.

The game started at 3.30pm. I did not have with me a stopwatch but rather just a H Samuel Everite watch or perhaps a more appropriate moniker would be a "Never right" watch that I had bought for about £2. The Mohill team had started brightly, kicking into the goalposts at the hostelry end. The umpires stationed there were our man, John Gallagher and Gortletteragh's John Patrick Sorohan.

The wild kicking resulted in the ball heading into the river countless times and together with the scuffles breaking out all over the pitch, the afternoon turned into evening. It was now six o'clock but I estimated that there were at least 15 minutes remaining to play before the full time whistle could be blown.

We never got that far. In those spartan GAA days, games were often played with goalposts which had no nets. I was positioned around the middle of the pitch when one of our forwards kicked in a long ball towards the Gortletteragh goal. John Gallagher of Mohill flagged for a goal and John Patrick Sorohan of Gortletteragh flagged for a point.

I was too far away to give a verdict. There was no 'Hawkeye' in Gortletteragh in those days! I went in to consult the umpires. Both men were adamant about their verdict. In the circumstances I felt I had no alternative but to abandon the game as I had a duty of care to the players as referee. I had to write a report and send it in to the county board.

As I had many friends on the Gortletteragh team, I made a point of sending a very mild version of events and did not mention the many fights that took place. The chairman of the Leitrim Co Board was the pipe smoking Fr. Sean Manning. He was a wonderful GAA man and held players in great esteem.

As the smoke from his pipe curled up towards the ceiling, he said in his droll voice: "I think there is more smoke than fire in this." He ordered that a replay take place with Mohill having home advantage this time.

Many years later at the funeral of one of our most fervent and passionate supporters, Teresa McGowan, who attended that match, an official in the club gave the graveside oration. He made reference to this particular game, the rows, and the ball being in the river half of the time as well as the disputed score.

He also mentioned that Teresa and I ended up in the river, presumably having been thrown in by the Gortletteragh side although I have no recollection of this. Apparently though Teresa got involved in a skirmish with the Gortletteragh players having taken exception to some of their heavy tackles on the Mohill players.

In his oration, the speaker recounted what had happened before and during the game and that the match was the longest in the history of the GAA. By abandoning the game at 6.15pm, with about 15 minutes remaining by my reckoning, I think it should be in the Guinness Book of Records as just that.

*Peter Gordon is a retired businessman and father of five grown up children. A proud Leitrim man, he has resided in Dublin for many years. His hobbies include, gardening, walking and supporters his native county's GAA teams.*

# Why Silence Is Golden After Picking A Team

## Jackie Napier

One of the great unwritten rules in GAA circles is that a selection committee never reveals the content of a meeting on how a team was picked. In 1936, the Wicklow county board appointed a committee of five, one from each district, north, south, east, west and a representative from the county champions, who at the time were Bray Emmets.

Bray had seven players on the team, including the captain. All went well until the team reached the Leinster Junior Football semi-final which took place in Aughrim against Dublin.

One of the selectors was away on holiday when the committee met to pick the team. Two of the selectors said they were unhappy with the Bray Emmets goalkeeper while the other two were not in favour of changing a winning team. Two votes for and two against. As none of the selectors was the chairman there wasn't a casting vote. It was decided that the names of the two goalkeepers should be put into a hat and the one that was drawn out should start.

The Bray keeper lost out and his replacement played against Dublin. The winning streak continued. All was well until the method of selection was revealed. One of the selectors bragged that it was he who had written the name of the other goalie on both pieces of paper. The Bray Emmet's player had no chance of his name being picked from the hat.

It would never have been an issue only for the loose-tongued selector. For the All-Ireland semi-final against Cavan, the team was scheduled to meet at Barry's Hotel in Dublin before the game in Croke Park. The seven Bray players decided that they would not go to the meeting and there was a real fear that almost half the team would not turn up for the match.

Fortunately that was not the case as the Bray lads met their fellow county men in Croke Park. They were welcomed with open arms and assured that their goalkeeper would have his place restored. Wicklow not only got the better of Cavan that day, but beat Mayo in the final as well. The seven players played both matches.

# Days Of Great Escapes And Mysterious Disappearances

Sean O'Dwyer

Trains and matches were synonymous, a harmonious parallel of excitement on match days or, more to the point, match mornings. Young lives were enriched in those early days in Carrick-on-Suir when special match-day train excursions were laid on.

It was a captivating sight, those cultural groups of men walking steadily towards the station, be-capped and solidly shod, topcoat slung over one shoulder and a brown paper parcel under the other.

Supporters, especially younger ones, wore badges and nicely designed paper hats that remained intact if the day was fine but if it rained there would be a stream of blue and gold ink running down the back of your neck.

Having food with you was important to keep the hunger pangs at bay for the long day ahead and the smell of freshly cut ham was as much part of the occasion as incense is of benediction, a tradition now defunct – the sandwiches that is.

As we distanced from the three GAA club hurling mad town, Swan and Davin pilgrims – usually staunch rivals – were now singing from the same hymn sheet as we left the town behind for our 'noisy neighbours' (St Mollerans who competed in the Waterford championship) to sulk in if we were victorious or to rejoice in if the unthinkable happened and we had squandered the day.

The Munster Final of 1959 was the occasion of my first match-day train journey to Thurles in the company of my sports-mad cousin, Liam Slattery, a former excellent dual player with Killenaule who became RC Archbishop of Pretoria in South Africa. We boarded at Laffinsbridge railway station on our pilgrimage to hurling's capital.

Other great venues have their own stories but for me that first dawn left a lasting impression. There is something very Irish about Liberty Square, even the name seeps of revolution and rebellion. This sacred place with its historical, cultural and sporting background is the spiritual home of hurling and the perfect pitch for the birthplace of the GAA.

The tradition of Gael camaraderie between rival supporters was always to the fore – apart from the odd defector – as they mingled in the town's sea of colour.

Through the eyes of a child, I saw the famous Christy Ring play but his display was overshadowed by an eventful sideshow. The biggest Cork man I'd ever seen bedecked in cape and sombrero stood with a spreadeagled posture on the touchline deliberately obstructing our view and that of the big Waterford contingent behind him.

Several requests to move were returned with nasty expletives by the bully along with a dare to a Waterford supporter who he had just described as 'a leprechaun.'

Up sprang the lightweight to the cheers and a standing ovation from the crowd. Without extra expense, they were then treated to the greatest exhibition of underdog victory since David slew Goliath. Waterford won the double that day – the fight and the match.

Three years later and with a licence to wear my own county colours, I was back on the same railway platform in Laffinsbridge, only this time our destination was Kingsbridge (Heuston Station) Dublin. At an early Mass in Killenaule, the congregation comprised match-goers and those who were psyched in meditation and aspiration for All-Ireland back-to-back victories. Oh yes, and a prayer for a good display from Killenaule's representative Tom Ryan.

The gods were with us as Tipp overcame a great Wexford side and the local hero scored one of the goals of the century. But for the unfortunate rude interruption of an unexpected narrow defeat to Waterford in the 1963 Munster championship which was then run on a knock-out system and with no chance of a back door reprieve, that Liam Devaney-inspired victory over Dublin two years previously could, and most probably would, have been the first of a record breaking five-in-a-row for Tipperary.

Such an achievement would have been a fitting tribute for that team and in particular for the peerless Mick Roche – a hurling colossus, class personified as well as being a great clubman and amazing friend. The great sportswriter Con Houlihan summed him up best of all when he categorised him in a sporting trilogy with Muhammad Ali and George Best as the greatest exponents of their respective codes.

It was the privilege of watching such class that drove us in our thousands to travel to the big matches. The train was always the people's friend and I need hardly add that there was a sense of romance about that mode of transport, especially on match-day expeditions when the atmosphere was electric.

There was no public address system on the train in those days which was particularly noted on the Laffinsbridge to Thurles line because whenever the train stopped for no apparent reason, panic would set in and aficionados would begin to worry about having to 'watch' the match on the wireless with commentary by the legendary Michael O'Hehir in some pub in Laffinsbridge or Horse & Jockey.

It never happened as far as I know but the return journey could be even more precarious as some bright sparks were known to dislodge some of the rear carriages much to the horror of those who found themselves in a stationary position or worse, in reverse. This actually happened. I know because I was one of the lucky passengers who witnessed 'The Great Escape' to purposefully borrow the apt title of the famous film of the day.

My friend Dan, a passionate Killenaule man, tells a story about a man called Jimmy. He was an extremely parochial man who enjoyed the simple life and rarely strayed beyond the confines of the parish jurisdiction until one day to the surprise of hurling enthusiasts, he decided to join them on a match-day train excursion to Thurles.

On arrival at the crowded station, however, Jimmy mysteriously vanished into thin air and small groups of searchers failed in their efforts to find him. News spread to the village and surrounding area and it soon became the topic of all concerned who were now enduring a period of anguish.

Sometime later word of Jimmy's 'departure' was conveyed to the Laffinsbridge railway station office much to the shock and dismay of his friends and villagers who on hearing the sad news were gathered in grief and consolation at the local Laffinsbridge pub.

As the hours passed that night, talk of funeral arrangements were in progress when suddenly to the shock of all present Jimmy miraculously appeared at the front door dubiously explaining that he had mistakenly walked onto a train scheduled for Dublin.

From that day on Jimmy, taking centre stage and with the encouraging effect of a few 'large bottles' would proudly boast of his 'experiences' in the metropolis and always with the opening line: "It was the day I was in Dublin for two days!"

*Sean O'Dwyer is from Carrick-on-Suir, Co Tipperary. Married to Helen, they have one son, Ryan. A retired shopkeeper and wholesale confectionery salesman to shops and supermarkets, his hobbies are Gaelic Games and soccer.*

# A Case Of No Sliotar, No Game

## John Arnold

It's hard to imagine nowadays that a championship game had to be abandoned because there was a shortage of sliotars but that actually happened during a game in Cork.

In the year 1960, the club in the parish was affiliated as St Bartholomews. They entered the East Cork JBHC. The draw pitted Bartholomews against St Coitins from the Ballycotton area. This game was fixed for Midleton on Sunday May 8. The club looked for a postponement of the fixture due to a parish Mission.

This was agreed and the refixture on June 16 saw St Bartholomews win easily by 12-4 to 1-7. Shanagarry Rovers beat Cobh in another first round game with the winners meeting in Round Two.

It was Sunday September 18, three months after the first round, when St Bartholomew's faced Shanagarry Rovers in Castlemartyr at 7.0pm. The Shanagarry side were well on top and led by 4-6 to 2-1 with six minutes to go. With no wire behind the lower goals – and a field of corn growing behind the pitch, both teams had lost several sliotars.

The last St Bartholomew's sliotar was driven into the field by John O'Brien, and whether this was by design or chance, no one knows for sure even to this day.

The referee, Mr Coughlan, asked both sides for a sliotar but none was to be had. A search of the cornfield commenced but no sliotar was found. The time had passed eight o'clock and darkness was descending. The referee had no option but to abandon the game.

The replay was played on Sunday October 9 at 3.30pm and this time there were plenty of sliotars available. St Bartholomew's had learned their lesson of the first day and trained hard during the three weeks interval. They ended up winning easily by 3-6 to 0-4.

# Four Years In The Young Life Of A GAA 'Sham'

## Barrie Henriques

'Barrie, you have got to learn to kick with your left foot as well," said my mentor Sr. Fursey, who was a member of the Presentation Convent in Tuam, the town of my birth.

It's 1947, just two years after the terrible second World War in which countless millions lost their lives in the defence of small nations – thousands of them Irishmen.

Ration books were a prized possession, where coupons for a half pound of butter and two ounces of sugar demanded a custodial severity reserved for the crown jewels in the Tower of London.

A tyre and tube for a bicycle – the working man's Rolls Royce – was worth the price of two milch cows and a gallon of petrol was worth 'London' as you would hear said in conversations around the town.

Our convent school team was getting ready for the annual challenge between Pres and the Boy Scout cubs team on the lawn in front of the opulent residence of the 100 or so resident nuns.

I scored a goal. My Dad was there and being a very staunch and proud Corkonian, I suspected that he was proud of me too. Sr. Fursey was proud that we managed to beat the scouts.

A nun who was a GAA football manager? Well Sr. Fursey was no ordinary nun and this was not her first sojourn into GAA management. There were teams before us, who were coached, and encouraged by the nun from somewhere outside Connemara, who could kick a football with either foot, with a force that would knock a small pony sideways.

There were a lot of young lads who cut their footballing teeth under the watchful eye of the kicking nun. Recorded in archival stories of GAA folklore are names like Seán Purcell, Frank Stockwell, Jack Mangan and others. That trio is enough to gild any roll of honour. Fast forward to 1956 and you will hear of the greatness of Sr. Fursey's most iconic acolytes.

After that match on the convent lawn, my uncle Willie (Kelly), who was secretary of one of the most famous football clubs in the history of the game, Tuam Stars, made me a member of the Stars club, and gave me a shilling for my First Communion in 1947.

While Tuam people were 'shams,' and the lads outside the town were called 'buff shams' their football teams were known as the Stars to every 'sham.' Willie and my mother were brother and sister. My Grannie was May Stockwell. I'm sure you can see where this is going.

Every waking minute of my young life then was an amalgam of all things GAA, and in particular football. I never saw a hurley until the early 1950s but that too is another story.

The Stars football pitch back then was called Parkmore and several All Ireland semi-finals were held there in the earlier part of the last century. It was sited in the middle of the 100 acre Tuam Racecourse. Getting into it – one entrance off the Dublin Road – was easy for us youngsters from that area. We lived at No 9, Tubberjarleth, a sizeable social housing development. At the time I was waiting in Parkmore for "the lads" – Seaneen, Frankeen, Mangan and Mayo's Pat Doherty to arrive on their bikes for training. My job was to kick the ball back to them when it went behind the goal.

Often it took me two kicks to get it back, but I was 10-feet tall "playing" with those big lads, one of whom was my cousin.

They were all destined to be forever engraved in the annals of greatness whenever men discussed Gaelic Football. Eight years later I jumped on him in the middle of Croke Park after Galway had beaten Cork in the '56 Final, and my colceathar had created a scoring record that has never been beaten. He scored 2-5 of the Galway total, which will now last forever, as it was a 60-minute final and all the scores were from play.

We were both crying.

Back to the racecourse – the final two furlongs ran parallel to the Dublin Road, surrounded by the 12-foot high stone wall. As a matter of fact, the infamous Tuam babies Mother and Baby home, with its 12-foot high wall and unwelcoming timber door, also ran the length of the race track on the opposite side of the Dublin Road.

Getting to the pitch you had to cross the race track. The last ditch in the steeplechase course was but a hen's kick to your right. Seating arrangements in Parkmore consisted of five rows of railway sleepers on concrete supports along the entire length of one side. It was a big venue that time in Connacht as Tuam was considered a very central location geographically, with a railway line and decent approach roads.

I remember attending a couple of provincial finals in the place. I saw Galway play Roscommon and I recall it if for nothing else than seeing the great Jimmy Murray, Eamonn Boland and a full-back by the name of Brendan Lynch playing.

Mayo played Galway in another Connacht Final there. Galway weren't great at the time, and Mayo were the talked about team of the era.

It wasn't exactly sexy to have an interest in the GAA in that era. Media coverage was abysmally sparse – it was virtually apologists' copy. Whilst Michael O'Hehir arrived down to do the Galway races, with special interest in the plate and the hurdle, he would always do Tuam Races on the third day of his visit. However, he never came west of the big river to do any GAA games until much later in his career.

My Uncle Willie, who lived with my Grannie on Bishop Street, lived by the mantra that if you couldn't do the job right, you shouldn't bother doing it at all. For Sunday matches he lined Parkmore from a bucket of whitewash (he got the water from our house) and a hand-held brush. When the weather was inclement, he lined it from bags of sawdust that he got at the local sawmill on the Athenry Road.

But it was the Street Leagues I remember best from an all-consuming GAA life model. Fr. Fitzsimmons, a curate attached to Tuam Cathedral, was the organiser and mentor to a burgeoning youth movement in the town.

I felt as though there were thousands at every match. There certainly were many hundreds present and our Dublin Road team had great players like Tommy Brosnan, the Brennans, Henehans, Holians, McNamaras, Murphys, Cloonans, and O'Garas. Brosnan later won a minor All Ireland with Galway in 1952 – the county's first. Bishop Street's Brian Waldron was also on that team.

They beat Cavan 2-6 to 1-3. We had to wait until Tommy came home on the Monday to find out who won. Galway Road had a captain who was probably one of the greatest young footballers in Tuam at the time, the iconic, brilliant, internationally acclaimed playwright, Tom Murphy.

At local level, we had some murderous senior club games in Parkmore. I couldn't be kept out of the place. My mother didn't want to let me go because I would be scampering in among the players in the middle of the field at half-time, and being of very slight stature, she felt that I could be trampled to death if anything unseemly happened, as was often the case.

I remember one wet Sunday at a game between Carantrayla and Cortoon. There was always a certain feistiness between most sides, but there was most certainly a little more between the aforementioned combatants.

A Cortoon player was 'anointed' with a vintage Muhammad Ali right uppercut. The perpetrator was set upon by the entire parish who swarmed onto the pitch. I was among them in my best Sunday short trousers, and my rubber dollies- light canvas slippers with a very light rubber sole. They were only for Sunday wear.

The poor Carrantrayla lad ran like an escaping convict down the racecourse. The baying hordes behind him were looking for revenge. I was with them. One of my Sunday best dollies fell off my foot, but undaunted, I charged on in top gear. As the pack reached the entrance to the straight at the top of the racecourse, the 'hare' had a dilemma as he was fast approaching a 12-foot obstacle.

Looking behind, his options were a long way from optimal so he had no choice but to jump into a thick blackthorn bush, which was growing underneath the wall.

"We have him now lads," roared one of the chasing pack. "He won't get out of that thorny tree."

Ali made it to the top of the wall, and before he "lepped down" on the other side, he paused atop the wall where a big smile broke out on his face.

"Ye bastards won't ketch me now," he roared with a triumphant smirk on his face.

A wag down below remarked: "Jazus lads, if we could put a saddle on that lad, he'd win the Plate next year."

On the way back from the chase, St Anthony came to my rescue ... I found the missing rubber dollie near the final fence... there is a God!

Around this time a Street League for adults was started up as well. I remember the battles between our lads (Dublin Road) and Ballygaddy and recall seeing the likes of Purcell, Stockwell, John Nallan (Mayo), Pat Doherty (Mayo), Possie Connolly, Tony Mongan, Miko Kelly, Murt Burke, Jimmy Moran (Leo's Dad – Sawdoctors), Bomber Leo, Jamesy Corbett, Brosnan, Waldron, 'Scoff' Brennan, Pakie Shaughnessy, Tommy Varden, and many others throw everything they had on the pitch for the sake of the little serfdom in their area. As they would say in Tuam: "Twas mighty shhtuf sham."

Uncle Willie told me that there were moves afoot to build a new stadium in Milo Campbell's field behind the Railway Station. This was a stadium mind you. We were the first town in Ireland to build a stadium. It was more posh than a pitch.

As I said, Tuam was the epicentre of all GAA Provincial activity, being not too far from the Roscommon and Mayo borders, with a railhead not 100 yards away from the stadium. It was also the first GAA stadium in Ireland with a raised playing surface, very much in the style of the Croke Park I saw for the Railway Cup Finals in 1952.

The sideline seating facilities were way ahead of the Croke Park model.

## FOUR YEARS IN THE LIFE OF A YOUNG GAA 'SHAM'

In Croker for my first visit in 1952, railway sleepers were the seats, whereas in Tuam Stadium, the sideline seating – I think I counted 18 rows all around the pitch – were solid concrete. It was the first in Ireland to lay a cinders sub surface. The cinders came from the coal-burning sugar factory about three miles down the railway track.

My granduncle, Paddy Quinlan was an engine driver for CIE based in Tuam. In his spare time, this genial soul would take his engine down the line, hook up to 4/6 wagons full of cinders and bring it back to the goods siding next door to the stadium. It was built by Tuam people, for the town. Every evening, a vast number of working men would go to the stadium.

People with horses and carts, donkeys and carts would carry the cinders to the stadium after their suppers. There were teams of men with shovels, wheelbarrows, and spades waiting to spread the cinders.

No hymacs then as it was a case of everyone bringing their own working tool. Costs were kept to a minimum commensurate with the enormous community effort. No grants from any source; no rich benefactors; Tuam people had to "ride their own bikes" to make their state-of-the-art stadium their legacy for future generations. And, you know, they are still proud of it down there.

We kids were not idle in this great movement. We marched in twos to the site along with the rest of the lads in the CBS to pick stones. The Jarlaths' lads had their days too, even though many of them were not even Galwegians; they came from all over Connacht.

On May 21, 1950 (The Holy Year), Cavan played Mayo, and Galway played Dublin to mark the opening of the stadium. As if he wasn't busy enough, Willie brought me in by the hand. My Ma gave me a tanner, that was the silver coin with the greyhound on the front and the harp on the back. It was a king's ransom to me. I still have vivid memory of John Wayne, Barry Fitzgerald, Victor McLaglan, Ward Bond and the enchanting Maureen O'Hara making their way to their seats-suitably escorted by officials vying with each other to get their photograph into the 'Tuam Herald with one or other of the stars.

At that time they were filming The Quiet Man over in Cong about 22 miles away.

Following the decimating National Sugar factory strike that lasted from 1948 until 1950, my Dad was forced to get work in Ballyshannon. The workers in all four factories and their families ware close to starvation as a result of that lockout. Dad eventually got a job in the first turf-burning ESB power station, and our hearts were broken as my mother loaded the five of us into the cab of a furniture removal truck for our new life in a town we knew nothing about, called Portarlington on the Laois/Offaly border.

I couldn't get Tuam or the faces of all of my cousins out of my mind. I missed Parkmore. I missed the hype of race week in Galway and Tuam. I missed my uncle Willie; Frankeen, the Stars, and Purcell. I missed Tuam.

But you know, to this day, I doubt if any young lad outside of the town of Tuam has ever had the indoctrination – you might even call it radicalisation – that one Francis Finbarr, Anthony Jarleth Henriques (endearingly known as Barrie) was exposed to over that four-year semester in Parkmore on the rudiments of our great game.

It turned me into a GAA soldier for life …and sure why wouldn't it when you consider the tutors I had.

*Barrie Henriques was born in Tuam, Co Galway in 1940 but became known nationally as a sports journalist operating out of Kilkenny after returning from London in the early seventies to buy a pub in Callan. Married with four children, one deceased, he has edited the Kilkenny GAA Yearbook for over 30 years.*

# Playing With Two Legends Of Different Eras

## Seán O'Sullivan

Not too many people can make the claim of having played on the same team as the legendary Mick O'Connell and also replacing the inimitable Eoin 'Bomber' Liston during a game. As Con Houlihan would say – now read on!

Being from Kerry means that football talk is never far away during our waking moments, while constantly present also while we sleep. It is not just something we turn on the evenings after work; in truth it is a massive part of our DNA.

One day at work when as always I was talking proudly and passionately about The Kingdom a colleague asked me if I ever played for Kerry.

I told him that I came on for The Bomber and also played with the great Mick O'Connell. And yes, all in that previous sentence is true in one sense but overall is not as it seems.

Let me explain: When I was growing up I played for O'Rahilly's Ballylongford and we were part of the divisional team Shannon Rangers for the county championship. One evening in the early eighties, the Rangers were playing a team from Clare (who came across on the Killimer Car Ferry) in Ballylongford in a challenge. I was walking to the village when I met Jackie Walsh, who did play with Kerry, and he told me the Rangers were short a number of players and asked if I would play?

I was a goalkeeper and was thrilled to be asked. By the time I'd gone home to get my gear and arrived back up at the pitch, the game had started. Jackie told me to go in goal and who was standing there in civvies only Eoin 'The Bomber' Liston.

Looking resplendent in jeans and casuals, he was delighted to shake my hand as he escaped without having to dirty his clothes by diving to make a save or being knocked down by over eager forwards wanting to leave a mark on him.

Back in the office, my esteemed colleague looked at me and smiled at the story. It was if to say "fair enough that's plausible" but now explain Mick O'Connell to me.

Micko is the supreme god of Kerry football after all, having played for The Kingdom in three decades from 1956 right up to 1974.

So I told him my O'Connell story. In the late eighties, I emigrated to New York and got a job in construction. The union delegate over the construction was Tommy Hennessy from Ballylongford and he was involved with the Kerry GAA in New York at the time.

I decided to get involved also as the GAA community was and is a great network when you are away from home. My friends Chris and Noel Larkin used to travel to Gaelic Park or Van Cortlandt Park in the Bronx for training. At that time only the Kerry team could train in Gaelic Park by permission of John Kerry O'Donnell.

Some evenings Hennessy would arrive at the park and watch us train from the bleachers. On one particular evening he arrived with Micko, who was working as a shop steward for the 18A union at the time. They watched us train under the guidance of Pat Burrows from Tralee and later 'Connell', as most people called him, came out onto the field to demonstrate some free-taking techniques. This he did perfectly despite the fact that he was wearing a pair of construction boots.

Needless to say I was in awe of the man as the last time I saw him play was in a national league game in Tralee. That day he came on as a sub but it was very much towards the end of his career. It was the first time I ever saw a player get a standing ovation from the crowd and the memory still gives me tingles.

But back to New York. In the next training session, O'Connell togged out and as a 24-year-old, I estimated that he was about twice my age.

We played a game of backs and forwards and he was on my team. He was marked by my friend Chris who played at full-back in front of me in the goal. The maestro showed us that class was permanent by kicking four points.

The following Sunday we were playing Cavan in the championship and Micko arrived in the dressing room and togged out. The manager told us all to be quiet and read out the team. In goals – Seán O'Sullivan, and went all the way up to the full forward position when he declared... number 14, Mick O'Connell.

And there you have it. I did indeed line out in New York with the great Mick O'Connell for Kerry and don't forget I also came on as a sub for the Bomber.

*Seán O Sullivan is a native of Ballylongford in Kerry. He works as an environmental technologist in Limerick and is a lifelong member and activist in the Ballylongford GAA club.*

# The Soccer Man Who Led Rebels To Hurling Paradise

Frank F Murphy

Derry Cremen never played hurling. Soccer was his sport and he was to pay a terrible price for his love of the beautiful game. A misdiagnosed hip injury in his late teens, allied to the crude orthopaedic treatment of the 1940s, left him on crutches all his adult life. Yet he was to inspire a generation of youngsters in Ballinlough that backboned the glorious era of Blackrock and Cork hurling in the 1970s.

There is no signpost for Ballinlough. Even natives are somewhat unsure of its boundaries. It meanders from the City Hall to Beaumont Quarry and lies between the Well and Blackrock Roads. It is centred roughly on that stretch from Our Lady of Lourdes Church to Driscoll's shop and it was from a low wall outside that shop that Derry Cremen oversaw his dominion.

A young parish in the 1950s, those of us that grew up in Ballinlough were all first-generation country boys and we had three beacons held up for us by our parents: the church, education and the GAA. We got plenty of scope for all three as we sported and played around the newly built housing estates and the former market gardens of Ballinlough.

Derry was the fulcrum of our young lives. Like the Pied Piper we gathered around him at Driscoll's wall every lunchtime and his influence was totally benign. We lapped up his stories of Timothy Jim O'Keeffe from Ballintemple, who played international soccer for Ireland; of Fulham, Farrell, Fagin and Flood, the great Shamrock Rovers quartet of the 30s, of Jimmy Turnbull, the Englishman who scored 63 goals in his first season with Cork F.C. and, of course, it was from Derry we first heard of Gah and Balty Ahern, of Eudie Coughlan and Maree Connell, of Jim Hurley and John Quirke, that pantheon of hurlers that had brought glory and honour to Cork and Blackrock.

Derry was the key holder of 'Jocks'... the home of a local man who was confined for many years in hospital. It was there we would gather in the evenings and watch Derry struggle against his infirmity as he repaired hurls for the minor team.

He'd place a broken chair with a metal vice attached on the kitchen table and we'd jostle each other to hold the hurl steady while Derry bound on the steel band that protected the hurl from cracking and gave it balance and power.

I remember the first time he spliced a new St. Lua hurl and handed it to me. "There", he said, as I stood speechless, "you'd stop a swallow going through a barn door with that."

I had arrived!

Derry never tolerated bad or uncouth language or conduct in his company and card playing in Jock's was taboo. The talk was hurling, pure and simple. We'd sit around the open fire and drink in the anecdotes of our elders as they relived clashes with the Glen or the Barrs or trips to Thurles to see Christy Ring take on 'The Rattler' Byrne in mortal combat in the 'Hell's Kitchen' that was the Tipperary goalmouth. We'd go home drunk with the excitement of it all and wonder would we ever play hurling for the Rockies or, dare we dream, with Cork?

We hurled up and down the Ballinlough Road, along Sundrive Park, our home ground, Belmont Park and then, for excitement, we'd travel 'away' as far as Pic-du-Jer Park – a whole bus stop away. A match could go on for hours and we'd only grudgingly hold up proceedings to let the No. 14 bus pass.

Teams would be replenished or diminished as players were called home to have their tea or do their homework. The match carried on regardless and players could be dismayed on their return to find the opposition had scored five or six goal in their absence. The battle would be re-joined and away we'd go again, skin and hair flying. I remember the first time a group of us ventured down to Church Road and our dismay at finding it was a field.

A field. How could you play hurling in a field?

As we progressed from primary to secondary school there grew up around Derry a generation of young hurlers from the locality that began to bring honour and glory to Cork and Blackrock. The year 1956 saw Derry's first success when his U-15 team, captained by Mick Waters, won the City Divisional title. It was only a 'C' grade competition but, remarkably, no fewer than eight of that team were to win All-Ireland medals.

Four of Derry's prodigies were to captain Cork All-Ireland winning minor teams and in 1968, Cork lined out in an All-Ireland Minor final with seven of Derry's boys in the starting fifteen.

Eventually there wasn't a park or road in Ballinlough that didn't boast an All-Ireland medal holder or an African Missionary priest. Of particular joy to Derry was to travel to the SMA Novitiate in Newry, Co Down to see his first captain, Mick Waters, ordained a priest just a few months after he had starred for Cork at midfield in the 1966 All-Ireland final.

Within three short years Derry was dead, taken from us much too early while still in his forties. How could a man of such a quiet disposition and with no background at all in hurling have produced such a generation of talented players?

Those were different times, of course, and you'd get short shrift now if you tried to play hurling on the Ballinlough Road. But there was something innately good about Derry that both attracted us youngsters to him and inspired us to embrace the sport of hurling and The Rockies club.

There is a great deal made now before big matches on the TV of 'fair play' and 'respect'. Derry Cremen preached that doctrine to us youngsters 50 years ago and he did so without any flags waving or banners flying, His simple ways taught us honesty and integrity; that you don't take shortcuts or cheat. Above all, he taught us that success doesn't count unless you earn it fair and square; integrity has no need of rules.

I've no doubt that angels led him into paradise.

*Frank F Murphy was born, bred and still lives in Ballinlough in the family home. His brother Simon won All Irelands at minor, U-21 and senior with Cork, the latter when beating Wexford, the land of his father, in 1970. (Additional information from Kevin Cummins).*

# Stuck Up Player With The Flour Power Togs

### Jamesie Murphy

During 'The Emergency' in the 1940s, there was a scarcity of all kinds of material for making clothes. Housewives begged shopkeepers to keep the white flour bags for them when they became empty.

These 20st bags bore the brand names of Odlums from St Mullin's and Heart's Delight, a product of the Waterford Flour Mills.

The bags were used for lots of things including making sheets, bibs and aprons for the women as well as making togs for the hurlers and footballers.

One such footballer worked in Waterford city where some of our local girls were also employed. He was a stuck-up kind of lad and barely bade the time of day to his neighbours from the same parish.

However, on the Sunday his team were playing football and your man trotted out in style rigged out in his flour-bag togs. One of the team's female followers to whom he had barely spoken to all week shouted out: "Will you look at your man, not a word to us all week, and now he thinks he is God's gift to women, with Heart's Delight blazed across his arse".

# The Pitch With The Humped Back Middle

## Pat Healy

When you are born and bred into the GAA, it is galling not to have your own team represent you with your own parish name on the club crest.

In 1978, a group of us felt that way and held a small meeting in the old national school – which has since become a community centre – to see if we could reform our club.

There had been none in the parish for quite some time which meant the neighbouring clubs like Belmullet and Kiltane could pick two or three of our best lads to play with them, leaving the rest to twiddle their thumbs.

Our first push to reform saw 20 players declare and immediately we decided to order football boots for them. That was because a number of our volunteers had never worn a football boot in their lives and did not know what size to order.

So with the problem of having sufficient numbers now solved, our next task was to find a pitch. That was easy to do as I had a field, not perfectly flat, which I knew would be good enough for football purposes.

That said I must show my gratitude to great GAA men like Dr. Mick Loftus and Paddy Muldoon who allowed us play in my field for years until we got our own new, proper pitch.

You could see I suppose in hindsight why the opposition might be miffed at having to play on our pitch.

They ran the gauntlet from arrival to departure as they had to initially criss-cross a stream to enter and then to exit the playing area. That was after togging out in the hayshed, which while warm and luxurious for calves and cows, had little other than shelter to commend itself to humans in the 20th century.

They also had to come to terms with the trajectory of the pitch as there was a high mound in the middle. When I say 'high' let me give you an idea of what I mean. Neither goalies nor fullback lines could see what was happening at the other end of the field due to the elevation in and around the half-way line.

# GRASSROOTS

The unusual trigonometry certainly took a bit of getting used to, hence visiting teams found it difficult to beat us. Needless to say we had loads of objections but the local GAA hierarchy stood by us.

We entered the club in the North Mayo junior championship and had a good run of victories despite or maybe because of the 16th man on our team – the brokeback mound we called our pitch. There were also a few game-time issues such as retrieving the ball when it errantly landed in the field beside our pitch. There was a resident bull there which took his job of minding the cows to the extreme by chasing any human who dared to enter his territory.

For all that, there were many fine players who graced our temporary home pitch including the former Mayo player and All Ireland winning manager with Galway, John O'Mahony.

In 1989, I shed a tear of joy one day in Croke Park at the mention of our beloved Glenamoy club underneath the name of the Mayo goalkeeper, Gabriel Irwin.

Gabriel went on to win an All-Star goalkeeper award that year – just over a decade after our grassroots came together and made sure youngsters such as he got the chance to play for club… and now for county.

*Pat Healy is a native of Glenamoy, Ballina, Co Mayo. Married with five children, he officially retired a few years ago. His hobbies cross all sports but is a particularly avid GAA fan.*

# The Day The Bomb Dropped On Kerry In 1982

## John B. Keane

I didn't make it to the All-Ireland football final, and I gave up watching it on television because of a faint fluttering at the rear of the breastbone. I upped and hopped into my car and skedaddled for the quiet slopes of Cnocanore, one time gathering place of the Fianna and still standing serenely in similar contour. Not a solitary Christian was abroad. I parked my car five hundred feet up and proceeded on foot to the summit.

I had hardly gone a hundred yards when I encountered an old lady with a rosary beads in her hands.

"Well Moll," says I, "How are you?"

"Praying for the boys," she said, "praying they'll do better in the second half and how are you yourself Johnny B?"

"Couldn't stick the excitement of it," I confessed, "so I came out here to get away from it."

"Yerra come on to the house aweenach," she said, "and we'll watch the rest of it. Jack is inside and he'll give you something to calm you."

We went towards the house which was flanked on either side by two of the largest and most haw-hung whitethorn bushes I had ever seen. Along the way the briars were draped with shimmering blackberries. I picked a handful and handed them to Moll before picking a handful for myself.

"Blackberries are the boys for the bowels," she said confidently, "and when I was a girl they'd be picked before now. No one bothers these days. We used to make jam of 'em and jelly and pies and bottle the juice for the winter, great for colds. You could mix it with wine or whiskey too."

"How's Jack?" I asked.

"He's cranky these days," she said, "and if Kerry don't win, he'll be worse."

In the house he sat all wrapped up in the television. No colour here, just plain black and white.

"If we knew you were coming," said he sarcastically, "we'd have made balls of butter for you."

He rose and produced a bottle of Paddy Flaherty from the cupboard. He poured a decent dollop into a glass but took none himself.

"I'm drinking all morning," he explained, "went into Nolan's after Mass and swallowed my fill."

We sat, all three of us, and watched the game. After five minutes I rose and explained that I could endure it no longer.

"Sit down you cowardly custard," he called as I walked out the door. Outside it was like the aftermath of a nuclear drop-out. No being stirred as I drove homewards. The roads were entirely deserted. It would never be as lonely again unless human life was wiped out by the bomb or if Kerry were going for five in a row again.

I got home in time to see the bomb of the day drop. It was a despairing kick but an inspired kick. The minute Seamus Darby fielded that dropping ball the Fates stopped smiling on Kerry. You may smirk at this, but I believe that Darby was born to score that last-minute Offaly goal. Pierpoint was born to be a hangman and Piggot to be a jockey and so Darby was destined from the moment of his birth to do what he did when he did it.

That's fate for you.

That night when the post-mortems were all concluded my daughter appeared wearing her five in a row jersey. Earlier in the day she had been inconsolable, had shed bitter tears after the final whistle had sounded but now hope was springing anew and all the thousands of five-in-a-row jerseys would be worn just for the craic, at least those that had been bought before the game.

I had an inkling before the game that Kerry might not win when I read of the argument between Tralee and Killarney spokesmen as to whether the reception should be held in Tralee or Killarney. Surely this was flying in the face of the same fates that placed Seamus Darby in a certain spot at a certain time. It was the kind of talk that simply begs defeat.

Offaly won squarely and fairly but Kerry went down gracefully and in my book the manner of their defeat was their finest achievement since 1975.

(Seamus Darby writes: The following year after that match, I was in John B's pub in Listowel one summer's night with my wife Verrone, enjoying a pint. The place was heaving and the crack was mighty as the great man mingled with his customers and his son Billy kept the drink flowing from behind the bar. I didn't think I was recognised until the owner put up his hand, called for ciúnas and said: "Ladies and gentleman, we have among us tonight the man who climbed the highest branch of the highest tree to slay Kerry last September." As the crowd applauded, I was totally dumbstruck but also humbled that this great man of words would describe my goal in such terms. The honour lives with me and will to the end of my days. Thanks you John B.)

## THE DAY THE BOMB DROPPED ON KERRY IN 1982

*John B Keane, (1928-2002) is a legendary Kerry playwright, whose body of work both entertained and educated Ireland's people as they made the transition from fledgling state to modern nation. Among his best known work was The Field, which was adapted for the silver screen in 1990. Richard Harris received an Academy Award nomination for his performance as Bull McCabe in the Best Actor category.*

*John B, who was also an essayist and novelists, owned a landmark pub 'John B's' in his native Listowel with his wife Mary; they had four children, three sons Billy, Conor, John and daughter Joanna.*

# The Man Who Scored Twice With The One Shot

### Donal O'Shea

The parish of Meelick Parteen and Ardnacrusha straddles the Limerick border and over the years they played collectively and separately and in 1971 Meelick and Parteen went their separate ways.

In 1917 Meelick won the Clare Intermediate Hurling Championship. One of the players Paddy White was afterwards shot in Spike Island during the troubled times. Another member of the side Jack Liston made history. He is the man credited with scoring a goal and a point with the same puck of the ball. The cover of the ball went over the bar and the inside went under and both flags were raised. A photograph of this team proudly hangs in The Cusack GAA Centre in Carron.

Two Ringrose brothers John and Tom were also members of that team and their extended family went on to star in other sports; Billy in equestrian and Gary in rugby.

The power station was one of the major catalysts that helped form the club. Thousands of workers assisted in the building of the Ardnacrusha power station. Calling themselves the "Shannon Schemers" they played and trained in the field at the back of the present post-office. With the club registered, it fielded two teams and many joined in the games... even the German contractors.

In one such match the referee John Walsh, father of the late Irish Times political editor Dick Walsh from Cratloe, reported to the county board that four languages were used. English, Irish, German and bad language.

With the completion of the station the 'Schemers' disbanded and the games in the parish returned to normal.

# Forgetting My 'Name' While Playing Féile Illegally In Roscommon

Joe Connolly

Back in the early seventies, I was a butcher boy in a summer job in Ó Mearas when I got a phone call at work one day – we had no phone at home. It was from Harry Murray who had a few shoe shops in Galway city though he originally hailed from and kept strong ties with Knockcroghery in county Roscommon.

He asked: "Are you doing anything this evening?"

I said "no" so he told me he wanted me and another player, Mícheál Glynn, to play a hurling match for St Dominic's against a very strong Four Roads team in the Roscommon Féile final.

I was 15 which was the age limit at the time for this competition though later it was reduced to 14 years of age. I think Mícheál would have been overage but that was the least of our worries as we were going into another county to play as bangers under assumed names.

It was good training though as years later Mícheál and myself were on the Castlegar team that won the All Ireland senior club final in 1980.

When Harry asked me if I'd play I told him I'd be delighted to except I had no hurl with me and obviously no gear as I wasn't expecting to have to tog out that day. He told me not to worry as he would phone ahead and arrange to have two hurls and two sets of togs and socks as well as boots ready for us.

We were met outside the town. Harry had a bit of a name for bringing lads down from Galway so if he was seen driving into the pitch in Athleague it might have looked a little bit suspicious. He was well versed in what to do. We pulled up about a mile outside Athleague and were transferred to local cars where we were given the gear and in my case a very small juvenile hurl – way too small for the size I had become at almost 15.

As I recall, we were told that a family had left the area to go to England some time before and two of their sons were very handy hurlers. For the life of me I can't remember their names but I was to be one of the brothers and Micheál got the other name. That way, there was some sort of story line to go with the fact that Four Roads might not have encountered the two new players for a few years.

Four Roads were a cracking outfit and were maybe five or six goals ahead at half-time. I was at nothing with this little hurl so I asked if I could get an adult hurl to play with for the second half. I hadn't made much of an impression up to then.

The second half started and at last I was able to play now that I had the proper equipment. I got three or four goals fairly quickly and there was a sense of expectation that we could come close if not win the match.

The referee was a Christian Brother who knew every good hurler in the county and once I started getting the scores, he was baffled that he hadn't noticed me on the local circuit before.

So while there was a lull in playing awaiting a puck out after I scored one of the goals, he ran over to me and asked me my name. I looked at him in total shock. For the life of me I couldn't remember the new name I had been given before the game.

I had to think fast. All I could come up with was to hold my stomach area and tell the ref that I had a fierce pain. He looked at me somewhat perplexed as I dramatically slumped to my knees for a few seconds. Then when the goalie pucked the sliotar out again, I got up and made a note to keep well away from the ref for the rest of the match. Just to be sure, I went over to our mentors on the touchline asking what my name was in case the official did catch up with me again. I remembered it for the rest of the match but have long since forgotten what name I operated under that day.

Anyway, we played as a team transformed in the second half and the competitor inside me thought with about five minutes to go that we could win the game.

I looked down the pitch and seeing my Castlegar teammate, Micheál, roared at the top of my voice: "Come on 'Cashel', we can do this." That's what Castlegar was known as and it was out of my mouth before I realised I was a Dominick's man for the day.

Fortunately no one seemed to notice what I'd just shouted. We lost by a point or maybe two but such was the comeback that the supporters and officials were very proud of our efforts and gave the team a rousing reception as we came off the pitch.

Micheál and myself were very disappointed at the outcome though we were treated royally when we were fed in Jimmy Murray's after the game. The journey back to Galway was shortened because it had been a great game to play in, and Harry was delighted at how we fought back.

## FORGETTING MY 'NAME' WHILE PLAYING FÉILE ILLEGALLY IN ROSCOMMON

Four Roads had a very sturdy, not for moving corner-back named Liam Dowd and when I was going through after scoring a few goals, he gave me a tackle to end all tackles. It was so hard that I can still feel it.

About three or four years later I was talking to the lads in UCG about Four Roads, he informed me that he was the player who tackled me in that Féile match which he remembered well. We have been life long friends since.

A few years ago, I was at a funeral in Dublin and I met Dom Cox at it. Dom also played in that Féile game and was by far the best player we had. All those years later we started talking about the game as if it was only yesterday.

When Harry died a few years ago, I thought how he had brought so many friends together for me in those Féile days and other ones like them.

The big shock for me is that this is the 50th anniversary of our cross-border excursion into Roscommon for that match.

Looking back now, I am convinced it was all for the best that we lost because if we had managed to win, there was no way that Mícheál and myself would have got away with being part of another club's team for a long national Féile weekend.

In the end everyone got something out of the game; we were beaten but showed great heart to fight back and give the St Dominic's supporters something to cheer about. Our opponents, Four Roads, rightly represented their county in the national finals in Tipperary because they were the best Roscommon team to do so and deserved their win.

*Joe Connolly is the former Galway hurling captain forever immortalised for his All Ireland winning acceptance speech in the Hogan Stand in 1980.*

# Three Amigos Who Caused Havoc At Every Turn

### John Caplice, Mallow, Co Cork

Mick, Pete and Davey went to every match that was on.

Davey was very excitable. He watched games through a haze of smoke, getting so worked up with the ref once that he confused himself by putting the box of matches in his mouth while throwing away the pipe.

Mick, a pure countryman, couldn't bear to miss a hurling match. He was close to 25st and his car was consequently always low to the ground when carrying him. Pete was well known around the place for his nerves and irritability but also for his deep match analysis: "They're only a pack of woodbines, not a player in 'em".

They knew every trick and shortcut, creating their own brand of mayhem wherever they went. Mick, driving in late to a match one day, was so busy watching it out across the passenger window so as not to miss any action, crashed his Ford Anglia. His devotion cost him one bumper and one front door for the other parked car.

But it was Davey, launching an extra sliotar into a melee in the square that caused the most havoc at an U-14 match played at dusk. That was Davey's first and last time being allowed on the sideline. From then on he was condemned to watch from outside the wire next to Pete who himself had been barred for tampering with a loose goalpost.

Pete, acting as umpire and finding a little movement in the west post, gave it a timely push that forced a wide into a point. That had been Pete's second chance. Previously he had called for a 70 and ran 10 yards down the end line before realising his mistake and waving the wide. Everyone agreed Pete should be allowed another go until the goalpost incident. Needless to say, his umpiring days were over from that day forward.

A trip to a Munster final in Killarney saw the three in a hotel in the town for their dinner. Mick, being accustomed to his wife emptying a large pot of spuds onto the table every day couldn't believe his eyes when the waitress served them three small potatoes each on a side plate. Mick stuck a fork in one and called after the waitress "you can be bringing them on, they're done enough."

# Three All-Irelands – The Good, The Bad And The Bubbly

### Dan Kerr

I attended my first All-Ireland final in the 1930s. The events of the day have left an impression on me to his day. We travelled by train from Clones to Dublin. There was a long delay, just outside of Drogheda. This held us up for more than an hour. We were very late arriving into Dublin. It was a setback especially for men who had expected to be able to attend Mass before the big match.

Most of my friends decided to forego Mass and go straight to Croke Park. Jimmy Murphy, the treasurer of Clones GAA club, knew where we could go to a late service, so I went along with him. I was crestfallen after Mass finished because I was certain that my chance to see the final had passed me by. Jimmy already had his ticket, so I decided to accompany him as far as Croke Park, to have a look around, get something to eat and find somewhere to listen to the match on the radio.

As I was walking alone down by the canal bank, I noticed a few men were taking off their boots and shoes. They crossed the canal on wooden planks to the opposite bank, just behind the Cusack Stand. An array of helping hands, who were already inside hoisted them up over the wall into the stadium. I joined the brave souls crossing water and then high barriers to get to their sporting Shangri-La.

I was so grateful when these strangers pulled me up as well. I thanked them profusely and marvelled at the view I had before finding myself a nice spot from which I could sit down and watch the final.

I was less lucky at my second final. I started out in good spirits. Myself and three friends left Clones in my brother's hackney. This final was to be contested between the neighbouring counties of Meath and Cavan. The two Maguire brothers were playing on opposing teams.

We decided to go to Dublin via Cootehill and Kingscourt. There would be too much traffic on the main road. Our journey was going well. We were looking forward to seeing the match. Suddenly, a car appeared from a by-road and drove into the side of our vehicle.

We were knocked sideways through the air, sent tumbling over a hedge before coming to a standstill on the marshy ground of a low-lying field. Scrambling through the upside-down doors in total shock, we were thankful when we checked to see that none of us was injured. A crowd of people passing by in another car stopped and helped us to get out of the field and back onto the road. However, by then and with the car in a poor state, we knew we had no chance of making it to the final in time for the throw-in.

As it happened, we were further delayed when the guards arrived to investigate the crash and take copious notes about the incident. They said we could makes statements at Clones Barracks. My cousin, Fr. Eamonn Murphy, stopped on his way to the final and with all of us in no humour to travel after the crash, we passed on our tickets for him to sell to GAA people outside Croke Park.

A local farmer towed our car out of the field with his tractor. We were delighted to find that the car could still start. The left-hand side of the car was badly damaged and the mud wing was hanging off. We tied it up as best we could so that we could use it to get home. The journey back was a slow one. We stopped in Kingscourt to have dinner. Our friends were surprised to see us and the state of the car was a major topic of conversation. When we recounted our adventure, they were thankful that we escaped from the accident without a scratch on any of us. We also won the court case that followed a month later in Navan.

Fortunately, I made it to another All-Ireland final. Myself and Paddy Reilly had two Hogan Stand tickets. We travelled by train to Dublin. Paddy had scheduled to meet his girlfriend, later his wife, who was arriving by train from Belfast, where she was working as a nurse. We got a big surprise when we met her as she had brought along a nursing colleague who was really eager to see the football final.

Paddy paid for our meal which wasn't like him. He turned to me then and said that he would not like to see the girls standing for an hour in the queue. In the end, chivalry won out. I gave in and we handed over our tickets to the women.

Paddy and I spent the next hour pushing and shoving to get into the match. We didn't get a great view from the terraces. During the match I said to Paddy: "I'm sure the girls are enjoying themselves." We were far from it.

Several years later, I met this girl again at Paddy's wedding. As we toasted our glasses of bubbly to the happy couple, she thanked me for giving her the ticket on the day.

*Local historian and GAA stalwart Dan Kerr was born in Clones, Co. Monaghan 100 years ago on June 5, 1921. He is a prominent former player and follower of Clones St. Tiernach's football and hurling teams and won a county football championship with his three brothers in 1938. Dan was on the staff of the Great Northern Railway (GNR) from 1937 until the closure of the Clones station in 1958. During the Emergency, he was a member of the local LDF. In later years, he was a member of Clones Civil Defence and gave assistance following the Clones bombings in the 1970's. A native Irish speaker, Dan continues to enjoy conversing in his native tongue.*

# Injured For Bloody Sunday Game

### Alice Glover

My father, Thomas McAuley, was born in 1884 and played for Parnells and Geraldines in Dublin. He won an All-Ireland medal when playing for Geraldine's GFC who captured the 1908 All Ireland championship.

He was picked to play for the Dublin team against Tipperary on Bloody Sunday in 1920. However he injured his knee and couldn't play. It was probably fortunate for him in the circumstances.

As an injured person, he was unable to work and the GAA sent a bag of coal by way of compensation in recognition of his position.

My father and mother walked to Croke Park to attend the matches for many years. It was the highlight of their week but there was always the sadness with them of what happened when the Dublin and Tipperary teams and the crowd was indiscriminately shot at by British forces on that fateful day.

# There Is An Isle Of Hurling, Though I Didn't Know It Then

## Mae Leonard

I didn't know him back then when the Limerick minor team won the All-Ireland hurling championship in 1958. In fact, I had never seen a hurling match in my life. Coming from The Parish (There Is an Isle) in Limerick City, I was heavily into rugby, rowing and swimming. Hurling didn't even enter the equation.

I didn't know him throughout the early years when his hurling skills were developed to the point where he was one of the chosen few to wear the green and white of his county. But, thanks to my mother-in-law, I have been afforded the privilege of sharing her pride, excitement and devotion to his and Limerick's GAA career of over 60 years ago. I inherited her scrapbook, a diary of everything to do with the hurling career that I really know very little about.

But it is not just the scrapbook itself. It is the way it is lovingly put together or I should perhaps say not put together. Nothing is in proper sequence. There are no dates on the yellowed newspaper clippings and there are reports of matches between teams from clubs that have long since faded away. There are action pictures that any press photographer would be proud to claim. There are home-made badges and paper hats all stuck between pages of the huge old diary of 1958.

Now leafing through it, some of the pasted-in items become dislodged and in my mind's eye I can see her, his mother, mixing a bowl of flour-and-water paste. It is probably late at night when she has the eight of them asleep. Then she takes the most recent newspaper match reports and pictures, carefully cuts around them, applies the paste and smooths them onto the pages with her son's face scowling up at her. He never seemed to smile in those press pictures.

The one I like best is a mid-air clash with a Waterford forward when he clears the sliotar away from the goalmouth. I've heard Limerick followers describe him as talented, strong, reliable, always first to the ball, solid and skilful in holding his half-back position. But I think the best description of him is in an article by An Mangaire Sugach, Manachin Seoighe, in the

Limerick Leader sometime in the early 1950s. Manachin was in attendance at a Limerick hurling match when he overheard a supporter remark: "Boy! That Leonard is a quare hawk." And, no matter what way you look at it, that's admiration indeed.

By the time I met him and we started to see each other regularly, he was playing on the Limerick senior team. And then came the time he had to meet my parents.

My mother suggested that I bring him to tea one Sunday evening and, horror of horrors, he was late. When he finally arrived he had a black eye, three stitches over his right eyebrow and his knuckles were raw and bloodied.

However, he was welcomed and, over mother's high tea, my father, a rugby follower all his life, pulled out all the stops to discuss the greats of current-day hurling – Tom McGarry and Dermot Kelly of Limerick; Jimmy Smyth of Clare; Donnie Nealon and Tony Wall of Tipperary; Pat Fitzgerald and Jimmy Brohan of Cork.

Things went just fine and my father would joke about it afterwards in his father-of-the-bride speech: "When this fellow came across the bridge into The Parish famed for rugby, carrying a hurley, everyone stared at it and asked – 'What's that?'"

◆ ◆ ◆

When I first met my mother-in-law, she was hanging out a set of jerseys in the Wexford colours on her washing line. Our meeting was totally unexpected and a bit of an embarrassment for both of us. I was wearing a bulky Civil Defence uniform and heavy boots. My boyfriend, her son, and I were on our way to a Civil Defence exercise when he remembered that he had left his notes at home and, having collected me, he had to return to pick them up. I was waiting in the car when my eyes were drawn to the explosion of purple and gold fluttering in the county Limerick breeze. His mother saw me and came over to investigate who was this city slicker that her son was dating. She eyed me nervously – I was tongue-tied.

"The jerseys", she said, "It's my turn to wash them."

"But they're Wexford jerseys." I said.

That broke the ice. She laughed and told me that the chairman of Ballybricken – the local team – was a fan of the 1950s Wexford hurling team – in particular the skill of the Rackard brothers. So, when it came to the purchase of a set of new jerseys for his team, the chairman persuaded the committee to change from their original red and black to the purple and gold of Wexford hoping that the players would be spurred on to greater things.

## THERE IS AN ISLE OF HURLING, THOUGH I DIDN'T KNOW IT THEN

That evening, fanned by the jerseys on the washing line, she said that I should come to a match in Caherconlish the following Sunday. I made up my mind, there and then, to go and promised myself that I'd be properly dressed next time I met his mother.

I was big into dressmaking at the time and my Mam, on a shopping trip to Dublin, bought me a length of navy and white heavy kind of gingham in Cassidys. I set about making a dress to impress... and did. My new white dainty slippers were perfect with the dress. Yes, I was thrilled with myself as I cycled out to Caherconlish on that sunshiny Sunday.

The pitch was a good bit outside the village on a bog road that led to Caherline but it was easy to find it by following the line of bicycles propped up against the ditch. It surprised me to see there were no locks on the bicycles but I watched as everyone removed their pump and took it with them. I did likewise.

The players were lined up on one side of the field. A man stood with a pile of purple and gold jerseys on the ground in front of him, list in one hand, he lifted up the neatly folded jerseys in numerical order. A name was called and the player was handed his numbered jersey. The man got to number 15 and paused. The four remaining players waited anxiously as the final name was called out. There were no jerseys for the three substitutes.

The opposing team was from the neighbouring parish – South Liberties – kitted out in green and gold stripes – the rivalry between the two teams was fierce and the comment from those around me was enlightening, to say the least, throughout the game. "Ah lookit him – great pair of hands but no legs!"

I spotted my future mother-in-law at the other side of the pitch. Now I was confident that I could meet her again this time looking a lot more presentable not to mention glamorous.

Some chance.

Towards the end of the match there was a sudden shower of rain. There was no shelter to run to and this city slicker had neither coat nor umbrella. My carefully curled hair turned into rats' tails. The navy of the gingham ran and my new dress became a mass of inky blobs and my dainty white slippers sank into the mud. In great haste I went with my pump, collected my bike and before himself and his mother could see the state of me, I cycled back to the city, dripping all the way.

I had my own life apart from the hurling hero. I won my very own Bonn na hEireann with the Irish Red Cross. My team from Limerick won the Presidents Trophy and were regaled and presented with our trophy and replicas at Áras an Uachtaráin. I had the very great honour and pleasure to converse with Bean de Valera in the garden of the Áras after the ceremony. And I won a place also on the Limerick Camogie team but the least said about that the better. My swimming career was more beneficial to me in the long run. I went on to train as a swimming teacher and that became my career for some 35 years.

◆ ◆ ◆

I'm going to a hurling match. Having lived with rugby all my life this is totally alien for me. My hero's mother convinced me to go with her three sons – one of whom is now my husband. I know she wants to have her first grandchild, our little daughter, all to herself for the day and as there are bound to be celebrations Après Match – a sober driver is required – that's me. The Munster Hurling final between Tipperary and Limerick is being played in Killarney and the rivalry is such between them – they could not – or would not – agree to a venue closer to home. Limerick are hot favourites and that's why, in our thousands, we're on the road to Killarney.

As we drive out of Limerick City the three brothers are talking about the great semi-final game that Limerick played against Cork. There is absolutely no way they can be beaten today by an 'iffy' Tipperary team. So, in high spirits we're going to Killarney for the match this Sunday, July 25, 1971.

The traffic is thickening up as I drive the brothers through Patrickswell. I am concentrating on the road while my passengers name the Limerick hurlers who live here – Tony O'Brien, Sean Foley and the Bennis brothers Richie and Phil. On to Adare and I recite a few lines from Gerald Griffin's poem – Sweet Adare.

– 'The wild flowers in the vale are breathing
There winds the Mague as silver clear
among the elms so sweetly flowing
Wild roses on the bank are blowing.'

Is anyone listening to me? Not a chance. They're talking about Jim Hogan, the Limerick goalkeeper who lives here. Through Newcastle West and Abbeyfeale the traffic is bumper to bumper and moving at a snail's pace. Farther on up a winding hill it's at a standstill and we get out of the car for a breath of Kerry air. A woman comes to the gate of a cottage with massive royal blue hydrangeas. I chat with her and she shares with me her secret of turn pink hydrangeas to that shade of blue.

The scent of turf smoke rises from the valley below us. "Lyreacrompane." She says and in a lilting voice as beautiful as a blackbird's song, she goes on to tell me that John B Keane, in his youth, spent a lot of time there with his cousins.

## THERE IS AN ISLE OF HURLING, THOUGH I DIDN'T KNOW IT THEN

In fact, he came across the plot for his play The Field in Lyreacrompane and he wrote too about the Matchmaker – the man with three names – Dan Paddy Andy.

Too soon the traffic begins to move on and I wave goodbye to Lyraecrompane and the woman who shared the secret of royal blue hydrangeas with me.

Back in the car the talk is of hurling again. They're discussing the Cregan brothers – and there is yet another pair of brothers on the Limerick Team – Pat and Bernie Hartigan. This conversation is so one-sided I dare to ask: "What about Tipperary's Francis Loughnane, the great Jimmy Doyle and Babs Keating?" That drew the comment: "Ancient monuments."

Killarney welcomes us with a drenching shower and we're directed into a field of mud to park the car. Mercifully the rain stops as we make our way to Fitzgerald Stadium. Ten minutes into the game Limerick have scored two goals and three points. The Tipperary players seem to be tripping over each other. Babs has kicked off his boots and socks and is playing in bare feet. By half-time Limerick are in a comfortable lead. My lads are in such high spirits they don't even notice that it's pouring rain. I leave them and go back to the sanctuary of the car. Sometime later three drenched, disenchanted brothers climb in to join me.

According to them, Limerick were robbed. Apparently, Tipperary woke up in the second half and won the match by a point. So much for Tipperary's "ancient monuments." There was a great goal scored by Limerick's Eamon Grimes but another by Willie Moore that was disallowed. There were mutterings of a dry sliotar hidden in a towel being passed by Donie Nealon to Babs Keating for a 21-yard-free. That won the match. There were no celebratory drinks for the Limerick brothers on Sunday July 25, 1971. It was straight home to my mother-in-law who formed a bond with her little granddaughter that lasted for the rest of her life.

Oh, I nearly forgot, the ancient monuments of Tipperary beat Kilkenny too to win the All Ireland Final in Croke Park that September.

◆ ◆ ◆

The young man boarded the Limerick-bound train at Thurles and placed a brand new hurley, very carefully, on the table between us before sitting down opposite me. I couldn't help myself – I had to reach out and touch it. Rough. It was rough and not as smooth and refined as the hurleys I used to know – in fact the word that flashed on my mind was 'clumsy'. I'd never before seen a hurley with a bas that shape. The young man noticed my puzzled expression and said – "It's a Kilkenny Hurley."

"A Kilkenny Hurley." I repeated. "Ah! You bought it in Kilkenny?"

"No, I bought it in Thurles."

"Oh."

I looked at the hurley again noticing that the bas seemed to be extra wide. And the penny dropped. – "Ah now I have it. You're a goalkeeper."

He made an annoyed sound with his lips and shook his head – "No. I'm a free taker. That's why I bought a Kilkenny hurley."

"Oh."

End of conversation.

I opened my Ireland's Own to read before I could aggravate him any further. But the question niggled me all the way to and from Limerick until I got back home to Kildare again.

"Is there such a thing as a Kilkenny hurley?" I asked the All Ireland medal winner of our house, telling him of my brief encounter on the train.

"No such thing as a Kilkenny hurley." He assured me: "That fellow was only having you on."

And I believed him, for after all, he's a man who knows his hurleys. In fact, I accompanied him when he went to buy one, years ago to that old Limerick Sports Store, Nestors.

Several hurleys were shown to him that day – then one by one he measured them against his hip for the correct height. That narrowed his choice down to about six or so. Next, he explained to me, the grip and the weight depended on how light and comfortable the hurley felt when swinging it with one hand. Patrons in Nestors that day gave him a wide berth. There was a close scrutiny of the curve of the grain right down to the bas that narrowed his choice to two. Of those two the final one had to have a perfectly turned heel and toe and a slim ankle. So, between the grip, the bas, the weight, the height, the heel, the toe and the ankle – it took so long I did not want to be drawn into the process ever again.

Once back home it was checked again – this time for flexibility and that's when the beauty treatment began. The hurley was given a very close shave with a piece of broken glass until it was streamlined to the point where you could see the satin sheen of the grain in the ash wood. There was a loving massage of linseed oil to help with its elasticity and durability and it was left to rest for a couple of days before the finishing touches were added. The bas was bound with a steel hoop and the grip was bandaged with insulating tape so that it wouldn't slide out of his hands during a game. When my hero lined up with his team in Croke Park he swung his hurley confident that he and it were both capable of giving their best for Limerick. And they did.

Sixty plus years on things have changed in the world of hurleys. I was talking to a man from Kilkishen in Co. Clare who makes hurleys for a living. And when I recounted my conversation with the young man on the train, he told me that, yes, there is such a thing as a Kilkenny hurley.

Not alone that, you can get a Clare, Waterford or Galway model or you might even like to have one with the Treaty Stone embossed on it, if you're lucky enough to be on the Limerick team. It really is a matter of choice, the man from Kilkishen said, just like golfers choose clubs – hurlers now have the choice of several designs – it's all about the strike, the control and balance of the hurley – a free-taker would know exactly which model suits him best.

So, the young man on the Limerick train knew that. Over 60 years ago, my Limerick hero didn't know there was such a thing as a Kilkenny hurley, he just honed his own one to win his All Ireland minor medal.

◆ ◆ ◆

My Limerick Hero is out in the garden now digging potatoes for the dinner. Having reached four-score years he is not as fit as he used to be. One of the most treasured images I hold in my mind is of watching himself and his Co. Kildare grandson, both wearing their green jerseys leaving for Croke Park that September in 2018.

They came home smiling… And they were smiling again in 2020. This time Covid-cocooned in armchairs wearing green jerseys in front of the television when Limerick made us all so proud again. Luimneach Abu!

*Mae Leonard is a proud Limerick woman who has lived all her married life in Co Kildare. Once upon a time she played camogie for Limerick and captured the heart of a Limerick hurler. The well-known journalist is also an award-winning author of short stories and poetry.*

# High Spirits See Galbally Home

John Cummins

On Sunday August 21, 1994, the senior football panel, which incidentally is the club of Limerick hurling manager John Kiely and who was on the team, travelled by bus to Clare to play Doonbeg in a challenge game. It was exactly a week before lining out against Fr. Caseys Abbeyfeale in the county SF final.

After an entertaining game, the team were invited back to Tubridy's Pub for food and the team management allowed the players to have 2/3 pints before the long trip home.

On the way back to Galbally, the players asked to stop off in Newmarket and after a bit of persuasion, the manager Johnny Wallace said they could stop for two drinks.

Shortly after entering a pub, music started up and the craic was mighty. One of our bright spark players inveigled a local woman to ask Johnny to get up for a dance. That manouevre bought us a few extra hours in the place.

On the way home we needed a watering stop at a local farmer's field where we had to climb a gate to relieve ourselves. When we got back, locals were outraged to see us in such high spirits a week before the county final.

One of the players, yours truly, lost his glasses climbing the gate but during the week another player, John Dunne, stopped and found the glasses on his way to Limerick.

Incredibly, Galbally drinking and dancing exploits had no negative impact on the team which won its first senior title by 3-17 to 1-13.

It's been said since that the trip to Clare bonded the team and gave them a great sense of togetherness on the day. The starting team had five players under 22 who had never socialised or interacted with the 10 or so older players over 30. The spirit created on that trip was the best thing that could have happened – but every now and then I get a cold sweat when considering what would have happened had we lost.

# Is Maith An tAnlann An tOcras

### Eilís Uí Bhriain

Bhí seanfhocal ag mo mháthair: "An leaba a chóirigh tú duit féin, luífidh tú uirthi," agus is minic a smaoiním air agus mé ag strácáil leis an saol. Phós mise Déiseach 40 bliain ó shin, ach ní raibh a fhios agam go raibh dílseacht do bhratach 'gorm-is-bán' na nDéise sa chonradh pósta! Cheap mise gur thuig Liam, m'fhear céile, go raibh mise mar Chorcaíoch tiomanta, sáite chun na súl i gcúrsaí peile agus iománaíochta Chorcaí. Bhí sé de nós agam a bheith ag dul siar ar éachtaí Christy Ring, Jack Lynch an tIar-Thaoiseach agus a leithéidí. Nach raibh an ceart agamsa mar Chorcaíoch dílis? D'éist Liam gan fhocal as ach thug mé faoi ndeara nach raibh mórán mar fhreasú le cloisint uaidh ach gnúsacht íseal agus a cheann sáite i leathanach spóirt an "Dungarvan Leader"- bhreac sé orm go raibh sé ag tabhairt 'bodhaire Uí Laoghaire' do gach aon fhocal as mo bhéal.

Bhí go maith is ní raibh go holc agus ár gclann ag fás aníos agus thosnaigh na leaids ag imirt leis an gclub áitiúil nótálta, Caisleán Uí Liatháin. Bhí an-suim acu san iomáint, go háirithe Gearóid agus é ag plé eachtraí na gcluichí le Daid. Chaitheadh sé féin agus Seán na huaireanta amuigh sa ghairdín ag déanamh aithrise ar aclaíocht Joe Deane nó ag iarraidh máistreacht a ghnóthú ar ghearradh an chamáin le scil Uí Ailpín agus é ag tógaint poc sleasa ón dtaobhlíne. D'éireodh seisiúin traenála níos déine gach aon bhliain ag druidim le Cluiche Ceannais na Mumhan agus bhíodh comhrá domhain idir Daid agus Gearóid maidir leis an imreoir ab fhearr i dtaca le pocanna saora nó an cic pionóis agus araile.

Ní dheanfaidh mé dearmad choíche ar Chluiche Ceannais na Mumhan 2004 agus diospóireacht gan stad idir Daid agus na leaids óga faoin ócáid stairiúil a bhí le teacht i nDúrlas Éile agus an dá fhoireann ab fhearr in aghaidh a chéile, Na Déisigh in éadan Na Rebels! Bhí Gearóid cinnte go mbeadh an lá le Corcaigh don dara bliain as a chéile ach a mhalairt de smaoineamh a bhí ag a athair agus é machnamhach, ciúin. Thug mé faoi ndeara gurbh é sin an 'caper cliste' a bhíonn ag na Déisigh in amanta mar sin, "Is binn béal ina thost!" Bhí na ceapairí ullamh agam agus mála pacáilte ag Gearóid. Bhí sceitimíní an domhain air féin agus ar Sheán ag imeacht cos in airde an doras amach: Daid mar Dhéiseach fíorbhródúil agus an t-ál ina dhiaidh le bratacha Chorcaí! Ní raibh spás domsa agus dár ndóigh thaitin cúpla uair suaimhnis liom sa bhaile ag féachaint ar an scáileán agus ag lúireach liom féin faoi imeachtaí an chluiche. Bhuel, tá a fhios ag an saol Fódhlach faoi thoradh an lae sin, deirtear gurbh é sin an taispeántas ab fhearr riamh i gCluiche Ceannais na Mumhan; Corcaigh 1-21 Port Láirge 3-16 agus pointe amháin eatarthu ag an deireadh.

Bhí cupán tae uimhir 10 á ól agam nuair a bhris an chlann an doras isteach chugam: Déiseach caithréimeach, ardghlórach agus Na Rebels óga tuirseacha in ísle brí á leanúint. Bhí sé deacair creidiúint gur bhuaigh Port Láirge le 14 imreoir tar éis do John Mullane a bheith curtha den pháirc le cárta dearg agus é ag béicíl "I love me County!" I ndáiríre bhí trua agam dó an lá sin. Sheas na Déisigh an fód ina ainneoin sin áfach, b'iontach an cruinneas agus an scil ó Paul Flynn le gach poc saor díreach thar an dtrasnán, cúl 'cool' ina measc. Bhí Gearóid cráite ag filleadh abhaile ach bhí sé sásta caint faoi chluiche den scoth agus 9 bpointí, gan chomparáid scóráilte ag a laoch Joe Deane. "Beidh lá eile ag an bPaorach" arsa mise leis nuair a chonaic mé nach raibh ocras air don dinnéar agus ag cur in iúl dó nach raibh Corn Mhic Cárthaigh imithe as radharc Na Rebels go fóill.

An bhfuil a fhios agaibh, a chairde Gael, cad a tharla ar 12ú Meán Fómhair an bhliain sin? D'éirigh le Corcaigh an ceann is fearr a fháil ar fhoireann Chill Chainnigh! An toradh – Corcaigh 0-17 Cill Chainnigh 0-09 (agus Niall McCarthy mar Laoch na hImeartha).

Bhí mise ag ullmhú na gceapairí bagúin arís don lucht taistil an mhaidin sin agus chuir mé ceist ar Ghearóid agus é ag cogaint an bhricfeasta faoin seans a bhí ag Corcaigh an bua a bhreith leo. Seo an freagra a fuair mé agus a bhéal lán ag cogaint:

"A Mham, is cosúil le ceapaire bagúin fíorbhlasta é Cluiche Ceannais na hÉireann, braitheann sé ar an ocras atá sa bholg...agus inniu táim craosach!"

*Eilís Uí Bhriain ó Bheanntraí ó dhúchas, iriseoir Gaeilge le Avondhu Press, an-suim i gcúrsaí iomanaíochta agus timire na Gaeilge ó áit go háit, pósta le Liam, cúigear clainne.*

# Fun And Games On And Off The Field

## Nudie Hughes

You play many parts in your time as a Gaelic footballer; on any given day you could be the hero or villain of the piece. One thing for sure is that one day you are a cocky youth thinking nothing can stop you and before you know it, you turn into a frustrated veteran wondering how come it is no longer so easy and natural to go out and play as it used to be?

Until your last day in your club, county or provincial colours, you set out to play the best you can and hope to pick up some trophies along the way. I'm fortunate that this happened both individually and for my club and county team. While I'll always regret not reaching an All-Ireland final when Monaghan could and maybe should have a few times, well it's not the end of the world, is it?

At this stage of life, it's the friendships and the situations – some funny, some quite mad – which are the real rewards in my memory. Indeed, it is the offbeat memories that stay with you down the years. There won't be many people who would put a Railway Cup occasion up as one of their top recollections but that's how it is for me.

The Railway Cup still meant a lot to the players when I started out on the scene and maybe it meant that bit more to Ulster players than the other provinces. In training for games together we'd nearly kill one another to get on the team and then we'd go out and enjoy each other's company when we went to Kerry or Dublin or Mayo to play in semi-finals or finals of the competition.

One year we were due to play Connacht in a semi-final on a Sunday in Castlebar and five of us went down together by car on the Saturday afternoon. Myself and Fran McMahon of Armagh met up in Monaghan and drove together to Castlepollard where we caught up with the other Armagh car containing Jim McKerr, Brian McAlinden and Denis Stephenson. We travelled the rest of the way together and were the first to arrive at the hotel located on the way into the town.

I was last to get my gear out of the car boot and by the time I arrived in the foyer I could hear the receptionist telling the four lads that the players' room arrangements had yet to be allocated.

"Mr McEniff (Brian McEniff our Manager from Donegal) said he would assign the names when he arrived," she explained.

Brian wasn't as well known or as easily recognised back then as a hotelier in the northwest area as he is now so I felt I was on solid ground by making a decision to impersonate him.

As the other four boys looked very gloomily at a receptionist who clearly wasn't for turning, I piped up from the doorway: "Yes, I'm here now. Brian McEniff. Sorry I'm a bit late. Give me a look at the sheet there and I'll fix up the names straight away."

The lads twigged what I was up to and were delighted they wouldn't have to hang around until the real Brian arrived from Donegal.

Naturally I assigned the best rooms with four-poster beds to the Armagh lads and put my fellow Monaghan player Ciaran Murray in with myself in one of those deluxe rooms.

I proceeded to go down the list and gave McEniff and Art McRory from Tyrone, who was over the team with him, a half decent room to share as well. After putting our stuff in the rooms and seeing how high the beds were, I thought it would be a bit of fun to assign one of the four-posters to a man small in stature in the Ulster backroom team.

The best part of the impersonation was putting players from different counties who had been flaking each other in the championship games a short time before into the same rooms. In particular, I knew there had been skin and hair flying between Tyrone and Down that year so in the big room, I stuck them all together on top of one another.

By the time the manager arrived, all the damage had been done and to listen to fellas spitting fire at the dinner table that evening was priceless.

"Why am I in the same room as that bollix who split me the last time I marked him?" moaned one of the discontents.

I think there were 25 or 26 in all and after putting names for the bigger rooms of five and eight as well as the luxurious doubles, the night got more and more hilarious as fellas had no choice but to bed down beside sworn on-field enemies.

Even to the present day, anytime I meet Brian McAlinden, it always comes up in conversation and when Fran phones me from Chicago, he'll invariably throw in the line: "Nudie, do you remember the ructions you caused that night in Castlebar?"

It's hard to recall it without laughing out loud at the sour faces on lads and the mumblings under their breath about the stupid way McEniff had made the arrangements. The saving grace for me was that we won the match the next day and everyone was on a high. They all forgot about the way they were thrown together in the hotel, and instead we went out to celebrate in a nearby pub. Ulster players had a great bond forged from nights like that.

Speaking of the Railway Cup, I nearly had a unique record in the competition because after winning medals at right full and right halfback, I was captain for two further years when I played at right half forward and right corner forward. We lost both games. It would have been a bit of history for the one player to win four Railway Cup in the four different positions along the right flank.

I started out as a defender, at corner back and ended up playing a lot in the forwards. My favourite position was centre-back because I was good at reading the game. As the great ice-hockey player Wayne Gretzky once said: "I skate to where the puck is going to be not where it has been." I found I could do that more easily in the centre-back position. You could anticipate the play and be there when it arrived.

No matter where you play you have to do an apprenticeship in learning your football trade.

Being brought up in a big family of seven boys and seven girls meant you had to know how to fight your corner. I did, from the time I was knee high to a grasshopper.

I grew up at a time when fellas my age played nothing but football and there was always only one ball available.

It was the reason I developed a philosophy of getting on the ball as much as possible because the way I looked at it, if I had it, I could dictate the play.

I suppose because I got used to playing in that way that I was a very confident player. Even when I came into the senior county set up in Monaghan under Seán McCague, I never doubted my ability against the best of opponents.

He actually singled me out one day when I was 20 and we were playing in the 1979 Ulster Final. He pointed at me to the older lads and said: "I know what Nudie is thinking – he is going out to play the game of his life today."

I was. For me football was a game to be enjoyed – and as I went along, I learned how to enjoy it beyond the winning and the losing.

Kerry's John Egan, one of the greats, God rest him, ended up a good friend of mine but only after he had taught me a few on-field lessons. I remember in 1980 when Sean O'Neill was over Ulster we were playing a semi-final down in Munster. I was corner back at that time and I knew all about his prowess. However, I wasn't prepared for his line of chat which threw me off my job of marking him tightly.

"What's that lad writing up on the scoreboard?" he asked me.

I couldn't see that the guy was doing anything but he insisted that I look closer. As I glanced across, John was gone from my side and in the blink of an eye, he had the ball in the back of the net.

"That's the last time you'll do that to me," I told him.

He smiled. Afterwards we met up for a drink and did so most times we played against each other. The Kerry lads were always very friendly and as I said, I liked to get to know players beyond meeting them on the pitch."

Over time I was grateful to John for that lesson. When I moved into the forward line, I used his cute off-putting ways several times myself. In a 'derby' game with Cavan, I was being marked by their corner back Damien O'Reilly and once the match started I kept looking up at the crowd in the hill.

"How many would you say is in that section?" I asked him. "Would you say there's 15,000 there?"

Gerry Sheridan, who was the Cavan fullback, heard what I was at and kept shouting over to Damien: "Don't listen to that fella, he's trying to trick ya."

I kept pestering Damien as I had nothing else to do because Cavan had all the possession up the other end. He didn't bite at first but when I kept pointing at the hill, he yielded to temptation to look up into the crowd just once. As he did, the ball was quickly transferred into our attack. It came in over his head. I moved, caught it and stuck it over the bar.

Gerry was furious: "I told you not to listen to him." He didn't for the rest of the game.

I did the same to a young Tony Scullion up in Ballinascreen in an Ulster championship replay against Derry. I talked and talked over the first 15 minutes and had 1-2 to my credit in that time. Tony was a good student because he stopped listening after that and as every GAA follower knows, he seldom gave the player he was marking a kick of the ball for the rest of his career. I suppose I was his John Egan.

Probably the greatest legacy of this and the other games I played in was the fact that in my time, lads wanted to circulate with players from other counties. I don't think that happens as naturally today and it is a loss.

I mean I can still slag Ambrose O'Donovan about how his tackle on Dave Byrne cost us an All Ireland final appearance. That was '85 and it's the one that still gnaws at my gut. We were eight points up against Kerry when John Kennedy's shot hit the top of the upright and landed in Ger Power's hands for a goal.

They got 1-2 in the following five minutes and suddenly there was a replay. Davy was lording it that day and Ambrose's tackle was a bit delayed but not dirty. Kerry knew how to win a game they should have lost while we lost a game, the replay, which we should have won the first day.

Ambrose and I have jousted over that down the years on social occasions but in fairness to him he was doing the best he could to get his team over the line and I respect that totally.

You get these unlucky losses just as the odd day you find yourself in the headlines when really it's the sporting gods who are looking after you. That certainly happened for me near the end of my career when I was 34 and no longer able to run around and dictate play.

It was the semi-final of the Ulster club against a very strong Kingscourt outfit played in their place in 1991. The overriding memory I have is that they had new dressing rooms up on a hill above the pitch.

It probably didn't help my energy levels that I was just back in time to play from a rugby World Cup match in Murrayfield between Ireland and Scotland.

Like ourselves, Kingscourt had six or seven players on the county team and it was a full-blooded affair. At half-time I was totally spent thanks to all the off the ball running I had to do on top of the late nights in Edinburgh.

When the referee Michael Cranny from Down blew the half-time whistle, all I wanted to do was sit down and catch my breath for a minute. After doing so, I decided I'd better leg it up to the dressing room or the half-time pep talk would be over. By the time I'd negotiated the steep slope up to the new facilities, I was the only player still outside. In fact as I opened the door, our manager was finishing his speech and the lads were getting ready to go back down.

I sat down for another rest at the spot where I had togged out and before long Cranny was whistling for the restart. Without my realising it, everyone was waiting for me to return and as I walked into the pitch, I got a big applause from the crowd.

The ref was about to give me a ticking off when I said: "Michael at my age, I'm lucky to get back at all after having to climb that hill."

People who heard my answer began to laugh – some of the crowd nearby, Michael himself smirked and even my marker Pat Faulkner was shaking his head and smiling as I walked up to take my place beside him.

About five minutes into the second half, Pat was out ahead of me for the ball but slipped. This allowed the ball to arrive in my hands unmarked and all I had to do was tap it into the net. The most fortunate goal I ever scored.

A short while later, the ball evaded their defence and again I happened to be in the right place at the right time to get a second goal.

Normally Cavan and Monaghan supporters would be the best of enemies when they played each other but this time they could see the funny side of what had happened. Here was I finding it hard to get back out onto the field in time and now I was the hero with two quick second half goals.

*Eugene 'Nudie' Hughes is a native of Castleblayney, Co Monaghan and is a former Ulster Championship ('79, '85 and '88) and national league (1985) winner with Monaghan. He also won two Ulster club titles with Castleblayney Faughs in 1986 and 1991. He was the first man from the Farney County to be honoured as an All-Star in '79 and ended up with three awards in his career. A former salesman, he has two grown up sons, Ciaran, who also played for Monaghan and Conor, both of whom also play with Castleblayney.*

# Dubs Win On Back Of Our Dollymount Tidal Wave

## Maeve Edwards

Imagine, if you will, the following scene; The date is Sunday, August 18, 1963. The time is 2.45 pm. The place is Dollymount Beach on the north side of Dublin.

A car comes to a halt on the soft sand just above the tide line. The sun is high in the sky.

All four doors of the car open simultaneously, and out pour a medley of children, a mother, a father, a baby in a bonnet, and finally a slightly dazed family dog. The mother spreads a red tartan rug on the side of the car facing the sun and settles herself down with the Sunday papers and a few cushions taken from the armchairs at home. The children change into their elasticated swimming togs, blow up their rubber rings, and take off at high speed for the sea, the dog at their heels. They are filled with excitement at the blue sky, the approaching tide, and are oblivious to that touch of autumn in the air that signals a return to school only a few short weeks away.

But it's the father of this family we must watch. He seems beside himself and cannot settle to anything. If truth be told, he has taken no part in the preparations for this day, other than to drive his entire family to Dollymount beach. It was his wife, the mother of all his children, who had packed the picnic, sent the children off to search for their swimming togs, locked up the house, and made sure they had everybody on board before they set off.

Now the father is twiddling with the dial on the car radio and soon – success at last – Micheal O'Hehir's voice can be heard loud and clear. The father sighs with relief and settles himself down in his deckchair as Amhrán na bhFiann wafts over the sand dunes. Yes! You've guessed it! Dublin are playing Down in the All Ireland senior football semi-final.

Up and down the beach, other families are setting up camp in a similar way and out of every car door comes the same sound. O'Hehir is in fine voice today. The children return from their swim and wrap themselves in their towels, shivering. They watch their father and recognise his excitement.

Sure, isn't he always the same at this time of year? They ask their mother if it's time for the picnic, but she says "not yet" and sends them off with the baby to make sand castles. Now the father is on his feet, not able to contain himself, and the children know that the early signs are good for Dublin.

The voice from the radio proclaims: "Another point for Dublin!"

The children play with the baby, burying his feet in the sand. He's enchanted with the day and bangs his bucket and spade together in delight. The father is on his feet again, shouting, stamping, crying: "Go on, go on!" The voice has reached a new crescendo: "And it's a goal for Dublin. Dublin has scored a goal!"

"Go easy Eddie," says the mother, as he lifts the baby up into the air in triumph.

She lays out the plastic beakers on the rug and calls the children to her. She pours the tea and carefully unwraps the pile of sandwiches. The older children had made them that morning, piling slice after slice of buttered fresh pan until there seemed to be a mountain of bread. Another child had chopped the tomatoes and onion, and one by one the bread was filled, sliced in two, and wrapped in grease proof paper. The children settle down on the tartan rug, and reach for a sandwich. They are right in believing that nothing can compare to the taste of a tomato and onion sandwich which has been stored for a couple of hours in the boot of a car on a hot summer's day.

In years to come, the sound of that commentator's voice will bring back the memory of those days; sitting on the red tartan rug, their mother's face upturned to the sun, their father so young and carefree. And always they grow nostalgic and find themselves wondering should they chop up a few tomatoes and make themselves a sandwich.

"Daddy, is Dublin still winning?"

"They sure are. Down can't catch them now!"

"Have a sandwich, Eddie before they're all gone!"

"No, Alice, don't you know I can't eat when Dublin are playing!"

"Sure Dublin will win, aren't they miles ahead!"

"It's not over until it's over!"

Under the shadow of Croke Park, the father's brother, the children's Uncle Jimmy, is in his back garden listening to the game on his transistor radio. He's in the same state of heightened excitement as his brother, three miles away on Dollymount beach.

Uncle Jimmy hears the roar of the crowd coming loud over the rooftops from Croke Park and he knows with absolute certainty that Dublin has scored again. He has a moment of trepidation in case his ears are playing

# DUBS WIN ON BACK OF OUR DOLLYMOUNT TIDAL WAVE

tricks, until Michael O'Hehir confirms it on the radio: "Yes, it's a second goal for Dublin. Hill 16 is going berserk in a sea of blue!"

The children finish their picnic and ask can they go for another swim, but their mother tells them they must wait half an hour. The father, delirious with joy at Dublin's success, looks around him as if emerging from a dream.

The tide is in, Howth Head is where it always is, the children are freckled with the sun, the baby golden haired.

"Anyone want a game of football?" he asks.

The children cheer and jump to their feet.

"Bags be Dublin," they cry.

"No, I'll be Dublin," says the father. "You lot can be Galway. We have five weeks to prepare for the Final!"

*Maeve Edwards is a native of Clontarf in Dublin but now lives in Bray, Co Wicklow. A grandmother of two, her writing has been shortlisted for many awards over the years.*

# First Hurling Game Ever Played

## John Arnold

The familiar voice of Mary Fitzgerald from Kildinan in our parish was the reporter. Mary has travelled the world, often going 'behind the lines', in places of extreme conflict and danger.

Now living in Marseilles, Mary was detailing facts on the Covid situation in France's oldest city. She referred to the 1720 Bubonic Plague which claimed up to 1,000 victims a day at its height. Events were planned to mark the Bicentenary of that awful event but had to be cancelled.

Mary went to Bartlemy National School and her family farm in the townland of Glenagoul in Kildinan has special significance in GAA history.

On this farm in the autumn of 1741 a hurling game was played. The earlier famine and terrible cold weather of 1740 and early 1741 had come to an end leaving tens of thousands dead in Ireland. However by the late summer of 1741, the weather had improved and a harvest of sorts was saved.

The local landlords were relieved and in probable thanksgiving to their workers, the MacAdam Barry chief in Lisnagar organised a hurling team and sent out a challenge to meet them in a game.

A team from Tipperary led by Denis McGrath answered the call. What is regarded as the first Cork v Tipperary hurling game was played in Glenagoul at that time but down the centuries the question still remains…who won?

According to the Tipperary side, their men claimed victory and commissioned a poet to write a glowing account of the match.

"Not so," said the Cork scribe Sean Ó Murchu, 'Na Raitineach' from Carrignavar, who wrote several verses stating in no uncertain terms that Cork were the victors …is it any wonder we have such fierce rivalry between the two counties to this day?

# The GAA, The Guards...
# And All Things In Between

## Pat McGilloway

Growing up in what was a sports mad part of Galway in the 1950s, I knew I wanted more than anything to be a member of a GAA club that represented my parish.

Down the years, we had many good players in Kiltormer who were forced to play with other clubs nearby because we didn't have our own in the village.

I was still at school in Garbally College when I decided to do something to change all that in the mid-fifties. I'd say I was probably no more than 18 at the time.

A few of us around Kiltormer felt it was the right thing to do. So with the innocence of youth as my driving force, I gathered a shilling a man from 18 fellas at Larkin's Corner and then four of us went to the Galway County Convention in Loughrea.

Jimmy Brennan, Martin Lowry and Mick Markham accompanied me on the day we officially registered the club. This allowed us to play in the Galway hurling 1956 championship. We hadn't enough young lads around to play minor so a few of our own, my brother Seán among them, played with Ballinasloe and ended up winning the championship.

Once we became an official part of the great GAA fraternity as a proper club, I knew there would be a constant demand for money. I used to run dances and concerts in the Crystal Ballroom, courtesy of Frank Campbell.

I was delighted when we had enough to buy our first set of jerseys. I inveigled my mother, May, to travel up to Dublin with me as I had registered the club colours as maroon and white – we would be the only club in east Galway with county colours on our backs.

We bought the set in Clerys on O'Connell St. Then we travelled the short distance over to Hector Greys in Liffey St. to buy white numbers that my mother stitched on the 18 jerseys when she got back home.

The coincidence of that day in Dublin was revealed to me years later when I found out that the man who had sold us the jerseys was Laurence

Kilkenny – then a salesman in Clerys. Laurence remembered us coming in and buying the Galway colours. He was the uncle of Ollie and Tony, two Kiltormer stalwarts who went on to win All-Ireland and All-Stars in their careers.

Back in the late fifties, there were few official games compared to today. There were minor, junior and senior championships in counties but little else.

Local tournaments were a big part of the GAA activity back then; for instance I can remember a crowd of us cycling over to Birr to play in a seven-a-side tournament. There were always unusual prizes for the victors and the year we beat Mullagh in the final (who had the great Tony Reddin in goal), we got suit lengths as our prize.

Tony and Seanie Duggan were vying for the Galway goal and it was only when Tony ended up playing for Lorrha in Tipperary that he became such a household name. He is considered by many to be the best goalkeeper of all time, having been selected on both the GAA's Team of the Century and Team of the Millennium.

Funny to think that Tony was getting nowhere against Seanie in the pecking order and when Tipp were short of a goalkeeper they offered him a job. He went across the river and became a legend with three All Ireland medals.

◆ ◆ ◆

The McGilloway name arrived in this area when my father became the local Garda sergeant in Killimor, some seven miles away from Kiltormer in 1933.

My father was originally from Fahan in Donegal and joined the guards in 1922 while my mother was from Cavan; her people were cattle dealers. She went into the drapery trade and was serving her time in Curleys drapery shop in Killimor when she met my father in 1935.

He had been posted from Killarney to Tralee and then Galway at a time when Patrick Larkin had a guesthouse in Killimor. This man had written the first hurling rules for the GAA, and was a leading light in the Land League. He had just come back from America and my mother and father moved into the house with him.

Larkin was a fierce republican, and this was reflected in the names he chose for his USA-born children – Emmet, Robert Parnell and Patrick after Padraig Pearse. I was born in his Galway home and his son, Parnell and daughter Mary, were my godparents.

As there had been no hurling team in Kiltormer for years before I got involved, Patrick had lined out in his playing days with Meelick Eyrecourt. He was the goalkeeper with Galway in the first All Ireland against Tipp which they lost by 1-1 to 0-0 in Birr.

The only way to get a game in such circumstances was to throw your lot in with a neighbouring club...in our case Clontuskert or Mullagh or some other parish close to them. For instance, Marty Lowry was from Kiltormer but played in 1939 with Mullagh and was also on the Galway team that won the junior All Ireland.

I grew up in this vacuum with my pals where we had no local club to call our own. That changed in 1956 when we registered the maroon and white colours for Kiltormer and I was delighted when shortly afterwards, Fr Jack Solan arrived in our parish. I knew him as my history teacher in Garbally, but more importantly, he was a great hurling man from Clare, who had won many honours there and with Munster.

Fr Jack arrived just before the East Galway junior final of 1959. We won the divisional title easily enough but he over-trained us for the county semi-final and we became too muscle bound and ended up losing.

He had a massive influence in the club and was involved when we got a pitch in 1961. Initially after we affiliated, it was my job to organise a pitch for county championship matches.

The fact that my father was the local sergeant gave me a bit of clout in this regard. Eyreville had a big demesne just across from the garda station and there was a particular bit of ground right inside the wall known as 'The Lawn'.

On one side there was a raised bank – to us it was like the Hogan Stand. I approached the owner, Stratee Eyre and his daughter Charity, and asked them if it was possible to use that land for matches.

He was delighted to help out and it was music to my ears when he refused to charge us rent. We held championship matches there from 1956 onwards and later when I asked Stratee if he would do a deal down the line for the pitch if we could raise the money to buy it, he assured me that he would.

Fr Jack's arrival meant the club pursued this line and it was he who got the deal across the line to own that part of the Eyreville ground.

By the time that was done, I was in the guards and was deeply involved in rowing. I was living in Dublin and naturally had less involvement in what was going on in Galway. In 1969, the Kiltormer club we had formed decided to amalgamate with neighbouring Lawrencetown and Clontuskert and the new club colours were changed to blue and white.

They have done remarkably well since then, winning five senior county titles and one All Ireland club title. It was also a source of great pride for me to see Conor Hayes captain Galway to back-to-back All Ireland titles in 1987 and 1988.

I remember the first day his father Michael came working as an insurance inspector in the area. He married into a local family and another of their sons, Joe, was a brilliant hurler and would have been on those Galway teams if he hadn't sustained a serious knee injury.

For some reason, the founding of Kiltormer GAA club in '56 and following years has been airbrushed out of existence. I don't know why because it is part of the history, just as the coming together with the other areas in 1969 is.

◆ ◆ ◆

There is a great bond between the GAA and the Gardai; by this stage I'm sure hundreds of serving members have won provincial and All-Ireland medals at various levels of competition.

From the time in the late fifties when I began training to join the force, I could see the advantage of being from a hurling county. As soon as you arrived in the Garda Depot, mentors from Dublin clubs like Faughs, Civil Service, Lucan Sarsfields and many others would approach fellas from hurling strongholds. If you were in any way handy, you could have a game every Sunday.

Accordingly, although always officially playing only for the club I founded back in Galway, I played league and championship games in four other counties – Dublin, Roscommon, Westmeath and Kildare.

Before joining the guards, I had the honour of marking the legendary Jobber McGrath when I played for Raharney against Rickardstown in Westmeath on one occasion. At that time I was so fit from rowing and hurling training that I got on a lot of ball that day. My biggest problem, aside from marking the Jobber, was to turn down their county board's request to play for them in the National Hurling League that winter.

I missed out on going to the Olympics in Rome in 1960 by less than half a second with the Garda Boat club. I won two rowing All Ireland championship with garda and was bowman on the Leinster team that won the interpros in 1959. Our crew failed narrowly to qualify for the Rome Olympics in 1960.

Although rowing was taking over my sporting life, hurling was also important and one of the proudest days in my life was when I captained Kiltormer to its first championship win in the East Galway junior hurling championship in 1959.

When I joined the guards, the person in the bed beside me during training was Seamus Quaid. His Garda number was 13497 and mine was 13498 and during our time together I nearly ruined his inter-county career.

It was a typical schoolboy prank where I set up the bed in such a way that it looked fine but collapsed once he put his weight on it. In the fall, he broke four of his toes.

He was playing for Limerick at the time but had to cry off the team for the Munster semi-final. If it had got out what had actually happened, I'd say I would never have been allowed to finish my training.

Seamus and I became great friends and even though he was posted to Wexford and I was placed in Dublin, we always stayed in touch. If he had to come up to Dublin either for a court case or for some other reason, he would always stay with us.

I remember fondly his last visit to our house two weeks before he was killed in the line of duty in early 1980 by the IRA when he was only 42.

A lovely man and a great hurling enthusiast, he threw in his lot with Wexford as soon as he arrived down there and won an All Ireland medal with them in 1960.

Myself and himself often played together in Dublin with the likes of Lucan Sarsfields, Civil Service and Faughs. That didn't mean we got involved; we didn't, we just turned up for a match on a given Sunday and were gone as soon as it was over.

◆ ◆ ◆

Hurling that time was tough and you had to meet fire with fire. I remember one Dublin game when a fella drew across me so ferociously with the hurl that he got a very long suspension from the game.

Ironically, the worst injury I ever got occurred while playing a practice match among our own recruits in Dublin.

I went for the ball with a lad from Kerry and whatever way the hurls collided, he chopped my left thumb straight off.

We were playing on a bad old pitch and the ball was coming and it hit a tuft of grass and hopped up and he pulled and my thumb was underneath. When I got the belt I heard the lads say: "Oh Jesus." They knew it was serious.

A bigger and more immediate problem for me was the fact that I went blind for a few minutes. Then when my sight returned, all I could see was blood pumping out of the wound two bones sticking out. One of the mentors drove me down to the hospital while I sat in the passenger's seat cradling my thumb with my right hand.

I went into Dr Steevens' Hospital and it took them six hours to stitch the thumb back to the hand. And to their credit they did a great job on it.

In games in that era, time wasn't nearly as exact as it is today. Watches were scarce and I can remember playing for Kiltormer against Closestoken when the second-half alone lasted for an hour and a quarter.

We were a young team and they were seasoned performers. That's not to say that all our lads were young as we had two or three 40 year olds looking after us out on the pitch. They had a habit of never going out to face the enemy without getting a few slugs from a whiskey bottle to fortify them for the challenge ahead. And they were right in this case.

There was holy murder during the game, they took lumps out of us and the referee had to continuously stop and start the play.

However, all the brutality was forgotten once the final whistle was blown. After that particular match, I was standing outside just talking to a couple of fellas. I was about 21 or 22 at that stage. One of their players passed by and in a friendly gesture, he gave me a slap with the heel of his hurl on my hip and said: "Well done, Pat."

There was absolutely no malice involved but whatever way he hit me, I ended up with a hip injury that followed me around for 20 years. Eventually I had to have an operation and the surgeon found there was a chip from that belt still causing damage. It gave me a heck of a lot of trouble over the years but after the surgery, the hip was perfect again.

There were no two days the same in the guards in the Ireland of the nineteen seventies and eighties, by which time I would have gone up the ranks to detective sergeant.

Over the course of my career, I was involved in dozens of murder cases and was fired at during an armed robbery in Dublin.

Without doubt though, the biggest headline case I was ever involved in was the arrest in 1982 of Malcolm McArthur when he was apprehended in the house of Paddy Connolly, the then Attorney General, who coincidentally went to school in Garbally as well.

I was standing beside Connolly when he got permission to make a phone call that Friday night. We didn't know whose number he rang and we could only hear what he was saying down the phone. Pretty soon it became obvious, he was talking to the then Taoiseach, Charlie Haughey.

We heard him explain what had happened with McArthur. He also mentioned the fact that he was going to America the following day. As events transpired, he flew out but had to return within a few days whereupon he resigned his AG post.

McArthur had stayed as a guest in Connolly's place and during that time went with him to a match in Croke Park. They bumped into the Garda Commissioner and a general discussion among the three took place on the murder of Meath nurse, Bridie Gargan, and Offaly farmer, Donal Dunne.

Following McArthur's arrest, Charlie described what had happened in the following terms – "it was a bizarre happening, an unprecedented situation, a grotesque situation, an almost unbelievable mischance." Later former government minister and journalist, Conor Cruise O'Brien, coined the acronym GUBU out of that quote.

While I enjoyed being in the force all my life, my first love was art and I made many friends through painting and drawing. I forged a strong link with Faughs GAA club years after playing for them when former Limerick hurler Ned Rea asked me to colour a black and white photo he had of the 1970 Faugh team, Dublin senior champions that year. It is still hanging in the clubhouse.

I also did a painting of Michael Cusack which is now part of his museum in Carran, Co Clare, his birthplace. I had worked on it years before and had almost forgotten about until my sister visited the centre and recognised it. I think it is also on a fair few websites as well.

As I now am in my mid-eighties, I look back with special fondness on the good times playing GAA afforded me and so many of my peers.

I suppose my favourite moment in retrospect was one evening showing my granddaughter, Ali the Dublin junior hurling medals I won in the late fifties and early sixties and seeing her eyes light up.

"I'm going to get one like that some day," she said. And she was true to her word.

My daughter Martina was always involved in Lucan. They were gathering a good squad of young camogie players in the area. Not only did Ali (Twomey) go on to win many more medals than I ever did, but she has become a stalwart of the Dublin team over the past number of years.

Maybe that explains better than anything else the great debt we owe the GAA for giving us the honour of handing down such aspirations from one generation to the next.

*Pat McGilloway is a native of Kiltormer, Co Galway. Aged 19, he was founder of the local GAA Club in 1956. A former detective sergeant in An Garda Siochana, he married Gretta in 1961. They have four adult children, 11 grandchildren and one great granddaughter, Mia. His hobbies include art, photography, golf and travel.*

# Cameo Mocked By Hands Of Time

## Paul Mulcaire

There is an annual game Buffalo play against NYPD on the day before the first round of the Connacht championship.

At 53, my playing days were well behind me at the time in 2019. But my son had come up through the youth programme and at 17 had real potential. I asked the manager to put me on for five minutes so I could say that we had played together in Gaelic Park. He said that wouldn't be a problem.

Seán Harte, a cousin of Mickey's, reffed the game. Seán is now the Canadian Co Chairman but is a darned good ref too. The game started on a fresh chilly evening in Gaelic Park. I'm all decked out in my Fenian shorts and socks with just a t-shirt on.

Just before half-time, the hallelujah moment came as Connor, the coach and manager, tells me to go in at full forward. So my son Jack and I were not only playing together but were both in the full-forward line.

Jack high-fives me as I run by him. Now to get my excuses in first... the surface on the artificial turf was very worn. Almost immediately, Jack won a great ball in and his movement drew the goalkeeper out of position. Jack could see how open I was to score and passed.

All I had to do was punch the ball into the empty net but in my anticipation of scoring, the ball slipped and bounced on the hard surface like a stone skipping across water. I took off after it as optimistically I thought I could still retrieve it.

What my head was thinking didn't telegraph further down my torso. My legs became confused and I only succeeded in tripping myself up.

"Seán surely someone pushed me?" I pleaded. He laughed. "Paul, it wasn't meant to be."

"Dad, please get off the field, you're embarrassing the family name," Jack whispered. With my tail between my legs, I returned to the sideline.

By game's end, I somehow persuaded Conor to let me back in and this time, there was a much better outcome... honestly, I didn't fall down once!

# A (W)hole New Ball Game In This Minefield

Peter Makem

Back in the early 18th century, lead was discovered underground in the Derrynoose district of Co Armagh, a country area south of Keady and bordering Clontibret in Co Monaghan.

This led to local mining of a sort but the mine is chiefly remembered for the incident when some of the lead was commandeered and used to make ammunition for the United Irishmen.

A more organised mining industry followed in the early decades of the following century and lasted until the mid 1800s. Ironically, some of this lead was used for ammunition by the British armed forces for the various imperial ventures they carried out across the world in those days. Almost two centuries later, the mounds of slag can still be seen dominating this area like little drumlins.

When a Gaelic football club was set up in Derrynoose in the 1930s, it was immediately attracted to a very level piece of ground in the vicinity of the mines which fortunately was just the size required for a decent playing field. This field had earlier been used for sports days run by the parish and for the odd kick-about by those locals interested in Gaelic football but with no formal outlet. The mines at this time had been unused for almost 100 years and there was little sense of danger as cattle and horses had grazed there all the time.

However, what the people didn't realise until much later was that the mine ran directly underneath the football field on a straight line from one goalpost to the other. Only one man knew all along about the strange secrets of the field, but he kept those secrets to himself.

Now and again after periods of prolonged rainfall, the field would flood and a small lake would emerge in a gentle hollow. Peter John Cowan, who was the actual owner of the field, had such knowledge of the ground's topography that it appeared he could see what was happening below the earth's crust.

When the lodged water had to be removed, he'd arrive with a crowbar and focus on a certain spot in the puddle. He could be seen jabbing around in the lake until he found the bulls-eye he was looking for. Then he would work furiously with the crowbar until he had burrowed an underground opening. Once that happened the water level drained into the abyss below and in an hour or so, it would have totally disappeared.

Funnily, no one else quite knew how to find the exact spot like Peter John. It was his secret, a special ownership, in his own special field. Whether it was the remnant of an old air vent or some dislocation caused by a sinkage below, no one ever could fathom the exact spot – which made the owner indispensable to the community.

From time to time a few Derrynoose players would voice fears that some day in the middle of a game, players jumping for a high dropping ball might vanish on landing and spend the rest of their lives playing in the darkness of the underworld.

It became simultaneously a joke and a warning in those conversations. This GAA pitch had the power, or at least the threat, that didn't exist anywhere else. It was something opposing teams were teased about while referees, particularly those considered to be somewhat hostile to the home colours, were often cautioned that they should watch their step before body and whistle disappeared into Hades for eternity.

Thus, the Secret of Derrynoose was no idle thing either to locals or other Armagh teams playing in the 1930s. A local hall was built beside the field for socials, dances and general fundraising around that time. The hall reflected the vicissitudes of local life, sometimes being closed for years on end, depending on the interest of the various committees and was finally closed down in the early eighties.

One morning in 1983 a local man driving past on his tractor noticed something 'strange' had occurred overnight at the side of the hall. He turned his vehicle and headed back for a closer inspection. He was met by a huge hole in the ground as wide as a whale's mouth. He ventured to the edge, threw a big stone down the vent and eventually heard an echoing sound from deep in the underbelly of the ground.

This was part of the same stretch of mine that ran underneath the football pitch. It seems that the expulsion of underground water and the rotting of wooden pit props had forced a seismic weakness.

Later a local mechanic claimed, perhaps apocryphally, that he had buried 13 car wrecks into the chasm along with loads of machinery lying around his premises, old gates, fireplaces, buckets, mattresses, and everything he could find to try to fill the hole, but soon recognised it was an exercise in futility.

Eventually some mine officials ordered work on the gaping aperture so that the danger was sealed off from the public. It emerged from the geological examination of the area that if the opening had been one yard closer to the hall, the corrugated iron building, or at least part of it, would have slid into oblivion.

For a long time afterwards people thanked the man above that the hall had been closed before a catastrophe took place in the community. Back in the late 1980s, the Derrynoose club created a new state of the art playing field and clubhouse over a mile away from the old field. The opening game between Armagh and Monaghan was in fact one of Joe Kernan's first games as Armagh manager in 2002.

I was present on that historic day for the club and I recall imagining a stranger coming over to me and saying: "Do you remember those mines running right beneath the old field? Well, according to a map I've seen, that whole vein of lead runs under this new field as well."

*Peter Makem is a native of Derrynoose, Co Armagh and is a writer and journalist. A former Armagh GAA manager, he is married to Catherine and they have two children, Grainne and Colm. Peter belongs to a musical family, including his grandmother Sarah, the traditional singer, and Tommy, his uncle, of international fame with the Clancy Brothers.*

# Moving The Goalposts 1927-style

John Arnold

On Sunday June 26, 1927, Aghada junior hurlers travelled to Rathcormac to play the home team in the East Cork League. The Rathcormac pitch at the time was a roadside field in the townland of Knocknaboola on Jack 'Knock' Barry's farm. The local club noticed that a large crowd of spectators were outside on the road, not paying the 6d admission fee.

They were obviously going to view the game by looking in over the ditch for free. The home club decided that as funds were low there was no point in providing free entertainment.

Shovels were procured and the four goal-posts dug up. These were then moved to a field closer to the river Bride which couldn't be seen from the road. Holes were dug, posts re-erected and the game went on.

The spectators had no choice but to part with their 'tanner' (a sixpenny bit) to view the contest. In fairness they got great value for money as the game was a thriller.

The Cork Examiner reported the game as follows: "Both teams seemed equally matched and possessed of a truly sporting spirit. Rathcormac won by 1-2 to 1-1."

# How Quick Thinking Flattened A Bigger Opponent

Dermot O'Brien

A football story from Kilkenny... now that's a bit unusual.

In the rural parish of Windgap, football had been the main game for many years with some good teams representing the area.

However, in the late 1950s and early 1960s it lost ground to hurling in our area, though it still had its enthusiasts. As a small rural parish with only a cluster of houses and some 200 inhabitants, it was difficult to field any team, not to mention a football one, particularly in underage competitions.

The man over us was a football enthusiast who never shirked a task no matter how difficult. He had played the big ball game himself through the years and felt that there was a duty to line out in both codes. And so, he turned to the youth and took over our U-16 team.

The problem with a small club in the secondary code was getting enough bodies to field a team. We had some good players but needed to call on many younger lads of 12 and 13.

At that level, a year is a long time, not to speak of two or three. We also had very little opportunity to practise as hurling took centre stage most nights in the field.

And so, it came to pass that our small young team was gathered together, and with no fewer than 10 players in the trainer's own Volkswagen Beetle, we set off to play our championship game. The remainder of the team got a lift in another car.

As we were togging out on one side of the pitch, we looked across and saw our opponents getting ready. We immediately became anxious as they looked much bigger than us and even more worryingly, some looked a good bit older. Anyway, our trainer was not to be put off and encouraged us to go out and take them apart.

From the off we were fighting a losing battle as the size advantage became more obvious as the minutes ticked by.

By half-time, despite our honest efforts, we were a cricket score in arrears. The other club had better players, particularly the ones who had long since been introduced to the art of shaving. We had a few big fellas ourselves and in particular had one lad who was actually the biggest of all 30 on the field.

There was no pep talk during the interval about how we were going to stage a magical comeback in the second half or anything like that. Instead our trainer brooded for quite a while before telling us to sit down and relax. Obviously he was concocting something in his mind but even the most optimistic of us felt sure he couldn't help us escape from the severe beating that lay in store on the resumption.

Just as the referee blew the whistle to signal us back onto the pitch for the second half, the trainer told us to form a tighter circle around him.

"Listen," he whispered to the group, "the first time any of you get the ball, pass it to him (pointing at our big centre back)."

He then drew attention to the field alongside the GAA pitch, which had a drain and ditch separating them.

"You see that field of barley over there with the ears full ripe and nearly ready for harvesting?"

Addressing the big defender, he instructed: "When you get the ball, I want you to kick it as far as you can into the middle of the barley. Will you do that?"

The centre-back nodded in agreement and our trainer sent us back out, confirming that he would be closer to the corn pitch than the field of play.

He then smuggled our ball in a bag to a young lad, told him to bury it in the car as this was vital to his plan.

On the aforementioned field of play, we were once again being thrown around like rag dolls as the bigger and brawnier opposition dominated in every facet of the game.

Once or twice when one of their moves broke down, we tried to execute the trainer's plan by working the ball to our big kicker -but were thwarted.

Finally, about eight or nine minutes into the second half, the big fella himself rose majestically to catch one of our own kick outs. Fortunately, he landed only 20 yards or so from the boundary on the barley field side. Following orders to a tee, he thumped the ball as far as he could over ditch and dyke. We all watched it sail long and high before coming down right in the middle of the corn field.

The young helper, who had 'disappeared' with our own ball, ran like a whippet to mark the spot where the ball landed. Our trainer went in hot pursuit or at least as fast as his ageing legs would allow. By this stage the ball had disappeared under the long stems of barley. The young helper acted like an expert 'spotter' and said "there it is" as he pointed to a particular spot. The trainer praised the young assistant and instructed him to leave the rest to him.

One or two of their officials were by this time scaling the ditch in their efforts to help retrieve the missing ball. They were greeted with the good news from the trainer: "No worry, lads, I've found it."

As they were still nearer the pitch, he threw the ball in their direction. By the time it got back to the pitch, it was noticeable that not only had the ball got smaller, but it was no longer capable of holding air.

Efforts to revive it through pumping proved futile as the noise of air going into the bladder was followed by an even bigger sound of air escaping from it. At this stage our opposition were becoming very suspicious about how the ball had been punctured.

Our trainer, wearing a face of choirboy innocence suggested that it could have been caused by the broken bottle that he saw strewn under the barley when the ball landed.

"I'd say that's what happened alright," he said hoping the excuse would hold water, if not air, with the opposition mentors.

It didn't. You could see they were seething but without evidence suggesting nefarious actions by our man, they had to swallow on their suspicions.

After seeking firstly our ball, which had also mysteriously disappeared and then the prospect of getting a ball from another club – not an option as it was an evening throw-in and the light of the late August evening was fading rapidly, the referee had no choice but to abandon the game.

So, a potentially bad evening on the pitch turned into one of intrigue as we set out for home in the knowledge that we had not lost the game – we had merely been part of an abandoned spectacle. And believe me, it was a spectacle for all the wrong reasons from our point of view.

On the way home in the Volkswagen Beetle, we were delighted that the man who had put us in this terrible mess, also managed to extricate us from it. One of the players innocently asked the driver what had really happened to the ball?

The trainer, with a wry smile, took out his swiss army knife from his pocket and held up a sharp point that was designed to take stones from a horse's hoof.

"Make no mistake about it, lads, that was a victory for us tonight. They would have humiliated us if they had played the full match. What's more, they really didn't deserve to win as they were using over-age players."

We all agreed with that remark. Then the trainer told us what had driven him to puncture the ball. "When I looked over as we were togging out, I saw that they only had one ball. Once I saw we had someone with a huge kick in him, I knew I would deliver a different half-time pep talk than you've ever heard before."

Once again we all cheered at his cleverness – and our victory, if not on, well certainly off the field.

By this time we were well on our way back to Windgap and our trainer was already thinking ahead. "We'll be ready for that crowd the next day. I promise you that. We'll throw in a few of our older and bigger but young-looking players. Aye, and we might bring in one or two from across the border as well. One thing I guarantee you lads is that we will surprise them again."

The man was true to his word. The next day we played we had a much-changed team... and this time, we won pulling up.

*Dermot O'Brien is a Windgap, Co Kilkenny native who now lives in Bray, Co Wicklow. Married with four adult children, he has served Bray Emmets GAA club as Chairman, Treasurer and PRO over the years. His hobbies include watching GAA games especially Kilkenny and Bray Emmets, golf, reading and family... not necessarily in that order.*

# The Summer Of Sweeney And Ballygar

## Noel Hughes

While Ballygar's Mattie McDonagh was powering his way to All-Ireland glory for Galway in 1956, a quiet revolution was taking place a bit closer to home.

Ballygar, on the Galway/Roscommon border is famous for its carnival, started in 1945, and still going strong.

One of the carnival organisers in 1956, Joe Sweeney, also managed the Ballygar minor football team, who that year were short a few bodies.

Always an enterprising man, Joe played a visit to Ahascragh who had no minor football team that year. And after a great chat, out came the transfer forms.

Bertie Concannon, Padraig Fitzgerald, Ollie Mitchell, myself and Geoff Fallon from Castlefrench were only too delighted to be given the opportunity to play football.

Joe had some surprisingly modern training tactics and the team went into an intensive programme under his watchful eye – sometimes involving separate training sessions for the Ahascragh contingent.

He seemed to have planned every minute of that outstanding season with unheard of amounts of training and uplifting team talks.

Remember, in those days you just turned out for matches and fitness was just something you had naturally.

The opening game of the campaign was scheduled in Ballygar against neighbours Newbridge.

However, Joe hadn't counted on the Ahascragh players being required to play hurling elsewhere on the same day when he had arranged the transfers.

An emergency meeting of officials decided that, all going well, with 10 minutes to go in Ballygar, the Ahascragh contingent would all be substituted, pile onto the one car and drive as fast as possible to Mountbellew in time for the throw-in.

However, this was contingent on us securing the right result.

Taking a big chance we decided to really go for it from the outset. We hit them with all we had in the first half and built a sizeable lead that we held on to until the appointed time.

The great escape went according to plan. Off we came and the ancient Vauxhall Wyvern was driven football boot to the floor at a maximum speed of 40 miles per hour as we held onto our hurls and prayed for a safe delivery.

I say 40 with certainty as it was impossible to get an extra one-mile an hour out of that car.

That car was the reason we were able to play for both clubs at all. It was also to prove a very reliable getaway vehicle.

The rest of the season with Ballygar went like a dream with lots of training and uplifting team talks from Joe as the tiny club began to believe that a county championship could be a reality.

The county final was against Caherlistrane in Tuam and after a tight match Ballygar came through to win the first title in memory. Sweeney's methods had worked and the area rejoiced.

Plans were quickly laid for a massive celebration dance in Ballygar where the players were to be honoured. The home of the carnival was set to fete its favourite sons and it seemed as if the whole town had turned out for the occasion.

All the players arrived in their best suits; this was to be the crowning glory of a not-to-be forgotten year.

One by one the players took to the stage to be presented with their medals, to be greeted with a quiet word from Joe.

Anyone looking on could have been forgiven for thinking that he whispered in each ear: "Well done. We are so proud of you."

In fact, what he actually said was: "Smile and don't open the box, whatever you do."

While the boxes had arrived, the medals as we would say now, were in transit.

Each player played his part and raised the boxes high. It was all put right two weeks later when we each got our medals delivered by hand by the maestro himself. The medals' episode wasn't the only unforgettable piece of quick thinking from that season.

After playing another junior hurling match in Mountbellew for Ahascragh, it turned out that there was no referee organised for the subsequent game between the home side and near-neighbours Newcastle.

I don't know why they asked me – maybe it was because I was tall and I had a car – but as a 17-year-old I just shrugged my shoulders and agreed.

The match went very well and was extremely tight between two evenly-matched teams. Going into the last seconds Newcastle led by a point, and, battling to equalise, Mountbellew gained possession just inside their own half.

One of their players was blatantly fouled, but kept going, and I was happy to give him the advantage he clearly wanted.

With a singular intent, on he went, passing players, soloing, and building up to the grand finale – roared on by his teammates.

With the posts closing in, and no one looking capable of halting his gallop, the player got to 10 yards out, looked up, steadied himself – and promptly skewed his shot wide.

When the ball was pucked out, I blew for full-time, delighted with how it had all gone, and headed off to Brigges Pub in the square in Mountbellew.

I was having my pint of orange when I heard a roar from the other side of the crowded pub: "That's the fecker that cost us the match."

I hadn't anticipated the level of passion referees are expected to absorb – and I certainly didn't expect what came next.

The shouter then stood up, still incensed that I hadn't blown for a free, cracked the empty pint glass in his hand on a bench and came towards me with the jagged end – intent on leaving a lasting memento.

Without thinking, I made for the side door and kept running to the car – grateful for every bit of training Joe Sweeney had given us.

It may have only done 40, but that was faster than the guy with the broken glass could run. And his reaction also made up my mind about refereeing – I never did it again.

*Noel Hughes is a native of Ahascragh, Ballinasloe, Co Galway. A retired civil servant living in Dublin, he is married to Pauline and has three sons. His hobbies revolve around sport. An enthusiastic watcher of all codes, he currently plays golf but has participated in 16 different sports over the years.*

# Winning While On The Run

## Stan McCormack

This is the unique story of Kilbeggan Shamrocks GAA football team who won seven Westmeath senior football championships between 1919 and 1935. The club won a number of those titles during one of the most difficult times in Irish history from 1918 to 1922. At least seven of the players were on the run, raided, or had their houses broken into while they played for the team.

Local hero John McGuinness managed to turn up for one match in Rochfordbridge, while on the run. The word spread amongst the crowd that McGuinness was going to play and luckily, he escaped before the end of the game but all agreed that the score was: 'McGuinness 1; The Auxiliaries 0.'

It was ironic that the GAA pitch was provided in 1890 by the McManus Family, who owned a distillery in Kilbeggan back in 1782 under the name of Matthias McManus. It was his son, John, who was local leader of the 1798 rebellion which took place on the main street where a number of local people were killed. John McManus was convicted of treason and executed in Mullingar.

In September 2019, the then GAA President John Horan attended the celebration in the Parish Centre for the 100th anniversary of Kilbeggan winning their first title in 1919. They beat Kinnegad St Patrick's on November 2, 1919 by 1-7 to 1-1 in front of 3,000 people.

The victory heralded a golden era for Kilbeggan, though matches were restricted in 1920 and 1922, because of the political situation or they would have won more.

Kilbeggan attracted some strange characters in this era like David Stack a Kerryman, related to Austin Stack, who was an excise officer in Locke's Distillery. He wore a kilt and carried a blackthorn, which he engraved with three emotive dates in Irish history -1798, 1803, and 1867.

Mick Lynagh, a famous runner in this era, was refused permission to play with Kilbeggan because he had taken part in a race sponsored by the Evening Herald, the ruling being he competed with British soldiers and had to be suspended but he was later re-instated.

# Micheál's Voice Transported Us To The Land Of Tír Na nÓg

## Art Ó Súilleabháin

Micheál Ó Muircheartaigh loved the Irish language and never forgot his roots in Dún Síon, outside Dingle or indeed his roots in the Irish language. He was a teacher by trade and remained working in primary or secondary schools until he became a full-time commentator with RTÉ in the mid-1980s when Michael O'Hehir was forced to retire due to ill-health.

From 1949, when he commentated in Irish on the Railway Cup final, to his last commentary, on the international rules test match of 2010, the voice enthralled us. His calling card was how he slipped us nuggets of information: "We have listeners like Nellie O'Connor from Blarney, she's 95, and she attended the Thunder and Lightning Final of 1939" to moments of sheer ad libbing class: "Pat Fox has it on his hurl and is motoring well now... but here comes Joe Rabbitte hot on his tail... I've seen it all now, a Rabbitte chasing a Fox around Croke Park!" or "The stopwatch has stopped. It's up to God and the referee now. The referee is Pat Horan. God is God."

As you can see, the redoubtable Micheál had a special way with words.

Unknown to his vast following, he chose one afternoon in 2004, while at the height of his powers, to transform McHale Park in Castlebar, into the land of Tír na nÓg, like only he could do.

The affable Mic man, considered the greatest commentator in Ireland, was not only gracing this small community with his presence, but would do something no one, not even in their wildest dreams, could have expected.

I'd invited him down from Dublin to launch a project I'd initiated for children in primary schools across Mayo. It was called 'Scéim Inste Scéil', a scheme to encourage children to tell stories as Gaeilge. I wanted the children to hear the voice of a great storyteller, one who painted pictures better than any television could show them.

I wanted the children to experience the skill and presence of a gifted raconteur. Micheál fulfilled that role with his usual nonchalance and with his inimitable encouragement for the Irish language. Like Yeats before him, he was among schoolchildren and was truly enthralling. He beguiled them with stories of his own.

He launched the project, stood patiently for photographs with the various classes and then engaged with the children about their interest in sport. He discovered that at noon on that very day, one of the classes that had come to listen to his stories, (Snugboro National School, from just outside Castlebar), would be playing the Final of the Mayo Cumann na mBunscol hurling, at McHale Park in Castlebar, just down the road from the Mayo Education Centre.

Then the true spirit and generosity of Micheál emerged. The children could not believe their ears when he suggested that he might go to McHale Park with them. He would not only watch the game but he would do a live commentary on their final, a match that would mean as much to the children as any All-Ireland final in Croke Park.

Our guest had a hurried lunch and refused to take any sort of payment for his appearance and expenses, saying that if his presence helped promote Gaeilge in the schools, that he was delighted to be involved. He then hastened to McHale Park in Castlebar where he would honour his promise to the young hurlers of Snugboro.

He used his easy influence to gain access to the official commentary box and did a live commentary over the tannoy on that Cumann na mBunscol hurling game. Needless to say, true to the nature of fairytales, Snugboro won the match. The team had pictures taken with their hero and Micheál rejoiced in their success.

My own son Arthur Óg ran out onto the pitch afterwards to ask the great man to sign an autograph for him. Naturally he did so and made the young lad feel 10 foot tall in the process.

Personally, I was left with an abiding and a precious memory – that of a national icon being energised and completely engaged in the lowliest of Gaelic games, a primary schools' hurling match in Mayo, and making it sound like the most important encounter of its time.

His gift to us that day left a lasting impact as these primary schoolchildren were made feel like gods of the GAA, thanks to the magical voice of a man conjuring up images of greatness among the young.

*Nár laga Dia a spiorad, nár laga Dia a dhá shúil agus nár laga Dia riamh a ghuth.*

*Art Ó Súilleabháin is a native of Corr na Móna in Co Galway on the shore of Lough Corrib. He is a retired director of Mayo Education Centre and Fulbright teacher (2017/18) at the Catholic University of America in Washington DC. A father of six, Art is the author of a number of children's books.*

# Whatever Happened To The Fahey Cup?

Tommie Kenoy

In 1983, Kilmore GAA won its first and so far only Roscommon SFC title. It was a huge achievement for a small rural club with a population of less than 1,000 and around 80 adult club members.

One of its stars was Gerry Connellan, an All-Ireland U-21 winner in 1978 and a member of the Roscommon team that reached the 1980 All Ireland SF Final after which he received an All Star award.

The winners of the Roscommon SF Championship are presented with the Fahey Cup which was presented to Roscommon GAA by the family of JJ Fahey.

JJ was Roscommon Co Secretary during the glory years of the 1940s during which Roscommon won two minor, one junior and two All-Ireland senior titles. He was a tireless Co Secretary who played a significant role during Roscommon's glory years.

Needless to say the Fahey Cup was at the heart of a week-long celebration following Kilmore's historic win. It was proudly displayed on the top table at the club's AGM, at the club's annual dinner dance and was taken on a celebratory tour to London.

The New Year dawned and things quietened down as plans were put in place to defend the title in 1984. That was until the Co Board asked Kilmore to return the cup. No problem. Except that when the club officers went looking for the cup they couldn't find it.

Consternation all around. Every house, pub, hedge, ditch and drain in the parish and beyond were searched but no joy. The cup was missing and in spite of a forensic search no a trace of it was ever found.

All types of theories were put forward; it was left in London; it was stolen and melted down; it fell into the Shannon when the club were celebrating in nearby Carrick-on-Shannon; the Parish Priest brought it with him when he was transferred to a different parish. No substance could ever be attached to these or other theories and the mystery of the disappearing Fahey Cup has never been solved.

The club had the somewhat difficult task of contacting the Fahey family to tell them the bad news and to offer to buy a replacement. And that's what happened.

The "new" Fahey Cup is still presented to the county champions today 38 years after the original mysteriously disappeared.

*Tommie Kenoy is a native New Yorker but has lived in Kilmore, Co Roscommon since 1957. Married to Teresa, he is a former member of An Garda Síochána and was chairman of Roscommon Co Board from 1990 to 1998. Tommie was also secretary of the Club Players Association and is a member of Kilmore GAA Executive. His hobbies include angling and golf.*

# By The Way, You Wouldn't Be Anything To...?

## Peter Nolan

From growing up to grown, from childhood to young adulthood and even now, in what I will euphemistically call middle age, I have been asked this question over and over. At Gaelic grounds, in bars, at Irish events, and in recent years online; usually on Facebook, where I am sometimes mistaken for the man himself.

The question empowers those asking to somehow be transported back into their childhood. Men who played the game with or against him. People far too young to have seen him play but who have heard the name across the years in the stories told by their fathers, or more likely grandfathers.

His name, my name. And always, I have been proud to answer: "Yes, I am his son."

When I tried my hand at the sport myself, I heard them say: "If you're half the footballer that your father was, you'll be doing alright."

I never felt slighted by that. Always, I knew that half as good would be plenty good enough.

And often I would hear their stories. These reminiscences were seldom new to me but each teller brought his, always his, own passion to the telling.

"When he kicked the ball the stands shook." Ok, that was a new one. A man stopped my mother in the street outside of their home in Ireland to tell her that one a few years ago. A brand new tale to stack upon the pile of stories that through the decades combined to make a legend of my father.

There was the free kicked over the bar from alongside "Lefty's Box" at Gaelic Park in the Bronx. 70 yards if it was a foot and as my father himself has often said ... "it gets longer every year."

Another ball that went a long way was one kicked down the town. During a tough match against Laois, apparently fed up with having to clear ball after ball, his frustrations got the better of him, and finally when yet another one of his clearances came right back to him he let fly, kicking the ball out of the pitch, over the stands, and out of the stadium. That ball may still be rolling down the streets of Portlaoise half a century later!

Recently I was contacted on social media by a man I did not know. He told me that his father idolised mine and that when he coached him as a boy in the skills of Gaelic football he would punctuate his demonstrations with the remark, "that is how Peter Nolan would catch the ball."

One image that has stuck with me came at the height of the celebrations for Offaly's dramatic All Ireland hurling victory over Limerick in 1994. My father and I had attended the match together, following the crowd to the post match celebrations at the Dublin hotel where the heroes of the day were toasted.

In the midst of this joyful chaos, a man I would describe as 'hardy' approached my father and with tears welling told him that he had been his idol as a boy. To see that expression of vulnerability coming from this man has stayed with me across the years.

And then there were the introductions made possible by that name.

In 1979, I was playing for the New York minors. We were stationed in Tuam and so a few of us were brought to the dog track by one of my father's former rivals, the legendary Sean Purcell. My dogs lost every race that night but Purcell and his fellow 'Terrible Twin' Frank Stockwell, whom I would also meet on that trip, were vocal in their admiration for my father, easing the blow of a handful of pounds lost.

Some years later while on our honeymoon, my wife and I stopped at a well-known pub in Waterville, Kerry. I was aware of the owner's identity but never expected to meet him. In fact, we had stopped by to say hello to a friend we had known from New York that worked in the bar in question. Then as we sat down while attempting to decipher whether the locals at the bar were speaking English or Gaelic, the great Mick O'Dwyer himself came out to meet us.

The famous Micko was generous with his praise for my father and greeted us like old friends, making for a warm welcome and lovely memory.

The best of all the stories and the biggest piece of my father's legend was, of course: "We'd have won the All Ireland (in 1961) if they had brought your father back."

"That auld priest" was to blame, the story went. The priest in charge of the County Board had refused to bring my father back for the All Ireland semi-final versus Down in 1960 or the All Ireland Final the following year.

Given that Offaly fell to a Down team that is regarded as one of the finest of all time by just two points after a replay in 1960 and then by a single tally in the 1961 Final, it is easy to see how my mother was sometimes referred to as "The woman who lost the All Ireland."

With no disrespect to the great men of that Offaly team, I've lost count of how often I was told in no uncertain terms that had my father

## BY THE WAY, YOU WOULDN'T BE ANYTHING TO...?

been repatriated in 1960 or 1961 that the breakthrough of 1971 would have occurred a decade sooner.

With no Sam Maguire to his credit and few if any televised images to document his prowess, all we are left with to document my father's career, like those of his contemporaries, are yellowed press clippings and the word of mouth accounts of those who saw him play in the flesh.

Clippings and stories handed down from generation to generation and even if the question comes less frequently as the years pass, it still comes.

"You wouldn't be anything to Peter Nolan from Offaly, the great footballer?"

The question has never changed and neither has the answer.

"Yes," I say proudly, "I am his son."

*Peter Nolan junior is a native of New York who has maintained strong Irish roots by living in Ireland for a time and playing football here for his father's home club of Clara in Offaly and for Offaly and New York in the USA. Married with two adult children, he is a creative writer and sports writer for numerous publication in the US.*

# Player's Name Taken For Unholy Moment

## Seamus McRory

In a lifetime of wholehearted involvement in the GAA, former Tyrone All-Ireland final manager, player and official, Art McRory has seen many great matches, got much satisfaction and made many wonderful friends throughout the 32 counties. He has also accumulated a wealth of funny stories and unusual incidents. The following anecdote stands out from the rest.

It was a club challenge game in Tyrone during the latter half of the 1950s. About 15 minutes into the game, the Angelus bell rang out and, at once, the referee blew a long blast of his whistle. He immediately dropped to his knees as did 29 players in prayerful obedience.

One new player, who was not familiar with the tradition of the area, stood alone and in angry frustration he bellowed loudly: "What the blazes is going on here?"

When the referee and the other players had finished their reverential recitation of the Angelus, the extremely annoyed official stood up, took the name of the dissident player and cautioned him severely as to his conduct.

# Inch By Inch, Row By Row

## Joe Kernan

I lived many years of my life as a GAA club manager and then as a county manager trying to balance on the high wire between giving players nuggets of good information without overloading their minds in the pursuit of our goals.

The Chinese philosopher Lao Tzu probably put what I am trying to get across best of all when he said: "To attain knowledge, add things every day. To attain wisdom, remove things every day."

I don't know what GAA club he was a member of, but he could have been overlooking my work down in Cross or later with Armagh because that was the first and last commandment of what I tried to bring to the football set-ups I was involved in.

It was never a case of one voice because I knew from my own experiences that players soon get fed up listening to 'una voce'. As I grew in experience, I also got better at taking away parts of our session to help them in the long run.

I was a great disciple of the Al Pacino's speech from the film 'Any Given Sunday.' Even now that "inch by inch, play by play" speech which he delivered in the dressing-room at half time makes the hairs stand on the back of my neck.

"We claw without fingernails for that inch," he told his US Football team as they sought a way back into a game that seemed beyond them on the scoreboard. It was perfect to use on the team bus going to Croke Park as it made its way through the crowd. It focused us so well.

I liked that concept of working harder than opponents and every now and again would bring in a big name to hammer home that message to the players.

Former great players like Meath's Colm O'Rourke and Tommie Dowd and Donegal's Martin McHugh – fellas who had been there and done that – were a great help and opened up the possibilities that were there if a group was prepared to work hard for it.

I never did manage to get Alex Ferguson to take a Tuesday or Thursday spin across from Old Trafford to Armagh for county or club training, but I admired his team's commitment to fight for everything until the final whistle. You saw how that paid dividends against Bayern Munich in Barcelona in the Champions league final in 1999.

Brian Cody's Kilkenny had more than just the black and amber colours in common with us in Cross. Like Ferguson, he believed that hard work was a God-given talent and his talk helped our fellas in the Armagh squad believe that the harder we worked as a group, the further we would go on big days.

Seán Boylan, the former Meath manager and a great friend of mine, was someone I knew would leave our group enriched. His visit gave us sporting insight and intuition that was of enormous benefit – and I will come back to one big game in particular a little later.

That other great sage, Mick O'Dwyer, also answered my call when I was looking for signposts to keep us on the right road.

Like most others of my era, I greatly admired the Kerry team of the seventies and eighties which Micko developed into one of the best teams ever to tie up laces. I also liked what the three Ulster teams of the 1990s who won All-Irelands – Donegal, Down and Derry – did to achieve success. I make no apology for saying that we adapted some of their plays into the Cross and Armagh blueprints.

People think that Micko's Kerry teams were all about hand-passing and short interplays but I watched many times when Jack O'Shea would pick up a pass out of defence and he'd have it in to the Bomber with a long kick. Meath's team of the 90s were great with their use of the diagonal kick... and we used that to good effect for sure.

All the while I was adapting little parts of other teams' games, I did so mindful of what talent I had and how I could best use it. I wanted us to evolve our own basic structures. I remember one night seeing our goalkeeper Benny Tierney trying to work the ball out short to one of the McNultys in the fullback line. It ended up being intercepted. So having used Alex Ferguson's 3Ls equation of – 'Listen, learn and lead' I called Benny over for a quiet chat. "Do that one more time and Paul Hearty will be starting in the goals," I warned him.

I told him we needed to get our clearance out to the spaces in the half back line where even if things did go wrong, there was time for the defence to readjust.

In Croke Park in the final, Benny started a move out to Barry O'Hagan on the wing, he transferred it into Aidan O'Rourke who sent a diagonal ball across to Stevie McDonnell... and he kicked the crucial point with 12 minutes to go which saw us win by 1-12 to 0-14.

Micko's talk to us was full of wisdom. I asked him how could I have my team in better fettle than the opposition on the big day.

"Keep them fresh," he replied simply. "You can't beat that and neither will the other team if you get it right."

Neither Micko in the time he played, nor myself in my time a decade or two later, ever saw much example of that. I remember we'd be at it hammer and tongs in training the week before a big match trying to ensure we got picked.

He believed the players should be so hungry for action and for the sight of a ball that when they ran out on a big day, they would be gagging to get off the leash.

Eamon Coleman (RIP), the great Derry manager, was of similar mind to O'Dwyer but had a different way of saying it.

"How do you know when a team is ready, Eamonn?" I asked him one time we were together talking football.

"When they're atin' grass," he said.

I didn't know what that meant, so I asked him to explain.

"When a fella goes for a ball in the championship and gets knocked off it, he doesn't give up, but gets up and goes after it again and again and again. That's what atin' grass is," he emphasised with a smile on his face.

I used the memory of those two conversations to taper off in the weeks before big matches. Instead of 40 minutes of a practice game, I'd cut it back to 30 in the run up to a big game.

The players would nearly be in revolt and often told me we weren't doing enough. I remember one time Ronan Clarke was coming back from injury. Ronan was as honest as the day is long and wanted to do too much too soon. Our physio told me not to let him do more than 15 minutes to keep him ticking over.

I had two teams every night at training – the players and the backroom team. I asked the latter only to do their job and part of that was telling me when a fella should and should not push himself.

After the 15 minutes, Ronan begged me for 10 more minutes but I wouldn't let him. He was very unhappy but the way I looked at it was if he broke down in that 10 minutes or was unable to train the following week, it would be far worse.

Tony McEntee was injured early in the year we won the All Ireland against Kerry but we got him fit enough to give us some time in the second half. Most people wouldn't know this but in those final minutes, Tony intercepted five balls and every one of them ended up with an Armagh player. For a fella who had struggled the whole year with injuries, that was a helluva contribution to our cause when you added up the inches he gave us that day.

Armagh journeys had many bumps along the road – we were beaten three years by Meath, Kerry and Galway who went on to win All Irelands in the time immediately before we made the breakthrough in 2002.

I used to look at Munster rugby who were almost there but not quite in Heineken Cup finals when Northampton beat them 9-8 in 1999-'00 and Leicester edged home 13-9 in 2001-'02. Like ourselves they got there because they believed, even though they had to wait a little longer than us before delivering in '05-'06 when beating Biarritz 23-19. This is the image that stays with you – remember the big screen in Limerick that day – when a team gets over its hard luck stories and times of desperation to land the big prize.

In the times we were losing All Ireland semi-finals and looking a little short, I kept putting positive images in front of the players and making them believe they could go the final inches. When Paul O'Connell talked to them, it was a kindred spirit telling us that we could touch the sky if we believed.

Which brings me back to Seán Boylan. It was on a dirty December night in 1999 and we were looking to win our third All Ireland club in four years.

We had won Ulster and I wanted to keep the lads up for the challenge. I told them we would have a very special guest trainer the next night and you should have seen the reaction when Seán ran out onto the pitch. He decided that the best thing to do was play 20 minutes of football. I could tell from the boys' reaction that they wanted to be up for it in front of the renowned Meath trainer. They were "atin' grass" trying to impress him that night. If I'm honest, I'd have been more than happy just to have got that 'lift' from Seán's visit but we got an awful lot more by the time he'd finished with us.

One of our really good players went down with an almighty roar up at the top goals during Seán's session and I was worried over the seriousness of his injury.

Seán assessed the player's leg injury and asked me to help him lift the young lad over to the sideline. Then he called the rest of the lads down to the other end of the pitch. He told the group: "Boys there's nothing wrong with him, he has a bruised shin and he'll be dead on in a day or two. Remember this though, an injured player is no good to you. You have to move on immediately if it happens in a game, you have to be prepared because this will happen sometime to you as a group."

Three months later we were playing Dublin and Leinster champions Na Fianna in the All Ireland final on St Patrick's Day in Croke Park. One of our greatest ever players, Jim McConville, was having a stormer but broke his ankle after 20 minutes or so. Shortly after we had two or three more injuries. Most teams would have been crestfallen if that happened, thinking "this is not our day."

Since Boylan's visit that night, we'd talked about fighting for inches every step of the way. We had talked about players getting injured and instead of thinking our chances were diminished, we had talked about clawing with even greater energy to win those inches for our team.

Between the time Jim was carried off and half-time, we kicked five points without reply. The injury seemed to affect the Na Fianna players more than us because they stopped playing. Maybe they thought they had us when we got those injuries. We had prepared for such moments and didn't panic. We had it drilled into each player that no matter what happened, we played on to the final whistle. Donal Murtagh, our full back, went beyond the pain thresholds to stay on the field despite a serious injury to his elbow in the first half. And he made a tackle that saved a certain goal near the end which would have brought them back into it. We ended up winning 1-14 to 0-12.

Afterwards Geezer (Kieran McGeeney) was devastated having lost in Na Fianna colours. He asked me how we had managed to win three titles in four years and by then I had a clear picture in my mind. "Simple," I said. "We come to win."

It was a victory achieved in Croke Park on the biggest day of a club team's year, but it was one fashioned down in the grassroots of the club's practice pitch on a dank and dreary night far, far away from the bright lights of All Ireland final day.

My motto always was – "if you play safe, you lose"... you have to have a go for it every day you go out.

*Joe Kernan is a former Crossmaglen Rangers and Armagh player and manager who led both teams to unprecedented Ulster and All-Ireland glory during his terms in charge. He also served as Ulster manager and was appointed Ireland's international rules football manager for the 2015 series against Australia. A two-time All-Star, he is married to Patricia and they have five grown-up sons.*

# Priest Left Holding Glass Of Water

### Nioclás Ó'Griobhtháin, Co PhortLáirge

Martin Curran and his two friends left Mine Head in Old Parish, Co Waterford, cycling to Dungarvan for 7am Mass – a distance of 10 miles before catching the train to Dublin for the 1948 All Ireland final on September 5.

When they reached the church the parish priest, Fr O'Farrell was standing at the door welcoming worshippers in and marched the three boys down to the front pew of the church. This meant their plan to exit early was thrown in tatters; it also meant that they would be late getting their tickets at the railway station.

So Martin came up with a plan before Mass began that at Holy Communion, he would pretend to be overcome with a weakness. His two friends would then assist in carrying him down the middle aisle of the church. As they were doing this on the way out, who should they bump into again but the redoubtable Fr O'Farrell, who insisted on fetching a glass of water for Martin.

What were the trio to do? Desperate moments call for desperate actions. As the priest went across to the vestry to get the water, up jumped Martin from his friends' grasp. They hightailed it to the railway station, deciding they would find an explanation for the concerned Fr O'Reilly at another time.

They even joked after they had secured their train tickets and were on their way to that match that they hoped Fr. O'Farrell wasn't still holding the glass of water.

Their journey had a happy ending as Waterford went on to beat Dublin in the final on a scoreline of 6-7 to 4-2 in front of 61,742 fans.

# Uplifting Twist In Marathon Final Series

## John Lennon

When Tubbereclair and Ballynacargy, known locally as 'Bal,' reached the Westmeath Junior football final in 1967, little did anyone think it would take four games and seven months of hard labour before a winner would finally emerge.

Tubberclair had last won the Carmelite Cup in 1951 and were hungry for victory over a major rival. And so they took to the late autumn and winter training in '67 with a great zeal despite the fact there were no pitch lights, dressing rooms, hot showers or any sort of gym facilities.

Training was done in the old schoolhouse with a road run in the dark or with flashlights to warn the little vehicular traffic that was about at the time. The lamp was invariably carried by the trainer on his bike who oscillated from front to back waving his light and shouting for the slackers at the rear to quicken their pace.

The fact that those sessions took place on several occasions in driving rain helped because when the team ran out on the first Sunday of October in Cusack Park Mullingar to face the mighty men of Bal, they were met by driving stair rods – the worst day of the year.

It was a day for trying to gain possession of the ball and 'lurrying' it as far as possible. Tactics went out the window; it was a case of "let God direct it" when ball was transferred from foot.

The game ended all square and in truth both sides were happy that they had lived to fight another day. The replay was fixed for the last Sunday in that month and produced an entirely different type of game altogether.

Half-way through the second half, Bal were eight points ahead and cruising into the home strait. Tubberclair, in their green and gold colours, had a great fighting spirit and their forwards showed tremendous resolve in winning virtually every ball kicked into them. They whittled away at the lead and with a minute left, they had levelled the game.

Bal mounted a last gasp effort to snatch victory and forced their opponents to concede a 50. Fortunately for us, the resultant kick fell just short and the fullback rose majestically to catch it on the edge of the parallelogram.

Most people thought the referee would then blow the final whistle but as the defender attempted to clear the ball, the official awarded a 14-yard free directly in front of the goal to Bal. Naturally this led to mayhem on and off the pitch – it looked for sure that Tubberclair would lose by a point.

However, as the kicker placed the ball to take the free, two Tubberclair players climbed up the posts like Batman without his cape and stood on the crossbar across the length of the goal. Two others attempted the same thing but only got to swing from the crossbar.

This unusual and novel attempt to mount a defence against a free stopped the kick from being taken and ultimately when a Tubberclair player lashed the ball down the field, it led to a pitch invasion by spectators, forcing the referee to abandon the game.

The local newspaper, the Westmeath Examiner, under the headline 'Extraordinary Ending To JFC Final – Players Man The Crossbar,' recorded the details of the ending as follows: "Two Tubberclair players perched themselves on top of the crossbar, preparing to block down what would likely have been a point. A couple of non-players came in to have a discussion with the referee. This number increased and before long the pitch was filled around the goalmouth with spectators. Clearing the area now was impossibility and the referee had no choice but to abandon the game. Despite the fact that play could not continue, there did not appear to be any blow struck or attempted."

At a subsequent county board meeting, the game was firstly awarded to Bal before by some strange quirk of fate, it was agreed that a replay was the best course of action.

Three months later, in the early spring of 1968, the third game of the Junior Co Final series began... this time with a referee specially brought in from Co Louth to officiate.

Once more it was a very fiery affair and, you guessed it, once more it ended all square. It went to extra time and even with that, the sides were tied on the scoreboard.

And so like the Meath-Dublin series which would follow many years later in 1991, the fixture entered a fourth game.

By now the cuckoo had arrived in the New Year and the third Sunday in April was a standout day. The exploits of both teams had drawn attention from across the county so that when they ran out onto the pitch for the fourth encounter under the same 'foreign' referee, a massive crowd greeted them.

By now both sides knew each other's inside leg measurements but it was Tubberclair who refined their tactics to suit better than their rivals.

## UPLIFTING TWIST IN MARATHON FINAL SERIES

Once more both sides put on a gripping spectacle for the supporters and we finally got the chance to bring the Carmelite Cup back to 'the village of the rose' after winning by 1-10 to 2-2. The Westmeath Independent, in a banner headline over a picture of the squad and a match report, stated 'Tubberclair Win Marathon Junior Title'.

Even at this remove of over half a century, those of us who saw action talk fondly of the time we had to pull out all the stops – including our 'assault' on the crossbar to get our hands on one of the hardest won medals of all time.

*John Lennon is a native of Tubberclair, Co Westmeath. A widower, he is a former member of the club. He now resides in Ballymore and is still active in the local GAA club.*

# Officiating At An Unusual Pitch Battle

Tom Farrell

I refereed for 30 years in Dublin and the only regret I have at this stage is that I didn't ever get to officiate at a senior final.

In retrospect, I was probably a bit too independent for the county board's liking but when JJ Barrett, a journalist I respected for the passion he as a Kerry man brought to Dublin GAA, said I was one of the best, well, that was good enough for me.

In those 30 years with the whistle, I came across many funny and strange things on the capital's GAA beat.

One of my first memories when I was only a matter of weeks reffing came from a game played in a pitch at Rowlestown in the Fingal league.

The ground was very sparse then, with no clubhouse or facilities like they have now. However, it wasn't that which irritated me on the day. There was a crowd of about 100 along the sideline but one in particular was admonishing my decisions at every turn.

I glanced across a few time and noticed that as well as being quite elderly, he had a stick which he constantly waved in my direction.

Finally I snapped, blew the whistle and told the officials and the crowd that I was not going to restart the game until the elderly man was ejected from the ground.

"You can't do that," one of the Fingal Ravens officials whispered politely to me.

"Why not?" I asked, a bit put out that he too appeared to be questioning my authority.

"Because he owns the field," he replied.

That story reminds me of another at a time when places like Fingal did their own leagues not really under the county board's supervision. A young lad who had started out reffing asked for advice when taking charge of matches "out the country."

A colleague enlightened him as follows: "Any time you are down to referee in Garretstown, arrive earlier than usual, take a walk around the hedge to see if there are any gaps… you might want to know where they are later."

# Antrim On The Cusp Of New Era When Troubles Took Hold

Declan Bogue

For those signing up to the Provisional wing of the Irish Republican Army, the choice was spelled out to them before they took their oath.

The fluffy stuff, the romance and all that, they got from monuments and old songs and stories about the glory of Old Ireland. The Belfast Brigade would dispense with niceties.

Being lucky was to spend the best part of your youth in prison while those outside were socialising and going to college, enjoying relationships, getting married, having families.

Could be worse though. Chances were, you could be mown down in a gun battle or blown up by your own bomb.

Fitting in a bit of Gaelic football? Sure, they had that four days a week in the Long Kesh cages.

Winning a senior championship while on active service? It happened one man. Maybe more. We'll come back to that.

In the meantime, picture the scene in the Aztec Stadium Mexico, when Brazil are crowning themselves the greatest most flamboyant and adored soccer team of all time as they hammer Italy 4-1 to lift the World Cup on June 21st, 1970.

On the same day, another team in a shade of yellow had arrived. The latest batch of great Antrim footballers had come along and beat Down in Casement Park, denying them a place in the Ulster final for the first time in 12 years.

In midfield, the huge figure of Frank Fitzsimons blotted out the cerebral Joe Lennon of Down. The All-Ireland champions of 18 months ago were gone.

But Fitzsimons was jumpy about the whole thing. Once the game was over, he got offside. Staying about wasn't an option for someone in the PIRA.

Onto July 5th and Taoiseach Jack Lynch makes an appeal for every illegal firearm in Belfast to be dumped.

The night before, the British Army stormed the Lower Falls Road, seizing ammunition and arms and placing the residents under curfew.

That included the Antrim centre-back Billy Millar who was smuggled to Newry for the Ulster semi-final. Antrim beat Monaghan 2-10 to 1-8, Aidan Hamill's two goals and Andy McCallin's threat carrying them through.

Derry, inspired by Eamon Coleman and Mickey Niblock beat them by four points in the Ulster final, but as 1970 made way for 1971, the footballers of Antrim would have been forgiven for thinking of themselves in a good place.

This is where dates get hazy, memory clouds over.

A lot of the time, that's intentional. Some of this information is sensitive.

Here's what we can nail down in sporting terms.

In 1969, Liam Boyle captained Antrim U21s to an All-Ireland U21 Championship. A few years later he was in prison.

The Antrim Vocational Schools team win an All-Ireland in 1968 beating Galway, and lose to Mayo in the 1971 final.

St Mary's Christian Brothers won the MacRory Cup in 1971.

Antrim seniors were in the Ulster final of 1970.

But society in 1971 was curdling. Belfast was at the epicentre.

On January 13th, there were riots in Ballymurphy. Two days later, Ardoyne went up in flames.

From February 3rd, the British Army began conducting a series of house searches in Catholic areas of Belfast, prompting rioting and gun battles that lasted days.

Three days later, the first British soldier was killed by the IRA. Gunner Robert Curtis, a 20-year-old from Newcastle-Upon-Tyne was in Belfast less than a month and found himself dispersing a crowd in the New Lodge Road. Trying to evade a nail bomb blast, he was caught with a rake of fire from a Sterling submachine gun.

The same night, a Catholic civilian Bernard Watt and IRA man James Saunders were killed in north Belfast by the British Army.

The most stark statistics come in the raw data. Between police, British Army, paramilitary and civilians, there were 16 deaths in 1969 and that rose to 26 a year later. 1971 had 171 deaths. 1972 had 476.

Throughout 1971, word was everywhere about the old British RAF base outside Lisburn that was being converted into a prison. It became known as Long Kesh.

It was opened on August 9th, when 342 men and boys were lifted from nationalist homes and interned without trial. Fourteen of them – the Hooded Men – were subjected to days of continuous torture. So as long as internment remained a policy, many others had to go on the run.

In that environment, family traditions came into play. Frank Fitzsimons' father Francis had been a Republican in the 1940s. His mother was an O'Rawe, another staunch family.

"I have to be honest, my family was steeped in Republicanism," he begins.

"My mother and father, the way it was in my house was family first, country was next and county was after that. Those were the things that kept us going at the time, and they were hard times.

"My father was interned, my brother was interned. I had two brothers sentenced, I had a sister on the run with me. And my mother, well she wasn't on the run, but I couldn't tell you what she was at. I was only one of many."

But for years he played for club, county and his province.

"Football back then was the Holy Grail to us. You loved the club. I'll give you an example. I travelled from Cork in the back of a container lorry, just to play a match.

"I was just in Cork and a fella called, he said he could bring me up. Five hours in the back of a container lorry. But I wasn't the only one. There were a couple of lads who would have done the same. We loved the game that much."

Others not from the same traditions were drawn in. Mickey Culbert was left-half forward on the U21 team that won the All-Ireland in 1969 and was a social worker getting married in August. He was far away from the 'unemployed barman and bookies' runners' stereotype of an IRA man. He had relatives that fought in the First World War.

"I wasn't a Republican, per se, I was more aware that things were not right. Basically, I was more Civil Rights-ish," he says.

"But when we are talking about the currents of change, probably the major change was coming and it had nothing to do with me, was internment in 1971.

"The build-up of stuff was going on around us. I worked in the city centre as a civil servant. And everything changed, there were no buses, people were walking to work. I remember walking down the Falls Road down to the top of Albert Street and there was a massive, massive mound of empty shells. The British Army must have been firing heavy machine guns.

"I wasn't paying any attention to the republican movement at that stage. My interest was still in the GAA, basketball and my girlfriend. To get up and down the Falls Road was very difficult from where I lived to where she lived.

"Within our club, there were rumblings that something wasn't right. A lot of fellas left and later on you realised what was going on. They had political differences with other fellas."

He continues: "I would always have had an underside of support for violent republicanism. I think probably the books you used to read about the IRA in the '20s and '30s and stuff. I know it might sound ridiculous. But my sympathies would have been with the IRA. And gradually I came to realise that the British Army weren't there really, as they had said, to protect the nationalist areas from the B Specials and the RUC.

"I came to that realisation with internment in 1971. That was a major catalyst for me. 'This is like other countries, they are an invading army,' which gradually led to me thinking, 'ah, I might have to do something about this myself.'"

Andy McCallin didn't want any of that. He was more concerned with perfecting his football and hurling and becoming one of the best exponents of either code in the country with St John's and Antrim. His father, Andy senior, was chairman of St John's and they only had eyes for the GAA.

He won an All-Star in 1971, Antrim's only such award in football, in the first year of the scheme. Seldom can an All-Star have been won in such trying conditions.

He acknowledges that: "Life was difficult. I was going with the wife, she lived in Beechmount at the time and I got over the barricades and would have walked the Falls Road, because you daren't get a taxi or transport, and then walk home.

"You are trying to get to work, and in the middle of the night the bin lids are banging away like mad because that was to tell everybody the Army was about.

"But the things we had to go through in those times, and we did! I lived 600 yards from Casement. John Burns (Antrim full-back) lived on the other side of the town in Glengormley and he was able to make it to Casement come hell or high water."

Domestically, subtle changes became massive. Entire clubs split between those who supported the 'Officials' and the 'Provisionals.' One club house was emptied one night and firebombed as the in-fighting between republican factions raged.

Watching from as far away as America was Bob Murray. He had been a veteran of the Border Campaign in 1956 to 1962 and entered Crumlin Road gaol at just 18 for a ten-year sentence after an arms raid in Belfast.

Once he got out, he made for America. He was only there a matter of months before he was conscripted into the American Military. They didn't ask about previous experience.

The pay was poor, but he discovered how to get a bit extra.

"You got $55 a month if you jumped out of the aeroplane, so I joined the

82nd Airborne Division. And that almost doubled my pay. Most of the time I was in America. There was a skirmish in the Dominican Republic once, but you were only in for two years," he says.

He was working for NORAID (The Irish Northern Aid Committee, an Irish-American body that fundraised for the Provisional IRA) and looking at the front page news of American newspapers throughout 1971 when he decided to come home.

"I was involved before I went and I came back again. I didn't spend any more time in prison, but I was arrested many, many times," he says.

As soon as he got back, he got back involved with his club, St Paul's. In times of curfew, the ability to go down to your local club and drink there in relative safety was a small comfort.

Maintaining a full programme of games was in itself another part of the resistance.

"It was sort of normal, the games were very important and very important for kids. You always kept the show on the road and we could get stopped going to games. We would be held up. But the games went on regardless.

"Everything went hand in hand. The war was going on, on a daily basis. It was going on in the street you were living in, and when you were going to play football and hurling."

The sound of a helicopter above head was a constant throughout 1971.

Fitzsimons had to be secretive about his whereabouts. He saw little of his children for many years. Whenever there was a team photo, he would duck out and warnings were delivered to newspaper reporters to put his name down as AN OTHER.

Yet, he played throughout that summer.

He even went to America and played a few games with the Cavan team in New York and came back to captain Antrim in their Ulster Championship first-round 0-8 to 0-4 defeat to Derry.

Special Branch were gathering intelligence on GAA activity though and made a swoop once.

"We were playing Sarsfields one day at their pitch and the helicopter landed. But I got away. There was a massive crowd there that day, back then you could have had 600 following the football, it's not like today. But I got away, there was a lad sitting in a car and I just jumped into it and he got me away."

There were other audacious escapes, including one night in Glenavy when he was captured and in a police car. His captor took out a packet of Gallagher's Blues cigarettes and after Fitzsimons' request for one was turned down, he headbutted the policeman and forced open the door, making for safety when he and his accomplices all scattered in different directions.

But the most daring of all was the county final of 1971 in Casement Park. Lámh Dhearg won their very first title with Fitzsimons at centre-back, fending off McCallin's St John's who came with a late flurry of scores.

In the Ulster club, they were drawn to play Bryansford in Newcastle. But word came that a raid was in the offing. Fitzsimons stayed away.

Another day, Culbert was playing for St Gall's against St John's in Corrigan Park, half-deafened by the rotating blades of helicopters.

"It would have been around that time," he recalls. "Low-flying over us. It was only later in the day when we realised they were taking the men from the Maidstone Ship (a prison ship moored in Belfast harbour) and moving them out to the new jail at Long Kesh. That was the flight path."

In late July 1972, the biggest British Military operation since the Suez Crisis, Operation Motorman was launched with 22,000 soldiers deployed to take back control of nationalist 'no-go' areas.

Part of it was to take over Casement Park.

The following week, the Belfast clubs staged a protest and arrived outside the ground, before playing a series of small-sided games up and down the Andersonstown Road.

Being on the run, taking part in battles, the occasional snatched visit to relatives was a way of life. There was nothing glamorous about any of it. Prison or death was still only seconds away.

In 1974, Fitzsimons was charged and did a deal of sorts, admitting he was a member of Sinn Fein, getting three years.

Once inside, he introduced a Gaelic football league between the different huts in the compound.

"You had four huts, A, B, C and D," he explains.

"'A' would have been the Tyrone lads, who would have fought with their fingernails. 'B' would have been Derry, 'C' was Down, and 'D' was Antrim. Antrim was always the best team. We had one of the best players in jail at that time, Liam Boyle (captain of the U-21 team in 1969)."

Clubs and counties sent in footballs and equipment. Some had snazzy rigs in the colours of their county, although they could have stood up by themselves with the stench.

Fitzsimons recalls going down to a hut to see an inmate, Dal Delaney who was in a bad way. People said he wasn't far from death.

"So down I goes to him and the cell is like a Grotto. I said, 'Well Dan, what about you?'

"Ah, I am gone big man, I am gone," came the reply.

This was Antrim's day to play Derry and Fitzsimons went back to his hut to get togged. While there, he told another to fetch what homemade poteen they had left and run it down to Dal in the 'Derry' hut.

"The Gaelic pitch was right beside his cage. We were playing the lads in that cage and they were Derry lads. I was playing away and could hear this shouting halfway through the game, 'Get into that big bastard! Hit him!'

"And who was it? Dal Delaney swinging on the cage. He got better very quick with the help of the poteen!"

He adds: "The whole secret inside jail was to keep the morale up. Everyone can get a blue day, they get blue days now. But whenever you are in jail, with a big sentence hanging over you, and you see friends walking out every other day...

"We used to cut up rough in the games. I have to say this about jail, there were so many good lads, the only thing you were missing was seeing your family. And you could see them once a week. Other than that, we had plenty of sport. The Tyrone men would have played all day. And the screws were scared to come in."

Nowadays, Culbert helps former Republican prisoners as co-ordinator of COISTE, leaning on his social worker background. But he put down 16 years in Crumlin Road prison and Long Kesh after being found guilty through the Diplock judicial system of the murder of a UDR officer in Lisburn.

While inside, he was the results man.

"Every week I was smuggled in the GAA results," he says.

"You used to shout out the results. The Irish News had a column with a narrow long piece of results from all the counties. So it was cut up and rolled up very tight, smuggled into jail. And I used to call out the results.

"So they came in every Monday. And you would hear the odd cheer from those inside if their club had won a big game."

Around this time, Antrim football fell off a cliff. In senior football championship, they won four games between 1970 to 2000. Internment and The Troubles decimated them.

Casement Park is still off limits to them, this time by more subtle means, a lack of will from political Unionism contributing to its' ongoing dereliction.

"It went on too long. The Troubles," adds Fitzsimons (Frank also had a son named after himself, who both played for and managed the Antrim senior football team and brought St Enda's Glengormley to the All-Ireland Intermediate final in February 2019).

"What we took from the British Army and what we gave back was unbelievable. People think the IRA had thousands and thousands of men. You had the support within your own community, but as far as soldiers went, you hadn't that much. And what you were working with wasn't great.

"The British, what they had, well you might as well as went out with a catapult."

*Declan Bogue is from Garvary in Co Fermanagh. He grew up playing football for Tempo Maguires and hurling for Lisbellaw St Patrick's and has worked as a sports journalist for national newspapers in Ireland and England. His book 'This Is Our Year' which chronicled the 2011 Ulster Championship is acknowledged as one of the best books ever written on the GAA. He is married to Ciara and they have three children; Thomas, Lily and Ruairi.*

# Playing GAA In 'The Blacks' Before GAA Was Founded

Paddy Phelan

Snowflakes were drifting across the skyline as Fr. Edward Walsh administered the sacrament of marriage between Edmond Wall of Sean-Baile-Anna and Catherine Kiely of Curradoun at St. Mary's Church Tourneena on February 4, 1864.

In an arranged marriage agreed by both sets of parents, the bride and groom were given little or no vision of each another before their wedding. The bag of money as dowry had to be handed over to the groom's family before the bride walked down the aisle. Catherine was well-spoken, good hearted and as it turned out, a stunning beauty to boot. Edmond was more than pleased to rest with her.

They soon found they could both handle a pike and a gun as they roamed the sloping fields and golden glens near their home, where almost 200 years before in early 1670, the bold 'Faylin', the bard of Armagh, walked and rested in Edmond's ancestral old thatched home.

'Faylin' of course was Oliver Plunkett in disguise and on the run with a bounty on his head. The Penal Laws at that time were to the fore and on a Sunday the people would walk quietly through the woodlands to the Mass House which was located at Sean Baile Anna.

Fr. Nicholas McGanney was the parish priest and silence was the order of the day, as discovery meant terrible consequences. Twenty-three years previous to this time in 1649, two Franciscan priests were drowned in the River Nire at Sean Baile Anna whilst fleeing from Cromwellian soldiers. The place is still known today as Pól na Sagart.

Two years before Edmond and Catherine's marriage in 1862, a beautiful Catholic church named St. Helena's was completed at Glenanore, Ballymacarbry. In 1864 a new schoolhouse was erected close to the church. As a new generation grew up around Edmond and Catherine, their thoughts turned more and more to the provision of a field for sport so youngsters could play their native Gaelic games together without fear or favour to any over lords in the village.

Twenty years before the GAA was officially founded, Edmond and

# GRASSROOTS

Catherine outlined their plans to dig, clear and level three acres of heather-clad land at the summit of Sean-Baile-Anna. After much debate the couple employed the Cross family who were diggers of ditches to carry out the work.

Noonan's forge at Sean-Baile-Anna crossroads played its part in keeping the implements in working order. After a lot of sweat, blood and tears, the pitch in The Blacks, as the area was called, was completed in 1875.

Talk about a couple being ahead of their time...they not only preceded the foundation of the GAA but were socially involving a community through a love of sport. That is remarkable at any time, but in the decades after the famine and during the occupancy of Britain and its ownership of Irish land at the time, it was both inspired and inspiring that a young couple would take such a lead.

It was a move that served not only that crop of youngsters but also succeeding generations across almost a century during which 'The Blacks' was the centre of the universe for local football and hurling activity.

It was indeed a mighty blessing for the area, one that was given initially by Fr. Will Power P.P. in 1875 at the opening of the facility. Plenty of water flowed down the sparkling Glea-Da-Buí stream on the pitch's eastern bounds before some 89 years later, another playing complex took over the mantle of sports centre for the area.

The pride at all times was the village ... your village. Down the decades for almost 90 years, when the cows were milked and the butter made, the people would assemble there on a summer's evening to pass their time in sporting pursuit. Games, mostly on Sunday, were by and large ad hoc fixtures between neighbours, though on special occasions, there would be more formal meetings between different villages.

Sometimes as you played in or attended such games, you could clearly hear the whistle of the steam train rolling into the railway station in Cluain Meala, eight miles to the north across the mountain.

Many of the participants in those games would later shed bitter tears before boarding this train on the first part of their journey to foreign lands – some never to return to their native place. God rest them.

By 1890, six years after the founding of the GAA in Thurles, local and district championships were becoming common across the landscape. The Nire football team competed in the West Waterford championship and played Kinsalebeg on Dungarvan that year. Although beaten by three points they gave as good as they got, the final score being Kinsalebeg 1-3, The Nire 0-3.

Even in those far off times, romances blossomed ... as on the occasion of

## PLAYING GAA IN 'THE BLACKS' BEFORE GAA WAS FOUNDED

February 11, 1904. Bridget Ryan of Knocklasheen married John Jack Wall, the strapping son of Edmond and Catherine Wall (and my grandfather) in Fourmilewater Church.

By 1920, the new generation of boys and girls in the football field were playing their part in the War of Independence and Civil War. By 1930 the field had a new lease of life. Dinny McGrath of Knockaun, who is 100 years young as I write this in early 2021, recalled the story to me some months ago.

He played with the Gap team, which was a selection from the villages of Knockaun, Knockavanni, Kilkeany and Shanballyanne. Dinny said it was not unusual to have 300 or more spectators at a match in the Blacks in the 1930s. In a famous game fought out between the Gap and Glenanore, Paddy Sean Brazil of Glenanore broke his leg but made a full recovery.

In the summer of 1956, Jack Phelan along with his brother Ned, brought the Phelan Cup to the football field in The Blacks, a field were Jack and Ned played in their youth. Members of the Nire junior football team, who were county champions in 1942, also played football in the Blacks in the 1930s.

It was indeed a historic place to play and a source of great pride in our family that my great grandparents had the prescience to see how bringing a community together under the one sporting umbrella could make such a difference to the growth of our culture and social enlightenment.

*Paddy Phelan is a native of Waterford and is the great grandson of Edmond Wall. Married to Josephine, they have six adult children and 10 grandchildren. A dairy farmer, he has represented his farming colleague on both the board and advisory committees of Waterford Co-op for four decades.*

# Policeman Flew Under The Ban

## Anon

In October 1967, the English newspaper The Sunday Mirror highlighted the case of GAA player Andrew Buchanan.

Back then in the good old ban days, Andrew worked as a member of the British police force in Moseley, Birmingham. For those who may remember the then GAA rule: "British soldiers, navy men and police shall not be eligible for membership of the GAA."

In Wicklow, Baltinglass had annexed another crown by accounting for Newtownmountkennedy in the senior final. However, the Mirror highlighted the fact that maybe the result should be reversed. And there was precedent on their side as in 1906 when Cork beat Kilkenny in the All Ireland hurling final, their goalkeeper, Jim 'Sonny' McCarthy was a reservist in the British Army.

A Kilkenny objection was sent to the Central Council and upheld, resulting in the game being replayed without McCarthy.

Six decades on the Mirror highlighted the story as much to show how archaic this rule was as to rain on Balto's parade.

Buchanan flew home regularly to turn out for his club and his style as a scoring forward made him a favourite of the team's supporters. The fact that he was a policeman flying over and back only added to the intrigue and mystery. This time the result stood with the GAA.

# A Giant Of The Alley Called 'Tatters'

## Éamon Ginnane

I learned my handball skills against the gable wall of the national school in Carrigaholt, West Clare. My job brought me to Westmeath and I played football with Athlone GAA Club and handball in Bealnamulla. I cycled the five miles to the club some evenings but Sunday mornings were the highlight of the week with a series of singles and doubles. And it was always Tom 'Tatters' Keegan who was the centre of attention.

'Tatters' was born in 1888. A well-built man of 5ft 8inches with an open face, he had a natural welcome and a roguish smile. He was an early riser. First thing in the morning he would dip his head in a barrel of rainwater outside his back door. Every Sunday, he made 7 o'clock Mass in the Friary in Athlone and later cycled out to the Bealnamulla handball alley on his old Raleigh.

He wore a pocket watch and chain, making a big display of taking it carefully from his pocket, flicking open the lid and pausing to check the time. Although he was great on the Gaelic field, it was in the handball alley where he shone. He was as fit as a fiddle because he was a 'mobile ganger' with the Great Western Railway. That meant he cycled miles from his home to wherever his crew was working laying the railway tracks.

There were all kinds of stories about how he had earned the nickname. I heard the true story from the local postman, Paddy Farrell. Tatters was a spectator at a GAA club championship game between Tubberclair and a team from north Westmeath. Tubberclair were being hammered in the first half. A Tubberclair selector spotted Tom in the crowd and even though he wasn't a club member, he was coaxed into their dressing room, given a club jersey and a pair of boots. There were no spare togs to be found so he played in his Sunday trousers (at the time, people dressed up in their Sunday best). He played an outstanding game and turned the tide for Tubberclair. When he arrived back in the dressing room, he looked down and roared: "My Sunday best is in tatters!' and the name stuck.

Tatters wasn't just a great handball player, he was an outstanding coach. The Bealnamulla alley was built on the verge of the old road to

Taughmaconnell and for a number of years had no back wall. Tatters would coach us to serve a long high ball because if our opponent failed to hit it in the air rather than letting it hop, he would have to run backwards, across to the far side of Taughmaconnell Road before he could return it.

Duggie Mahon, a nephew of Tatters, approached him to coach a team of Townies (myself included) in a tournament against the local country lads, who were being coached by a very skilful player, Jackie Fallon. Tatters was a great admirer of the legendary Cork hurling manager, Jim Barry, who always looked immaculate on the sideline in an Aran jumper. Tatters suggested he would do a far better job of coaching if we managed to find him an Aran jumper. He got the jumper. We got our coach.

The country lads were noted for their skill at butting, but Tatters had warned us to keep the ball high and skimming the side walls; the advice was good and the townies won out. Tatters roared: "Look at ye now – when ye first joined, ye couldn't even hit the ball with a bicycle wheel!"

He spent hours coaching, coaxing and cajolling players to perfect their skills. He continued to play handball into his eighties and was filmed giving an exhibition of his handball skills by PJ Devaney for RTE. At 84, he cycled out to the alley accompanied by his grandchild, Paddy Harney. They played for a while with Tatters passing on his handball tips and tricks to his grandson. It was to be Tatters last game at his beloved alley. A few weeks later he passed away. His trusty Raleigh now takes pride of place on a wall in Paddy's workshop.

The local handball community, young and old, attended his funeral. At his burial in Kiltoom cemetery, many were surprised by the Irish army honouring Tatters with a seven gun salute. However, Tatters was not only a giant of handball, he was also a man of great courage. He was awarded three medals for brave and honourable deeds as a captain in the War of Independence.

He was always on the run from the Black and Tans but was never captured – the bog and the forest were his safe hideaways. Whenever the Tans arrived at his home and failed to find him, they wrecked his house and terrified his family.

Tatters house was located on the bóirín leading to the 'Occupiers' rifle range. The army lorries drove past at top speed and woe betide any hen or duck that crossed their path. The driver was obliged to report any 'fowl' incident to his commanding officer, who would then compensate Tatters family for their loss.

Times were hard and money was scarce. Occasionally, when he heard the sound of approaching lorries, Tatters would release an ailing hen or a lame duck on the road. Just like on the handball alley, when Tatters saw his advantage, he took it.

*Éamon Ginnane grew up playing handball against the gable end of Carrigaholt national school and football in the West Clare pitches beyond. Married to Margo Flanagan, they have two daughters Sinéad and Síle. An employee of An Post for 47 years, he helped Athlone GAA Club to a magnificent five-in-a-row of Westmeath senior football championship titles from 1955-1960.*

# Getting Rid Of All Things English

## Anon

Yes, there was a time when the old adage "burn everything British except their coal" held sway with many people, particularly those in the GAA.

One such man worked in the civil service in Dublin and journeyed by train each day to the capital from his abode. This individual loved arguments and was known to stick rigidly to his own point of view. One day he got involved in a heated debate on the national situation.

At that time you could smoke on public transport and as a pipe smoker, he often used the facility of arguing to fill his pipe with tobacco. On this particular day, he couldn't find his matches and one of his adversaries generously handed him over his own box. He lit his pipe and as was about to hand them back when he noticed they were manufactured in England.

"What the hell are you doing with those English matches?" he asked his opponent, and without permission he threw the box out the window of the carriage.

The other guy was none too happy and in reprisal took up our friend's hat which was at the end of the long seat, examined it and saw it was also made in England. So without by or leave, he threw the offending object out the window.

At that point another man returned from the toilet and as he was about to sit down, saw that his hat was missing and asked had anyone seen it? No one admitted to how it had been ejected... however the carriage quietened for the rest of the journey.

# Rock And Roll Like Never Before

Enda McEvoy

Irrespective of the level they are competing at, when there's a buzz around a local team that is going well, the benefits for the club are tangible. One of the offshoots of a team in form is that it can bring enhanced sponsorship revenue to enable a club to expand its facilities. The added exposure makes it that bit easier to sell tickets as a part of fundraising activities. Sparking a general interest in the club within the local area can increase the pool of available players for its teams across all ages and levels as well as attendances at matches and club functions.

For the player, the benefits are perhaps not as clearcut as they are for the club, but they are there nonetheless. Naturally, from the sporting perspective there is the obvious advantage of enhancing one's chances of playing at county level. Playing with a team that is in with a chance of winning silverware can also offer the player something which is extremely beneficial.

It is called leverage and the player can potentially utilise this to his advantage in any number of circumstances. It can, for instance, increase the chances of getting a scholarship to a third-level institution. It may present the opportunity of a plum summer job, or indeed a full-time job from a club official or "a lad he knows," if the player makes it known that he may not be around to play in the championship that year because of a need to search for work abroad.

Leverage can be applied in certain social situations too. Many is the player who has punched well above his weight in the shifting stakes by virtue of his place on the local team.

The Rock GAA club, which is located outside the town of Mountmellick in Co. Laois, reached its first senior football final in 1998, just 28 years after the club was formed. By that time it was beginning to reap the rewards of a strong juvenile structure from the late eighties and early nineties. The club was also well represented in the Laois minor successes during the mid-nineties and this production line was starting to bear fruit at senior level.

Even though the club lost that 1998 final to Stradbally on a truly miserable December day at O'Moore Park in Portlaoise, it was confident that it had sufficient strength and quality to be involved in the mix for the foreseeable future. This optimism was tempered with the realistic assumption, that for a club of its size, the window of opportunity to deliver a Laois senior football title was not going to be open forever. There was no room for "if onlys" or "what ifs" in their pursuit of this objective.

Any opportunity in future would have to be seized and the club would have to do all that it realistically could to achieve it. This last point is underpinned by the unwritten understanding in the relationship between player and club – once the player shows dedication and respect to the club, then the club will do all it can to help the player.

This brings us neatly back to the subject of leverage. Volumes have been written about the age-old conundrum of club and county fixture scheduling within the GAA. The precarious nature of this scheduling can have serious repercussions for the club player and their planning of a holiday abroad. This is amplified by the fact that the months from May to September are (Covid-19 era aside) the most important in the GAA calendar, which is, of course, also the time of the year when people usually go on holiday.

Despite the best intentions and an almost chess-like attention to detail by players in choosing the most appropriate time for their week away, there are inevitable clashes with these plans when a championship fixture is rescheduled at short notice.

Such a conflict occurred with The Rock during the 2000 GAA season when some of the team had planned a holiday away in the sun which ultimately ended up clashing with the planned date of their championship quarter-final fixture against Portarlington in August of that year.

It's worth bearing in mind that this occurred before a time when the likes of a Ryanair flight was somewhat disposable and also before a time when, if you gave sufficient notice, you could cancel an online hotel reservation without ending up horrifically out of pocket.

Deposits had been put down earlier in the year and the balance paid off a few weeks in advance of flying out. Back then when you booked a holiday, you made a significant commitment to it. If that wasn't bad enough, the lads had already got their pesetas sorted out at a very favourable exchange rate, as the introduction of the Euro was still another 17 months away. The simple fact of the matter was that a holiday had been booked and, more importantly, paid for.

When the fixture ended up clashing head on with the holiday, strenuous efforts were made by the club to seek an alternative date once the issue had been flagged by the affected players. However, in an already extremely congested schedule, postponing the match was ruled out.

The lads' flight was leaving Dublin on the Saturday evening and the only available option from the County Board was an early afternoon throw-in on the same day. The burning question was whether that would leave enough time to make it to the airport after the match. We must also remember that this was before the current M7 motorway connected Laois with The Pale.

Could the club ensure the lads made their flight?

That word again – leverage. The lads had no need to worry. They would be able to strut around Playa del Inglés in their O'Neills shorts like a bunch of sunburnt Adonises, long before Paul Mescal made it fashionable to do so.

How many people have ever had the privilege of a personal garda escort from the midlands right up to the front door of Dublin Airport?

Unless you are royalty, a heavyweight politician or a rock n' roll star, then I'd guess that you haven't.

That's leverage for you.

The Rock GAA club enjoyed the privilege on that Saturday in 2000. Like something out of The Dukes of Hazzard, our lads tore out of the car park of Mountmellick GAA grounds after their match had ended. Leaving a cloud of dust in their wake, they were delivered at God speed with all the pomp and ceremony of an official state visit.

They travelled along the old Dublin Road that took them through Monasterevin, Kildare, Newbridge and Naas. Lord only knows who the bystanders witnessing this odd-looking cavalcade thought the VIPs in the Picasso actually were.

Some B-list boy band perhaps?

Supplied with a car fresh from the showroom of The Rock's main sponsor, George Delaney Car Sales, and prepped with the briefest of instructions by the garda leading the way – "Stick on your hazard lights and stay as close to me as you can. Got it?" – the driver, Pa, nodded in agreement and with his foot to the floor just about kept pace with the flying squad car as it sped along the labyrinthine country roads, straight through Newlands Cross in Dublin's Citywest and all the way north on the journey to the airport.

It had been a testing drive for the car's pilot as he was urged to keep pace during the 100 kilometres race so as to make it in time for the plane.

"Who do you crowd think I am, Michael fecking Schumacher?" he roared at one stage when it seemed like the squad car was pulling too far ahead. (Only he didn't say 'fecking').

Poor Pa was pumping sweat behind the wheel. "How am I supposed to keep up with him in this shaggin' Citroen against the yoke he's driving? It's no match for it," he exclaimed.

Once he arrived at the airport and the pressure was off him, he could relax for the first time that day. Earlier Jacko had ribbed him from the back seat while they were driving. "Sure Pa, you were chasing shadows trying to mark young Sweeney during the game and now you're doing the same here trying to keep up with the guards."

Pa showed his paces in the arm bending stakes too. Indeed, he set a new personal best. When he got inside the Departure Lounge at the airport, he skulled the first pint in about two seconds flat!

Once more, the lads followed his lead and when a few more went down the hatch, they reflected on a never-to-be-forgotten day in their own GAA history.

That's the beauty of our association. It has the ability to make the most ordinary of souls feel like superstars... if only for a day.

*Enda McEvoy is a native of Mountmellick, Co Laois, and upon graduating from NUI Maynooth, he began his career with Laois county library service. His only GAA-related claim to fame is that he once actually scored an own-point in a juvenile game with The Rock. He is an avid walker and keen local historian.*

# Winners Forged From Feuding Cornafean-Slashers' Rivalry

George Cartwright

Such was the rivalry between two Cavan clubs teams that after one particularly vitriolic match some players had to leave without their clothes. Here is how that came about. During the 1910s, Cornafean Naomh Fionnán was the outstanding senior team in Cavan GAA competitions. Though they were only formed in 1908 they won the county championship in 1909, 1910 and a four-in-a-row between 1912 and 1915. Championship final clashes with Bailieborough and Virginia were intense as the association continued to grow in the county.

Soon, a strong team began to emerge in Cavan town drawing on some of the disparate teams that had existed previously. Slashers, named after the heroic soldier Myles 'the Slasher' O'Reilly, soon developed into a formidable force and games between The Slashers and Cornafean began to take on a new intensity. It was typical town versus country, the townies from Cavan taking on the farmers from Cornafean. During these years the championship in Cavan was played on a league basis.

In August 1917, there was a crucial game took place between the teams in the Showgrounds Cavan, which was the Slashers home ground. With time almost up a Slashers player was injured and the referee decided to abandon the game because he felt it was getting out of hand.

The points were awarded to Slashers and a Cornafean player received a three-month suspension. Both teams won their other remaining games and the return fixture between the teams in Cornafean took on a new importance.

This game was played in October and was full of incidents. During the first half, Andy Donohoe, the Slashers goalkeeper, got a nasty knock against the upright and as a result, the goalposts collapsed. After a delay a Cornafean club official got a hammer and nails and did a quick repair job. According to The Anglo-Celt: "Donohoe got a nasty bash against the upright which was smashed and the whole structure collapsed. After hammer and nails were procured and after some amateur carpentry work, the posts were re-erected. The game was restarted and further controversy ensued as the referee blew the final whistle with five minutes to go with Cavan Slashers in front.

Slashers had caused a sensation and put Cornafean out of the championship in their own backyard. After the game both teams reverted to the Cornafean Gaelic League Hall adjacent to the pitch, which was used as a dressing room.

As some of the Slashers players were togging in, they were subjected to considerable unfriendly attention. In fact, they were forced to exit the hall through a window, a few without their clothes!

Some stopped and got dressed a quarter of a mile from the hall but others had to go back to Cavan town scantily attired indeed.

Leading Cornafean GAA official Paul MacSeáin gathered up the clothes that were left behind and travelled to Cavan town in a pony and trap the next day to return the clothes to the Slashers players. This game marked the beginning of an intense rivalry which was to develop between both teams during the next two decades.

Between 1920 and 1941 they met in eight county finals winning four each. An extract from the Cornafean GAA history 'Up The Reds' by George Cartwright (1990) gives further background to this rivalry especially during the 1930s: Games between Cavan Slashers and Cornafean were typical town-versus-country affairs. The Slashers were composed chiefly of a middle income group – shopkeepers, businessmen, government officials, teachers etc.

It usually included players from different parts of the country – Gardaí, army officers, railway clerks, etc who were employed in Cavan town. Hence the taunting description 'League of Nations'. As a team they depended on skill and speed and they had the advantage of knowing every blade of grass in Breffni Park.

Cornafean, in contrast, was a rural club. Their team was made up almost entirely of farmers' sons. They depended chiefly on strength and determination combined with a great will to win. Whatever happened on the football field was legitimate and all part of the game as far as Cornafean was concerned.

If a team beat them well and good, they adjudged their opponents the better team and all was forgotten afterwards. Cavan Slashers liked the game to be played to the letter of the law. They considered Cornafean to be little better than bogmen or savages on occasions, while Cornafean considered them to be whingers. Supporters of both sides were fanatical.

The Cornafeans had great pride in their club and they were extremely loyal to the red jersey. They often clashed with the town supporters who

## WINNERS FORGED FROM FEUDING CORNAFEAN-SLASHERS' RIVALRY

followed the Slashers. Off the field players from both teams were friendly and had a lot of respect and even admiration for each other.

The real beneficiary of the great rivalry was Cavan football because the successful All-Ireland winning teams of 1933 and 1935 were backboned by a large number of players from both clubs who were household names. Willie Young, Mick Dinneny, Packy Phair, Brian and 'Big' Tom O'Reilly, Ned O'Reilly from Cornafean and Terry Coyle, Tom Crowe, Louis Blessing, Paddy Boylan and John Molloy from the Slashers featured in these All-Ireland victories.

These stalwarts thrived on the fierce rivalry which existed between both teams. They honed their skills in these tough home and away encounters dating back to that infamous game in Cornafean in 1917. These games produced the kind of footballers that made All-Ireland winners.

*George Cartwright is a native of Cornafean and author of a number of GAA books including 'Up The Reds,' (1990), 'Breifne Abú' (2011) and his most recent, 'The Gallant John Joe' in 2020. A former school principal and chairman of Cavan Co Board, he is married to Lorraine and they have three grown up children, daughters Helen and Emer and son James.*

# The Match That Changed Football

Anon

A match between Waterford (composed mostly of players from Rathgormack and Windgap) and Tipperary led the brothers, Maurice and Pat Davin to devise the idea for remodelling the rules of the game.

The Davins wanted to get rid of the 'old style' of 34 players-a-side with wrestling the norm. The first match played under the new code was between the footballers of Callan and Kilkenny.

# Cusack Stand Intro And UDR Outtro

Micheál Rodgers

We were the four musketeers leaving the North to enjoy a day out at Croke Park.

For the record, there was my younger brother Eamon a bricklayer, club mates Dan McCartan a butcher, Eric Trimble (nicknamed Sykes) a fisherman and myself a joiner, from junior club Glasdrumman in Lower Mourne, Co. Down.

We were going to the All-Ireland football semi-final in Croke Park on August 24, 1986 between Kerry and Meath. We travelled in Eamon's gold coloured Vauxhall Vectra, parked at Drumcondra and joined the queue to get in to McGovern's pub on the northside.

The place was packed as we hosed a good few pints into us. There was no such thing then as a designated driver. The objective was simply pints – before and after the game. We finished with a round of double whiskeys before heading off to the game at 2.45 for the 3.30pm throw-in.

Tickets then weren't issued for semi-finals, it was a case of paying at the turnstile. We arrived at the Hogan Stand entrance to be told it was full. We joined the crowd heading along the walkway at the rear of the Nally Stand towards the Cusack. We could see there was a big crowd inside there too but also that there was ample room at both ends of the stand.

We arrived at the large metal-gated entrance to find they were shut; there were a few hundred people milling around hoping the gates would be opened to speed up the entry for the large numbers still outside. It was getting near throw-in and we began to panic. I approached a garda standing against the wall observing the crowd size and asked why the gates were closed.

"The ground is full," he said.

"It isn't, there's plenty of room at both ends, sure we seen that from behind the Nally," I pointed out.

"Nothing to do with me," he said as he moved away.

"If Peter Robinson was here, youse would let him in," I shouted after him.

(This was a reference to Peter Robinson and a crowd of loyalists who had invaded Clontiberet, Co Monaghan on August 7, 1986. Robinson was arrested and it was all over the news for days).

The Garda ignored me; the lads and I headed back over to the gates, hoping against hope that they would be opened. No such luck.

Then I had a brainwave – I got the lads to lift me over the high wall to the left of the solid metal gates... it must have been a good 10ft high. When I looked down I saw the padlock was hanging loosely on the bar of the gate. I jumped down the other side and immediately two stewards left their stations to apprehend me and put me out.

I waited until they were about 30 yards away, then I removed the padlock, drew back the metal bolt, threw open the gates and shouted: "Long Kesh couldn't hold me, neither will these gates!"

A loud cheer went up from the waiting hordes who rushed in. The stewards, seeing what was happening, beat a hasty retreat to where they'd been before.

We reached the next set of gates where the turnstiles were located, directly in line with the gable of the stand. Once again the gates were closed, so I directed our group up and over the wall to the left of the gates. We pulled each other up and jumped down the other side to the grassy area.

We walked behind the stand and down to the turnstiles at the Canal End terrace; we were livid as we could see there were still plenty of seats at the ends of the Cusack.

After walking down underneath the terracing at the rear we located a yellow door. We loitered with intent in the hope someone would unlock it and sure enough our luck was in.

Five minutes before the match started, two white-coated stewards came towards the door to enter the Cusack. We asked if we could get in too as there were plenty of seats. They smiled and said: "In you go, lads."

We got four seats in the upper deck and had a great laugh at not having to pay for a stand seat. I suppose if we hadn't been drinking we wouldn't have dared to do what we did, but it certainly paid off.

Kerry were captained that day by Tommy Doyle, and won on a scoreline of 2-13 to Meath's 0-12.

We went back to McGovern's after the game to "top up" before heading for Dundalk for a feed of fish and chips to fortify the constitutions. This was the era of the Troubles and a while after we crossed the Border, inevitably we were stopped by the UDR at Bryansford just outside Newcastle. They asked where we were coming from and Eamon replied: "Dublin."

They then ordered us to get out of the car.

We refused, telling them they would have to shoot us in the car.

We locked the doors and put the Wolfe Tone's rebel tape into the eight track stereo and turned up the volume.

They didn't know what to do, and after a short while, they went over to their land rover vehicles and drove off.

That was the culmination of a special day out for us – we still reminisce that it was a day of days from our youth.

*Micheál Rodgers is a native of Glasdrumman in Lower Mourne, Co Down and is a former chairman of Dundrum GAA. A building contractor, the father of two is an avid GAA fan, liking nothing better than to attend matches.*

# 'God Save Ireland' Played The 'Tans

### Stan McCormack, Westmeath

The Black and Tans and the Auxiliaries came to Ireland in 1920 and with all the troubles, no football championship was completed that year, while a number of prominent players were taken away by soldiers and the RIC.

In spite of this, five of the Kilbeggan panel played for Westmeath in the Leinster football semi-final in August 1920, when they were narrowly beaten by Kildare.

One January night shortly before midnight the following year, the lock on the door of McGuinness's house on Main Street, Kilbeggan, which was also a shop, was forced open and two attempts were made to burn down the house.

Members of the family fled across the road to Flynns' house and watched their home burn in front of their eyes. The raiders went to the bedrooms, collected clothes and dresses, and dumped them on the ground with paper.

Some Tans stood guard outside the shop while it ignited into a mass of flames. Even worse, the family dog was inside and when he barked, they shot him.

At 5am a bombing party arrived. One bomb which fell off the roof also damaged the houses of Messrs Scally and Flynn. The three sons (Jim, John, and Frank) were on the run at the time. The family had to move to the Harbour Rd outside the town and the building was not restored until 1929.

One of the most unusual events during the troubles was when the Black & Tans burned the local Dramatic Hall. They took the local communities musical instruments and walked down the street playing tunes, and surprisingly they were Irish tunes, including very oddly "God Save Ireland."

# Kerry Win 'Sam' In Cork Dearg Agus Bán Colours

David Devane

The story of the fabled 'Dearg agus Bán' – the colours of Dingle GAA Club – originated in the famous old city on the banks of the Lee.

Legendary club figure Jimmy McKenna was serving his drapery apprenticeship in the Queens Old Castle in the city of Cork when the legend of the jersey was born. Cork Co Board did its business with Queens Old Castle during the 1930s and a new set of jerseys was ordered for the county team with the old set being originally ordered – just like what happens today with a car purchase.

However, due to a dispute between the Co Board and the shop, the jerseys never found their way to Cork GAA. Instead the set wound up on the backs of the victorious Kerry men of 1939.

Upon his return to Dingle, Jimmy was appointed captain of the club, which had entered in the Kerry county championship but had not yet decided on the colours for the team jersey.

Jimmy convinced the club hierarchy to agree that 'Dearg agus Bán' should be the colours mindful that he could do a deal which he paid for himself with his old employers at Queens Old Castle for the set originally ordered by the Cork Co Board.

And so a small bit of history was created in 1938 when Dingle – clad in the 'Dearg agus Bán' – went on to win their first senior football county championship.

Amazingly, the following year the very same jerseys were worn by Kerry in their All-Ireland victory over Meath.

As both the Kingdom and the Royals wore green and gold, they tossed to determine who would get to play in their own county colours. Kerry lost the toss and had to find an alternative stripe, the rule being that the colours of the county champions be used.

The Kerry Co Board decided the team would line out in the blue of Munster but this was not well received by the reigning county champions. With a substantial number of players representing Dingle on the Kerry panel, Jimmy wrote to the board: "As county champions, Kerry will wear the red and white of Dingle. The Dingle lads won't play unless it's in the Dingle colours and we won't travel".

The county board acceded to Jimmy's ultimatum and Kerry beat Meath by 2-5 to 2-3 with Paddy 'Bawn' Brosnan, Bill Dillon, Billy Casey and Tom 'Gega' O'Connor lining out on that historic day in 1939. A bout of the 'flu unfortunately prevented Strand Street hero Sean Brosnan from leading the Kingdom out on that momentous occasion but another Dingle icon, the aforementioned 'Gega' hoisted Sam above his head sporting his native 'Dearg agus Bán.'

Dingle went on to win six Kerry county senior championships in a glorious 10-year period up until 1948 when some of the true greats of our national game wore the 'Dearg agus Bán' with pride while continuing to represent the Kingdom with distinction.

Canon Lyne summed up the mood of the Dingle locals when he addressed the crowds that welcomed the returning heroes of '39 home to Dingle by declaring: "This magnificent team wearing the red and white of Dingle has proved to the world that Kerry is the first football county in Ireland".

The following week the team displaying Sam together with mentors that included Jimmy and Canon Lyne, gathered in Killarney for an official team photo being obliged to wear the green and gold of Kerry. It is this photo that is the Official 1939 Team Photo until the present day despite not displaying the true story of how Dingle GAA once caused the Sam Maguire to be won by a Kerry team amazingly wearing the jerseys of the Rebel County no less.

*David Devane is a native of Baile na Buaile, Dingle, Co. Kerry and played for his local club as well as representing St Brigid's in Roscommon for a few years. Now residing in Pallasgreen Co. Limerick, the múinteoir bunscoile is married to Mary and they have one daughter Éadha.*

# A Sevens' Squad That Tamed The Wilds Of Boho

## Seán Treacy

Peter Ferguson recounted the story to me as if it only happened yesterday instead of over 60 years ago. As a youngster then, he remembered clearly that the excitement all kicked off for him after 11 o'clock Mass on a wet August Sunday back in 1959.

"Con Monaghan spread the word that there was a Sports Day and a 7-A-Side tournament in Boho. He had organised John James Moohan, otherwise known as 'The Jazzer', to drive a squad there. Only 14 at the time, I was told to tell my older brothers, Michael and Brendan, to be on the bridge for two o'clock sharp. Most pleasingly for a young lad, I was ordered to bring my own boots too... 'just in case we're stuck'.

"By the appointed time on the bridge we had a team of five, counting me, which was no good. We switched to Plan B and after much persuasion, we finally enlisted Josie and Francie Carty to join us on our safari to the wilds of Boho.

"Pat Casey declared we were all mad as we finally set off. 'The Jazzer' said his version of the Lord's prayer when he slammed on the brakes as we hit a biblical-like flood on the road near Braade. By the sheer power of prayer, the A90 kept going and by the bottom of the fall, she was back firing on all cylinders again.

"We made Boho Cross by 3.30pm to be met by another biblical storm of sand and gravel hurling down on us from the hills. In the Sports Field when we arrived, the girls were rocking sideways as they tried to dance a jig on the back of a half-covered lorry. The music came from a rasping accordion being played by a man in the cab with the passenger's window wound down.

"Big Jim Bannon was trying to MC on a PA system that had a mind of its own. For those of you who ever frequented one, it was the sort of sports day every parish put on once a year.

"The A90 owned by 'The Jazzer' suddenly became the centre of attention as it possessed the only car radio in the area. Michael O'Hehir was in full flow crackling across the airwaves. The reception was in and out as you'd expect. Down were playing Galway in the All-Ireland semi-final. The crowd gathered round, not a sound was made as they strained to hear the commentator's every nuanced word.

"There would be no sports activity going on there until the game was over, that much was certain. When the game ended the sun came out; things couldn't have worked out better except for poor Down, who would have to wait another year to make the historic breakthrough by winning their first All-Ireland in 1960.

"We all poured out of the A90 and headed for high ground. Con was jumping around like a young bull calf, telling the committee that he had competed for Ireland at the high jump and long jump, so these events would have to be organised to "facilitate an international."

"The local shop was open where half inch nails were purchased, some slating laths were rustled from somewhere for uprights and a young fellow's cane fishing pole was pressed into service to act as a crossbar. Now that Con the international was facilitated, the high jump competition was on.

"Eamon Ferguson jumped 4'8" before Con increased the level to 4'9" and so did Brendan with ease. Then Eamon fouled out. Con failed his first attempt at 4'10" while Brendan sailed over. Con failed again – the committee and the crowd held its breath – was the international going to be beaten by a 16-year-old schoolboy? He was.

"Undaunted, Con reckoned that he was a better long jumper and he would find consolation in that event. He didn't as Brendan beat him again. Even the committee began to enjoy the fare.

"Still unabashed, Con now told all and sundry that the 440 yards was by far his best event. Away they went twice around the field, we all waited for Con's finishing burst – it never came. Brendan and Eamon had a fierce tussle over the last 50 yards to finish in a dead heat, while the self-professed international's bad run of form continued.

"Then the GAA 'Sevens' started. We drew Belcoo, who like ourselves, consisted of a few old men and a few cubs. A see-saw battle was ultimately decided by a point scored from the left corner flag courtesy of my boot. 'The Jazzer' flagged it.

"Melanophy in the goals for our opponents said it was 'a good two-foot wide'. 'The Jazzer' said he had a two-foot starting handle in the car and he'd wrap it around Melanophy's neck if he wasn't careful. The referee agreed with 'The Jazzer' and we were in the final.

"Derrygonnelly, who were about to become senior league champions in Fermanagh, had played a 'derby' game against Enniskillen in the other semi-final. It was truly a dour struggle with skin and hair flying – certainly no place for 14-year-old cubs. Mick Brewster got the Gaels through with two great goals in the last minute.

"Derrygonnelly didn't like losing so dramatically, so they went home. It was us and the Gaels in the final but we now had just one small problem – there was no ball. You see Derrygonnelly owned the ball and after they lost, they decamped with it.

"Jim Bannon said there was nothing that could be done except to toss a coin. Mick Brewster called 'heads' and Con called 'tails' for us.

"The coin was tossed into the sky and came down tails; 'The Jazzer' let out a wild cheer and we collected a lovely set of silver medals. We headed for Garrison and dry ground, all the while mindful that Con may have lost his personal pursuits but had won out for us when it mattered most."

*Seán Treacy is a native of Garrison, Co Fermanagh and works in his own Estate Agency business, Fermanagh Lakeland Properties. Married to Sharon they have three children, Cianna, Grace and Sarah. A former player and administrator with the local club, Seán is also the author of 'Devenish, A Century in the Making.'*

# Hega's Verbal Assault On Tipp

## Kieran Burke, Cork

In the Munster championship between Cork and Tipperary at the Gaelic Grounds in the early seventies, Roger Ryan of Tipp and Tony Maher of Cork were having what Micheal O'Hehir would have called a right schmozzle at various times during the game.

They were two hard tough men for sure. A Tipperary fan in front of Michael Hegarty, known as Hega and myself in the crowd got a bit hot under the collar at one exchange between the pair and shouted: "Ah, the Cork dirt."

Hega was incensed. He possessed an incredible memory for incidents during matches going back to the late forties. He let fly with a litany of Tipperary foul play – according to him- going back a generation.

He rattled off the names in rapid gunfire fashion ...John Doyle, Musha Maher, Liam Devaney, all were indicted by 'Hega' who finished his tirade at the unfortunate Tipp fan (by this time rendered quite mute) with a flourish.

"Were you in Killarney in 1950?" he roared "when Tipp split open Gerry Riordan – and he wasn't even playing?"

# Earning The Right To Have A Jersey On The Coffin

## John Bermingham

The wait grew longer and the clouds greyer. I'd listened to the chug of every car passing over the bridge and scanned the road hoping a maroon coloured Austin A40 would appear. I'd sheltered from the rain under the eaves of Cummins old carpenter's shop and when it cleared I sat on Hackett's gate.

Car after car whizzed by and there I was still waiting; waiting and hoping that the next one would be Larry's. Then just as I was about to trudge home, the Larry Lonergan express would ramble into view.

"Hop in quick, John, or we'll be late," he'd say as he stuck the car into first gear for a quick take off.

"Late," I thought. "The second half should be starting at that stage."

We'd head off in a car full of baling twine, loose hay and burst bags of calf nuts.

The goalie, full-back and full-forward were squeezed into the front side – the rest of us in the back with the fodder and implements.

The nuts and bolts of Larry's day were strewn together with a bag of jerseys, a football and a pump.

We've now arrived and immediately the bag was emptied out onto the sideline. Mullinahone's one set of jerseys were unfamiliar with the inside of a washing machine and could hold the sweat of several teams.

It was a case of grabbing one of the better maintained ones as fast as you could or else you might end up playing with one sleeve hanging off.

Larry's team talks were short and sweet- "Do yere best lads!"

"Don't give them the first score."

"No fancy stuff."

"Watch the hop."

I loved to dribble the ball soccer-style out of tight situations; it drove Larry mad every time.

"Go down on it for heaven's sake," he would roar at me.

I could never see the sense of going down on it when a short pass along the ground would do the trick.

Back then I wasn't aware that soccer and Gaelic football were even different codes.

Sport didn't feature in our house.

I don't remember my father watching the All-Ireland finals. Yet I spent endless hours kicking plastic balls against the gable end of every shed in the place, trying to catch the rebound, jumping, diving, skinning knees, spraining wrists and painting goal posts on silage pit walls.

The first time I was ever at a match was the first time I played in one.

Twenty minutes to go. "You're going on," Larry said to me and another fella standing beside me on the sideline.

The jersey stretched so far down my legs that it came out through the shorts.

Swollen with pride, William O'Shea and I galloped onto the field.

We were an unlikely Gaelic football double act as we spent most of our time in Kilvemnon School swapping soccer stickers and dreaming of scoring the winning goal in the FA Cup final

I played football at every level for Mullinahone in Tipperary league and championship matches over the following 25 years. William never togged out again.

A full quarter of a century after my debut, the club was short a few players.

"Any chance you'd tog out?" I was asked.

I pulled on a Mullinahone jersey for the last time.

This time it just about fitted me.

Serious illness in 1994 curtailed my endeavours but upon recovery I had one sporting ambition; to play for Mullinahone again. I looked forward to framing the team photograph.

But when the camera was opened a few weeks later ...it had no film.

On the way home my neighbour asked how I got on.

I told him I came on for the last 20 minutes.

"Jasus," he asked, "A sub on a junior B team... tell me is there any lower form than that – and one time I thought you'd make the county?"

Kickham Community Park was opened in Mullinahone in August 1982 to coincide with the Kickham centenary celebrations. Fr Ryan, the local curate, was friendly with a senior official in Dublin GAA circles and he persuaded the famous Dubs to come to Mullinahone to play Tipperary in the opening game.

I was thrilled to be chosen to play for Tipperary against one of the greatest teams of all times. Just as we were about to leave the dressing room to parade around the pitch behind the Moycarkey Pipe band, the Dubs let it be known they were short a few players to start the game.

Some of them had mistakenly gone to Mullinavat instead of Mullinahone. A lopsided parade wouldn't look good.

Tipp decided to loan two players to Dublin until the missing stars arrived. Five minutes after donning the blue and gold, I took it off and pulled on the sky blue of Dublin.

The sideline was packed and spectators identified the famous Dubs as they passed by... Jimmy Keaveney, Brian Mullins, Tony Hanahoe, Anton O'Toole... they were all there.

"Jasus, where's Bermingham going?" was all I could hear.

As the referee's whistle blew a car careered onto the field.

Dublin didn't need me any more.

Tipp jersey back on, I galloped into my place at right half-back and shook hands with their left half forward for the day, Kevin Moran.

He'd already won two All Irelands and later played 71 times for Ireland.

I never played for Tipp again.

Later that week on the same pitch, I played for a soccer selection against FAI Cup winners Limerick Utd. I'd hoped to get plucked from obscurity, sign for Limerick who would later sell me on to Man Utd where I would get to team up with Kevin Moran again.

Unfortunately I spent the next 10 years milking cows.

Twenty five years after we lost a county semi-final by two points, the referee spotted my son Sean's name on an U-14 teamsheet and verbally floored him before the game began.

"We'd have won the county that year if your father hadn't missed that penalty with the last kick," he said.

On my way off the pitch after finally becoming South Tipperary Intermediate football champions, a neighbour shook my hands and delivered the immortal line: "You've enough done now to get the jersey on the coffin."

There were lots of memorable games along the way between 1971 and 1995. However, matches won and lost, points scored and penalties missed are not the abiding memories of my days in a Mullinahone jersey.

It's the memory of people like Larry Lonergan and Stephen Watters who brought us to games, organised leagues and gave selflessly of their time to ensure that we had the opportunity to run and play... until darkness came and the ball faded from view.

When I visit their graves, it is with a sense of tremendous gratitude that I recall those long evenings when I waited and waited at the top of the boreen for the sound of that Austin A40 to transport me and the others to those fields of dreams.

# GRASSROOTS

*John Bermingham is a native of Mullinahone, Co Tipperary. Married to Monika, they have one son Seán and run an award-winning tourist/forest enterpresi, Crocanoir, on their farm.*

# Opening Up A Brave New World

## Jim Berry

Former US President Ronald Reagan once remarked that "the greatest leader is not necessarily the one who does the greatest things. He is the one who gets other people to do the greatest things."

Back in 1966 the Kilmore/Rathangan GAA club in Wexford was your average team with the same outlook as most others. Players had a diet of working, training and playing matches at weekends.

That was until our great mentor, Fr. Paddy McDonald opened up a totally new world for us ... and told us we could go there.

Quite casually after training one evening, he put it into our heads that we should become one of the first clubs in Ireland to think big by going on a tour of America.

If he had proposed a trip to the moon – and this was before man landed there two years later – we couldn't have been more dismissive.

We all looked at him and laughed. We had no money, we had no contacts, we could hardly anticipate a trip to Dublin never mind the USA.

He kept a serious face as we made fun of his proposal and soon we saw he was totally in earnest.

Within 10 minutes, he spoke of his trip there the previous year and explained how it could be done. By the time we broke up that night, we had not only gone along with his idea but had pencilled in September 1967 as the month of our departure.

Talk about changing a humdrum existence into a community energised by the thoughts of seeing the Big Apple, Boston and Montreal. This was the stuff of films... and yet here we were already planning for this global tour.

Fr McDonald never saw obstacles, only challenges. He charted a plane through a travel agent and then made lots of badly needed cash as the plane was nearly booked out. There were 17 priests on it together with the great Wexford hurler Ned Wheeler.

He told us that we would all need to gather up £65 for our seats. He assured us that further expense could be met by both saving and fund-raising. To raise further money for accommodation etc, we did everything from sowing sugar beet, raising bullocks, running 7-a-side tournaments, staging carnivals to anything else we could put our hands on that would raise a buck. We paid €2 every week into a kitty so that we could save for the airfares in 33 weeks.

One of the big financial fillips we got for the trip was when a farmer in the area gave us his own contract so that we could grow six acres of sugar beet in his name. Contracts for such tonnage were hard to come by and the Sugar Company was alert to any farmer sowing a little over his contract. They had agents whose sole job it was to measure up what crop was sown and ensure it was consistent with the contract between factory and farmer.

Unfortunately our trip made national headlines and in an article on the Irish Independent detailing the various ways that we were collecting money for the trip, the sugar beet part was also highlighted.

The Sugar Company spotted this and there was hell to pay over how they could be doing this without a contract. Fr. MacDonald was in a spot of bother as was the farmer, but they knew there were GAA people in the Sugar Company and like all conflicts, they found a way to traverse the challenge through the GAA network.

It wasn't as though this planting was an easy way to make money. Sowing the beet was one thing but then the crop had to be thinned and that meant the players were on their knees many evenings from 6.0pm to 8.0pm before finding the relief of jumping on their bikes, cycling a few miles and taking part in training. Tough going.

As the countdown to the big day arrived, those on the trip all went to Mass in Kilmore Quay at 7.30am. It was the second Sunday in September. Fr. McDonald said the Mass and after that, it was a case of climbing on to the bus for the trip to Shannon Airport.

Excitement reached fever pitch as we saw our plane and embarked before arriving in New York at 8 o'clock that evening, having gained five hours on the journey west.

This was truly the trip of a lifetime as we saw the Big Apple slap bang in the swinging sixties. All human life was there and it seemed to be open for business 24 hours a day.

We enjoyed being tourists but then we knew we had two games to play in Gaelic Park. The first fixture was against the Monaghan club on the Friday evening and the second was against the Kerry club there as a curtain raiser to a big hurling match there on the Sunday.

We got $180 for playing them from the proprietor of Gaelic Park, John Kerry O'Donnell, after a lot of haggling.

The game against the Kerry club was a tough affair and when our goalie Fr. Phil Egan made a great save, he was kicked in the stomach by an inrushing forward and injured. Right through the game was a tough, rough affair with the local referee having no sympathy for us at all.

This led to an almighty dust up and in the end we were so disgusted that we walked off the pitch.

The big crowd that packed the place for the National Hurling League final between Kilkenny and New York, couldn't believe what we were doing, but we felt the local side had crossed the line.

We got a standing ovation from the crowd for having the bottle to walk off. This was supposed to be a friendly game but we had players concussed, needing stitches and one with a sprained ankle.

The New York officials were in a terrible way and it was a pity that Fr. MacDonald had done the deal of $180 for doing the curtain raiser before the game started or he would have had a great bargaining tool.

However, cool heads prevailed and John Kerry O'Donnell eventually pleaded with us as the Kerry players were anxiously waiting for our return.

We got an even warmer reception from the crowd for coming back on to finish the game. We had made our point and we reckoned that as we were on holidays, there was no point in making any further protest.

Afterwards a lot of the Kerry lads came down to Keenan's bar in the Bronx to mingle with us and their captain, the great Mike Foley, said that he would have given us the huge trophy only we walked off the pitch. They accepted they were the culprits as the crowd confirmed to them. But what happened on the field stayed on the field and a great night was had by all.

After that we headed to Boston for another game and then on to Montreal to the World Fair where we stayed in a hostel. We had been living it up in hotels before that. There we saw the first rocket that had just come back from the moon amongst many other wonderful things.

We took in the Niagara Falls on our way back to New York and arrived home to Wexford on October 1. What an historic and wonderful trip.

It brings me back to thinking of President Reagan again when he said: "Some people spend an entire lifetime wondering if they made a difference in the world. But, the Marines don't have that problem."

In our case, neither did Fr McDonald.

*Jim Berry is a retired Teagasc technician. Married to Anne Doody, they have four children, Seamus, Eileen, Diarmuid and Donal. A former Wexford hurler and footballer, the St Annes clubman is a former Co Board chairman and chairman of the Leinster Council.*

# Escaping A Lynching On Our Pub

## Sean O'Dwyer

Our family pub on Main Street, Carrick-on-Suir popularly known as 'Nancy Dwyers' was in county Tipperary but its clientele was mostly a Waterford supporting one in a unique three club hurling mad tri-border town.

On a Sunday matchday afternoon back in the late fifties our tap-room was unlawfully crowded for a radio commentary by Michael O'Hehir of a Munster hurling championship match between Tipperary and Waterford.

However the old 1950s wireless had the unfortunate habit of cutting out every so often so my job allocation as a 10-year-old and the only Tipp supporter in the room was to sit beside the elegant set and reactivate it with a sensitive touch that only I could muster.

After several short-circuits I was pleased with the success of my skilful touch and to this day I can still hear O'Hehir taking up the play with Waterford trailing by a single point..

"Seamus Power to Philly Grimes and in a lovely passing movement to Larry Guinan and now Tom Cheasty to Frankie Walsh to John Kiely... there's a goal on here for Waterford..."

Then disaster struck as the wireless went dead and this time my skilful touch deserted me.

Paddy 'Goggy' Sweeney jumped up out of his chair and in a fit of madness gave the old Bush wireless a wallop, causing a bang and a blue flash that lit up the darkened room.

The game might have continued in Thurles but it was a case of set and match in our pub.

Placing the blame on me for what 'Goggy' referred to as "the ulterior motives of the young Tipp fella" could have led to a riot, but while tarred with suspicion, the accusations were thankfully overlooked as 'Goggy's' lynching on Carrick's Main St was a more pressing priority for his Waterford supporting colleagues now that the radio was banjaxed.

# For And Against – The Leech Brothers In Louth Co Final

## Mickey Leech

The 1965 Louth senior football championship final will be best remembered as the 'Day of the Leech Brothers' as the four members played on that unique occasion – two for The Newton Blues and two for Drogheda's other finalist team, the O'Raghallaighs.

We were reared close to the Lourdes Hospital. There were six children the four of us boys and our two sisters Maeve and Gerty. Paddy played with the Feckins out in Termonfeckin for a while and Liam with Lourdes Rangers before the club broke up. Myself and Joey went from the Street League Harmons Gardens into the O'Raghallaighs.

I recall the night before the 1965 final. We were all at home having our tea and looking at television like it was any other Saturday night. Joey would hop the odd ball about how we were going to cause an upset and then my parents would dampen down everything by saying they hoped we all played well.

I went to the match on my own and the other three arrived separately. I think everyone except the Leeches thought it was a big deal that day.

It wasn't even a thing to us as brothers teaming up against the other two.

I was 20 when I lined out on that day of the final for the O'Rahhallaighs with my brother Joey, while Paddy and Liam for the Blues who were seeking to claim their fifth consecutive championship win.

There were a lot of headlines around my family being divided but to be honest about the match I can't remember any of that in our house. We just took the occasion in our stride.

To be truthful, when asked what I remembered about the day I have no great recall about what the match was like, the final score, or if I had scored or not.

It was only when I looked it up in the local newspapers that I saw we won easily enough before a crowd of nearly 4,000 by 1-9 to 0-5. We won the toss and having played with a big wind in the first half, we led by 1-6 to 0-1. I scored four points, one from play and Liam on the other side, accounted for three of the Blues five points on the day. I played left-half forward and Paddy was a right half-back but we didn't mark each other that day, we switched to avoid going head-to-head with each other. We didn't want to do that.

There was a bit of banter after the match, largely due to our first cousins Mick 'Muckie' McKeown and his brother Paddy, known as Sparrow, who also played very well that day for the O Raghallaighs. My mother Maisie and their mother Mona were sisters and were full of devilment after the game... talking up what we had achieved. My brothers Paddy and Liam had won so much by then with the Blues team that I think they could accept the odd loss.

I suppose the Cuchulainn Annual of 1963, which was the then a coveted GAA year book, told our story best. "In 1963 Paddy, Liam, Joey and Michael collected no less than 12 medals during the season and helped bring all the major trophies in Louth football to Drogheda. Paddy and Liam were on the Newtown Blues team that won the county senior championship, the Cardinal O'Donnell cup and Old Gaels Cup. Joey and Michael were part of the O'Raghallaighs side that captured the county junior championship and Wolfe Tones Cup. Michael also won county minor championship and Drogheda minor league medals with O'Raghaillaighs."

As you may tell, our family weren't hung up on achievements but one thing I am really proud of is the fact that Paddy, Liam and myself each captained the Blues to win Louth senior football championships – a unique honour in any family. Liam would go on to become a Blues and Louth legend for the rest of his career.

Anyway, it was all an eight-day wonder because Paddy and Joey gave up football fairly soon afterwards. Liam went on and ended up winning nine senior medals. I won three with the Blues and of course that memorable one with the O'Raghallaighs in 1965.

Some months after that county final, I decided to throw my lot in with the Blues and went for a transfer from the O'Raghallaighs but was shot down by the county board. It forced me away from GAA for a year and then when I thought I was eligible to resume my Gaelic football career, the Co Board heard that I had been playing soccer to pass the time and suspended me the evening before I was due to play my first GAA game with the Newton Blues club.

Eventually when I did return, my first game was against Roche Emmets who let it be known that they were playing the game but under protest. Although the Blues won the match, Roche Emmets objected to my playing and won the case. It was referred to the Leinster Council who wouldn't make a decision on the issue, thus handing it back to Louth Co Board. They had no problem suspending me under Rule 27, which was a big thing at that time.

When my ban ended, my new club – the Blues – played a Louth team in a challenge and we hammered them. After that performance I was picked by Louth to play for the county, but the night before the match, the Louth chairman came into the pub where I worked and told me not to travel the next day because I was suspended again. I can't even remember what for, but I think it had to do with the 'garrison game.'

When my brother Liam heard about it, he was disgusted and pulled out of the county team in support of me.

The GAA was like that back then, but we both decided not to hold a grudge and myself and Liam ended up playing for years in the Wee County colours and for the Newton Blues.

Footnote: Having the name Leech in the sixties and seventies automatically confused people because of the great Shamrock Rovers legend who shared my name. I remember being in Maher's Pub in Dublin when the Dubs under Heffo were making waves in the 1970s. I had gone to a match in Croke Park and later went up to the pub for the after-match craic.

That night the other Mick Leech was in the pub as well, though I didn't know it at the time. A voice came on over the pub's intercom: "Mick Leech is wanted at the door," and the two of us went out and as it happened, it was a fella looking for me.

However, I shook hands with Mick, who was a great goalscorer when the League of Ireland meant something. We had a chat for a few minutes before shaking hands and going our separate ways.

*Micky Leech is a native of Drogheda and a former Blues and Louth star player. Predeceased by his wife Phyllis, they had three children Orla, Robert (RIP) and Michael and four grandchildren. Mickey is now retired though he keeps active by cycling.*

# A Case Of Writing To Myself
## Larry Ryan, Dublin

When you're secretary of underage boards in a county, it is surprising the number of peculiar correspondences you have to deal with in the course of a season.

For instance when I served as secretary of the South Dublin juvenile board in the early sixties I also happened to the secretary of Kilmacud GAA club at the same time.

A dispute arose between another club and my own so as club secretary I had to write to myself as board secretary on the matter. The letter began – 'Labhrás, a chara'... and ended – 'Mise le meas, Labhrás Ó Riain' not once but twice.

Sometime later at the Dublin Minor Board, there was an objection to Ballyfermot De La Salle (it may have been Ballyfermot Gaels at the time) on the grounds that some of the names on their team list were not in Irish. The Ballyfermot defence was that the names were Hebrew.

One of the funnier stories from that era was when a manager of an under age team was stopped by a guard on his way to an U-13 county semi-final. The guard was about to speak when the manager said: "Yes, I know I have 10 young lads in the back of the car but it's a county semi-final and we're already late."

The guard, instead of admonishing him for having too many bodies in the vehicle, took out the keys to his squad car and said: "Right, I'll stick the siren on and you make sure you keep up."

# Tight Timetable For Railway Station And Football

Dick Stokes

My late father Jack Stokes was born in the townland of Whitewood, near Streamstown, in Co Westmeath in 1888. Growing up in the 1890s, the GAA had not yet become as strong a feature of life in the area as it would subsequently.

In those days the only ball game in the area was cricket. There were several small clubs around, promoted by a number of 'big houses' and involving their staff and tenants. A regular feature of such occasions was the provision by those big houses of a half-barrel of porter (16 gallons) for the players when the match was over.

The nearest club to my father was in the townland of Bracknahevla. This club had a boys' team with which he played a number of games. One doesn't normally associate cricket with sports injuries, yet he told of one nasty knock he sustained – and it had a somewhat amusing aftermath.

Standing chatting with a group of boys while the men were practising, he heard an extra loud crack when the ball was struck. He looked around – just in time to be struck in the face by the cricket ball. It was very painful and left him with a blackened and swollen face, but thankfully no long term damage.

The next day he was in school when an inspector called. He gave various individual tests to the boys. The test he gave my father was to write a description of how he got his colourful and puffed-up face. My father claimed he had no trouble doing that and was commended by the inspector.

Everything changed, however, when my father was about 12 or 13 and attended a local sports meeting where he saw his first Gaelic football match. He was immediately 'hooked' and, as he said himself, he never looked at cricket again. From then on, he played Gaelic football on men's teams when he was only 15 and was in his early forties before calling a halt to his playing career.

He started out with 'flapper' unaffiliated teams, bunches of lads coming together unofficially to compete at local sports and tournaments. This was common practice in the early years of the 20th century and a feature of the increasing popularity of the GAA. It was grounds for an objection at the time if a properly affiliated team included a player who had in the current year lined out with a 'flapper' team.

When I was growing up all my family were keen GAA people, involved in both football and hurling, a legacy of our father's interest and involvement in Gaelic football. Much of his recollections centred on the early days of the GAA and his involvement in teams in Westmeath, Mayo, Roscommon and Galway where his employment with the Midland & Great Western Railway took him. He died aged 97 years and, fortunately, had tremendous recall to the last, committing some of his memories to paper. I am happy to draw on them.

We heard much about the aforementioned 'flapper' teams, illegal players 'imported' by clubs, hard men he saw in action and 'shmozzles' he came through. He recalled one game he played in Westmeath where the opposition had a standout player whom nobody seemed to know. Two days later, he was on duty in Ballinasloe station when the same player arrived to collect a consignment of goods for the shop he was working in. They had an interesting conversation.

However, despite playing in Roscommon, Galway, Mayo, Longford and Cavan, depending on where his job as a railway signalman took him, he won only one medal in his whole career. That was in 1918 when Westmeath Co Board ran its first intermediate football championship.

He was then playing with a new team that had been set up in his home area of Bishopstown, near Streamstown. And as by now he had been permanently assigned to Streamstown railway station, he threw in his lot with them. The team reached the final of the new competition, beating a team from Walshestown, near Mullingar in Tyrrells field, Loughnavalley, which is now the ground of Loughnavalley football club.

Little or no detail is available about the match – neither the score nor the lineout of the Walshestown team, but he often related a quirky story about how the day went for him.

He was rostered for duty in Streamstown that day, so he persuaded a colleague Tom G to deputise in his absence. Up to half-time Bishopstown were doing well, but as he entered the 'huddle' with the rest of the team at the interval, he spotted his relief signalman at the event on the sideline. He rushed over and demanded to know who was looking after the signal box.

"Oh," said Tom, "I asked Jim D to do it."

Now my father knew that the same Jim D had little or no knowledge of the signalman's work. Luckily, it being Sunday, there were very few trains...

but there was one due shortly after the end of the match. So he played the second half, but would stress that he didn't remember one kick or tackle or score, as his mind was focused on getting back to the station to let the train pass safely.

As soon as the match was over, he jumped on his bike to cover the five miles-plus trip to Streamstown. He knew it would be a tight call to get there in time and indeed he heard the train whistling as he reached the entrance to the station. This just about gave him enough time to pull the signal and open the road for the train. It was a testament to his fitness that he was able to make it after playing a fairly strenuous game.

His medal was truly hard-earned, and sad to say it was later stolen, along with handball medals and a War of Independence medal when his house was burgled in 1978. Some money was taken too, but losing his medals troubled him most.

Still, it has to be said that he never measured his football career in terms of trophies won, but rather in terms of the enjoyment it gave him ...except for that day when he had to beat a train in a race against time to Streamstown Station.

*Dick Stokes hails from Streamstown, Co. Westmeath and is a retired HSE official. Married to Kathleen, they have two daughters and a son. As well as having a lifelong passion for the GAA, he is interested in traditional music and local history.*

# A Lucky Escape On Bloody Sunday

Larry Ryan, Dublin

Joe Norris was a native of Carnaross in Meath but won three All-Ireland medals with Dublin, 10 Dublin county medals with O'Tooles, was on the Ireland team in the Tailteann Games of 1924, won a Railway Cup Medal with Leinster in 1929 and at the age of 39 was a sub on the Leinster team the following year.

Joe was an outstanding player of his time and it begged the question – "Why wasn't he picked to play for Dublin against Tipperary on Bloody Sunday, November 21, 1920 when he was in his prime?"

The reality was that he was due to play but missed out for the following reason – he explained that he was in charge of a barrel of porter the previous evening and the event he was at turned into an all-night party. So late in fact that he went to 5am mass on his way home in Church St.

After mass he went into his house, lay on the bed but many hours later woke up under the bed in a state of total confusion. Mindful that he had a game to play, he washed himself and despite still feeling under the weather, headed to Croke Park. By the time he arrived, he was struggling even more, so much so that the captain of the Dublin team took one look at him, told him he was in no condition to play and sent him home.

# Wartime Champions Deprived Of Medals Due To Gold Scarcity

Fintan Mussen

Nowadays when a team wins a county championship or other competitions, the presentation of the cup and medals is a mere formality. Modern players and supporters may be surprised to find this was not so when Clonduff won the 1944 Down championship. On that occasion the cup was presented alright but no medals were available.

The 'Emergency' or Second World War was still going on and the consequent restrictions applied to almost every sphere of life. One activity that ran into difficulties was the purchase of gold and silver, the supplies of which metals were strictly controlled.

This affected wartime brides, who found their wedding rings, reluctantly admitted by the British government as necessary items, to resemble brass rather than gold, so small was the proportion of precious metal in them. Like other articles on sale, they showed the mark of austerity. "Utility" was the official jargon to describe such goods.

As Ireland was neutral south of the border, the jewellers' windows in Dublin attracted longing looks of Northern brides-to-be and other potential purchasers of gold and silver. Those who were tempted to buy ran the risk of detection – even long after they had secured the precious goods.

The stamps on such items revealed their origin. Purchasers were liable to heavy fines with the real threat of their articles being confiscated as well. Not only were they contravening UK regulations on purchase tax and custom duties, they were also breaking the Irish government prohibition on the export of precious metals.

Winning football teams were dissatisfied with the prospect of having medals of inferior quality in the unlikely event of their availability in the North. It was hardly surprising then that Gaelic football trophies were not considered as priorities by the Stormont and London authorities.

County Boards responsible for providing the medals for winning teams were faced with a difficulty. Some of their members made the suggestion that they should award a sum of money for the purchase of suitable medals and that the team should then arrange the purchase of the trophies they preferred. This expedient was adopted and explains the reference to the award of money instead of medals that was made from time to time in the Gaelic columns of the press.

Naturally though, the eyes of some club secretaries turned southwards. So it was with Clonduff. The medals were ordered in Dublin and an arrangement was made to have them posted to a friend residing in Co Louth. The set could then be collected by someone travelling south for that express purpose.

However, this practice was not unknown to the customs authorities and officers were stationed in the post offices of the border towns to inspect suspicious packages. The Clonduff medals were detected in Dundalk and seized by the officials. The addressee was notified that the packet awaited collection in Dublin Castle. At a meeting of the Clonduff committee, it was agreed that a member who volunteered to do so would call at the Castle and seek to negotiate the "release" of the impounded medals. So off he set by bus to Newry, branch-line train to Goraghwood and thence by rail to Dublin.

After stating his business to the porter, he was admitted to an outer office and given a form to complete. As it was bilingual he followed the GAA preference and filled it out in Irish. The form was taken into an inner office and eventually a civil servant, who was obviously an Irish language enthusiast, came out and began a friendly conversation.

As the details of the purpose of the Clonduff delegate's visit emerged the tone of the dialogue changed and soon the official was delivering in fluent Irish a lecture on the duty of GAA committees to give a lead to the young people of Ireland to keep the laws of their native government.

It was a scandal that they should be involved in smuggling. Someone had initiated this scheme to defy the regulations and unless the delegates could furnish the name of the party, there could be no business done.

The Clonduff representative truthfully replied that he knew nothing of such matters as he was a new arrival on the committee and in any case, even if he did know the answer to such a question, he would consider it highly improper to give it in view of the circumstances.

The official left briefly in high dudgeon and soon returned, bringing a superior official as he had promised. He later proceeded, with greater calmness, to convey more or less the same information in English, adding a veiled hint at possible prosecution for all who had organised the purchase and dispatch of the goods.

The Clonduff delegate made a vain appeal to his interlocutors to

## WARTIME CHAMPIONS DEPRIVED OF MEDALS DUE TO GOLD SCARCITY

consider the exceptional circumstances of a championship winning team deprived of their medals and the absence of any commercial move in trying to provide them. He had to leave in the end without success.

The medals were eventually released after further negotiations at a later date but by that time Clonduff had almost reached their next county championship final.

*Fintan (Finty) Mussen is a former player, team manager, chairman and secretary of Clonduff GAA Club. He is also a long-time member of Down County Board and Ulster Council. A brother of Kevin, who became the first man to take Sam Maguire north of the border as Down captain in 1961, Finty is a former primary school Head Teacher. His late wife Margaret designed the club's crest based on the local Legend of 'The Meadow of the Ox.'*

# A Whiter Shade of Pale Green

### Louis Brennan, Co Laois

Borrisokane GAA club in North Tipperary was formed in 1885 and throughout its history there were other clubs affiliated in the parish including Eglish (Aglish) in the 1930s and the 1950s.

One of the most auspicious events in the short history the Eglish club was the junior hurling defeat against Kilruane McDonaghs in 1958 on a 3-8 to 1-4 scoreline.

Eglish played in their 'Lily White' jerseys while Kilruane wore green. During the course of the game a Kilruane sub was introduced wearing a white shirt.

The following is a synopsis from the Nenagh Guardian which reported on the activities of the North Tipperary GAA board meeting. Eglish wrote objecting to their opponents being awarded the match because the Kilruane sub L.S. Haverty was not properly attired.

The chairman quoted Rule 104a which stated: "The referee shall see that the players are properly attired."

Mr L. White (Eglish) said Haverty played in a white shirt. The Eglish players were also attired in white jerseys while Kilruane McDonaghs had other subs with green shirts who could have been used.

When this player came on he scored two goals. Eglish players inadvertently passed the ball to Haverty in the white shirt, thinking he was one of their own.

Eglish were winning until that switch and Mr. White said he would consider it a fit subject for an objection. He felt that if the match had gone on without that substitution, they would not have had to move their goalkeeper outfield.

Mr C Heffernan, Kilruane Rep, queried if the objection was in order relative to use of Irish and the proper address etc. The chairman indicated that the document did not conform to the rules. Following further discussion, the objection was lost and the board agreed to return the £1 objection fee to the club.

Mr White thanked the chairman for the ruling and for the generous offer of returning the fee.

# Chairman Sends Off County Secretary And Future GAA President

### Seamus McRory

This is the story of how a referee who happened to be a County Chairman sent off his own County Secretary during a game. That same County Secretary would in later life rise to become President of the GAA. But first a bit of context.

In 2013, GAA delegates from every county in Ireland and from every unit of the Association abroad attended the annual GAA Congress held in Derry for the first time. This was a splendid opportunity for the Gaels of our native county to showcase all that is good and much that is great about the GAA in our native place.

As an occasion of brilliant organisation, informed debate, spectacular entertainment and pure unadulterated enjoyment, those three days will live long in the memory, especially for those who visited our city and county for the first time.

Amongst the gathering of 350 delegates was a young-at-heart, 94-year-old man who has surely created a national record for the most Congresses attended. Almost 70 years previously, in the mid-1940s, he attended his first Congress in Dublin and he has missed very few in the interim. To put the enormity of that achievement into perspective, the vast percentage of those who attended the 2013 event were not even born when our legendary personality made his Congress debut.

Paddy MacFlynn was born in Magherafelt in 1918 and became a founder member of the local O'Donovan Rossa club as well as its first secretary, at the tender age of 16, in 1934.

As a player Paddy was also a member of Derry's first county minor team and he won a senior county championship medal with Magherafelt in 1942.

After representing Derry in an administrative capacity at Ulster and Central Council levels, he moved to Ballynahinch in Down to take up a primary school teaching post in the late forties. In 1953 he was appointed principal of Gilford Primary School in the parish of Tullylish, which was the home place of the famed McCartan brothers of the 1960s Down senior All-Ireland winning teams.

In quick succession, he became chairman of the East Down District Board as well as the Mourne County's representative on the Ulster GAA Council, becoming its chairman between 1961 and 1963. For the 18 years between 1955 and 1973, the multi-talented South Derry native also served as treasurer of the Down County Board. In 1964 he was selected as Down's representative on the Central Council and he remained in that position until he was chosen as the first President-elect of the Association in 1978.

The following year he assumed the illustrious office of President of the GAA. This most quiet and unassuming of Gaels has given over three quarters of a century of total commitment to every facet of Ireland's premier organisation. He really epitomised what loyalty to the ideals of the founding fathers of the GAA is all about.

However, lest some people might think that I am about to bestow on Paddy an honour only befitting the GAA's first candidate for sainthood, I must now recall, for posterity, some of the more human and should I say endearing qualities which he has shared with many of us. Before I explain the implications of what our erstwhile saint did, I must confess that I have a vested interest in the great man's one time errant behaviour!

Paddy and I have known each other for many years. We met at many gatherings, including the official opening of my adopted Longford Slashers club complex, during his GAA presidency. More pertinent, however, one of his longest established and closest GAA acquaintances, the late Paddy Larkin, lived in my native parish of Lissan in South Derry for almost 20 years. The latter's wife, Cassie, was the much admired and respected school principal in our local primary school. But I digress somewhat. Now to the kernel of the story.

As I stated earlier Paddy played for his club in the 1942 Derry County final. The referee appointed for the game was his county board colleague, the Chairman Paddy Larkin – a fellow teacher and friend of MacFlynn's.

To add novelty to the scenario, MacFlynn was also Co Secretary at the time. As both were natives of South Derry and with transport scarce in wartime, they naturally travelled together, northwards, to the game in Dungiven.

Though the Rossa's were winning a lot of possession in the match itself, their small forwards could not cope with the tall, stronger Glenullin defenders. To counteract this forward fragility the commanding figure of centre half-back MacFlynn was switched to full-forward. Nearing the end of the game, MacFlynn gave a full-blooded charge to the Glenullin full-back, putting him not only over the end line but also into the railing surrounding the pitch.

Referee Larkin immediately took MacFlynn's name and sent him off. In a totally dispassionate manner, the Co Chairman had dismissed his Co Secretary.

After the game, the pair togged in, gathered their belongings and drove home together. There was no bitterness, no rancour, just two GAA aficionados recalling the merits of the Rossas victory and the demerits of Glenullin's performance. They acted completely oblivious to anything remotely untoward having occurred on the field of play. Each one, instinctively, knew that the rules of the game were greater than personal prejudices or camaraderie. Those parameters were confined to an hour on the football field.

Ten days later Larkin and MacFlynn travelled together again for a meeting of the then disciplinary committee of the Co Board. As his sending off was the main subject of the evening's business, MacFlynn had to obey proper protocol and sit outside the decision-making room while his case was being heard. But as the Magherafelt man was the only board member who really knew the rules regarding proposed suspensions, the Chairman left the meeting, every so often, to check with his errant Co Secretary to ensure that he was properly suspended under the appropriate rule.

It was agreed on the advice of Paddy, the Co Secretary, that Paddy the Co Chairman should propose that under the rules of the then Official Guide that the correct decision had been applied in the game i.e. the referee was entitled to send off MacFlynn under Rule 105c i.e. for a player indulging in dangerous play.

Accordingly, it was jointly agreed between the two officials that the Magherafelt centre half-back should be suspended under Rule 64 for the term of one lunar month. This was done and accepted in a spirit of mutual trust and complete integrity. There were no further appeals or any CHC hearings or friends, legal or otherwise, pleading for clemency. The friendship of the two Paddys endured for over 50 years until Paddy Larkin died in the latter half of the 1990s.

At the 2013 Congress which I mentioned at the outset, I met Paddy MacFlynn for the last time. Before I left him I asked him to confirm again the authenticity of that famous story which had occurred 71 years earlier in 1942.

"Seamus, it's a long time since I told you that story for the first time and it is as true now as it was then. Anyway I might never see you again so I'd better tell the truth," he added jokingly.

Sadly I never did see him again as he passed away seven months later in September of the same year. One can say for certain that no one in heaven rejoiced more in October 2019, than the redoubtable Paddy MacFlynn, when Magherafelt O'Donovan Rossa, under inspirational captain Danny Heavron, won their first Derry Senior championship title in 41 years and 77 years since Paddy's famous win in the blue-riband of Derry football. The Gaelic footballers of Magherafelt had once again brought the ultimate honour to their legendary founding member.

*Seamus McRory is a Derry native, now living in Longford. A retired primary school principal, Seamus and his wife Olive are the parents of Diarmuid and the late Mairéad. He is a keen GAA follower and has authored six books: The Voice from the Sideline (1997), The Road to Croke Park (1999), The All-Ireland Dream (2005), James McCartan, The King of Down Football (2010), The Dove of Peace (2013) and Born to Lead (2019).*

# GAA's Global Story Eloquently Told By Ladies From The Land Of The Rising Sun

Páraic McGrath and Joe Trolan

Japan and Ireland may have only had official diplomatic relations over the past 60 years but the connections between the two countries goes way back to the early 18th century.

Back then in 1704 a man from Waterford, Robert Jansen, found himself captured in Kyushu but survived to tell the tale. In 1872 a Japanese Meiji Government trade mission visited St James's Gate and sampled our national beverage when a man called John Fenton from Cork wrote the music for "Kimigayo" – the Japanese national anthem.

Most famously a man called Lafcadio Hearn, son of an Offaly man, lived most of his life in Japan and to this day is revered there as a famous writer and poet but interestingly enough is a distant relation of Eric Elwood, formerly of Galway GAA, Ireland and Connacht Rugby.

In more modern times, the two governments agreed in the mid 1980s to develop programmes that allowed young Irish graduates travel and work in Japanese companies for a period of one or two years. These helped to further strengthen the ties and afforded the graduates wonderful opportunities to learn first-hand how these iconic globally renowned Japanese companies were at the cutting edge of manufacturing and technology and also learn about Japanese culture.

Such graduates, including myself (Páraic) landed in the Land of the Rising Sun with eyes and mouths wide open, had no prior knowledge of Japan or its people, but within a few months had started telling our new Japanese colleagues and friends all about Ireland and the Irish.

Central to these stories was the GAA and our national sports which in my own case saw me bring some hurls, sliotars and a Gaelic football to the three schools that I was working at so that I could demonstrate to bemused school kids my limited hurling and football skills.

By 1992, about 40-50 young Irish professionals were meeting regularly in different bars in Tokyo. Soccer and rugby teams were formed but it was only after a chance encounter with a young Australian businessman called Gerry Moran, that the idea of an International Rules Game was first mooted.

Meetings were arranged, format and rules agreed, a pitch was booked and a month after that first chat, the first ever Gaelic football team in Japan took the field against the Tokyo Goannas, the Australian Football team based in the city.

We competed for the 'Ned Kelly' Cup over four quarters, alternating between the Gaelic and the oval "footy" with the game ending in a draw – probably a fair result. I used my own family connections to secure a free set of sleeveless style green and gold Irish jerseys from O'Neill's with 'Ned Kelly Cup Tokyo 1992' emblazoned across the front.

We repeated the event in 1993 with the Aussies winning comfortably. Jerseys were obtained for free again by this time writing a letter to Joe Connolly, who was then running Connolly Sports with his brothers. They agreed to supply us with the set that we wore proudly onto the pitch at Nishi Chofu in Western Tokyo on November 27.

The Ned Kelly Cup is still played today between the two clubs and now 30 years on from that first match, it is great to reminisce with former players about the first ever Gaelic football team in Japan and how we managed to bring the GAA to our adopted homeland at the time.

In 1995, Japan GAA was founded and since then they have been growing their player base from mainly Irish players to its 2021 variation which sees 14 different nationalities with a majority of Japanese especially amongst the ladies team.

In 2016, the two governments decided that 2017 was going to be a year full of events to celebrate the 60th anniversary of diplomatic relations between the two countries. The DFA in Tokyo contacted us on the Asian Co. Board about what we could contribute from a GAA perspective, for example a game in Tokyo between different teams.

We decided to go further and after some lengthy discussions with key contacts in the GAA especially Iar-Uachtarain Aoghan O'Fearghail & Gearoid O'Maolmhichil secured a 12-minute playing slot during the half-time break of the All-Ireland football semi-final scheduled for Croke Park that August. Luckily for us, Dublin won their qualifying games to be one of the teams which meant a full house of 82,000 people were going to attend. What happened next was memorable, thrilling and never to be forgotten.

The Japan GAA & UCD International Ladies teams left the changing room a few minutes before the half-time whistle and when it was sounded, sprinted onto the field as if they were about to participate in their own All Ireland final.

Following in his father PJ's footsteps by refereeing in Croke Park, Paraic started the match and in the first few minutes, Dublin legend Brian Mullins, who has been a major influence in the growth of UCD's Ladies Gaelic Football was yelling instructions like he had never left the sideline. His promptings made the battle even harder in front of the capacity crowd.

Remarkably, media interviews went on simultaneously to the football action on the field with several of the Japanese ladies stepping away from being subs to chat. Up and down the field the two sides went with great football being played in an open and flowing game. In the end after a quick-fire 12-minute game, the score ended 1-3 to 0-2 in favour of UCD international Ladies.

At the final whistle the ladies received a standing ovation as they walked off the pitch. It saluted a truly momentous experience for Japan GAA and their ladies team. Back in 1995 when Japan GAA was established, I don't think the founders ever thought that one day the Japanese jersey would grace the hallowed turf of Croke Park, or that their ladies team would be heroes for a day as their name became forever associated with Croke Park and the evolving GAA story.

*Páraic McGrath is a native of Claremorris, Co Mayo and is son of former All Ireland final referee, PJ McGrath (RIP). He left Ireland for Japan in 1990 but now lives in Australia. After many years with the Asian GAA Board, he is a referee and member of Garryowen GAA in Melbourne. A Business Development Executive, he is married to Clara with three children and also dabbles in triathlons.*

*Joe Trolan was born in Ballinascreen, Co Derry and represented his county in the 1991 All Ireland minor semi-final against Kilkenny before studying and working in the USA. He now works as an Assistant Professor of Sports Management at Hankuk University of Foreign Studies in Seoul, South Korea. Married to Helen, he is the Games Development Officer for the Asian GAA Board and loves to run every day.*

# Getting Ready For Grassroots, Volume Two

If you have managed to get to this point, maybe the thought has struck you that you too have a GAA story to tell. If so, your tale could become part of *Grassroots, Volume Two*, which is earmarked for publication in late 2022.

Already we have a cornucopia of great stories pencilled in for that publication (see list below), including a contribution of my own. At this stage the second book is rapidly filling up but if you want to become part of the next collection, please email me at pj@gaastories.ie or write to

Ballpoint Press
4 Wyndham Park
Bray
Co Wicklow

Below is a selected list of those already earmarked for the collection.

**Stories**
A Tale Of Two Penalties – Tom Hunt
Memories Of Hughes Shop – PJ Cunningham
Behind The Goal – Paul Holland
Belfast Haunting – Pat Lynch
Cap For Sam – Maura Flynn
Seamus Darby and Connor's Cowboys – Mary O'Connor
Hurling In The Glen – Tom Aherne
Don't Mess with A Fermanagh Woman – Liam Keane
When Mayo Were World Champions – Michael Larkin
Mixed Fortunes – Michael Walsh
Clare Stories – Padraig MacMathuna
Reservoir Dogs – Joe Kearney
Pride And Loyalty – Declan P Gowran
The Giant Haystack – Mark McGaugh
Troubles And Strife In London – Barrie Henriques

A Horrific Day in the GAA – Sean Nugent
Refereeing With Stopped Watch – Eamon Moules
Fun in Buffalo – Paul Mulcaire
Mucky Business Afoot – Betty Deveney
Team Groupies – Rosemary McDermott
Cavan Memorabilia of '47 – Brian McCabe
Any chance of a loan of your left boot? – Michael O'Brien
Day Of Four Goal McGee – Willie McGee
Boat, Train and Bicycle Pains – Ann Curran
Cut The Grass – John Hoban
Home Grown Heroes – Helan Calvey
Rosaleen's Medals – Florrie Wise
Terry Wogan's Day in Rathnure – Maria Nolan
The Green Above the Red – Sean Hallinan
The Battle of Rathoe – Sean Kehoe
Cultec Hurley – Tom Wright
Where One Appearance Might Lead – John Mannion
A Trip To Dunmanway – Aodh Ó Broin
Imports For The Big Day – Vincent Cryan

**Poems**
Up For the Match – Moira Gallagher
Grace before And After – Ned Cuggy
Win, Win, Win – Sean Hallinan
Song of the Hurler – Gerry McLaughlin

# PJ Cunningham

PJ Cunningham once played senior club and county U-21 football before later in life occupying selectorial and manager roles on the sideline at both levels.

A former deputy editor of the *Sunday Tribune* and *Evening Herald* and sports editor of the *Irish Independent*, he has been a sports columnist with various publications for 20 years.

Cunningham is the author of five books, two of which – *The Long Acre* and *About That Goal* (the story of Seamus Darby) – were shortlisted for Irish Published Book of the Year in 2014 and Sports Book of the Year in 2019 respectively.

He has also compiled and edited with Dr Joe Kearney three collections of books on rural life – *Around The Farm Gate*; *Then There Was Light* and *From The Candy Store To The Galtymore*.